Rethinking Humanitarian Intervention in the 21st Century

RETHINKING HUMANITARIAN INTERVENTION IN THE 21ST CENTURY

Edited by Aiden Warren and Damian Grenfell

EDINBURGH
University Press

Edinburgh University Press is one of the leading university presses in the UK. We publish academic books and journals in our selected subject areas across the humanities and social sciences, combining cutting-edge scholarship with high editorial and production values to produce academic works of lasting importance. For more information visit our website: edinburghuniversitypress.com

Edinburgh University Press Ltd
The Tun – Holyrood Road
12(2f) Jackson's Entry
Edinburgh EH8 8PJ

Typeset in 11/13 Sabon by
Servis Filmsetting Ltd, Stockport, Cheshire

A CIP record for this book is available from the British Library

ISBN 978 1 4744 2381 6 (hardback)
ISBN 978 1 4744 4442 2 (pbk.)
ISBN 978 1 4744 2382 3 (webready PDF)
ISBN 978 1 4744 2383 0 (epub)

Contents

Notes on Contributors   vii

Foreword   xii

Abbreviations and Acronyms   xiv

Introduction   1
Aiden Warren and Damian Grenfell

PART I The Evolution of Humanitarian Interventions in a Global
     Era

1 Rethinking Humanitarian-Military Interventions: Violence
   and Modernity in an Age of Globalisation   15
   Damian Grenfell

2 Peace in the Twenty-First Century: States, Capital and
   Institutions   43
   Oliver P. Richmond

3 The Evolution of Economic Interventions and the Violence
   of International Accountability over the longue durée   74
   Bronwen Everill

4 Changing Patterns of Social Connection across
   Interventions: Unravelling Aberrant Globalisation   94
   Paul Battersby

PART II The Limits of Sovereignty and the Ethics of Interventions

5 A Framework for Reimagining Order and Justice:
   Transitions in Violence and Interventions in a Global Era   117
   Michaelene Cox

6 Humanitarian Intervention? Responding Ethically to
   Globalising Violence in the Age of Mediated Violence   145
   Paul James

7 'Manifestly Failing' and 'Unwilling or Unable' as
   Intervention Formulas: A Critical Assessment   164
   Ingvild Bode

8 Interventions and the Limits of the Responsibility to
   Protect: Regional Organisations and the Global South   192
   Joseph Hongoh

9 Regulating the Abstraction of Violence: Interventions and
   the Deployment of New Technologies Globally   216
   Aiden Warren

PART III The Politics of Post-intervention (Re-)Building and
          Humanitarian Engagement

10 (Re-)Building the World: Local Agency and Human
   Security in the New Millennium   247
   Trudy Fraser

11 Who Rebuilds? Local Roles in Rebuilding Shattered
   Societies   267
   Susan H. Allen

12 Transforming the Discourse of Civil-Military Interaction
   in Humanitarian Environments   287
   Vandra Harris

Index   311

Notes on Contributors

Susan H. Allen directs the Center for Peacemaking Practice at George Mason University. She is a scholar-practitioner of conflict resolution. Her main focus is on reflective practice and research that emerges from practice contexts. She has substantial expertise in intermediary roles and coordination among intermediaries, evaluation of conflict resolution initiatives, and theories of change, indicators of change and evaluation in conflict resolution practice. She has engaged long term in conflict resolution in the South Caucasus, as well as contributing to a variety of conflict resolution initiatives in Eastern Europe, Eurasia, the Caribbean, South America and Africa. Susan Allen's current research centres on catalytic workshops. Her work has been supported by the US Institute of Peace (Peace Scholar award, Grant program), the One Foundation, USAID, the UK Conflict Pool, the US State Department, the William and Flora I. Hewlett Foundation, Compton Foundation, Catalyst Fund (with ACT) and the US State Department (with ACT).

Paul Battersby is Associate Professor and the Deputy Dean, Global and Language Studies of the School of Global Studies, RMIT University, Melbourne. His research and writing reflects the intellectual diversity of Global Studies at RMIT. He maintains an active interest in the history of Australia–Southeast Asia business and diplomatic relations, but his principal area of scholarship currently addresses contemporary issues of global security, international development and transnational crime. His most recent work explores complex patterns of globalisation and presents a new framework for investigating global crime.

Ingvild Bode is a lecturer at the University of Kent, Canterbury. Her overall research agenda covers the area of peace and security, with three particular research interests. First, the potential influence of individuals from diverse backgrounds on processes of policy evolution at the United Nations, particularly in relation to UN peacekeeping, thematic mandates at the Security Council and humanitarian affairs. Second, how changing post-9/11 US practices towards the use of force contribute to altering the UN Charter's use-of-force regime. Third, the roles and functions of narratives in conflicts and how these relate to questions of agency. Ingvild is the author of *Individual Agency and Policy Change at the United Nations* (2015) and the co-author, with Aiden Warren, of *Governing the Use-of-Force: The Post-9/11 US Challenge on International Law* (2014). She has also published in journals such as *Global Governance*, *International Studies Perspectives* and *Contemporary Security Policy*.

Michaelene Cox is Associate Professor in the Department of Politics and Government, Illinois State University, Normal. She teaches within the subfields of international relations and comparative politics, with specialisation in international humanitarian law and European politics. Her research agenda broadly addresses issues of quality of governance and human rights, and focuses particularly on conflict and cooperation, corruption and political participation. Michaelene has published three edited volumes, including *Social Capital and Peace-Building* (Routledge); a sole-authored book and several book chapters. Her articles appear in journals such as *Journal of Peace Research*, *Transition Studies Review* and *Journal of Common Market Studies*. She is currently working on a book about transnational corruption and armed conflict.

Bronwen Everill is an historian of the Atlantic World at the University of Cambridge. She is the author of *Abolition and Empire in Sierra Leone and Liberia* (Palgrave 2013) and the editor, with Josiah Kaplan, of *The History and Practice of Humanitarian Intervention and Aid in Africa* (Palgrave 2013). Her work has appeared in *Slavery & Abolition*, the *Journal of Global History*, *The Journal of Imperial and Commonwealth History*, and the *Journal of Translatlantic Studies*. She has looked broadly at the interactions between humanitarianism and imperialism in Africa in the modern period. Her current project investigates the ethical consumer movements of the early nineteenth century and their impact on antislavery thought, Atlantic commerce, and American and British political economy.

Trudy Fraser is Senior Fellow at Global Action to Prevent War, New York, and a United Nations-based consultant. She was previously a Postdoctoral Research Fellow with joint affiliation at the United Nations University (UNU) in Tokyo, Japan, and the University of Tokyo. Her work examines the efficacy of the United Nations in meeting the challenges of contemporary human security. She is the author of *Maintaining Peace and Security? The United Nations in a Changing World* (2014) and the co-editor of *The Security Council as Global Legislator* (2014) and *Perspectives on Peacekeeping and Atrocity Prevention: Expanding Stakeholders and Regional Arrangements* (2015). She received a PhD in international relations from the University of St Andrews, Scotland in 2011.

Damian Grenfell is Director of the Centre for Global Research and an Associate Professor in the Global Studies Program at RMIT University in Melbourne, Australia. He undertakes research on social change in the context of conflict, security and peace. Of particular interest is what occurs when diverse forms of political and social integration intersect in circumstances of military, humanitarian interventions, development initiatives and peace- and state-building efforts. These research interests are reflected in his co-edited collection *Rethinking Humanitarian Intervention in the 21st Century* (Edinburgh University Press, 2017). A significant aspect of Grenfell's research focuses on programmatic responses that attempt to mitigate violence against women and children.

Vandra Harris is Programme Manager of the Master of International Development and an executive member of the Centre for Global Research, RMIT University. Vandra's research focuses particularly on the interface between different actors in the development space, especially militaries, police and NGOs, as well as contact between local and international development actors. She has a special interest in humanitarianism(s), and in ethics in everyday practice. She is currently working on a project concerning the interaction between NGOs and militaries in complex emergencies and disasters, funded by the Australian Civil-Military Centre.

Joseph Hongoh lectures courses in Peacebuilding, Conflict Resolution and Development Studies at the School of Political Science and International Studies, University of Queensland. He is also an established facilitator, trainer and monitoring and evaluation consultant in the area of conflict resolution, peace-building and international development. Joseph is also an interdisciplinary researcher in state–society relations in conflict management and resolution, state-building as conflict management, the politics of development, community-based approaches to managing conflicts, relations between local and external interveners, as well as peace-building and post-conflict reconstruction.

Paul James is a professor at the University of Western Sydney, Director of the Institute for Culture and Society, and Research Director of Global Reconciliation, an international organisation based in Australia. Global Reconciliation has been doing work in zones of conflict around the world, including Sri Lanka and the Middle East, bringing people together in ongoing dialogue. Paul is a social theorist with three overlapping areas of research focus. The first is globalisation and its impact upon social relations, from national community to local community. The second is social change and the human condition, including the impact of modernisation on customary and traditional ways of being. The third is sustainability with an emphasis on sustainable urbanisation. These areas of focus are integrated through an approach to social theory called 'engaged theory', encompassing questions of social formation, social integration and ontological tension.

Oliver Richmond is Professor of International Relations, Peace and Conflict Studies, University of Manchester. His primary area of expertise is in peace and conflict theory, and in particular its inter-linkages with international relations theory. He is currently working on a book on peace and intervention in the twenty-first century. His most recent works have been on peace formation and its relation to state formation, state-building and peace-building (*Failed Statebuilding and Peace Formation* (2014) and *Peace Formation and Political Order* (2016)). This area of interest has grown out of his work on local forms of critical agency and resistance, and their role in constructing hybrid or post-liberal forms of peace and states (see *A Post-Liberal Peace* (2011)), as well as earlier conflict resolution and conflict management debates in international relations, including international mediation, peacekeeping and state formation debates. He has also recently published a *Very Short Introduction to Peace* (2014), which offers an overview of the development of related concepts, theory and practices.

Shirley Scott is a Professor of International Relations in the Faculty of Arts and Social Sciences, University of New South Wales, Sydney. Shirley's research and teaching focuses on international law as a dimension of global governance, demonstrating the complex interplay between power politics and international law. Shirley has published on a range of subjects including the use of force, climate change, Antarctica, international law and Australian foreign policy and the nature of US engagement with international law. Shirley is the Research Chair of the Australian Institute of International Affairs and a member of the Advisory Council of the Asian Society of International Law. She is currently undertaking a project on the scope for the UN Security Council to contribute to the governance of climate change adaptation.

Aiden Warren is a Senior Lecturer in the School of Global, Urban and Social Studies and a Researcher in the Centre for Global Research at RMIT University in Melbourne, Australia. His teaching and research interests are in the areas of international security, US national security and foreign policy, US politics (ideas, institutions, contemporary and historical), international relations (especially great power politics), and issues associated with Weapons of Mass Destruction (WMD) proliferation, non-proliferation and arms control. Dr Warren is the author of *The Obama Administration's Nuclear Weapon Strategy: The Promises of Prague* (2013) and *Prevention, Pre-emption and the Nuclear Option: From Bush to Obama* (2011), and co-author of *Governing the Use-of-Force in International Relations: The Post 9/11 US Challenge on International Law* (with Ingvild Bode) (2014), *Presidential Doctrines* (2016) and *Weapons of Mass Destruction: The Search for Global Security* (with Joseph M. Siracusa) (2017). He is also the Series Editor of the *Weapons of Mass Destruction* (WMD) book series.

Foreword

It has long struck me as sadly ironic that one of the principal tools at the disposal of global powers by which to respond to humanitarian disasters inflicted on societies by their own leaders, has been to bomb the very country whose peoples have suffered. Those whose research and work focuses only on the subject may be immune to the irony but I have found that for students coming to the subject for the first time, the juxtaposition of problem and solution often appears quite stark.

As the editors of this thought-provoking collection point out, other aspects of the practice and theory of intervention are just as deserving of reflection and ripe for fundamental re-evaluation. For example, while it may have become clear that regime removal does not of itself guarantee a better future for the citizens post-intervention, it is not so obvious that ruling out regime change after a Responsibility to Protect (R2P) intervention would as a matter of course protect the citizens. Presumably if a regime has no qualms about inflicting harm on its own people once it may well do so again, as the experience of Syria would seem to suggest.

And, whether or not intervention encompasses regime removal, the question remains as to what then? And what of those from the previous state apparatus who are removed if regime change is enforced? Although none of these issues are new, they have been the subject of particular concern to the international community since the failure to intervene in the Rwandan genocide and the decision to intervene without authorisation by the United Nations Security Council international during the Kosovo crisis in 1999.

The concept of the R2P has been the most tangible product of this review, and debate on the issues raised by intervention has, since the 2001 report of the International Commission on Intervention and State Sovereignty, generally been centred on the R2P concept. Advocates of the concept tend to be those who feel compelled to find a way by which the international community does not become complicit through silence in atrocities. Interestingly, many R2P critics would not want to be seen as endorsing the brutality but view themselves as realists who accept that interventions by the powerful tend to occur where there is a confluence of humanitarian concern and perceived national interest and indeed, in instances where national interest may in fact be the stronger motive.

The R2P concept has not moved debate beyond past conundrums, such as that of the appropriate authority, if any, to authorise intervention in the event of an impasse in the Security Council and how to ensure that the country involved does not then become bogged in a quagmire of seemingly never-ending instability as did Iraq. The spuriousness of the legal justification for the Iraq intervention together with the failure of the intervention on policy grounds have had long-lasting implications for the West. Together with Kosovo it arguably emboldened President Putin to annex Crimea and weakened the reaction of the West. The experience of Libya confirmed Chinese scepticism regarding R2P.

And so, despite having exercised some of the brightest minds for so long, valid solutions to the multiple complex issues raised by the subject of intervention have in most cases remained elusive. Hence the need to re-examine the issues in the light of recent experience. In moving beyond the confines of a debate on intervention centred on the changing nature of sovereignty, the volume has three central themes: the evolution of humanitarian interventions in a global era; the limits of sovereignty and the ethics of interventions; and the politics of post-intervention (re-)building and humanitarian engagement.

Case studies are varied and include Timor-Leste, Kosovo, Syria, Libya and Iraq. The editors of the volume are to be congratulated for drawing together a varied yet cohesive collection of papers to inspire further thinking on the vexed questions that confront humanity and contemporary geopolitics. I wholeheartedly commend the volume to readers.

Professor Shirley V. Scott
University of New South Wales,
Australia

Abbreviations and Acronyms

ADF	Australian Defence Force
AFRICOM	(US) Africa Regional Command
ANLM	Azawad National Liberation Movement
AQIM	Al-Qaeda in the Islamic Maghreb
AU	African Union
AUCISS	Commission of Inquiry on South Sudan
AUMF	Authorisation for the Use of Military Force
AWSs	autonomous weapons systems
BINUB	UN Integrated Office in Burundi
CIMIC	civil-military interaction
CMCoord	UN Humanitarian Civil-Military Coordination
COIN	counterinsurgency
CPT	Communist Party of Thailand
DPKO	United Nations Department of Peacekeeping Operations
DRC	Democratic Republic of Congo
ECCAS	Economic Community of Central African States
ECOMOG	Economic Community of West African States Military Observer Group
ECOWAS	Economic Community of West African States
EDC	European Defence Community
EU	European Union
FATA	Federally Administered Tribal Areas
FAWs	fully autonomous weapons systems
G77	Group of 77 at the United Nations
GA	General Assembly
GSPC	*Group Salafist pour la Predication et le Combat*
HCT	Humanitarian Country Team
IASC	Inter-Agency Standing Committee

ICGLR	International Conference on the Great Lakes Region
ICISS	International Commission on Intervention and State Sovereignty
ICRC	International Committee of the Red Cross
IGAD	Intergovernmental Authority on Development
IGO	intergovernmental organisations
IMF	International Monetary Fund
ISIS	Islamic State of Iraq and Syria
KLA	Kosovo Liberation Army
LAWS	lethal autonomous weapons systems
LRA	Lord's Resistance Army
MCDA	military and civil defence assets
MEND	Movement for the Emancipation of the Niger Delta
NATO	North Atlantic Treaty Organization
NCSROF	National Coalition of Syrian Revolution and Opposition Forces
NGO	non-government organisation
NLF	National Liberation Front
ONUB	UN Operation in Burundi
OROLSI	Office of Rule of Law and Security Institutions
OSCE	Organization for Security and Co-operation in Europe
PBC	United Nations Peacebuilding Commission
PRC	People's Republic of China
R2P	Responsibility to Protect
RMA	Revolution in Military Affairs
ROs	regional organisations
SCR	Security Council Resolution
SIPRI	Stockholm International Peace Research Institute
SSR	security sector reform
UAVs	unmanned aerial vehicles
UCLASS	Unmanned Carrier-Launched Airborne Surveillance and Strike
UMS	unmanned military systems
UN	United Nations
UNAMSIL	United Nations Mission in Sierra Leone
UNCTAD	United Nations Conference on Trade and Development
UNDP	United Nations Development Programme
UNMIBH	United Nations Mission in Bosnia Herzegovina
UNMIH	United Nations Mission in Haiti

UNMIK	United Nations Interim Administration Mission in Kosovo
UNOCA	United Nations Regional Office for Central Africa
UNOCHA	United Nations Office for the Coordination of Humanitarian Affairs
UNOMIG	United Nations Observer Mission in Georgia
UNOMIL	United Nations Observer Mission in Liberia
UNOMSIL	United Nations Observer Mission in Sierra Leone
UNOSOM I	United Nations Operation in Somalia I
UNOSOM II	United Nations Operation in Somalia II
UNOWA	United Nations Office for West Africa
UNSC	United Nations Security Council
UNSG	United Nations Secretary-General
UNTAET	United Nations Transitional Administration in East Timor
US	United States
WHO	World Health Organization
WMD	weapons of mass destruction

Introduction

Aiden Warren and Damian Grenfell

The need to fundamentally rethink interventions is before us. Driven by a combination of pressing humanitarian need as well as conceptual and theoretical dilemmas that limit the value of analysis, it is evident we are seemingly at the crossroads. The crises in Syria and Iraq – the human rights abuses, the destruction of cities and the attenuating flows of refugees into Europe – have only been enough to garner specific military action from external powers in ways closely aligned to national interests. There is the sense that despite being decades on from the end of the Cold War and notwithstanding the varying kinds of interventions in the name of humanitarian ends that have taken place, we have come full circle. For all their challenges and faults, at the end of the twentieth century Kosovo and Timor-Leste suggested that there was enough benefit gained by interventions that they had a future in global politics. The post-9/11 military invasions of Iraq and Afghanistan have, however, come to dominate discourse as wars fought overwhelmingly for state security rather than humanitarian ends (even though the latter are used instrumentally as a justification at times). Moreover, as events in Syria have unfolded, it has become even harder to discern who would be assisted, and to what end, by a large-scale intervention like those that occurred across the 1990s. The widening of Syria's civil war into a regional one, and the toll on civilians (approximately 260,000 at time of publication), reflects elements that are described in 'new wars' analysis, and yet are overlain with shifting forms of globalised warfare, intersections with terrorism, while reaffirming what appears to be more classical superpower rivalries (though now it is between different versions of empire and capitalism). It is such a riven mess that it is quite possible that the only 'end game' will come in the form of general annihilation.

The development of the Responsibility to Protect (R2P) doctrine

1

has ostensibly complicated conceptual and empirical debates over interventions, or at the very least have not shifted the boundaries of disagreements over the legality, the ethics of using military force, when interventions should occur, who should intervene, and whether they are effective. And there has been little shift in terms of understanding interventions within their more reductive dimensions; wherein advocates of interventions claim they are necessary and require immediate action in the face of significant human rights abuses, while in contrast, critics regard them as a ruse for military intervention or – particularly for the left – an excuse for imperial expansion.

While the end of the Cold War indicated that perhaps a new norm of military humanitarian intervention was emerging, the 9/11 terrorist attacks, the US 'War on Terror' and the different responses to crises in Libya, Syria and Iraq – particularly in the context of 'addressing' ISIS – have meant that the era of humanitarian intervention has entered a more perplexing period, or even taken a significant backward step. In 2011 the UN Security Council invoked the 'Responsibility to Protect' doctrine, endorsing a no-fly zone over Libya and authorising member states to 'take all necessary measures' to protect civilians under attack from Muammar al-Qaddafi's government. Western-led air strikes ultimately led to the ousting of Qaddafi, prompting criticism from Security Council members like Russia that the R2P doctrine was used to achieve regime change. These concerns, combined with those pertaining to the way Libya's post-intervention upheaval has affected the region, have given pause to humanitarian interventions backed by regional or international bodies.

In a context where layers to conflict appear to be so complex and fluid, it is difficult to imagine one book could 'rethink interventions' to the extent that is required. Nevertheless, a contribution to debates can be made. In this collection, several important choices were made in terms of how to bring a collection together that allows for the richness of an edited collection while also ensuring coherence. The task of 'rethinking' has meant many of the chapters are more or less underpinned by critical theory, with structures of power and the ends that they are deployed to serve never far from discussion (if not the direct focus of analysis). This in turn has meant that many of the chapters also have a concern for the 'local' with regards to interventions (influenced by the 'local turn' in peace-building analysis for instance), and that the kinds of problems that exist and the changes

2

that are needed are situated at the global level. In part a reflection of this bent to the essays, interventions are also treated across a wide spectrum of practice, from the legitimating claims used in foreign policies such as R2P and the 'use of force', the architecture of interventions from drone strikes to civil-military interactions, through to human security and peace-building. A broader approach to humanitarian-military interventions was taken in that peace-building, like human security, are as important components to interventions as the legal and ethical justifications that are used to initiate them. Both the decentred nature of conflicts and their complex trajectories mean that ostensibly different processes (for instance peace-building) occur and reinforce other elements (for instance peacekeeping) over the longer term. And yet despite the critiques, these are aimed at current practices, discourses and trajectories and what they tell us about the world today; no chapter argues against them.

As this collection will illustrate, despite the post-Cold War era initially offering many possibilities of attaining something towards humanitarian outcomes for those threatened by mass violence, not least innocent non-combatants caught in wars between state obfuscation and endemic violence, intervention debates appear moribund at the negotiating table. Inhibiting these possibilities has been the continuing pervasiveness of 'national interest'; to the extent that when interventions have occurred – from Haiti to Timor-Leste, Kosovo to Libya – they have been executed as an extension and maintenance of sovereign interests. Here, the rationale of states has been typically defined through the acquisition of natural resources, defining strategic balances, the containment of conflict and, in many instances, the continued dominance of compradors in former colonies. This tension between humanitarian demands on the one hand and national interest on the other continues to frame debates on interventions, often leading to analysis that attempts to 'unmask' state intentions by distinguishing between the rhetoric of political leaders and the motivating interests of given nation-states.

Similarly, there is substantive literature encompassing the ethico-juridical dimensions of interventions in the form of the 'just war' considerations, from *jus ad bellum* to R2P, or those in relation to the legal possibilities evident in the varying articles of the United Nations Conventions and broader infrastructure of international law. Often complementing this literature, at least in terms of evaluating the efficacy of interventions, is analysis that focuses on policy and practice; tracking for instance the changes in patterns of warfare and the subsequent transformation of peacekeepers to peace-enforcers, the gendered dimensions of humanitarian-military interventions, or the associated institutional decision-making processes. In embolden-ing the literature and discourse to this end, this collection attempts to build on these existing areas of debate, and in doing so, seeks to extend the analysis on interventions in three key ways.

Rather than limiting the discussion to the domain of the nation-state, the book will firstly examine the transition of interventions across the nexus of the global and local spectrum. As Chapters 1–4 (Part I, 'The Evolution of Humanitarian Interventions in a Global Era') reveal, on the one hand, there are the global political conditions that inform and shape the exercise of mass-military excursions from great distances away, while on the other, there are the local condi-tions in which interventions occur. In terms of the global context, this section seeks to frame its analysis in a way that challenges the sin-gular focus on the nation-state system even while it is acknowledged that the nation-state still plays a fundamental role in the process of interventions. Moreover, it refuses to separate the 'global theoretical' and 'local empirical' in its overall analysis.

In opening proceedings in Chapter 1, 'Rethinking Humanitarian-Military Interventions: Violence and Modernity in an Age of Globalisation', Damian Grenfell establishes a framework that calls for – as also the title of this book suggests – the rethinking of inter-ventions in which we move *away from* the common national inter-ests trajectories. The chapter begins with developing definitions of humanitarian–military interventions that have taken place after the Cold War's demise, arguing that the discourse surrounding the liberal peace paradigm have not delved thoroughly into understand-ing power relations between *interveners* and the *intervened*. Instead, what has transpired has been a conception of 'peace' that has worked to instil a type of modernity within conflict-riven societies, an effect strengthened rather than weakened in a period of intensifying glo-balisation. In pointing to Libya and Syria, as well as other sites in the global periphery, Grenfell contends that notwithstanding ongoing challenges, interventions will continue to have resonance in regards to the forms of reconstruction and humanitarian aid deployed by the international community.

In Chapter 2, 'Peace in the Twenty-First Century: States, Capital and Institutions', Oliver Richmond argues that analysis of interna-tional relations, peace, war, and interventions lacks the substantive historical depth that would otherwise enable us to explain difference between a number of key explanatory categories, including an episte-mological framework of emancipation; its focus on micro-level rela-tions of power; and the power relations inherent in centralised and vanguardist forms of empowerment envisioned in liberal internation-alism, international Marxism, global governance and neoliberalism. Richmond then proceeds to question the extent to which we can actu-ally move beyond the older ideas of peace and order, that so often delineate international relations and politics as occurring within the confines of power, structure and nature. In this regard, he looks at the degree to which difference, inequality and unequal power can be permanently managed by the state and international institutions, or continue to be moribund in a system of unequal power. Richmond's chapter then considers the extent transnational and informal net-works can be included in international politics, and whether relational ontologies can overcome the self-other, inside-outside binaries associ-ated with territorial sovereignty. Moreover, he asks, can the limits of nature be transcended in order to produce a peace of the twenty-first century, especially given the types of complex data now available, some of it for the first time, in the areas of society, economy, poli-tics, the environment, science and technology? Does the contempo-rary concept of 'global governance' capture these possibilities? How would divergent notions and practices of legitimacy be mediated (across different languages and cultures) and how would hierarchies by legitimised? In essence, Richmond's chapter examines the interven-tionary practices' relationship with peace and evaluates them accord-ing to what might be termed emancipatory theory for the twenty-first century.

Chapter 3 takes us in a profoundly different and vitally impor-tant direction with Bronwen Everill's 'The Evolution of Economic Interventions and the Violence of International Accountability over the *longue durée*'. Here Everill explores the different uses of eco-nomic interventions and their interlocking relationship with the evolution of humanitarian intervention. The chapter specifically focuses on examples from the African continent from the eight-eenth century to the present. Additionally, it examines state-level economic interventions – sanctions and aid, in war and peacetime – together as one form of pressure for conforming to humanitarian norms. Individual and corporate economic interventions are also considered separately as forms of intervention inherent to global capitalism. An examination of economic interventions reveals their interconnectivity, as well as their relationship to compulsion and physical force. By giving or withholding, states are able to intervene in the politics of dependent states, while individuals are able to determine the shape of global production. By looking at the long historical record of humanitarian intervention in Africa, Everill connects different forms of intervention: economic, military, capacity-building, humanitarian, individual, state and NGO. Ultimately, the chapter asks its readers to think about economic interventions as one form of humanitarian intervention that helps to bring these two strands of the literature together in ways that illuminate the ambiguities of intervention, and the relationships between intervention and power.

In Chapter 4, 'Changing Patterns of Social Connection across Interventions: Unravelling Aberrant Globalisation', Paul Battersby argues that the persuasive orthodoxy of international armed interventions in intrastate conflicts endures despite the erratic course, and outcomes, of foreign interventions in the Middle East over the past two decades. Here, there has been an assumption that order can be restored through the controlled application of limited military force. However, as the chapter conveys, notions of order, equilibrium or stasis implying systemic balances have been difficult to attain in an age of what he refers to as 'aberrant globalisation'. That is, because globalisation *is* aberrant in its complexity, and global dynamics do not produce simple choices between binary opposites of order and disorder, control or chaos, future interventions will, he argues, become even more complex. As such, Battersby's chapter calls for a more nuanced and contextualised understanding of global security, particularly in relation to understanding the global patterns of connection and organisation that generate and sustain *multiscalar* supply chains of violence.

Part II of the book ('The Limits of Sovereignty and the Ethics of Interventions') focuses on different areas of debate on the shifting forms of sovereignty and what these mean in both an ethical as well as practical–logistic effects. Indeed, as illustrated in Chapters 5–9 much of the literature has remained relatively stagnant. As just one example, the ramifications of waging warfare from an abstract technological distance (Libya, Iraq, Syria and Kosovo in comparison to Somalia) have often been explained in terms of military efficacy rather than on the political-cultural impacts of how such violence is enacted. While General Assembly debates in 2009–11 signified an apparent consensus with regard to the R2P domain, the international community still seems to be convalescing from the Western justification for the war in Iraq and the debauched arguments posited at the time on how regime change was somehow providing humanitarian benefits to the Iraqi people. The prodigious military métier of the United States continues to pose questions when it is ideologically opposed to military deployment for humanitarian purposes; evident in the Obama administration's commitment to 'days not weeks' of US military intervention in Libya, and little, if any, support on the ground in Syria. Concurrently, European states bemoan but contribute minimally in military capacity, while the privatisation of international relations and security – and therefore also of the succour and protection sector – present further complexities for an area already deeply in trouble. As an extension of these points, where possible, the authors in this section contemplate the limits of sovereignty, the ethics of interventions and even consider the future of interventions – particularly in relation to the degree to which humanitarian interventions will be destined to be caught in a quagmire of nation-state intransigence, national interest, the ambiguous fighting capacities of non-state actors, the ever evolving nature of technology and the movements of people escaping death or violence.

Chapter 5, 'A Framework for Reimagining Order and Justice: Transitions in Violence and Interventions in a Global Era', by Michaelene Cox, contrasts the interpretation and redefinition of sovereignty and intervention by Kofi Annan and Ban Ki-moon. Whereas Annan had found opportunity to interject a strong sense of moral authority into the ground-breaking R2P project, Ban drew upon mediation and bridge-building skills to shift the spotlight to its actual implementation. Primary responsibility for tackling their own problems still rested with the government and its leaders, he stressed, or otherwise engagement in conflict situations would be perceived to 'undermine their sovereignty, internationalize a problem or legitimize an adversary'. Cox's chapter evaluates developments beyond the state-centric model in face of contemporary challenges to order and justice. The chapter concludes with an emphasis on the need for political adaptability during periods of flux, and reminds us that whilst considering international, state and societal interests, the welfare and the participation of the human being is indispensable.

In further challenging both the definitional conceptions and ongoing limitations interventions, Chapter 6, 'Humanitarian Intervention? Responding Ethically to Globalising Violence in the Age of Mediated Violence', Paul James emphasises the capacity for interventions to often yield counterproductive and unintended

7

consequences. The main contributor to this short-falling, he argues, is that interventions are currently framed by an increasingly material and ideational abstraction that inevitably undermines humanitarian intervention efforts, however well-intentioned they may be. In the context of the material, James contends that in an era of drones and guided missiles, commanded by communications technologies that distort time and space, we subsequently blur the lines between war-fighting, execution and rightful intervention. Ideationally, we now pick and choose through the enumerated sections of abstract codes of conduct (such as R2P) while dispelling with virtue-based ethics through fervent speeches in parliament or congress about the need to act in the name of 'humanity'. This does not mean intervention should not occur, but it does suggest that the terms of intervention have to be fundamentally reconfigured. In this regard, James's chapter calls for a more meaningful approach that necessitates the capacity to establish ongoing regimes of mutual care, affinity, reciprocity and so on. Additionally, he argues that it is imperative to recognise the complexities of social difference where positive relationality – if realised – will engender opportunities for reconciliation and negotiation across the boundaries of difference. As such, the chapter concludes with seven defining sets of capacities that James deems to be provisionally fundamental in reconceiving societies in the aftermath of interventions and conflict.

In looking at the evolving interpretation of interventions in the post-9/11 context, Ingvild Bode, in Chapter 7, '"Manifestly Failing" and "Unwilling or Unable" as Intervention Formulas: A Critical Assessment', begins on an optimistic note by arguing that the inclusion of the R2P in the United Nations World Summit Outcome of 2005 marked a decisive shift in the evolution of interventions for humanitarian purposes. While the phrase 'manifest failure' corresponds to the 'unwilling or unable' standard previously used in this context by the R2P-defining International Commission on Intervention and State Sovereignty (ICISS), Bode admonishes that the 'unable or unwilling' standard has also been used to justify military intervention in a counterterrorism context; the formula warrants a more thorough examination of its legal foundations and policy practice. In adding to existing literature which considers either the counterterrorism or the R2P context only, Bode's chapter offers a critical examination of its usage across both contexts, and concludes with a summary of what these developments might indicate in terms of evolving intervention standards.

Additional limitations in the intervention domain are conveyed in Chapter 8, 'Interventions and the Limits of the Responsibility to Protect: Regional Organisations and the Global South', by Joseph Hongoh. Here, the author argues that the struggle in navigating the tension surrounding sovereignty as responsibility to protect actually obscures rather than enables productive engagements with the concept and practice of intervention. Referring to case studies from Africa, Hongoh suggests that integrating regional organisations (ROs) within the international–regional–national axes of R2P potentially restricts the broader conception of intervention. In undertaking this examination, he begins by providing an alternative reading of sovereignty as a responsibility that invests in the broader and enduring conception of intervention. In this regard, he demonstrates how regional organisations in Africa have perennially engaged with the questions of sovereignty, responsibility, protection and human solidarity within the broader frames of political and economic empowerment and emancipation. Lastly, Hongoh shows how the broader conception of intervention has the potential effect of producing transnational sovereignty, and in ways that are not imagined within R2P.

Given the evolving complexities of conflict in the twenty-first century, Aiden Warren argues in Chapter 9, 'Regulating the Abstraction of Violence: Interventions and the Deployment of New Technologies Globally', that the continual advancement of new technologies in theatres of conflict and more specifically, in the context of interventions, pose some very distinct challenges – and limitations – particularly in regard to notions of regulation, the associated moral, ethical and legal debates, and logistics that yield positive outcomes. Given the importance of new technologies, the chapter examines the advent and increasing use of drones, questioning their capacity to actually 'resolve' security issues and succeed as a viable option in humanitarian intervening contexts. Warren also considers the implications surrounding their utility and the 'dehumanisation of death', including those actors who are complicit in their science and construction. In the context of humanitarian interventions, the chapter interrogates the varying debates pertaining to the potential of drone usage and the security dilemmas that could arise should they continue to become a significant option in a state's intervening repertoire. Lastly, he argues, as technology rapidly advances and drones become wholly 'off the loop' in the form of 'killer robots', the chapter examines and rethinks what such additional complexities may spur in the context of future security scenarios.

In Part III, 'The Politics of Post-intervention (Re-)Building and Humanitarian Engagement', Chapters 10–12 illustrate that rather than separating the initial intervention from all the characteristic activities associated with state-building, peace-building and nation-building, these are each different aspects and moments in the broader act of intervention. These are interlocking moments that work to resolve different points of tension and conflict that blur into and depend on one another. By extending the definitional basis, the patterns of social connection and organisation that allow for such substantive 'interventions' can be properly analysed, not least by politicising what is meant by the suffix 'building'.

In advocating substantive actions, Chapter 10, '(Re-)Building the World: Local Agency and Human Security in the New Millennium', by Trudy Fraser, argues that any attempt to re-'build' or 'build' a society in the aftermath of conflict or mass violence *must* seek to engage with a revitalised and dynamic understanding and application of human security, and that the blueprints for such must strive to be resilient to externally imposed notions of failure or success. Drawing on case studies including the UN Peacebuilding Commission (PBC), Burundi and Afghanistan, the chapter calls for a human-security-based 'building' that includes local agents and stakeholders so as to allow for local agency and ownership by the community being 'built', even if that ownership is at odds with the 'builders'' notions of what local peace and security might look like. In this regard, Fraser argues, 'building' cannot exist in technical or normative isolation from the original community of the intervened. Ideally, the 'building' must be part of a consent-based, locally-relevant and resilient engagement by both the intervening parties and the intervened.

In building on the notion of a more nuanced approach, Susan Allen, in Chapter 11, 'Who Rebuilds? Local Roles in Rebuilding Shattered Societies', argues that rather than focusing on external actors, organisations, or states intervening to support that rebuilding, it is crucial to look at local roles in recovery from disaster, and how this can be emboldened so as to improve local-international partnerships. The understandings she presents differ from a state-centric or international-law-based understanding of the process of recovery from war. In this regard, societies that have been shattered must rebuild in multifaceted ways, including rebuilding civil society and electoral and economic systems and the range of social institutions. In undertaking her analysis, she draws on the case study of rebuilding Georgian–South Ossetian relationships as a way to consider who rebuilds devastated societies, and the activities and roles that people can play in the overall process of developing functioning social structures in the aftermath of trauma.

In offering further insight to the politics of post-intervention (re-) building and humanitarian engagement, Vandra Harris, in Chapter 12, 'Transforming the Discourse of Civil-Military Interaction in Humanitarian Environments', explores the key non-governmental and military approaches to intervention, and how these point to civilian leadership in humanitarian environments. The chapter explores NGO–military interaction and how it can be reframed to improve outcomes for communities, drawing on qualitative research with NGO and military personnel as well as civilian and military guidelines. Reflecting on the claim that NGOs are the military's 'force multipliers' – additional tools that increase the impact of the military force – the chapter argues that even turning this around is unhelpful. What is needed instead is greater clarity around humanitarian and humanitarian-like action and actors. With governments funding both defence and development – the latter increasingly under a foreign affairs banner and with an explicit 'national interest' agenda – it can be understood that they view both as valuable in shaping international environments. Harris therefore concludes that it is imperative to have a clear understanding of how these two entities relate to each other, and how that relationship can function best.

Overall, the chapters in this book attempt to address three central themes pertaining to the evolution of humanitarian interventions in a global era; the limits of sovereignty and the ethics of interventions; and the politics of post-intervention (re-)building and humanitarian engagement. In considering international, local and community humanitarian responses, and the role that the UN, international NGOs, local NGOs, bilateral and government agencies continue to play in the twenty-first century, an emphasis on the diversity of theoretical frameworks and practices leading to heterogeneity in the processes of modern polity creation is given applicable attention. Additionally, the collection deals with the issue of the morality and legality of international interventions; non-military interventions (sanctions and aid); humanitarian intervention and Responsibility to Protect; state failure and terrorism; promotion of democracy; and international administrations. As such, the chapters provide a valuable contribution to those academics, students, instructors and intellectual communities engaged in research pertaining to humanitarianism, conflict and interventions and different conceptions of security and international relations, and who agree that the present challenges require a basic rethinking of interventions.

Part I

The Evolution of Humanitarian Interventions in a Global Era

Rethinking Humanitarian-Military Interventions: Violence and Modernity in an Age of Globalisation

Damian Grenfell

Latin 'intervenire': to come between, interrupt.

Introduction

While the proclaimed humanitarian-military intervention in Libya ended on 31 October 2011, five years later the country remains deeply unstable with the population facing various forms of violence and upheaval. The trial of Saif al-Islam Qaddafi in 2015, the son and heir to Muammar al-Qaddafi, resulted in a death penalty being issued by a trial controlled by the Libya Dawn Militia (Kirkpatrick 2015). This could not be carried out, however, as Saif al-Islam himself was a prisoner of an opposing militia (Kuperman 2013: 125–33) and thus beyond the reach of the court's sanctions. That the son of the former and executed dictator faced a death penalty that could not be fulfilled due to competing militias speaks to the violent dystopia that Libya has become. By 2016 Libya had come to resemble the very thing the UK Prime Minister David Cameron sought to avoid in 2011, namely 'a pariah state festering on Europe's border, a source of instability, exporting terror beyond her borders' (BBC News 2011). Confirmation of the acute failure of the Libyan intervention came from the centre of British power itself when, in September 2016, the House of Commons Foreign Affairs Committee published *Libya: Examination of intervention and collapse and the UK's future policy options* (House of Commons Foreign Affairs Committee 2016). This report found that the 'result was political and economic collapse, inter-militia and inter-tribal warfare, humanitarian and migrant crises, widespread human rights violations, the spread of Gaddafi regime weapons across the region and the growth of ISIL in North Africa' (p. 3).

When the current situation in Libya is considered against that in Syria – where despite the catastrophic loss of life there has been little political will towards a humanitarian-military intervention – then a basic requirement for a fundamental rethinking of interventions is required. The crises in both nations give rise to a whole range of questions with regards to why and how an intervention occurs in the first instance, of the form it takes, and in turn the extent to which the subsequent humanitarian and political ramifications of doing so are considered.

In the task of rethinking interventions, this chapter is informed by and concerned with current events, though it takes the opportunity to shift away from the common trajectories of debates in this field; in particular, as to whether interventions occur (or not) because of national interests. Rather, this chapter will focus on the process of interventions rather than sites of conflict for the period from the end of the Cold War onwards. In turn, the key argument is that interventions are bound up with an assertion of power by exogenous forces that reconfigure local populations not just within a liberal peace, but a modern nation-state, and that this tends to remain the case even in a period of intensifying globalisation. As per the discussion in the introduction of this book, a broader approach to interventions is taken here where it is argued that there is significant overlap between military humanitarian efforts, peace-building, human security and development. In rethinking interventions, the focus is on the power associated with recalibrating social relations in conflict zones via various mechanisms of intervention in a way that consolidates 'societies at risk' within a nation-state system.

The first section of this chapter is concerned with developing definitions of humanitarian-military interventions since the end of the Cold War, and to account for the massive expansion of capabilities that allow for a transgression of sovereignty in particular circumstances. These interventions – as it is argued across the second section – reflect the dominance of the West, as the deployment of material and discursive resources in sites of conflict conform largely to the contours of a liberal ideology. Building on and extending these arguments, the third section claims that critiques of liberal peace do not venture deeply enough into understanding power relations between interveners and the intervened. Rather, ideological assumptions of what constitutes 'peace' are manifestations of attempts to instil a particular form of modernity within societies, one that is clearly tied to the formation or consolidation of a nation-state. Keeping with the

16

broader argument that interventions extend beyond a phase of initial military actions, the following section uses the example of voting – as prosaic an act as it might be – to demonstrate one moment in such a process. The final two sections of the chapter take the prior arguments and contextualise them within debates on globalisation, a still largely unexamined area with regards to interventions. The unevenness of globalisation is identified as an important factor, in particular where some states and humanitarian organisations are able to extend themselves temporally and spatially, resulting in a counterintuitive claim that such unevenness is critical to the continuation of a nation-state system.

While the current situation in Syria typifies the diminishing will for large-scale interventions, many peacekeeping missions continue around the world. In one way or another, these are typically accompanied by a range of human security, development and transitional justice programmes that are delivered with an expectation of societal transition. And even then, while it is so difficult to predict what will occur in Libya, let alone Syria, the arguments made in this chapter may still have resonance with regards to the forms of reconstruction and humanitarian aid that may be deployed by the 'international community'.

Humanitarian-military interventions

The massive increase in humanitarian-military operations coincided with the end of the Cold War, as the veto-invoked gridlock of the Security Council – caused by the constant blocking of initiatives by the United States or Soviet Union – gave way to Western-led efforts towards humanitarian military interventions.[1] The most well known have included: Somalia (UNOSOM I 1992–3, UNOSOM II 1993–5); Haiti (UNMIH 1994–5); Bosnia and Herzegovina (UNMIBH 1995–2002); Liberia (UNOMIL 1993–7); Sierra Leone (UNOMSIL 1998–9, UNAMSIL 1999–2005); East Timor (UNTAET 1999–2002); Kosovo (Operation Allied Force/UNMIK 1999–) and Libya (2011). While such large-scale humanitarian interventions were concentrated in the decade following the end of the Cold War, a multitude of peacekeeping operations and long-term reconstruction and development efforts have continued to occur into the new millennium. Roland Paris (2004: 17) is frequently cited for showing the sharp upswing in peace efforts where 'from 1989 to 1999, the UN deployed thirty-three peace operations, more than double the fifteen missions that the organisation conducted in the four preceding decades'. From 1999 to 2014 there have been twenty United Nations (UN) peacekeeping missions,[2] and as of 2015 there have been sixteen active operations comprising a total of 106,245 uniformed personnel, 16,791 civilian personnel and an approved annual budget of approximately US$8.27 billion.[3]

The expanded number and complexity of interventions over the last two decades has also been accompanied by significant expansion in the global humanitarian infrastructure. In terms of the UN, this has included the development of the Peacebuilding Commission, the Peacebuilding Fund, the Peacebuilding Support Office, as well as additional offices within the Department of Peacekeeping Operations such as the Office of Rule of Law and Security Institutions (OROLSI). In financial terms, with thirty-three active conflicts and more than 51 million people displaced by war around the world in 2015, it is estimated that 86 per cent of UN funds are allocated towards conflict situations.[4]

In 2014 the entire humanitarian system comprised approximately 4,480 operational aid organisations, and 450,000 professional aid workers with combined humanitarian expenditures of over US$25 billion (Stoddard et al. 2015: 11). Further, significant resources have been invested in consolidating rationales for interventions, most famously the Responsibility to Protect (R2P), and other doctrines such as human security and efforts at improving civil-military coordination. To support the development of such discourse, a vast array of academic and institutional efforts have been established, such as the Human Security Centre, Human Security Report Project, International Coalition for the Responsibility to Protect and Global Centre for the Responsibility to Protect.

This significant infrastructure marks a decisive shift to a world where interventions are situated at the point of complex intersections across local, national, regional and global concentrations of power. In fact, and as will be argued later in this chapter, even the value of these scales are becoming more difficult to articulate as organisations are simultaneously drawn outwards to both the most abstracted and inwards towards the most local levels. Community-based non-governmental organisations (NGOs) deal with the most intimate problems of everyday life while also becoming key intermediaries in the deployment of national and international humanitarian aid. Regional organisations are frequently drawn in multiple directions; towards the site of intervention where they can claim legitimacy due to proximity while mandated by international organisations and resourced through transnational and global supply chains.

One result of this complexity can be the great diversity in how humanitarian-military interventions occur in practice; from how they are mandated, which organisations coalesce to lead and coordinate efforts, and whether the military component is limited to embargoes, no-fly zones or armed engagement on the ground. With all these differences however, definitions tend to revert to the basic point that such acts are militarily backed transgressions of a pre-established sovereignty aimed at ending humanitarian crises caused by conflict (Pugh 2012: 410; Suhrke 2012: 389; Piiparinen 2015: 1). The 'humanitarian' part of this is typically defined relative to the level and kind of violence; for instance large-scale massacres, ethnic cleansing and genocide that, as implied here by Weiss, are on such a scale that they effect political agendas elsewhere:

> the definition of 'humanitarian' as a justification for intervention normally requires a high threshold of suffering. It refers to the threat or actual occurrence of large-scale loss of life, massive forced migrations, and widespread abuses of human rights – in brief, acts that shock the conscience. (Weiss 2007: 13)

As is often the case with definitions, the closer one gets to the ground the greater the need for qualification and explanation. In the case of interventions however, even at the level of broader generalisation it is difficult to neatly summarise the complexity of what takes place. For instance, changing patterns of warfare have meant that both military and humanitarian efforts are increasingly condensed both temporally and spatially (Kolb 2015: 691; Malešič 2015: 981), and that actual warfare has come to be legitimated in terms of humanitarian goals for political reasons (Binder 2015: 712; Bryan 2015: 33). While the wars in Iraq (2003–11) and Afghanistan (2001–14) have at times been justified by humanitarian objectives (Massingham 2009: 805), these typically fall beyond the parameters of a humanitarian-military intervention given that the main objective has been military victory (Human Rights Watch 2004: 13–35; Massingham 2009: 805).[5]

Sovereignty is equally seen as essential in any such discussion of humanitarian-military interventions. Once viewed as largely sacrosanct, the prohibition on transgressing sovereignty has given way to the extent that some argue for exceptions in cases where humanitarian crises are occurring (Weiss 2009: 12–21). This has most clearly gained traction with the R2P Doctrine which sets out the criteria in which interventions should be based: the right authority, right intention, last resort, reasonable prospects and proportionate means (ICISS 2001). While some distinguish between R2P and humanitarian-military interventions (Adams 2012: 12), subsequent definitions of the latter have been clearly influenced by this doctrine, such as that offered here by Don E. Scheid (2014: 3):

> The humanitarian goal is to protect or rescue innocent people (i.e., non-combatants) from ongoing or imminent, grave, and massive human-rights violations – that is, from mass atrocities. The rationale is not punishment for past wrongs, but prevention. The intervention is conceived to be a last resort for averting or stopping atrocities such as genocide, crimes against humanity, or mass expulsions. (Scheid 2014: 3)

That the rationale of prevention embedded in these kinds of definitions is not consistently applied to practice typifies how interventions are always bound by political contexts, including the ways in which they remain shaped and influenced by national interests. While Libya was partly justified by R2P, it has still been critiqued in terms of the disproportionate use of force where NATO 'assistance to the rebels significantly extended the war and magnified the harm to civilians, contrary to the intent of the UN authorisation' (Kuperman 2013: 14). The presence of Russia in the Syrian conflict can also be understood as a response to what was perceived to be an abuse of R2P in Libya where Western countries deployed it as a ruse to achieve regime change. As such, while R2P has had some traction in debates, its selective deployment draws attention to the pervasive role of national interest and power expressed through interventions. From this point, the more orthodox terrain of judging whether humanitarian interventions are simply an assertion of state interest or undertaken for a combination of complex reasons (Lyon and Dolan 2007: 50) could be the point of exploration. However, the interest here is in drawing attention to the form of interventions themselves, and how humanitarianism is neither apolitical nor neutral, but rather bound up with complex and fluid flows of power between the interveners and the intervened.

Rethinking interventions

Despite the challenges of doing so, this chapter moves towards a different kind of definition of interventions, understood as a process that effects social transformation undertaken by organisational forces exogenous to a given site of mass conflict. While the immediate effort may be towards peace – typically involving the implicit threat or the direct use of military force – interventions incorporate a fuller gamut of activities over a longer period of time; state-, peace- and nation-building, development and human security, as well as transitional justice processes. These elements interweave in different ways, both programmatically but also temporally and spatially, addressing different areas of risk within conflict-affected societies. These tend to be deployed towards a particular kind of peace, with the effect of recalibrating societies so as to ensure a sustainable modernity (typically within a national form). While the stated objective of such efforts by those leading the intervention are humanitarian and often mixed with national interests, in practice they form a significant effort at altering the fabric of societies in an attempt to either sustain or, if necessary, create a new national polity.

This understanding of interventions has various points of difference to the more standard interpretation. Firstly, as suggested it extends the temporal framework from beyond the military act itself, drawing other processes (state-, peace- and nation-building) into consideration. In reality, the military, humanitarian and development phases of interventions are far more intermixed, sitting in connection with one another in terms of playing different yet complementary roles in the broader process of social change. Moreover, there is little sense of linearity as these different moments in interventions intersect in a range of ways.

Secondly, the focus here on change opens the way for a consideration of the effect on local populations rather than on the interveners. There is minimal space in this chapter to take this task up, though it remains an important element when much of the literature on intervention focuses on decision-making processes, ethics and international law, while populations in the sites of intervention are treated as either anonymous or passive actors in a highly turbulent set of circumstances. Thirdly, and as a consequence of this second point, it is possible to draw attention to power dynamics at the (often messy) intersection between intervening actors and local populations, which is discussed across the second half of this chapter.

This approach to defining interventions is informed by critical approaches taken by authors such as Oliver Richmond, Mark Duffield and David Chandler. In different ways these and other academics have demonstrated that interventions are neither neutral nor benign, but embedded in power relations between the intervener and the intervened, and are in turn often the cause of negative consequence (Duffield 2001; 2007; Richmond 2008; 2011; Chandler 2010; Richmond and Mitchell 2011). While these critiques differ substantially in approaches, it is not an undue generalisation to say that a key point of debate is the extent to which the 'principal aim of peace operations thus becomes not so much about creating spaces for negotiated conflict resolution between states but about actively contributing to the construction of liberal politics, economies and societies' (Bellamy and Williams 2009: 4–5).

For the purposes here, concepts of 'liberal interventionism' or a 'liberal peace' serve as an important pathway to both critically addressing interventions while also providing a platform on which to extend debates further. In short, liberal interventionism represents the idea that conflicts are used as an opportunity to rewrite societies as idealised versions of the political norms and systems of Western liberal societies (Selby 2011: 15). In this interpretation, the military elements of an intervention do not simply work to enforce a peace, but rather establish the political space necessary to make changes to foundational governing and economic structures. Richmond discusses how this liberal peace manifests in practice:

> [e]ssentially, what arises from this 'hegemonic discourse' of peace is what Mandelbaum refers to as the 'Wilsonian triad' which, because of its liberal intentions, is based upon a universalist understanding of peace as an objective of intervention (Mandelbaum 2002: 6). Consequently, this legitimates a broad swath of contested means deployed directly and indirectly in the process of intervention. This works on the logic that democratization, free market reform, human rights protection, and development, will ultimately create peace in post-conflict societies. This is exactly what the 'peacebuilding consensus' implies. (2004: 140)

This interpretation is helpful in understanding the emphasis in interventions – especially once primary security has been established – towards elections, constitutions and the establishment of rule of law, state-building, capitalist infrastructure and development activities, even before acute needs (such as food security) are sufficiently addressed.

This all said, such a claim to a generalised coherence might appear at odds with the daily realities of building peace. At sites of interventions, military organisations, NGOs and state-based aid agencies can be found cutting across one another in often highly compressed spaces. While networks of communication and coordination mechanisms may be established to various extents and levels of success, there can also be friction and competition with different agendas, objectives, histories and approaches (Cooley and Ron 2002; Higate and Henry 2009).

Taking a step back from the immediacy of the intervention on the ground, one can begin to see how the liberal peace thesis works to elucidate the assumptions and objectives that shape the institutional and normative fields of engagement, even across highly diversified sets of actors. While a peacekeeping force, or an actual military intervention with war-fighting duties, may appear almost contradictory to a humanitarian NGO, they are drawn together in order to secure the basis for a transition within societies towards a peace (Pugh 2004: 41). For NGOs who move from relief to development, aid agencies that fund into state-building and civil society, or a military force that either keeps or 'wins' a peace, there is an implicit collaboration in generalised efforts that tends towards a particularly formulaic response. The image of patrolling peacekeeping forces on election days is an obvious and tangible example of this kind of confluence.

The definition of interventions at the outset of this section though claims more than what is possible within the liberal peace thesis. Where Richmond writes above that the approach to peace 'legitimates a broad swath of contested means' deployed directly and indirectly in the process of intervention, the claim made here – and drawn out in the following section – is that the liberal peace is a manifestation of a deeper set of assumptions of interveners that in turn shape the attempts at social change in sites of interventions.

Executing modernity

The power of interventions to reshape societies should not only be understood at the ideological level – liberalism in this instance – but through the attempt to redefine the most basic and foundational assumptions of everyday life. Power is not just expressed through the preference for institutional formations or particular political arrangements, but goes to the marrow of social relations by attempting to recalibrate societies across epistemological, spatial and temporal formations to the point where there is some form of sustainable modernity. Here, ideology – as a systematic set of normative claims to a particular truth applying to all people – is understood as one manifestation of modernity that came into use in the rugged aftermath of the French Revolution (Steger 2009: chs 1–3). Understanding the liberal peace then as the dominant ideology in the context of contemporary interventions only goes so far in terms of giving a sense of the contours that shapes the downward power pressuring for change via interventions.

There is an extensive heritage in discussing what is meant by the terms 'modern' and 'modernity' (Harvey 1989; Eisenstadt 2002; James 2006). While it is often used to define a historical period (as in from the early enlightenment), here the emphasis is on particular patterns of social integration rather than historical parameters. In a purely analytical sense, a modern society is one where social relations are constituted in dominance of the disembodied (in contrast to the face-to-face) as particular forms of epistemology, spatiality and temporality gain social ascendancy. Hence, when the shift from agrarian to industrial society is used to earmark a transition to modern society (Gellner 1983: 13–18), or the formation of nations is discussed (Delanty 2006: 357–68), these are taken to be the manifestation of shifts in the deeper ontological layers of social relations. This is 'purely analytical' nevertheless in that it is simply a category for critical thinking, and no society can be categorised as purely modern as there are multiple social formations in play (James 2006). Hence the term 'in dominance' is used as a careful qualifier.

It would be rare that those involved in interventions would speak, or perhaps even think, in terms of their labour being towards the modernisation of a conflict-ridden society. While discourse might orient towards peace, democracy, development, security, gender and land reform, neither documents nor speeches tend towards using the language of overtly changing societies to the modern. Yet such an absence is indicative of the kind of power in play. Just in the same way the liberal peace thesis or other articulations of power (more post-structuralist, such as Duffield) are not articulated at the level of practice, such a silence represents the assumed appropriateness of modernity and the lack of need to defend it as such. This may be the case for a number of reasons, for instance that those involved in interventions do not tend to have to think in such reflexive terms about their own assumptions of how the world is. This of course may be in part due to the acute pressure people are put under when working within an intervention, but also as their own forms of reflexivity remain ontologically limited to their own modernity. To put this latter point another way, even the practice of adaptation to culture or context (phrased for instance as the 'local turn' in peace-building) tends to occur overwhelmingly within a set prescription of what the world should be like, rather than being able to account for, and even accept, basic difference.

Interventions vary enormously, not just in terms of scale and mandate, but also with regards to the attempts made at altering the dominance of forms of social integration. Whether it is an attempt to consolidate, buttress or create a modernity in dominance, it is likely to be more evident in what are often referred to as hybrid political orders (see Boege et al. 2009; Luckham and Kirk 2012). Conceptually, a 'hybrid political order' is one way of speaking of polities that comprise differentiated patterns of social integration where no one form is clearly in dominance. Such an approach can assist in correcting the analytical blindness when sites of conflict are rendered 'ungoverned', as Mallet argues:

> an appreciation of hybrid political orders provides us with a way of: transcending the reductive failed states and ungoverned spaces discourses which frame so much of international politics; locating the often multiple and sometimes invisible governance mechanisms present in post-conflict or 'ungoverned' areas; and understanding their place and role within the broader political community. (Mallett 2010: 74)

Returning to the core argument of this chapter, for all the social changes that interventions seek to affect (both conscious and otherwise), the preference for liberalism is one manifestation of a deeper set of modern assumptions. Where a society has significant patterns of social integration that might be classified as customary, indigenous, traditional, tribal or religious, then the attempt is to recalibrate forms of temporality, spatiality and epistemology so as to create the conditions for a sustainable modernity, one which is typically formed around the modern nation-state. This is of course not to romanticise forms of social integration that are not designated as modern, though it is to argue that different forms of social integration – customary, indigenous, traditional and the modern – are each capable of producing deep violence, inequity and injustice. While modernity is often assumed to provide a civilising pathway forward, the perpetration of violence, from domestic violence to drone attacks, remains a defining feature.

To speak firstly of spatiality, in modernity this tends to be homogenised, secularised, and subject to abstract division. Spatiality tends to be emptied out of specific meaning, understood as part of a greater whole and can be controlled and regulated from a distance, and divisions between 'public' and 'private' space emerge (Habermas 1991).

In the context of this chapter, borders become emblematic of modern space, and their precise establishment, often via satellite imagery, and regulation via treaty, is a constant source of concern where new nations are formed. Agnew (2009: 29) writes that 'territory . . . is particularly associated with the spatiality of the modern state with its claim to absolute control over a population within carefully defined borders'. In hybrid political orders, shifting to modern forms of spatiality is often at the heart of conflict over land between communities constituted in dominance at the indigenous or the customary, for instance, and that of systems of modern governance and capital. As such, agendas for 'land reform' and land use tend to come to the fore in the wake of interventions (UN-HABITAT 2012: 8, 45–63), often along with associated societal conflict (Cryan 2015).

Time, like space, has been conceived of in all manner of ways (see, for example, Gingrich 1994: 125–34; Adams 2006). Modern forms of time are understood as linear and measured by categories (i.e. years, months, days, hours, minutes, seconds). Imbued with a sense of progression, this is what Anderson ([1983] 2006) referred to as 'empty time', where strangers are integrated through a form of time produced at the intersection of the modes of communication and production. Such a form of time constantly resurfaces in the attempts to change societies post conflict. In the period since the end of the Cold War, and arguably part of the liberal peace, there has been a significant trend towards truth and reconciliation commissions (of which there have been more than forty). While institutionally framed in terms of peace and justice, such efforts can represent a profound temporal effect. Firstly, individual and community experiences are drawn into a 'national history' marked by sharp and distinctly modern temporality across the past, present and future (Wilson 2003). Secondly, the practices of such commissions tend towards integrating communities of people via temporal simultaneity, drawing people into either new or reconstituted versions of the nation through a sense of modern co-presence (Grenfell 2009).

Sitting in relation to these two, a modern epistemology is taken as one that is framed by a secular rationality and logic, a form of knowledge based not on convention, the divine or the sacred, but on reason. Other forms of knowledge are subsumed by a faith in the technical and the scientific. One example of this is the 'rule of law', a generalisable principle for social regulation based on a claim to logic that is understood to be autonomous to and outside of people (Vasil 2015). In such an approach, people are assumed to act ration-

26

ally, and the principle is articulated in a universal sense to all within a given temporal and spatial relationship (i.e. all laws in a modern democracy apply to everyone, including the law makers themselves, and at all times). In an interventionary context, rule of law principles tend to be embedded in regimes of 'good governance', popular in aid-agency development and seen as a preventative measure to further instability; working to promote merit as opposed to patronage, transparency as opposed to corruption, technical skills as opposed to localised forms of authority and knowledge.

The power of 'the vote' and modern elections

Of the different potential elements of a liberal peace, elections are frequently treated with enormous symbolic value and allocated very significant resources (Norris et al. 2013: 133). National ballots in Timor-Leste, South Sudan, Libya, Iraq and Afghanistan have each been seen as evidence of societal transition (Rose and Shin 2001: 332). Whether this is the case or not is another issue, as Hohe (2002: 84) wrote of early independence in Timor-Leste that 'so-called "new democracies" do not empower the population as long as the international community takes it for granted that only liberal-style elections represent the people's will and genuine choice'. Importantly for this chapter however, such elections work as one possible example with regards to demonstrating the ways interventions work to effect changes across the temporal, spatial and epistemological patterns of social integration towards a modernity.

In the lead-up to an election, whole sets of systems are set in place: party registration, membership, electoral councils, monitors, different laws, public education and so forth. Each of these not only work to reset social relations in the sense of determining the outcome of public conflict via non-violent means, but also create the conditions in which people may relate to one another, and to systems of governance. In terms of the latter, elections then become a vehicle for consolidating relationships across a territorial form. That people are conscious of being bound together with unknown others, and in ways that cut across clans, customs, ethnicities or religions, does not just occur spatially via elections. Just as the brief references above to the kinds of temporality that are brought forward by truth and reconciliation efforts suggest, elections can also be seen to have the same effect spatially. The embodied practice of voting in a national election occurs – and only makes sense within a modernist mindset – when there is a sense of a disembodied (imagined) community of people drawn together in temporal co-presence, enacting the same task and participating in the same generalised process of legitimating new states. To round this discussion of elections out, this whole process is predicated on the assumption of people working as rational agents, participating in a process where, in theory, all have an equal right before the law to participate and be subject to the outcome.

This form and projection of modernity tends to be articulated or directed towards a consolidation or constitution of a nation-state. Given the objective of confirming a citizen-state relationship within a territorial domain, state-building is about shifting social priorities towards forms of community that cohere around a nation, where people are held in abstract relation to one other across time and space – and in turn in effect either relegate or subsume, for instance, the authority structures of customary Timor-Leste (Hohe 2002: 77–8; McWilliam and Bexley 2008), the 'tribalism' of Libya (IDMC 2015) or South Sudan (Johnson 2014), the ethnic identities in the Balkans or the religious fundamentalism in Mali (Soares 2006). Hence the concern when elections are seen to play into and exaggerate social divisions (Wantchekon 1999: 245; Rose and Shin 2001: 346; Nikolayenko 2007) and in the reverse, the constant discourse of elections being a unifying moment for a nation (Tlakula 2007: 2; Kingsbury 2012: 18–19; UNDPA n.d.). Whether a new nation is being formed, or a nation-state thoroughly reformed in a shift away from dictatorship, elections can work as an attempt at reprioritising systems of governance and identity from a range of identities by promoting a 'unified society'.

Elections do not occur in a void, and traction may represent a significant shift in the political priorities, norms and patterns of social integration of people as they reimagine and participate in a newly formed political space. The different facets of a liberal peace do not sit in isolation of one another, and are only seen to become sustainable if there is a shift to, or consolidation, of a modernity within sites of interventions. It does not need to be absolute, but it does need to be to the extent where people are lifted into a form of modern space, time and knowledge to the extent that a sustainable modern national form is reproduced.

Before moving to the next section there are two final points. Firstly, that the focus in this chapter is on external intervention does not mean that the process is simply an inside-outside dynamic. The use of the term 'consolidating' modernity is deliberate in that interventions frequently take place in sites where elements of modern forms of sociality are already, to various extents, in place. The modernity of a nationalist struggle for independence generally means that there are at least a cadre of local elites and returning diaspora that can work with and share the agendas of exogenous forces, while having access to, and authority within, localised structures of power.

The second point here is to stress that the attempt at social transformation often works in limited ways, and can result in friction, resistance, fracturing and rupture between the attempts at change and local populations who are very often not just passive recipients (see Miller et al. 2013; Schia and Karlsrud 2013). In Libya, tribal identities and religious identities remain extremely powerful, while at the same time as forms of warfare and spatiality continue to evolve, both exogenous and endogenous pressures are brought to bear on attempts to forge a modern nation-state.

To summarise this section, ideology shapes the implementation of a range of deployed discursive and material resources that – whether consciously or not – aim at consolidating a form of modernity with power embedded and contested via the recalibration of epistemologies, spatialities and temporalities. In this way, a 'liberal peace' is the ideological manifestation of a form of modernity that is executed via broad-based societal interventions undertaken with the immediate objective of ending violence, and a much longer-term effect of attempting to achieve social transformation. Building on these discussions of ideology and ontology, this chapter now turns to its final section and seeks to place these debates within the context of globalisation.

Interventions in an age of globalisation

The years following the end of the Cold War saw a deep fracturing of many states around the world. As risks of violence between states appeared to regress, emerging was an acceleration of violence from within nation-states, a shift from interstate to intrastate patterns of warfare. Far from ushering in an era of peace and tranquility, history was splintering in the face of a series of conflicts that were deeply brutal and seemingly impossible to resolve. At times, these wars have been for secession (Aceh in Indonesia and Tamils in Sri Lanka unsuccessfully; South Sudan, Timor-Leste and the break-up of former Yugoslavia all resulting in new nations). Other conflicts have been between groups competing to control resources or attempting to redefine a polity (Sierra Leone, Rwanda, Haiti, Libya).

29

These conflicts have attracted much analysis and debate, some of which engages with the impact of globalisation. Authors such as Mary Kaldor and Herfried Münkler have famously classified these forms of conflict as 'new wars', made distinct in part by the impact of information flows and technology (Kaldor 2001; Münkler 2012). For Kaldor, new forms of warfare were marked by decentralised organisation and integration into a 'global' war economy (Kaldor 2001: 8–9), where the rise of identity politics emanated from 'established political classes' and the threats posed to them by globalisation. The often-contested concept of new wars was once part of a broader analysis of the intersection between violence and globalisation (developed in different ways by other writers such as Appadurai (1998) and Bauman (2001)). While such literature helps in understanding different arguments made through this chapter – including how the kinds of conflict have been seen to necessitate the vast up-scaling of humanitarian infrastructure – the focus here is on how interventions effect social change, and in this final section, in the context of globalisation.

The main argument for this final section demonstrates what may ostensibly appear a contradictory claim, namely that at times globalising processes inform interventions in ways that salvage and reconstitute national sovereignty. Rather than being an anathema to one another, globalisation in its unevenness provides for the potential exercise of power by nation-states. In other words, the temporary breach of sovereignty via an intervention is seen as the avenue to secure the longer-term sustainability of a nation-state, albeit one recalibrated by intensive attempts at societal modernisation and held in place by global processes. In order to make this argument, it is important to delineate two key aspects of globalisation and to clarify its analytical relationship to modernity.

Firstly, and in the briefest of terms, globalisation is understood as a process where people are integrated via disembodied relations across global time and global space. Giddens was one of the first thinkers working in the field to draw attention to how both forms of spatiality and temporality were undergoing acute change across societies.

> In the modern era, the level of time-space distanciation is much higher than in any previous period, and the relations between local and distant social forms and events become correspondingly 'stretched'. Globalisation refers essentially to that stretching process, in so far as the modes of connection between different social contexts or regions become networked across the earth's surface as a whole. (Giddens 1990: 64)

Where Giddens refers to stretching, here the emphasis is placed on the 'disembodied' (closer to what Giddens means refers to as 'disembeddness'). Where, across earlier periods of modernity, the nation was the dominant political community formed around a bounded space (territory) and time (history), under conditions of intensifying globalisation the intersection between space and time begins to alter where there is an intensifying incidence of temporal simultaneity globally alongside a de-territorialisation of social relations spatially per se.[6] In other words, people are drawn progressively into relations with one another that are not just regulated by a world time (as nations are), but for whom a sense of temporal coincidence with known and unknown others emerges, irrespective of how or where one is located.

A second key element to globalisation is the concept of a 'global imaginary', a concept developed by Steger. The conscious shift that has occurred whereby people see themselves as part of a global community is, following his arguments, having a fundamental effect on the ideational foundations that have shaped societies across modernity.

> I suggest that there is, in fact, something new about today's political belief systems: a new global imaginary is on the rise. It erupts with increasing frequency within and onto the familiar framework of the national, spewing its fiery lava across flattening geographical scales. Stoked, among other things, by technological change and cultural innovations, this global imaginary destabilises the grand political ideologies codified by social elites during the last two centuries. Thus, our changing ideational landscape is intimately related to the forces of globalisation, defined here as the expansion and intensification of social relations and consciousness across world-time and world space. (Steger 2009: viii–ix)

Giddens writes that 'modernity is inherently globalizing', and in doing so reminds us not to conflate the two terms. While the 'modern' is an ontological category where forms of social integration within society are increasingly organised via secular-rational logic, and where both space and time become 'emptied out', globalisation is taken as process – a 'modernity at large' to borrow Appadurai's term – that carries with it the modern epistemological premise, albeit recalibrated globally (Scholte 2000: 186–7).

In the context of this chapter, globalisation informs interventions in ways that can be seen to contain the 'violent anomalies' where conflicts begin to threaten the stability of a broader nation-state system. Globalisation and nation-states are in this sense not treated as in basic opposition to one another, but are far more roughly knotted and intertwined, not least in the exercise of power. As Steger argues, to 'pronounce the nation dead would be both inaccurate and premature, just as it would be myopic to deny the eruption of the global on all geographical scales' (Steger 2009: 14).

A key here is to focus on how globalisation is an uneven process. To put it another way, the population of some nations, cities or organisations have vastly higher access to technological interfaces that allows them to extend their activities across a global time and a global space (the control of satellites for instance, currency exchange and banking systems). In turn, this allows for the uneven deployment of resources, discursive and material – such as media, capital or military – leading to the sense of a neocolonialism or westernisation of cultures, even via the humanitarianism of interventions. This point will be returned to shortly, however for the moment it is important to draw out the importance of the unevenness, as in several ways we can see that through interventions the nation is far from a defunct form or polity.

The globalised nation-state and interventions

In making the final arguments of this chapter it is important to recognise that nation-states remain the basic 'imaginary' on which humanitarian-military interventions are politically and militarily organised. Nations are shaped by and drawn into a globalised world, and yet remain the basic organisational currency. There are instances where single nations play an integral role, such as the United States at the start of the Libyan intervention prior to NATO taking over (Crook 2011: 573; Blanchard 2012: 668), British forces in Sierra Leone (Hough 2010: 9) and Australia in Timor-Leste and the Solomon Islands. In the case of multilateral efforts – not least the United Nations – the legitimating and organisational patterns underpinning interventions remain dependent on the membership and support of nations-states. The basis for NATO's membership is Western European and North American nations, with ECOMOG in Sierra Leone and the African Union in Somalia also cases where nations formed the membership of broader organisational efforts.

The importance of nation-states as being the primary organisational basis on which interventions are mounted extends to how civil society coordinates humanitarian efforts. Organisations such as *Médecins Sans Frontières* and the Red Cross, essential in both immediate and longer-term work undertaken through interventions and through humanitarian crises, are organised nationally with central offices (both based in Geneva) that manage global operations, with respective offices in turn based and organised nationally.

Secondly, the nation remains the assumed basis for the broader political objectives of interventions. This is a point that appears to be taken for granted in the liberal peace thesis, though there is little sense that anything other than the nation is seen to ensure stability and peace. And in turn, even when there are considerations of other forms of community, they tend to be scaled hierarchically with regards to a centralised state bound to a nation. As such, in a world where virtually all space is regulated via the nation-state (including treaties of the sea, air, of Antarctica and so on) interventions can be seen as a way of either consolidating nations as they currently exist (Liberia, Sierra Leone) or in the creation of new states where the existing forms have been deemed no longer sustainable (Timor-Leste and Kosovo as examples). This in effect ties back to the earlier arguments of how the modernity of interveners is taken for granted, as national communities with a centralised state are taken as the natural outcome of interventions. Yet while the nation might remain the primary political imaginary in terms of how interventions are organised politically, globalising processes can affect in different ways the shape and reach of interventions, and in turn attempts at the modernisation of societies.

Perhaps the clearest way in which globalisation has affected interventions is in how flows in information can lead to increased political pressure 'to do something' in national publics far from the sites of violence. Action from war zones, like natural disasters, can be watched live as frontline journalists or the combatants themselves televise the violence before them. Here we return to Steger's notion of the global imaginary, a moment of cosmopolitan fulfilment where demands for political action transcend the particularities of nation-states. The image of a dead boy floating in the shallows of the Mediterranean in 2015 (a refugee fleeing Syria) is a case in point, even if it moved opinion towards the acceptance of refugees rather than a humanitarian-military intervention in Syria. Equally, media imagery can shape domestic responses both for and against interventions; pro-intervention in the US in terms of Haiti, and particularly in Australia and Portugal in the case of Timor-Leste, or in opposition to interventions, most famously the US domestic reaction to the treatment of those of its soldiers killed in Somalia in 1993.

While this media effect can be seen as a positive trend, especially when what may have once been virtually unknown events gain significant global attention (such as the kidnapping of girls in Northern Nigeria by Boko Haram), the implicit power relation that underpins this is rarely thought through. If an interventionary act is raised in part through the pressure brought to bear on a national government, then in effect that means that the conscience of a person in a distant and presumably safe space has more power to shape events than those actually facing mass violence.

Beyond this, however, globalisation can be seen as central to the ways in which the reconstitution of sovereignty occurs via an intervention. Just as warfare has adapted and changed in accordance to globalisation, then so has the ability to coordinate interventions; from military efforts through to peace-building, state-building and transitional justice. More research is required in this area, but nevertheless the argument can still be made that those technologies used in war-fighting are having an effect in humanitarian-military efforts. The coordination of no-fly zones as well as military targeting in Libya was dependent, by way of example, on simultaneous flows of information, notably via satellite systems. Even the tracking of Qaddafi up until the time he was executed (Adams 2012: 14) occurred via NATO-controlled systems of mass communication (also frequently referred to as the Revolution in Military Affairs or RMA).

> Key technological elements of this 'revolution' entail, for example, stealth technology (i.e. making one's own systems less prone to radar-detection), better surveillance by satellite or drones and an increase in the precision of weapon systems by either laser or GPS guidance ... The wars against Iraq (1991), Kosovo (1999), Afghanistan (2002) and Iraq (2003) were increasingly based on these RMA assets and turned out to be less bloody for the West than many military exercises held by NATO during the Cold War both in relative as well as absolute terms. It is safe to say that the deliberate effort to invest into high-tech weaponry has created an asymmetrical situation for classical interstate war scenarios where less sophisticated armies have hardly any chance of inflicting significant damage to Western armies in war when fighting a strictly conventional war without resorting to weapons of mass destruction. (Schörnig 2013: 221–3)

The 'asymmetrical' in this quote is a product of the inequity of power that allows certain states to undertake interventions by harnessing globalising processes, and in turn to coordinate practices that reflect and reinforce forms of modernity in different sites. This extends to other activities as well, such as the use of economic sanctions in interventions, and the ways in which financial flows are tracked, monitored and frozen when it is necessary to dissuade a political elite from certain actions. Rather than necessarily being an anathema to the nation-state, globalising processes are being utilised to buttress existing or create new national territorial forms, albeit via the agenda of intervening states. Such a power imbalance, however, is not limited to military affairs, but humanitarianism as well, a point made by Chandler with regards to the actual implementation of humanitarian activity.

> The world of humanitarianism is undergoing fundamental change through the assistance of new technologies, held to be transforming international assistance in humanitarian emergencies. Science, new mobile technologies and Big Data are reputed to enable communities to prevent, cope with and to bounce back from humanitarian emergencies in ways that were impossible before. Humanitarian actors, including United Nations agencies, international bodies and non-governmental organisations have all published official reports in which a broad range of new technologies – from Global Positioning Systems to mobile phones – are applauded on account of their empowering potential and their capacity to improve humanitarian tasks dealing with health emergencies, conflict prevention, underdevelopment and disaster risk management. (Jacobsen 2015: preface)

Some states and organisations have a far greater capacity to extend forms of human engagement (i.e. both military and humanitarian) across the globe which, when used in tandem with other sources of power, create the means for interventions to assemble resources in such a way that comparatively the interveners have a significant recourse to power that cannot be matched in the period following significant destruction and violence.

Conclusion

While liberalism is treated as the ascendant ideology in the post-Cold War period, there has been little question as to why an ascendant ideology has even been necessitated in the first instance. It is not just a matter of triumphalism, though of course even ideology (let alone ontology) can be so ingrained in the DNA of a society that once fought over, ideas are taken as if natural and common sense. Here, and in conclusion, it is suggested that even while globalisation allows for a temporal simultaneity – which in effect means we can know more about more, and more quickly – the complexity this has brought to both the practice of violence and humanitarianism has been immense. That the effects of one set of actions reverberate in an untold number of different ways has meant that there is a need for some kind of coherence, a practical necessity for a broad consensus so as to allow for a coordination of the exercise of power. Interventions are almost inevitably organised around coalitions of actors – nation-states, multilateral organisations, the United Nations, NGOs – and without a broad unanimity on the appropriate political trajectories it would be very difficult to hold such coalitions together in a way that was even broadly legible. This is not some unarticulated conspiracy, but a form of ideological convergence where a kind of need has been created as massive humanitarian efforts are mounted via abstracted process and disembodied relations across the world. At the end of the Cold War this was liberalism, though Libya and Syria may be an indication that this is giving way while being challenged by other sources of power (what Steger refers to as Jihadist Globalism). Either way, an intervention as explored in this chapter is – in an age of globalisation – organised around diffuse sets of actors that are linked by ideological and ontological sets of assumptions. These play out in concentrated spaces as a way of coordinating the deployment of power in sites of acute violence for both the production of forms of peace, and also to secure a modernity.

Notes

1. These rivalries can quickly re-emerge nevertheless, exemplified by Russian backing of the Assad regime in Syria at the end of 2015, including against those forces being directly supported by the United States and Western European countries (Averre and Davies 2015: 818–9; Baev 2015: 12; Dannreuther 2015).
2. Figure taken from the list of operations held by the UN Department of Peacekeeping Operations (DPKO), available at: http://www.un.org/en/peacekeeping/documents/operationslist.pdf.
3. Figure taken from DPKO fact sheet, available at: http://www.un.org/en/peacekeeping/resources/statistics/factsheet.shtml.
4. Figure taken from the World Humanitarian Summit, available at: https://consultations.worldhumanitariansummit.org/whs_Conflict.
5. As will be shown further into the chapter however, there are points where military objectives in wars such as Iraq and Afghanistan dovetail with those efforts of military-backed humanitarianism (Seybolt 2008: 2–5, 25, 43, 175).
6. The per se here is important, as typically it is the nation-state that glo-

balisation is written as if in oppositional form, whereas it is in effect the de-territorialisation of social relations across all forms of territory, including for instance the home and the workplace.

References

Adams, B. (2006), 'Time', *Theory, Culture and Society*, 23(2/3), pp. 119–39.

Adams, S. (2012), 'Libya and the Responsibility to Protect', No. 3, Occasional Paper Series, Global Centre for the Responsibility to Protect.

Agnew, J. (2009), *Globalization and Sovereignty*, Lanham, MD: Rowman & Littlefield.

Anderson, B. ([1983] 2006), *Imagined Communities: Reflections on the Origin and Spread of Nationalism*, rev. edn, London: Verso.

Appadurai, A. (1998), 'Dead Certainty: Ethnic Violence in the Era of Globalization', *Development and Change*, 29, pp. 905–25.

Averre, D. and L. Davies (2015), 'Russia, Humanitarian Intervention and the Responsibility to Protect: The Case of Syria', *International Affairs*, 91(4), pp. 813–34.

Baev, P. K. (2015), 'Russia as Opportunist or Spoiler in the Middle East?', *The International Spectator (Italian Journal of International Affairs)*, 50(2), pp. 8–21.

Bauman, Z. (2001), 'Wars of the Globalization Era', *European Journal of Social Theory*, 4(1), pp. 11–28.

BBC News (2011), 'In quotes: House of Commons debate on Libya action', BBC News, 22 March, available at: http://www.bbc.com/news/uk-poli tics-12809496, last accessed 22 December 2016.

Bellamy, A. J. and P. D. Williams (2009) 'The West and Contemporary Peace Operations', *Journal of Peace Research*, 46(1), pp. 39–57.

Binder, M. (2015) 'Paths to Intervention: What Explains the UN's Selective Response to Humanitarian Crises?', *Journal of Peace Research*, 52(6), pp. 712–26.

Blanchard, C. (2012) 'Libya: Unrest and United States Policy', *Current Politics and Economics of Africa*, 4(4), pp. 663–700.

Boege, V., A. M. Brown and K. P. Clements (2009), 'Hybrid Political Orders, Not Fragile States.' *Peace Review*, 21(1), pp. 13–21.

Bryan, J. (2015), 'War Without End? Military Humanitarianism and the Limits of Political Approaches to Security in Central America and the Caribbean', *Political Geography*, 47, pp. 33–42.

Chandler, D. (2010), 'Rethinking Global Discourses of Security', in D. Chandler and N. Hynek (eds), *Critical Perspectives on Human Security: Rethinking Emancipation and Power*, Hoboken, NJ: Taylor & Francis, pp. 114–28.

Cooley, A. and J. Ron (2002), 'The NGO Scramble: Organizational Insecurity and the Political Economy of Transnational Action', *International Security*, 27(1), pp. 5–39.

Dannreuther, R. (2015), 'Russia and the Arab Spring: Supporting the Counter-Revolution', *Journal of European Integration*, 37(1), pp. 77–94.

Crook, J. R. (2011), 'Contemporary Practice of the United States (United States Joins in Strong Measures Against Libya, Including UN-Sanctioned Use of Force)', *American Journal of International Law*, 105(3), pp. 568–611.

Cryan, M. (2015), 'The Long Haul: Citizen Participation in Timor-Leste Land Policy', *SSGM Discussion Paper*, 2015/13, available at: http://ssgm.bellschool.anu.edu.au/sites/default/files/publications/attachments/2016-07/dp_2015_13-cryan.pdf, last accessed 22 December 2016.

Delanty, G. (2006), 'Nationalism and Cosmpolitanism: The Paradox of Modernity', in G. Delanty and K. Kumar (eds), *The SAGE Handbook of Nations and Nationalism*, London: SAGE Publications, pp. 357–68.

Duffield, M. (2001), *Global Governance and the New Wars*. London: Zed Books.

Duffield, M. (2007), *Development, Security and Unending War: Governing the World of Peoples*, Cambridge: Polity Press.

Eisenstadt, S. N. (ed.) (2002), *Multiple Modernities*, Piscataway, NJ: Transaction Publishers.

Gellner, E. (1983), *Nations and Nationalism*. Oxford: Basil Blackwell.

Giddens, A. (1990), *The Consequences of Modernity*, Cambridge: Polity Press.

Gingrich, A. (1994), 'Time, Ritual and Social Experience', in K. Hastrup and P. Hervik (eds), *Social Experience and Anthropological Knowledge*, London: Routledge, pp. 125–34.

Grenfell, D. (2009), 'Reconciliation: Violence and Nation Formation in Timor-Leste', in D. Grenfell and P. James (eds) *Rethinking Insecurity, War and Violence: Beyond Savage Globalization*, London: Routledge, pp. 181–93.

Habermas, J. (1991), *The Structural Transformation of the Public Sphere: An Inquiry into a Category of Bourgeois Society*, Cambridge, MA: MIT Press.

Harvey, D. (1989), *The Condition of Postmodernity: An Enquiry into the Origins of Cultural Change*, Hoboken, NJ: Wiley-Blackwell.

Higate, P. and M. Henry (2009), *Insecure Spaces: Peacekeeping, Power and Performance in Haiti, Kosovo and Liberia*, London: Zed Books.

Hohe, T. (2002), 'Totem Polls: Indigenous Concepts and "Free and Fair" Elections in East Timor', *International Peacekeeping*, 9(4), pp. 69–88.

Hough, L. (2010), 'A Study of Peacekeeping, Peace-Enforcement and Private Military Companies in Sierra Leone', *African Security Review*, 16(4), pp. 7–21.

House of Commons Foreign Affairs Committee (2016) *Libya: Examination of intervention and collapse and the UK's future policy options,* Third

Report of Session 2016–17, HC 119, 14 September 2016, available at: https://www.publications.parliament.uk/pa/cm201617/cmselect/cmfaff/119/119.pdf, last accessed 22 December 2016.

Human Rights Watch (2004), *Human Rights Watch World Report, 2004: Human Rights and Armed Conflict*, available at: https://www.hrw.org/legacy/wr2k4/download/wr2k4.pdf, last accessed 22 December 2016.

Internal Displacement Monitoring Centre (IDMC) (2015), *Libya: Uprising and post-Qadhafi tribal clashes, displacement in a fragmenting Libya*, available at: *http://reliefweb.int/sites/reliefweb.int/files/resources/201503-me-libya-overview-en.pdf*, last accessed 22 December 2016.

International Commission on Intervention and State Sovereignty (ICISS) (2001), 'The Responsibility to Protect', Ottawa: International Development Research Centre, available at: http://www.un.org/en/ga/search/view_doc.asp?symbol=A/57/303, last accessed 22 December 2016.

Jacobsen, K. L. (2015), *The Politics of Humanitarian Technology: Good Intentions, Unintended Consequences and Insecurity*, London: Routledge.

James, P. (2006), *Globalism, Nationalism, Tribalism: Bringing Theory Back In – Towards a Theory of Abstract Community*, vol. 2, London: SAGE Publications.

Johnson, D. H. (2014), 'Briefing: The crisis in South Sudan', *African Affairs*, 1–10.

Kaldor, M. (2001), *New and Old Wars: Organized Violence in a Global Era*, 3rd edn, Cambridge: Polity Press.

Kingsbury, D. (2012), 'Challenges of Constructing Postcolonial Unity: Timor-Leste as a Case Study', *Asian Politics and Policy*, 4(1), pp. 15–32.

Kirkpatrick, D. (2015), 'Son of Muammar el-Qaddafi sentenced to death in Libya', *The New York Times*, 28 July, available at: https://www.nytimes.com/2015/07/29/world/africa/seif-al-islam-el-qaddafi-death-sentence-libya.html, last accessed 22 December 2016.

Kolb, R. (2015), 'Military Objectives in International Humanitarian Law', *Leiden Journal of International Law*, 28(3), pp. 691–700.

Kuperman, A. (2013), 'A model humanitarian intervention?: Reassessing NATO's Libya campaign', *International Security*, 38(1), pp. 105–36.

Luckham, R. and T. Kirk (2012), 'Security in Hybrid Political Contexts: An End-User Approach', JSRP Paper 2, London: London School of Economics.

Lyon, A. J. and C. J. Dolan (2007), 'American Humanitarian Intervention: Toward a Theory of Co-Evolution', *Foreign Policy Analysis*, 3(1), pp. 46–78.

McWilliam, A. and A. Bexley (2008), 'Performing Politics: The 2007 Parliamentary Elections in Timor-Leste', *Asia Pacific Journal of Anthropology*, 9(1), pp. 66–82.

Malešič, M. (2015), 'The Impact of Military Engagement in Disaster

Management on Civil-Military Relations', *Current Sociology*, 67(3), pp. 980–98.

Mallett, R. (2010), 'Beyond Failed States and Ungoverned Spaces: Hybrid Political Orders in the Post-Conflict Landscape', *eSharp*, 15, pp. 65–91.

Massingham, E. (2009), 'Military Intervention for Humanitarian Purposes: Does the Responsibility to Protect Doctrine Advance the Legality of the Use of Force for Humanitarian Ends?', *International Review of the Red Cross*, 91(876), pp. 803–31.

Miller, G., J. van der Lijn and W. Verkoren (2013), 'Peacebuilding Plans and Local Reconfigurations: Frictions between Imported Processes and Indigenous Practices', *International Peacekeeping*, 20(2), pp. 137–43.

Münkler, H. (2012), 'Old and New Wars', in V. Mauer and M. D. Cavelty (eds), *Handbook of Security Studies*, Hoboken, NJ: Taylor & Francis, pp. 190–9.

Nikolayenko, O. (2007), 'The Revolt of the Post-Soviet Generation: Youth Movements in Serbia, Georgia and Ukraine', *Comparative Politics*, 39(2), pp. 169–88.

Norris, P., R. W. Frank and F. Martínez i Coma (2013), 'Assessing the Quality of Elections', *Journal of Democracy*, 24(4), pp. 124–35.

Paris, R. (2004), *At War's End: Building Peace After Civil Conflict*, Cambridge: Cambridge University Press.

Piiparinen, T. (2015), 'The Interventionist Turn of UN Peacekeeping: New Western Politics of Protection or Bureaucratic Mission Creep?', *Journal of Human Rights*, 15(1), pp. 98–125.

Pugh, M. (2004), 'Peacekeeping and Critical Theory', *International Peacekeeping*, 11(1), pp. 39–58.

Pugh, M. (2012), 'Reflections on Aggressive Peace.' *International Peacekeeping*, 19(4), pp. 410–25.

Richmond, O. J. (2004), 'The Globalization of Responses to Conflict and the Peacebuilding Consensus', *Cooperation and Conflict*, 39(2), pp. 129–50.

Richmond, O. J. (2008), 'Liberal Peacebuilding in Timor-Leste: The Emperor's New Clothes?', *International Peacekeeping*, 15(2), pp. 185–200.

Richmond, O. J. (2011), 'Critical Agency and a Post-Colonial Society', *Cooperation and Conflict*, 46(4), pp. 419–40.

Richmond, O. J. and A. Mitchell (2011), 'Peacebuilding and Critical Forms of Agency: From Resistance to Subsistence', *Alternatives: Global, Local, Political*, 36(4), pp. 326–44.

Rose, R. and D. C. Shin (2001), 'Democratization Backwards: The Problem of Third-Wave Democracies', *British Journal of Political Science*, 31(2), pp. 331–54.

Scheid, D. E. (ed.) (2014), *The Ethics of Armed Humanitarian Intervention*, Cambridge: Cambridge University Press.

Schia, N. N. and J. Karlsrud (2013), '"Where the Rubber Meets the Road":

Friction Sites and Local-Level Peacebuilding in Haiti, Liberia and South Sudan', *International Peacekeeping*, 20(2), pp. 233–48.

Scholte, J. A. (2000), *Globalization: A Critical Introduction*, London: Palgrave Macmillan.

Schörnig, N. (2013), 'Unmanned Warfare: Towards a Neo-Interventionist Era?', in G. Kümmel and B. Giegerich (eds), *The Armed Forces: Towards a Post-Interventionist Era*, New York: Springer, pp. 221–35.

Selby, J. (2011), 'The Political Economy of Peace Processes', in M. Pugh, N. Cooper and M. Turner (eds), *Whose Peace? Critical Perspectives on the Political Economy of Peacebuilding*, London: Palgrave Macmillan, pp. 13–31.

Seybolt, T. B. (2008), *Humanitarian Military Intervention: The Conditions for Success and Failure*, Oxford: Oxford University Press.

Soares, B. F. (2006), 'Islam in Mali in the Neoliberal Era', *African Affairs*, 105(418), pp. 77–95.

Steger, M. (2009), *The Rise of the Global Imaginary: Political Ideologies from the French Revolution to the Global War on Terror*, Oxford: Oxford University Press.

Stoddard, A, A., K. Harmer, G. Haver and P. Harvey (2015), *The State of the Humanitarian System*, London: ALNAP Study.

Suhrke, A. (2012), 'Waging War and Building Peace in Afghanistan', *International Peacekeeping*, 19(4), pp. 478–91.

Tlakula, P. (2007), 'Democratic Elections in a Global Context', *Potchefstroom Electronic Law Journal*, 2, pp. 1–20.

United Nations Department of Peacekeeping Operations (DPKO) (2013), 'List of Peacekeeping Operations 1948–2013', available at http://www.un.org/en/peacekeeping/documents/operationslist.pdf, last accessed 22 December 2016.

United Nations Department of Peacekeeping Operations (DPKO) (2015), 'Peacekeeping Fact Sheet as of 31 August 2015', available at: http://www.un.org/en/peacekeeping/resources/statistics/factsheet.shtml, last accessed 22 December 2016.

United Nations Department of Political Affairs (UNDPA) (n.d.), 'Elections', available at http://www.un.org/undpa/en/elections, last accessed 19 January 2017.

United Nations Human Settlements Programme (UN-HABITAT) (2012), 'Toolkit and Guidance for Preventing and Managing Land and Natural Resources Conflict: Land and Conflict', *Toolkit and Guidance for Preventing and Managing Land and Natural Resources Conflict*, available at: http://www.un.org/en/events/environmentconflictday/pdf/GN_Land_Consultation.pdf, last accessed 22 December 2016.

Vasil, S. (2015), 'Transitional Justice in Timor-Leste: Examining the Effect of Mechanisms Within and Across "Life-worlds"', unpublished thesis, Centre for Global Research, RMIT University, Melbourne.

Wantchekon, L. (1999), 'On the Nature of First Democratic Elections', *Journal of Conflict Resolution*, 43(2), pp. 245–58.

Weiss, T. G. (2007), *Humanitarian Intervention: Ideas in Action*, Cambridge: Polity Press.

Weiss, T. G. (2009), 'What Happened to the Idea of World Government', *International Studies Quarterly*, 53(2), pp. 253–71.

Wilson, R. A. (2003), 'Anthropological Studies of National Reconciliation Processes', *Anthropological Theory*, 3(3), pp. 367–87.

World Humanitarian Summit (WHS) (n.d.), 'Serving the Needs of People in Conflict', available at: https://www.worldhumanitariansummit.org/whs_Conflict, last accessed 22 December 2016.

2

Peace in the Twenty-First Century: States, Capital and Institutions

Oliver P. Richmond

History does not repeat itself, but it often rhymes.

(attributed to Mark Twain)

The political forms that we once knew – the nation-state, sovereignty, democratic participation, political parties, international law – have come to the end of their history. They remain part of our lives as empty forms, but contemporary politics assumes the form of an 'economy', that is, a government of things and of men.

(Savà 2014)

The Cynic is a functionary of humanity in general: he is a functionary of ethical universality.

(Foucault 2011: p. 301)

Introduction

The last century has seen the creation of a fairer, more stable and prosperous state and international environment than so far ever seen in history, even when seen from the perspective of the citizen. Much of this has been based upon the growing mobility of people, ideas, capital, resources and technology. There has been a transformation since the nineteenth century, based upon a 'complex configuration of industrialisation, rational state-building, and ideologies of progress . . .' which led to a core–periphery system, and more recently to a more decentralised and polycentric world (Buzan and Lawson 2015: 1). That the subaltern positionality is essential in order to understand the conditions for emancipation, strongly supported by certain and probably powerful or influential elites, is widely assumed in critical, liberal and other reformist debates. For many, however, a legitimate reading of the progress seen over this period represents a Rostowian

43

shift from tradition to modernity, spanning thinking associated with Plato and Aristotle to Kant and Rousseau, and on towards modern liberal democracy and global capital (Rostow 1960). It is seen by many thinkers, especially those sympathetic to political, normative, legal and economic strands of liberalism, as a form of meliorism: that the adoption and dissemination of positive peace requires social, state and international reform, as well as the development of the human condition (Malloy 2013: 467). Indeed, fifty years ago, the International Covenant on Economic, Social and Cultural Rights, now rarely mentioned, placed many of these problems at the forefront of liberal international and state policy (GA 1966).

Some thinkers have pointed to the historical link between liberation and emancipation and progress (Linklater 1996: 280). Nevertheless, much of the literature on international relations (IR), peace, war – the suite of practices of intervention – lacks enough historical depth to be able to understand the difference between an epistemological framework of emancipation, its focus on micro-level relations of power, and the power relations inherent in centralised and vanguardist forms of empowerment envisioned in liberal internationalism, international Marxism, global governance and neoliberalism. Similarly, IR theory and policy rest upon a standpoint and suffers from the same Northern-centric 'provincialism'.

Many questions arise from this critical view raising problems of positionality and hegemony. Can we move beyond the older ideas of peace and order – and their associated rationalities and *dispotifs* – which simply implied that IR and politics had to occur within the confines of power, structure and nature, and develop a more maximalist normative and ethical vision for IR? Can difference, inequality and unequal power be permanently managed by the state and international institutions or will they too become victims of unequal power, as appears often to have been the case since the Second World War (Hurrell 2007: 32)? Can transnational and informal networks be included in international politics, and can relational ontologies overcome the self-other, inside-outside binaries associated with territorial sovereignty? Can discourse, language, mediation, negotiation and translation – an unstable 'army of metaphors'(Nietzsche 1999: 37) – be harnessed to the cause of peace and justice rather than war and nationalism? Can the limits of nature be transcended in order to produce a peace of the twenty-first century – especially given the types of complex data now available, some of it for the first time – in the areas of society, economy, politics, the environment, science and technology? Does the contemporary concept of 'global governance' capture these possibilities (Commission on Global Governance 1995)? Is 'governing the world' in its complexity even possible, at least in an organised and neat way (Mazower 2012)? How would divergent notions and practices of legitimacy be mediated (across different languages and cultures), and how would hierarchies be legitimised?

This chapter discusses the relationship of interventionary practices with peace and evaluates them according to what might be termed emancipatory theory.

International order and peace

Behind all of the proposals for a more peaceful international order in history, the old idea of a commonwealth looms, promising a broader public good for all while being territorialised, connected to power and the state (Elden 2013: 330). E. H. Carr saw the formation of European-wide institutions after the Second World War as both practical and necessary for such a process, which possibly led to a 'post-state international society' (Carr 1939; Carr 1942; Malloy 2013: 472). This would be necessary to provide a substitute for war, he thought, as an ordering mechanism, overcoming what Marx had identified as a destructive relationship between land, capital and labour (Elden 2013: 9). It would take the people away from their close, historical relationship with the soil, translated into the 'political technology' (Elden 2013: 15) of a nationalist state and territorial forms of sovereignty, towards a more pluralist form of community, perhaps even a global *polis*. Indeed, human rights, democracy and prosperity have slowly begun to displace sovereignty, authoritarianism and oligarchy in many parts of the world, and even territorialism has been under question as a basis for sovereign power. The second half of the twentieth century saw international institutions, law and norms gradually built into an established international peace architecture. After the end of the Cold War this was increasingly parallel to, and often in tension with, global capitalism.

However, if one inverts the traditional debates about peace in IR as emanating from political, state-level, international agreements, development and trade, as well as global governance, to a more subterranean view from local and subaltern agents that IR is based upon a broad suite of interventionary practices rather than a fixed system, then peace looks rather different. If the apogee of peace thought is

45

the liberal peace system, then the post-Cold War era has seen several attempts to develop a related 'right of intervention' to support that system, culminating in the Responsibility to Protect doctrine of 2005 (ICISS 2001). R2P has not managed to reconcile human rights with sovereignty, however, in the eyes of many of the world's states, which prefer the latter norm over the risk of intervention. It has placed the state above the subaltern in practice. At the same time, in countries where economics were seen to be the tools of politics, from China to Brazil, global capitalism has been adopted.

Thus, the international system itself is already based upon an 'interventionary order' related to neoliberal forms of peace, rather than a fixed structure of sovereign states. As opposed to the state-centric and international architecture we perceive to exist, the structure of IR is actually a system of interventionary networks, practices, and discourses, emanating from a core group of dominant states and actors across each region (the US, China, India, Russia, the UK, Brazil and the institutions they create or of which they are members, from the UN, World Bank and African Union to the European Union).

This alternative view, which problematises any notion of a fixed international order of territorial and states and global governance, can be ascribed to historical practices of intervention, from invasion to imperialism, trusteeship and now development, state-building peace-building and counterinsurgency (COIN) doctrine, linked up across time. This continuity means that how we understand peace in a historical context must also be reconsidered, evolving from a victor's peace, to a liberal peace, and now to a neoliberal peace requiring global capital and counterinsurgency securitisation. This represents a historical structure of intervention. At best this evolution has led to a negative form of hybrid peace.

Intervention and progress

Can peace be drawn from within the international/interventionary system (victor's peace, imperial peace, liberal peace, neoliberal peace) or must it be drawn from advanced thought and related vanguardism, or a specific positionality (subaltern, state, institutional, global, normative, instrumental and so on) and possibly resistance? Should progress be identified and directed from a vanguardist elite positionality, or from that of the subaltern? This is a debate which has been ongoing probably since Plato's and Aristotle's contributions. Kant and Hegel underlined its tensions in different ways: despotism versus recognition and justice. The experience of R2P, as its contemporary culmination, and the liberal peace experience, suggests the connection between intervention and progress is problematic, but also that subaltern contributions are similarly weak. Distant, elite governance fails to identify the correct issues, and uses broad brush tools.

Subaltern agency is weak and inaudible and is located in wider social, political, economic and environmental systems, in a reciprocal rather than dominant manner. This expanded agency does not mean more direct power, but it means complex possibilities for change and reform exist in unlikely agents and spaces. It is distributed rather than intentional agency, multitrack and multidimensional, forming swarms which are often incidental in nature (Dürbeck et al. 2016: 122). The so-called agentic pluralism it offers may well be the basis for legitimacy at the social level, but it is also the basis for hybridity and collages.

However, if intervention is the structure, rather than the states system, global governance, or global capital, then it can be assumed that dominant international actors (such as the US) have, at least since 1945, given up on the idea that the subaltern can bring about progress. An interventionary, hegemonic (albeit benign) rather than organic communitarian or cosmopolitan order was thus needed, one which inverted how peace is thought of – not as a static, negative peace between warring factions but a mediation of the structure by dominant states, government and capital in their favour. This was out of exasperation with the ability of the masses to bring about progress, defined as order, peace, security, social and economic advancement. On the other hand, the subaltern requires intervention to modify otherwise immutable structures of domination they face.

Modernity has attempted to resolve this problem through rights, liberal institutions and neoliberalism, as well as new technology. However, the increasingly densely networked and heavily cooperative international order, as it has developed from Westphalia onwards, remains heavily marked by power and exclusion in its own peculiar mix of US and Northern hegemony and state-centric multilateralism. Consent has not been forthcoming in the last decade or so from the rest of the world. Much credibility has been lost for the liberal international order since the Iraq and Afghan wars, and during the financial crises of the last seven years. Despite these difficulties, the international order is more networked, cooperative, interdependent and transnational than it has ever been in history. This is so with either of the modern state's current main forms – Western liberalism and neoliberalism, or 'managed' democracy and capital-ism elsewhere.

The problem with previous colonial, Marxist, liberal internation-alist, critical, neoliberal projects for 'peace' is that they tended to see intervention as a tool of power, emanating from static units or con-cepts (states, the international community, social justice or norms), using strategic, class or liberal vanguards who have both right and power to intervene at social or state levels. Their deeper subtext is that social agency can overcome direct and structural forms of power, and coalesce around a more emancipatory international agenda if given the chance. But they set that agenda on the basis of internal assumptions. On the Marxist side not many achievements can be seen in recent history, and the social democratic or liberal compromise between society and power certainly offers by far the strongest indication of the possibility of progress so far. Yet, much remains to be done, indicated by the social, which seems far from the capacity of the liberal. So the question for the local, positioned in the middle of such power relations and looking for a more progres-sive peace, is how to turn intervention in their favour for the goal of a more positive form.

Marxists, dependency theorists and post-colonial thinkers have very negative perspectives of the underlying power structures that modernisation has entailed, and in a democratic order, they count for a very significant global constituency. They often point to how capitalism has perpetuated existing power structures rather than reforming them into a more equitable and progressive framework. Indeed, many aspects of the recent liberal peace system, from self-determination, to democratisation, economic liberalisation and glo-balisation, have had contradictory effects. When part of a peace process, as they inevitably are, globalisation and neoliberalisation have sometimes undermined independence, the capacity of societies to resist oppression, equality, rights and democracy through reassert-ing neopatrimonial frameworks of authoritarianism over individual rights in contradictory processes – and yet in other areas they have improved rights and justice.[1] The longstanding struggle over the broadening of human rights towards new and more sophisticated generations has barely made any progress since the 1960s. In a slightly more sensitive manner, the UN's Capstone Doctrine pointed to how the legitimacy of a peace operation should be present in the eyes of local populations if such a mission is to succeed (DPKO 2008). The US and UK militaries have also recently made similar assertions. R2P was meant to secure the rights of the human over sovereignty, but this has been undermined by Northern and Southern objections. The 'post-2015 Development Agenda' puts these aims into a global material context of ever-increasing, sustainable, development across the world, however, which seems unlikely under contemporary forms of global governance.

As anti-colonial and post-colonial, development theorists and others have realised, the colonised, poor and oppressed are not merely subjects of colonialism, but implicated in it, meaning that in IR peace is implicated in war and violence just as much as they might be seen to emanate from a specific geographic context and state. This can be described as a state of structural war, drawing on the concept of structural violence, understood as the system of violence that cannot be removed without system reform. Such a perspective can only be understood from a subaltern positionality. The implication of how peaceful states and societies may be implicated in various ongoing wars opens up new vistas of understanding for the nature of a peaceful international order, the good state, political community and the social contract, questions of justice and material equality, and intervention: in other words for peace and the contemporary good life (or 'living well') (Rist 1996: 246). Either structural violence is tolerated in the existing system, or progress points to systemic reform directly connected to local multiple and complex local claims. Minor modifications to the system may not be enough to maintain legitimacy. Progress cannot be found in enforcing the existing system and its structural violence.

The progress that has been made over the last two centuries might be said to have occurred mostly because of what were initially idealistic and often underground civil and social forms of activism and mobilisation, which were adopted by leadership, eventually producing democracy. Such processes appear to support democracy and its social instincts. The symbiosis of the social and democracy has not therefore, as Plato once feared, supported impractical interests, led to tyranny, or as de Tocqueville argued, produced mediocrity – so far at least (de Tocqueville [1835/40] 2000; Plato 2006). In fact the symbiosis of market forces and bureaucracy point towards tyranny, used to prevent democratic claims for fairer resource distribution.

As T. H. Marshall (2009) argued, citizens in the west gained civil rights in the eighteenth century, political rights in the nineteenth century and social rights in the twentieth century – though unexpectedly, so far in the twenty-first century all three sets of rights are now under some pressure rather than converging, or a fourth layer of rights emerging. Over time, basic rights for citizens against their leaders, various versions of a social contract, a realisation of the need for localism, decentralisation, and more sophisticated notions of human rights (though mostly not yet implemented), have developed. This might be said to be increasingly represented in the international system, though not fully formally, through the so-called 'first UN' of member states, the second UN of international civil servants and the third UN of non-state, NGO and other civil society actors, or perhaps a fourth UN made up of those working in transnational, scalar and sometimes transversal networks in order to improve rights and needs provision around the world (Keck and Sikkink 1998; Slaughter 2004; Weiss et al. 2009: 123–42; Weiss and Abdenur 2014: 1753). When these converge with diverse societies around the world, peace may be said to have converged with the art of government.

However, there is the question of whether such developments should be embodied in the person, the citizen, the state or the international, how they exercise the relevant power and authority, with what legitimacy to maintain themselves. So far, the territorial state, and very specific states at that, dominate regional and global order, despite ever-denser transnationalism. Top-down and Weberian notions of state legitimacy are clearly in conflict with bottom-up Foucaultian versions of the agential subject. Both are sometimes in tension with liberal international norms, and global capital produces further and fundamental tensions with liberal rights frameworks.

There is also the unsettled question of whether democracy can be brought about undemocratically and whether peace can be brought about through violence, as Tully has pointedly argued (Tully 2013: 11). The evidence of the last twenty-five years suggests the answer to both questions is negative: every legitimate order needs viable tools of intervention to sustain itself. What constitutes legitimacy for order, its viability or consent for the tools of intervention remains open to debate. Violence must be a last resort, and cannot be present in substantive peace, even in structural form. Territorial arrangements appear to be essential for societies to formulate legitimacy, but multiple claims to a kind of territorial legitimacy often spark conflict because legitimacy often turns out to be majoritarian or exclusionary in some way, perpetuating inequality. This clearly cannot lead to a progressive order.

There has been much tension over whether intervention creates a universal but hierarchical world order, or entwined orders dealing with difference and inequality. There has, over the last decades, been a growing contradiction between state autonomy and a legitimate and binding international order. Struggles for autonomy, human rights and democracy, for decolonisation and sovereign equality, social and distributive justice, and cultural liberalism, as Bull and Watson once argued, have influenced the global milieu if not decisively (Bull and Watson 1984). Indeed, liberal thinkers envision that the liberal international order will continue to expand, either by 'infecting' other states, or through various forms of military, economic, social and political intervention, leading to a fuller realisation of universal human rights, international law, courts, collective governance and multilateral institutions, probably at the expense of sovereignty and unipolarity (Ikenberry 2011: 296). Eventually this might lead to a world state or federation, as well as a kind of global Marshall Plan in order to produce relative equality for its members.

Gilbert Rist points to US President Truman's 'Point Four' of the Marshall Plan as the start of this technical 'age of development', which should spread its proceeds more equally as a response to war, violence and inequality (Rist 1996: 70–5). It also established a system of categorisation with the US and 'peace-loving' countries at the top of its apex. He argues that Western- or Northern-centricism will also decline, as will related hierarchies, but the potential for humanitarian forms of intervention must remain (Rist 1996: 70–5). So far, however, some commentators on the history of liberalism argue that it has become an unwieldy framework of contradictions, little able to resolve its own contradictions and perhaps therefore not able to offer much perspective on how progress towards emancipation may be achieved, let alone more refined universal and multilateral institutions (Bell 2014: 691). From a subaltern perspective, injustice, inequality and instability, as well as systemic insecurity and a lack of sustainability remain all too visible to perhaps two thirds of the world's population. Between forty and sixty states are still regarded as extremely fragile today (Mcloughlin 2012: ch. 1). Of course, state fragility may also be necessary in some aspects in order to prevent state capacity from spilling over into predation. Furthermore, the so-called 'Beijing Consensus' has diluted the previous Washington or New York Consensus on the liberal peace, as has the widespread emergence of authoritarian capitalist states, managed democracy and oligarchical forms of capitalism (Hudson 2003: xvi). Even from the perspective of a citizen in an advanced democracy, the post-war and post-Cold War settlements look weakened: they may

assume the sanctity of democracy but dislike their elected governments (Micklethwait and Wooldridge 2015: 251) and feel powerless against the disruption of capitalism. They also detect strong
hints of bias, self-interest or imperialism in Western intervention and
US hegemony. Indeed, democracy and rights, self-determination and
globalisation appear to be unbalanced and irreconcilable, whilst also
being posited as the solution to war and producers of progress.

Thus, any interventionary order has to be built for the subaltern
(as the liberal peace system was assumed to be, with its emphasis on
democracy and rights). R2P and the liberal peace have made some
progress in this direction, but they are also closely associated with
the interests of historical power and capital, and so have attempted
to balance that power with subaltern claims. The latter often point to
structural arguments about the constraints of capital and resources,
resulting in a major legitimacy deficit. The subaltern perceives many
injustices in this historical order, though many also want to be part
of it.

So progressive peace may emerge when the subaltern sets the
parameters for interventionary projects, the latter using the direct,
structural and governmental power amassed at state and international scales. This points to how layers of intervention based upon
a denial of rights are met, with some time lag and significant power
limitations, by layers of more contextualised, though often globally
networked, peace formation. A progressive peace can only really
be decided by the subaltern in their everyday context, according to
their rights, needs, identity and expectations, and power has to be
harnessed selflessly and empathetically to this end (as participatory
forms of democracy suggest) if it is to achieve legitimacy. This makes
centralised systems of governance look distant and unresponsive.
Indeed, this might be seen as the goal of the great liberal thinkers,
from Kant to Locke, if only they did not have to compromise with
power. However, structural constraints as well as elite and hegemonic
interests represent implacable obstacles to subaltern claims, given the
limitations of critical agency. Furthermore, this raises the additional
problem of how to separate exclusive and probably conflict-inducing
local claims from those that are subaltern, pluralist, emancipatory
and sustainable, both intellectually and in practice.

Liberal and neoliberal peace versus emancipation

In keeping with the development of progressive thinking, from John Stuart Mill to Beatrice Webb, which drew on Hobbes's notion of a contract between rulers and the ruled as the basis for the state's legitimate authority, the idea of a public good being the aim of the state has become widely accepted. Furthermore, this public good should continually advance society's material interests, not just maintain its security as a static hierarchy (Micklethwait and Wooldridge 2015: 683). In the twentieth century, this process was often connected, after disarmament and security, with social welfare, a tradition that joined with those related to debates about emancipation and social justice emerging from at least the eighteenth century onwards on both the left and the right, and most often connected with different traditions of liberalism or social democracy. Capitalism as well as egalitarian governance have been seen as crucial elements of emancipations. A complex mixture of individualism, freedom, equality, consent, toleration and pluralism, along with rational scientific progress, in preference to autocracy and conservativism, were assumed to be important though perhaps distant markers of this body of thought (Bell 2014: 684). The mix of these elements have been balanced in different ways, times and contexts, leading to different sets of contradictions.

Since the Second World War the US has promoted human rights, democracy and capitalism as the core, progressive path for all states, upon the understanding that they are universal ways of producing legitimacy, dismantling power inequalities, preventing corruption and producing material and technological advancement. The UK introduced a health service, national insurance and universal education after the Second World War as a progressive reform for the state. Thus, such progressive thinking has in the last century been gradually extended to the state and to the international level through the UN system, in that its architecture should facilitate social progress across the planet. Consent has historically been the basis of such an order, rather than solely a balance of power or hegemony. Consent is thus enshrined in the rule of law and allied with clever theoretical, technological and bureaucratic capacity (Ikenberry 2011: 48). Underlying this train of thought is the sense that subaltern positionality is necessary in order to understand the conditions of emancipation. However, consent has been somewhat in tension with US hegemony, at the same time, especially with the recent neoliberal state model the US has been promoting more recently, as in Iraq (Richmond 2014). Also notable in the most recent era of revolutions across the Middle East and Mediterranean basin has been the assumption that the state is likely to use violence even against those resisting its predatory domination, but revolutionaries and resisters should exercise non-violence: an unlikely assumption in many ways.

Over the last one hundred years, many Western leaders have agreed that a liberal international architecture, backed by Western industrial and military capacity, is the only source of world order that can be legitimate, progressive and relatively stable. They have assumed that all societies maintain similar expectations of progress. Progressing from the individual to the ethical state and the cosmopolitan international community, as Alfred Zimmern once foresaw, a moral community was thought to be emerging (Zimmern 1936), which some argued would lead to a world government promoting the interests of peace. The massive expansion of international and transnational organisations and agreements since 1900 add support to a progressive view of the deepening of order in relation to socio-political progress. Yet, recently, a range of studies have shown that only a minority of peace agreements survive for more than a few years. This poses something of a puzzle about the longevity of the liberal peace.

Since the 1990s, however, many observers have assumed over this period that eventually, a 'global village' or global governance will emerge where peace will reign through more decentralised processes of cooperation (McLuhan 1968; Rawls 1999). Prescriptive liberal multilateralism, following American epistemic and political hegemony, has been essential to the process (Hurrell 2007: 59). Others have pointed out that transcending the state (particularly the 'competition' form of state, which tends not to deliver welfare or services, or legitimacy and solidarity for its citizens) (Cerny 1997: 269) is necessary, as the ontology and the ethical concerns of the contemporary, neoliberal state generally do not enable a broader solidarity, pluralism or distributive justice (O'Hagan 2013: 118–37). European approaches to regional integration, from Jean Monnet to the concept of 'normative power Europe', have tended to take this more nuanced view. These ideas have emerged from the historical debate in Europe on the emergence of world government via a federation of states and the emergence of an international social contract; perhaps most notably described by Rousseau as a 'Commonwealth of Europe' and Kant as a *civitas gentium* (international state), or even by Marx as solidarity across global labour. These perspectives tended to be based upon cooperative and inclusive rationalities of politics, leading to broadly multilateral, internationalist – rather than state-centric and exclusive – orders (Rousseau [1756] 1917; Kant [1795] 1917; O'Hagan 2013). They also have a strong sense of 'duties beyond ourselves', as Hedley Bull famously stated, and a need to overcome the limitations of the order/justice dichotomy (Dunne and McDonald 2013: 1–17). Elements of liberal internationalism, Marxism and more recently globalisation continued this push towards global progressiveness in different ways, whilst also carrying forward political stalemates over aspects of power.

The following four elements appear to be pressing: the balance between global capital and political and material rights: identity and pluralism; environmental sustainability; and historical and distributive justice. Thus, the emerging order of global governance (rather than a more centralised system of world government) cannot be self-interested, isolationist or unilateralist (Talbott 2008: 391). Such thinking about the evolving liberal international order can be linked to the political and philosophical notion of a 'commonwealth' – a united but also decentralised social, political and economic community based upon membership, rules and cooperation.[2] It denotes a republican political community in historical thought about progress and order, connected both with social welfare, democracy and a state aligned to the interests of its people. It offers prospects for both the political power of society and a form of international society, all ensuring that the state does its utmost to support domestic and regional peace and order.

During the recent Bush era, liberal hegemony emerged as a new form of imperialism (Ikenberry 2011: 254). New wars in the twenty-first century are increasingly *structural wars* – a complex mix of social, cultural, historical, political, legal and economic contests that span the global economy, the state and the city and involve both formal and informal, rather than sovereign, conflict. War, violence and conflict are in complex ways connected to the societies, states and international systems which seek political authority, order, rights and prosperity. Some seek to end violence, some maintain it for reasons of power or progress. The tools of the weak in such conflicts are often difficult to counter with the standard security instruments of the state and the international. Such wars comprise indirect, structural violence (along with the usual forms of violence) and seek to maintain state, economic, identity and social inequality.[3] They require new responses. Liberal peace-building and neoliberal

state-building, as well as development approaches, are often ineffectual in dealing with structural forms of war, and are caught up in a
crisis of legitimacy, related to the tension between American liberal
hegemony and its challengers (Ikenberry 2011: 10), the expansion of
the 'international society' (Bull and Watson 1984) and widespread
social dissatisfaction with globalised capital. This is even though
there are perhaps 130,000 UN personnel, among others, involved
in peace operations around the world (UN News Centre 2014).
Thinking is now turning once again to the question of how it may be
improved in the light of more sophisticated knowledge about what
has gone wrong in the most recent phase of history. The new 2015
Sustainable Development goals are one example of this new development, with their focus on ending poverty, inequality, providing a
wide range of services and sustainability.

The potential of a post-liberal peace

From these contradictions, the nature of a post-liberal and positive
hybrid peace can begin to be discerned. It would also have to be post-
neoliberal, if social legitimacy is to be achieved more broadly (Hudson
2003). Agonistic reconciliation of identities within a framework of
heterogeneity would be essential. A progressive vision of improving social rights and conditions would attract societies towards this
position. It would have to offer progress towards material equality
through the state as well as the market, on top of legal requirements
for the equality of all citizens. Thus the state must offer an eventual
prospect of pluralism and relative equality in norms, identities, laws,
rights, institutions and material standards. There would probably
be a basic agreement on the nature of a universal and global moral
community, in very thin terms, and the modes by which needs, rights,
interests and identities were mediated and adjudicated. It would need
to respond to nature, technology, consent and rights as mutually
entwined determinants of peace and justice, probably aimed at progress towards equality (Hurrell 2007: 308–16). It would need to deal
with the contradictions of being epistemologically led by the powerful and the wealthy but identified, felt and needed most acutely by the
subaltern. It would need to be very broadly legitimate, representing
the 'expansion of international society' that Bull and Watson (1984)
once foresaw, as well as stable and effective in bringing about progress. It would have to deal with historical and distributive justice
issues, and respond to basic matters of environmentalism.

Contrary to the views of many liberals, realists and constructivists since the 1990s, the pathway to peace, security and development points not to a liberal or neoliberal peace, but to a new form of progressive politics with the power of attraction to move populations away from processes of violence and its conciliatory and cooperative behaviour. This probably requires a major reform of the states and international systems, as well as of global capital and governance; a regrounding in empathy, the local and the everyday, and a willingness to share material resources across regions; and tackle global problems in an egalitarian spirit. It would be progressive in terms of rights and needs, offering the probability of continual improvement along a path chosen mutually by society members following their preferences. Liberal peace and the neoliberal state, along with the liberal international community, were staging points along this path in the twentieth century. A new stage would require a form of global social democracy, with a set of centralised institutions to agree on core issues and standards, but which must be representative of a decentralised framework of local politics. Too many of the current attempts to engage with pressing global issues involve a defence of old-fashioned sovereignty, an unwillingness to share internationally, a lack of empathy, an inability to accept local needs or differences or everyday legitimacy, an inability to tackle longer term global problems and a defence of old modalities and hierarchies of power in history.

Peace in the twenty-first century must now deal not just with open war, but structural violence – or perhaps in a more radical vein, in structural war of capital over society and the environment. Structural violence tends not to be highlighted by mainstream bureaucratic, organisation, structural and institutional approaches to IR, concerned as they are with conflict management or transformation. The trouble with these perspectives on progress towards both the 'good state' and an 'international community' is that they have been led by Western hegemony, and Southern states, societies and actors are concerned that without more historicised and equitable approaches to global order, justice will not be served for many in the Global South (Lawler 2005: 479; 2013: 25). A liberal ethic has emerged from liberal imperialism and liberal internationalism, but has been replaced by a neoliberal ethic at the expense of a more social state (Piketty 2013: 471) and international community, concerned with improving and safeguarding the lives and conditions of their populations as fairly as possible (an ambition dating far back in history, and mentioned frequently since, not least in the 'Declaration of the Rights of Man' in 1789). For many outside of the stable community of developed states, even the EU appears to be as much an example of hegemony and discrimination as an exemplar for a peaceful political order. Even UN peace-building, as in Central America, may be too threatening to existing power structures to be welcome in many countries, as the elites in Guatemala concluded after seeing what the UN tried to do in El Salvador in the 1990s (Stanley 2013: 32). The good state and the international community have to make moral sense to all their members. The global economy needs to escape the deep structures of domination that exist within capitalism (Picketty 2013: 234). This indicates a need for both a centralised capacity to address human needs across the globe through systems of intervention and redistribution in a commonly agreed framework of institutions, and a decentralised and contextualised framework in which human needs and rights can be negotiated and transmitted upwards. The new, more polycentric, post-colonial world of 'emerging powers' must be recognised, probably mainly 'from below' in bottom-up and ethnographic terms, as well as emancipatory demands for decentralised and more horizontal forms of governance (as opposed to the top-down approach of the liberal peace architecture). A social, cosmopolitan, and pluralist ethic for the international system would be necessary, and a significant move beyond the old mix of the Westphalian state with a liberal international system, and global neoliberal capitalism. Intervention for enablement would thus be required, providing a different (and more Southern) alternative to the contemporary Northern concern with effectiveness (Prashad 2012: 228). Thus the United Nations Conference on Trade and Development (UNCTAD), for example, is concerned with fair distribution of resources and the control of private capital and a right to well-being and social justice (Prashad 2012: 235), as reiterated in the Bamako Appeal of 2006, which sought to overcome North–South divides and replace what it saw as the Northern militarised and neoliberal consensus with a more sensitive form of democracy and solidarity (Prashad 2012: 243).

Progress, intervention and autonomy are thus balanced in an actively equalised, democratic (in legal and material terms) political system spanning the local to global scales. So far however, only powerful states and occasionally alliances of states have been able to carry the day in responding to violence and promoting reform, which has been limited to their own norms, preferences and interests. Existing transnational frameworks for the negotiation of peace and order have little agency when confronting large-scale problems (Weiss 2009: 264). However, drawing on critical theory as gathered together by Habermas, progressive forms of reason, law and democracy together provide the basis for dialogic methods through which conflict can be settled, and new and more emancipatory ethical political orders might be achieved (Habermas [1983] 1990). Such processes depend on complex networks in a post-colonial world of acute inequality and constantly emerging new layers of injustice in which the only universal is the mediation of difference. It means, as Stanley has observed in his assessment of UN attempts to build peace in Guatemala, both reforming power structures and building new national institutions that contribute to domestic and regional peace, as well as working through existing local institutions which carry legitimacy authority and know-how in situ (Stanley 2013: 8). Merging indigenous or customary law and praxis with liberal law and institutions is an agonistic task, of course. Furthermore, dealing with material inequalities that afflict local populations – often indigenous groups – and others is difficult in the context of existing mainstream thinking on the liberal peace. The state is in effect not well predisposed to dismantling power structures that support such marginalisation, nor can it often afford to deal with current or past injustice of inequalities. Furthermore, the more effective the international community is in dismantling oppressive power structures, the more elites elsewhere will refuse to cooperate with peace interventions or do their best to prevent conflict-affected citizens from playing a democratic role. Similarly, at the international level, the more peace demands structural reform, the less hegemonic power supports it.

The G77, for example, appears to be a space for a progressive debate about North–South redistribution, about what the problems are with the current system and what might be done about it. It is also an avowed supporter of anti-imperialism, socialism and the sovereign state, from the New International Economic Order of the 1970s to the New World Order for Living Well of 2014 (of the G77 plus China, now numbering 133 states). Its latest document adds public services to the list of human rights and seeks a role for the state over the corporation. It calls for decolonisation not from imperial powers but from capitalism. It wants to see a revival of the UN and the abolition of the Security Council (G77 2014). Yet, it also constantly reiterates the sanctity of state sovereignty, as if this were the best way of support human rights and development. History over the last sixty years has thrown significant doubt on this assumption.

The west has generally been more progressive on questions of existing versions of human rights and gender, and implementation, but not on socio-economic inequality. Of course, there is a wing of Western thought and ideology which would prefer an engagement with inequality, but since the 1980s it has been on the retreat. The last era of progressive politics in the West for many was in the 1960s and 1970s (Wilkinson and Pickett 2014: 11). All of a sudden, the Western-created and backed order appears to be caught between more progressive demands to which it is reluctant to concede, and autocratic or oligarchic tendencies, towards which it is veering perceptibly. The UN, EU and other Western-backed structures of global governance and their key state supports are at best now seeking to stabilise the current order, with all of its imperfections. After the experience in the 2000s in Iraq, direct intervention is off the agenda, even where peace is threatened, creating obvious risks. Such concerns need to be taken seriously. There are some signs that they are, but there is much disagreement over what to do next, as with the new development goals of 2015, which have been developed through a global consultation of social and elite actors. Such consultation may well raise important issues like global inequality and justice, but persuading states to agree and act is a different matter.

Yet international actors have responded to such obvious problems in a rather negative way: they are protecting the old liberal peace model and are unable to develop an alternative, though they are trying to create space for localised forms of consultation, at least to a limited degree. Local peace-building is regarded as something of a challenge for international actors, even the UN: either they support it despite it having different goals and processes to theirs, or they want to ally with it in order to nudge it towards a liberal social contract. It is widely accepted, somewhat ironically, that social and economic rights have diminished in the post-Cold War world, even though many of the claims of the world's conflict citizens revolve around them (hence the revived G77 interest in a new statement about progressive politics).[4] There is little appetite for discussion of social justice even amongst an international community that claims it supports the most advanced state and international system ever seen in history. It is generally seen by policy elites in the international civil service as being an issue that is too complex and too long term for the current system of international relations, organisations and states to respond to. Thus, the international peace architecture rapidly becomes technocratic as a defence against its own ethical limitations, and states and donors easily return to sovereignty as a legalistic form of managerialism.

World leaders from the US, the UK, India, China, Brazil, the UN, the EU and others have recently implied a new or reformed order is in the offing, or is necessary, and that the leadership of the West and its old architecture is no longer plausible nor legitimate (BRICS 2014). Even the much-criticised World Bank is undergoing a quiet internal shift. The G77 is pushing for a wider engagement with development from the perspectives of the recipients. A new consensus is being sought, even if it seems unachievable. Military intervention is increasingly deemed unlikely or impossible, the state is returning, political space is absent where progress can be mediated and inculcated, but international actors, donors and personnel are responding. The usual 'mission' and 'programming' approaches are now old-fashioned and arrive far too late, with too few resources and limited local legitimacy. Security Council, General Assembly, Secretariat or World Bank and donor leadership is compromised from a number of perspectives. It is probably in denial about its legitimacy and capacity. There is also concern about a lack of global leadership capable of taking an ethical position vis-à-vis peace.

In the UN system, 'non-mission-setting policy'[5] indicates a possible response for peacekeeping missions, along with the use of other new techniques and new technologies, where a crisis occurs and there is little possibility of consent or support for an intervention. International mediation is now widely seen as having widened from state-centric post-violence settlements to broader matters of political affairs where entry points to stimulate an improved order may be found.[6] This is also connected with the UN's recent 'rights up front' approach (Ban Ki-moon 2013). It is connected with a revival of human rights, high ethical standards, prevention, local legitimacy and authority, and the acceptance of widely differing contexts. This may mean material assistance without political engagement in some cases. However, the United Nations Department of Political Affairs (DPA) has moved to a focus on building or assisting the social contract, as in Libya through its 'constitutional coordinator' meaning that the intersection between power and the state, politics and society is ever-present in any revamped form of intervention.[7] Of course, this has so far been unsuccessful in Libya. There is a slow response emerging to the dilemma the UN currently faces: it cannot rely on great power support, it cannot use a blueprint, cannot intervene, but as yet there is no visionary resolution of this problem available which would regain the moral high ground lost during the last decade.

In the light of the above arguments a positive hybrid peace might have some of the following dynamics or possibilities:

1. it would start from inclusive politics envisioned as progressive and sustainable in its local contexts;
2. as society is often based upon exclusion, small groups of progressive actors would be able to form alliances without willing outside actors;
3. it would have cultural, social, historical, political, economic, material and identity elements;
4. each of these elements would be contingent on context, the state and the international;
5. the tensions between the elements in (2) and (3) would be resolvable through politics and external processes of mediation;
6. politics would not be about merely the management but the treatment of problems;
7. the political system would not depend on self-help and resilience;
8. it would actively seek progress and improvement for all its citizens through equal access to service and resources;
9. the polity would be aware of intervening factors from beyond that context, whether they be new and better ideas or incursions by the predatory forces of nationalism, militarism or capitalism;
10. it would be able to seek assistance from outside in responding to such challenges without undermining its own pluralism;
11. it would maintain its own identity without threatening or displacing that of others;
12. it would maintain its own temporality despite that of others (industrialised modernity, for example);
13. it would be responsive to contingency and flexible enough to respond to internal challenges for progressive improvements;
14. progressive politics would seek sustainability in environmental and social terms;
15. institutions and economic frameworks would be tools to this end, operating within the boundaries of material and geographic (i.e. structural) constraints.
16. the international system would operate to enable co-operation and progressive equalisation, not through centralisation (which is open to significant abuse) but through decentralised networks of exchange;

17. the polity would be de-territorialised and the international community would focus on redistribution.

This would mean that security would be thought of as human security, and that frameworks of meaning and structure, such as interests, norms or the state itself would be much more closely defined by its subjects' perspectives. The international would act as the supporter of human security, rather than the protectors of sovereignty and markets.

Systems of representation would have to be far more participatory rather than bureaucratic or technocratic. Democracy would emanate from systems of representation, through which claims are made and authorised in a social context, which in turn would feed into formal participatory democratic institutions that are also connected to an international community or society.

Law would reflect progressive thinking from within society and from the international level. The state would be the vehicle for these systems which would collate and act upon the claims of the population, supported by the international community.

Power would have to be purposefully fragmented in order to allow these many systems of representation to support security and produce law that would be widely consented to, from local to global scales.

These systems would rest on a progressive understanding driven by a bottom-up understanding of how inclusive and equitable systems need to be built, including an understanding that the goal of such a scalar framework of progressive politics would be sustainable for the long term.

Thus, social and economic systems can be evaluated and reformed only from the most exposed and precarious position in any polity from the local to the global. This is because the more secure and the wealthier can afford to moderate their expectations without significant discomfort or structural violence. Those individuals and communities most exposed to direct or structural violence cannot be expected to sacrifice what they do not have in terms of security, resources or identity, and thus, the signals they send – albeit faint – are the most important for the reconstruction of any political, social or economic system. As the historical evidence points to the loss of legitimacy any system faces if it does not respond to these signals, and the system's tendency to revert to authoritarian power when challenged by them (because it maintains the interests of the powerful establishment), the contradiction between subjects, legitimacy, power and sustainability has to be addressed by any new turn in peace praxis.

Through these (arguably) utopian indications that can be drawn from modern debates on peace, it can be clearly seen that the removal of direct violence, and the redressing of structural violence and their linkages with the post-Cold War settlement (the liberal peace), indicates that levels of violence (including structural violence) are widely perceived to be far too high, even in states supposedly at peace. In other words, debates on peace indicate that old understandings of the difference between peace and war (state-centric, 'world' or civil war) are long outdated. Furthermore, the nineteenth-century system of nation-states based on territorial sovereignty, overseen by twentieth-century international organisations aimed at moderating the negative behaviour of states and guiding them towards liberal progressivism, is no longer adequate. Global levels of structural violence widely pertain, and require a better and more progressive peace settlement even in states and regions (such as the US or EU) supposedly at peace. Networks and assemblages of violence, responding to a range of injustices, perceived and structural, need to be engaged in a new peace settlement, which itself will be aimed at providing a complex assemblage and networked solution to the widely varied structural, normative, temporal, political, social, economic and geographic conflicts that travel with globalisation. Injustices across these terrains required networked and hybrid peace settlements across a global terrain of difference.

In the past, debates around these matters have aimed towards uncovering the conditions of a world state or a world confederation (Wendt 2003: 491–542), but a more realistic and practical approach under current conditions appears to be to think about a mobile and networked peace under an emancipatory form of global governance, meaning that it would be post-liberal and not territorial, though it would have to be legally and bureaucratically organised in order to maintain economies, redistribute resources and knowledge, enhance human security and so on.

Making sense of the current peace architecture and its possibilities

Table 2.1 depicts the effects of the liberal and neoliberal peace, and the negative and positive realities that have instead emerged from Cambodia to Afghanistan.

Table 2.1 Graduations of contemporary peace
Liberal to variants of hybrid peace

Perspectives level	Type of peace			
	1990s Objectives	2000s Objectives	Reality of last 25 years	Goal of peace engagement
International	*Liberal peace*	*Neoliberal peace*	*Negative hybrid peace*	*Positive hybrid peace*
	Positive peace, democracy, human rights, markets, human security.	Negative peace, compromise on democracy and human rights, peace is unstable because of growing inequality.	Negative peace; internationals tend to see hybridity as cooptation, outdated and a compromise on norms and refuse to accept local ownership.	Negative peace; internationals tend to see hybridity as cooptation, outdated and a compromise on norms, though they may accept the need for local ownership. They are concerned about the pluses and minuses of networks and mobility.
Regional	*Positive peace*	*Negative peace*	*Negative hybrid peace*	*Positive hybrid peace*
	Model is the EU and a social democratic member state	Model is ASEAN and a neoliberal or authoritarian state	Regional organisations tend to offer rhetorical rights and development but focus on power sharing and neoliberalism	As above
State	*Negative peace*	*Negative hybrid peace*	*Negative hybrid peace*	*Negative/positive hybrid peace*
	Limited resources and consensus means difficulties in placating interests, constitutional reform and institutional implementation and material support.	State simulates compliance but acts as a predatory actor, supported by global markets. Peace is unstable.	State focuses on elite interests only/ cooptation of internationals, predatory behavior towards society.	State may play a role as mediator of societal and international interests, or focus on elite interests only. But the state is under pressure to reform from below and above in contradictory directions: society wants human security, capital wants opportunities, mobility and sustainability.

Table 2.1 *continued*

Perspectives level	Type of peace			
	1990s Objectives	2000s Objectives	Reality of last 25 years	Goal of peace engagement
	Negative hybrid peace	*Negative hybrid peace*	*Negative/positive hybrid peace*	*Positive hybrid peace*
	Material issues, inequality inefficiency and coordination, cultural, customary and identity clashes with liberal norms.* Static and unequal.	Local inequalities and resources issues are not dealt with directly. Modernisation ethos undermines cultural and identity frameworks.** Mobile and networked.	Local/state interests and identities dominate*: static and unequal	Material issues, rights, inequalities are dealt with, while identity, culture, culture, and historic forms of association are able to adapt themselves.† Mobile, networked, pluralist and sustainable.
Outcome/ model of peace	*International trusteeship model*	*Global governance model*	*State/local ownership only model*	*Mixed mode, enablement and local ownership model*

* Liberal peace and negative hybrid peace appear to be the second-best contemporary outcome.

** Neoliberal peace is the worst outcome.

† Positive hybrid peace appears to be the best contemporary outcome.

Breakdown of negative and positive hybrid peace

Negative hybrid peace	Positive hybrid peace
International/regional level	*International/regional level*
Ceasefire, transitional agreement.	Internationals reconcile to local- and state-level forms of legitimacy and difference.
Lack of democracy and human rights.	
Local power structures and hierarchies dominate.	Internationals may normatively or ideologically disagree.
Lack of gender equality.	Internationals supply the necessary resources for human security without conditionality.
Centralised state controls power, or state is 'collapsed', 'fragile'.	
Threat to regional and international order.	Internationals recognise the need for local autonomy, legitimacy and authority.
Decentralised power dominated by custom, tribalism, warlordism and so on.	
This is unsustainable; but despite these factors, basic order is maintained.	
State level	*State level*
State is based on socialism, or centralized ideology.	The state balances international and domestic forces, norms, needs and expectations
State is authoritarian or oligarchical.	The state supports the security, rights and material interests of its society.
State is dominated by neopatrimonialism.	

Table 2.1 *continued*

State level	*State level*
State preserves a range of historic hierarchies and inequalities/structural violence. However, these systems maintain order (in the short term at least).	The state provides justice. The state represents local interests and identities at the international level. The state negotiates for more progressive politics at the international and local level. The state is locally and internationally legitimate.
Local level	*Local level*
Rights and needs are not dealt with. Identity is curtailed. System is not pluralist. Historic structural violence continues. State is predatory. International norms reject local legitimacy. These dynamics maintain order though domination.	Rights, needs, justice and identity are incorporated in a progressive politics. State responds to local claims for the above. International also responds to local claims.
Negative hybrid peace maintains order through maintaining structural violence, which requires territorialism, immobility, and inequality.	*Positive hybrid peace represents local legitimacy and consensus, reflected in the state, and supported (though perhaps not condoned) by the international. Mobile, networked, pluralist and sustainable.*
Power/the state/elites dominate order. Very susceptible to a return to negative peace but has potential for a shift to positive hybrid peace.	*Local norms, identity, needs, justice and consensus shape order: finely balanced between improvement and regression.*

Conclusion

As Kant wrote, in a universal community wrongs committed in one place are felt everywhere (Kant [1795] 1917; Archibugi 1992: 295–317). This is even more relevant in the new era of instant, global mobility, communication and translation, which applies not just to functional communication, but also to the understanding and mediation of one's positionality vis-à-vis others in justice terms. Norms, institutions and law across the international, the state and civil society reflect both the need to respond to wrongs as well as reflecting power. Inequalities of all sorts are increasingly being seen as 'wrongs', meaning the nature of political legitimacy at the global level has now irrevocably changed. Similarly, matters of environmental and intergenerational legitimacy have now made their appearance on the international scene. Power cannot deal with these claims by denying them: power must now respond by accepting and engaging with them. The international architecture, the state, globalised capital, technology and epistemology must be aimed at these bases for the formation of social legitimacy within the constraints of progress, in order to iron out the current, crippling, contradictions over legitimacy from these different sites, networks and processes. In this sense, legitimacy needs to be understood in ethnographic, sociological and normative terms, not just in terms of law, process and efficiency. Legitimacy is related to the social provision of consent through consensual systems of political decision-making, in other words (Brasset and Tsingou 2011).

Can justice be achieved in progressive mode against the grain of deep historical-material and geopolitical structures of world politics? In preliminary terms, we can point to some key qualities of progressive thinking, starting with national and global material and legal equalisation of society over time, which attracts the support and consent of populations in democratic scales, from local to global. It also demands pluralism, solidarity, public truth-telling and peaceful means of dispute settlement within civil society, across all sectors of society, and scaled up to the state, regional and international. It is probably true to say that this ambition, spanning the great thinkers of politics and international relations from Plato to Kant (or Plato to NATO, or the warfare state to the internationalised welfare state and onwards to the globally governed neoliberal state, as is often argued to represent the history of progress in different quarters), is closer to being achieved, and more plausible than ever before. Nevertheless, history, material and geopolitical structures, and human-contrived injustices, still stand in the way. Their presence is obvious and responses are increasingly clear, but political will is often lacking because of the threat that any such response will pose to long-standing and entrenched power structures: militarism, social hierarchies, international hierarchies, the control of capital and material distribution. Democracy dictates that challenges are dealt with according to the will of the majority, but while democracy pertains in some states, there is as yet no form of international institutional democracy, though the subaltern voice is the loudest. Furthermore, the various interest, ideological, epistemic and material groups and stratifications that currently claim expert knowledge often see democracy as a hindrance to their authority on the question of progress. Yet, local knowledge, legitimacy, and context are all vital in the construction of political legitimacy. It has become commonplace to argue that just and stable political solutions have to be found on the local level where legitimacy is least abstract and where inequality and diversity are at their highest, though this is also where power is least able. This raises the question of how to overcome power structures that anchor inequality, and how might, by implication, local legitimacy, power and international intervention ever be reconciled.

To begin to sketch out the possibilities for a positive, hybrid peace is already an act of hegemony, and must be done with ethical and methodological sensitivity and recognition of power imbalances. What we see from the above diagrams is that a positive hybrid peace as understood by society may well be a negative hybrid peace from the state or international level where concessions may be made. Likewise a positive peace from the international level may appear to be a negative hybrid from below. What the local may experience as a negative hybrid peace may well be a positive or positive hybrid peace from above. In other words, if peace is representative of a social contract, and the state and the international are outgrowths of this, than progressive and emancipatory processes are subjectively understood according to their positionality in time (history), space (territory), resources (materiality), norms and identity factors. One person's emancipation or positive peace may be another person's loss. One person's hybridity is another person's concession. Positionality matters, and the view from below, from the subject's position, is probably the most politically legitimate in democratic and developmental contexts, even if it is not the most suitable for modernisation, development, global security or Northern interests as seen from the elite perspective.

Notes

1. For an important discussion of this paradox in the MENA region, see Hinnesbusch (2015).
2. See definition in the *Oxford English Dictionary* (1989).
3. This concept of structural war adapts Galtung (1969) and Kaldor (1999).
4. Confidential sources (2014).
5. Confidential source (2014).
6. Ibid.
7. Confidential source (2014).

References

Archibugi, D. (1992), 'Models of International Organization in Perpetual Peace Projects', *Review of International Studies*, 18(4), pp. 295–317, available at: http://www.danielearchibugi.org/downloads/papers/models. pdf, last accessed 27 December 2016.

Ban Ki-moon (2013), 'Renewing our Commitment to the Peoples and Purposes of the United Nations', United Nations Secretary-General, 22 November, available at: https://www.un.org/sg/en/content/sg/speeches/2013-11-22/renewing-our-commitment-peoples-and-purposes-united-nations-scroll , last accessed 28 December 2016.

Bell, D. (2014), 'What is Liberalism', *Political Theory*, 42(6), pp. 682–715.

Brasset, J. and E. Tsingou (2011), 'The Politics of Legitimate Global Governance', *Review of International Political Economy*, 18(1), pp. 1–16.

BRICS (2014), 'Fortaleza Declaration', Sixth BRICS Summit, available at: http://brics.itamaraty.gov.br/media2/press-releases/214-sixth-brics-summit-fortaleza-declaration, last accessed 28 December 2016.

Bull, H. and A. Watson (eds) (1984), *The Expansion of International Society*, Oxford: Oxford University Press.

Buzan, B. and G. Lawson (2015), *The Global Transformation*, Cambridge: Cambridge University Press.

Carr, E. H. (1939), *Twenty Years Crisis,* London: Macmillan.

Carr, E. H. (1942), *Conditions of Peace*, London: Macmillan.

Cerny, P. G. (1997), 'Paradoxes of the Competition State: The Dynamics of Political Globalisation', *Government and Opposition*, 32(2), pp. 251–74.

Commission on Global Governance (1995) *Our Global Neighbourhood*, Oxford: Oxford University Press.

Confidential source (2014), personal interview, UN Department of Political Affairs, New York, 1 April.

Confidential sources (2014), personal interviews, UN Department of Peacekeeping Operations, New York, 31 March.

de Tocqueville. A. ([1835/40] 2000), *Democracy in America*, Chicago: University of Chicago Press.

Dunne, T. and M. McDonald (2013), 'The Politics of Liberal Internationalism', *International Politics*, 50(1), 1–17.

Dürbeck, G., C. Schaumann and H. Sullivan (2016), 'Human and Non-human Agencies in the Anthropocene', *Ecozon*, 6(1), 118–36.

Elden, S. (2013), *The Birth of Territory*, Chicago: University of Chicago Press.

Foucault, M. (2011), *The Courage of Truth: The Government of the Self and Others*, vol. 2, Lectures at the College de France, 1983–84, London: Palgrave.

G77 (2014), *New World Order for Living Well*, 14–15 June, available at: http://www.g77.org/doc/A-68-948%28E%29.pdf, last accessed 27 December 2016.

Galtung, J. (1969), 'Violence, Peace, and Peace Research', *Journal of Peace Research*, 6(3), pp. 167–91.

Habermas, J. ([1983] 1990), *Moral Consciousness and Communicative*

Action, trans. C. Lenhardt and S. W. Nicholsen, Cambridge, MA: MIT Press.

Hinnesbusch, R. (2015), 'Globalisation, Democratisation, and the Arab Uprising: the International Factor in MENA's Failed Democratization', *Democratisation*, 22(2), pp. 335–57.

Hudson, M. (2003), *Global Fracture: The New International Economic Order*, 2nd edn, Ann Arbor, MI: University of Michigan Press.

Hurrell, A. (2007), *On Global Order: Power, Values and the Constitution of International Society*, Oxford: Oxford University Press.

Ikenberry, J. G. (2011), *Liberal Leviathan*, Princeton: Princeton University Press.

International Commission on Intervention and State Sovereignty (ICISS) (2001), 'The Responsibility to Protect', Ottawa: International Development Research Centre, available at: http://responsibilitytoprotect.org/ICISS%20Report.pdf, last accessed 28 December 2016.

Kaldor, M. (1999), *New & Old Wars: Organized Violence in a Global Era*, Cambridge: Polity Press.

Kant, I. ([1795] 1917), *Perpetual Peace: A Philosophical Sketch*, London: Allen and Unwin.

Keck, M. E. and K. Sikkink (1998), *Activists Without Borders*, Ithaca, NY: Cornell University Press.

Lawler, P. (2005), 'The Good State in World Politics: In Praise of Classical Internationalism', *Review of International Studies*, 31(3), pp. 427–49.

Lawler, P. (2013), 'The 'Good State' Debate in International Relations', *International Politics*, 50(1), pp. 18–37.

Linklater, A. (1996), 'The Achievements of Critical Theory', in S. Smith, K. Booth and M. Zalewski (eds), *International Theory: Positivism and Beyond*, Cambridge: Cambridge University Press, pp. 279–98.

Malloy, S. P. (2013), 'Pragmatism, Realism, and the Ethics of Crisis and Transformation in International Relations', *International Theory*, 6(3), 454–89.

Marshall, T. H. (2009), 'Citizenship and Social Class', in J. Manza and M. Sander (eds), *Inequality and Society*, New York: W. W. Norton & Company, pp. 148–54.

Mazower, M. (2012), *Governing the World: The History of an Idea*, London: Allen Lane.

Mcloughlin, C. (2012), *Topic Guide on Fragile States*, Governance and Social Development Resource Centre, University of Birmingham, UK, available at: http://www.gsdrc.org/docs/open/con86.pdf, last accessed 28 December 2016.

McLuhan, M. (1968), *War and Peace in the Global Village*, New York: Bantam Books.

Micklethwait, J. and A. Wooldridge (2015), *The Fourth Revolution*, London: Allen Lane.

Nietzsche, F. (1999), *Philosophy and Truth: Selections from Nietzsche's Notebooks of the Early 1870s*, trans. D. Breazeale, Amherst, NY: Humanity Books.

O'Hagan, J. (2013), '"With the Best Will in the World …"? Humanitarianism, Non-state Actors and the Pursuit of "Purposes beyond Ourselves"', *International Politics*, 50(1), pp. 118–37.

Oxford English Dictionary (1989), Oxford: Oxford University Press.

Piketty, T. (2013), *Capital in the Twenty-First Century*, trans. A. Goldhammer, Cambridge, MA: Harvard University Press.

Plato (2006), *The Republic*, trans. R. E. Allen, New Haven, CT: Yale University Press.

Prashad, V. (2012), *The Poorer Nations: A Possible History of the Global South*, London: Verso.

Rawls, J. (1999), *The Law of Peoples*, Cambridge, MA: Harvard University Press.

Richmond, O. P. (2014), *Failed Statebuilding*, New Haven, CT: Yale University Press.

Rist, G. (1996), *The History of Development: From Western Origins to Global Faith*, trans. P. Camiller, London: Zed Books.

Rostow, W. (1960), *The Stages of Economic Growth: A Non-Communist Manifesto*, Cambridge: Cambridge University Press.

Rousseau, J.-J. ([1756] 1917), *A Lasting Peace through the Federation of Europe/ State of War*, trans. C. E. Vaughan, London: Constable.

Savà, P. (2014), '"God didn't die, he was transformed into money" – An interview with Giorgio Agamben – Peppe Savà', *Libcom.org*, 10 February, available at: http://libcom.org/library/god-didnt-die-he-was-transformed-money-interview-giorgio-agamben-peppe-sav%C3%A0, last accessed 27 December 2016.

Slaughter, A.-M. (2004), *A New World Order*, Princeton: Princeton University Press.

Stanley, W. (2013), *Enabling Peace in Guatemala*, Boulder, CO: Lynne Rienner.

Talbott, S. (2008), *The Great Experiment: The Story of Ancient Empires, Modern States and the Quest for a Global Nation*, New York: Simon & Schuster.

Tully, J. (2013), 'Citizenship for the Love of the World', lecture at the Department of Political Science, Cornell University, 14 March.

United Nations Department of Peacekeeping Operations (DPKO) (2008), *Capstone Doctrine: Peacekeeping Operations: Principles and Guidelines*, New York: DPKO.

United Nations General Assembly (GA) (1966), 'International Covenant on Economic, Social, and Cultural Rights', available at: http://www.ohchr.org/EN/ProfessionalInterest/Pages/CESCR.aspx, last accessed 28 December 2016.

United Nations News Centre (UN News Centre) (2014), 'In summit-level meeting, Ban announces review of UN "blue helmet" operations', UN News Centre, 26 September, available at: http://www.un.org/apps/news/story.asp?NewsID=48884#.WGKmHboZyC0, last accessed 27 December 2016.

Weiss, T. G. (2009), 'What Happened to the Idea of World Government', *International Studies Quarterly*, 53, pp. 253–71.

Weiss, T. G. and A. E. Abdenur (2014), 'Introduction: Emerging Powers and the US – What Kind of Development Practice', *Third World Quarterly*, 35(10), pp. 1749–58.

Weiss, T. G., T. Carayannis and R. Jolly (2009), 'The "Third" United Nations', *Global Governance,* 15, pp. 123–42.

Wendt, A. (2003), 'Why a World State Is Inevitable,' *European Journal of International Relations*, 9(4), pp. 491–542.

Wilkinson, R. and K. Pickett (2014), *The Importance of the Labour Movement in Reducing Inequality*, Centre for Labour and Social Studies, July, available at: http://classonline.org.uk/docs/2013_04_Thinkpiece_-_labour_movement_and_a_more_equal_society.pdf, last accessed 28 December 2016.

Zimmern, A. (1936), *The League of Nations and the Rule of Law 1918–1935*, London: Macmillan.

(Endnotes)

3

The Evolution of Economic Interventions and the Violence of International Accountability over the *longue durée*

Bronwen Everill

Introduction

Since the late eighteenth century, economic interventions have been a crucial component of both voluntary humanitarian action and international interventions. From sanctions to wartime aid to developmental and state-building projects and specific humanitarian commercial campaigns, economic tools have been, and continue to be, used by international powers to undermine or bolster state sovereignty.

However, the use of economic tools of intervention, while offered as a peaceful alternative to military intervention, is often connected to the escalation towards military intervention, rather than forestalling it. Attempts at intervening economically in situations with defined 'human rights abuses' or 'crimes against humanity' have had mixed results, sometimes even exacerbating the humanitarian crisis. Equally confusing has been the conflation of democracy with human rights, which has allowed intervention to be cast in a humanitarian way in support of regime change when leaders have disregarded the results of elections or suppressed democratic rights.

By looking at the long historical record of humanitarian intervention in Africa, the connections between different forms of intervention – economic, military, capacity-building, humanitarian, individual, state and NGO – become clearer. Given the contingent relationship between economic, diplomatic and military interventions that can be seen in recent examples ranging from Afghanistan to Zimbabwe, Sri Lanka to Syria, Libya to Ukraine, it should be clear to observers of humanitarian intervention that if economic development is a historical process, so too is humanitarian intervention. Thinking about economic interventions as one form of humanitarian intervention helps to bring these two strands of the literature together in ways that illuminate the messiness of intervention, and the relationships between intervention and power.

This chapter will explore the different uses of economic interventions and their interlocking relationship with the evolution of humanitarian intervention. It will specifically focus on examples from the African continent, stretching from the eighteenth century to the present, though the cases examined will share broader themes with developments outside of the continent. Additionally, the chapter will examine state-level economic interventions – sanctions and aid, in war and peacetime – together as one form of pressure for conforming to humanitarian norms. Individual and corporate economic interventions will be considered separately, as a form of intervention inherent to global capitalism. Overall, an examination of economic interventions will reveal their interconnectivity, as well as their relationship to compulsion and physical force. By giving or withholding, states are able to intervene in the politics of dependent states, while individuals are able to determine the shape of global production.

Economic interventions in the literature

While the field of intervention studies is expanding, few have looked back in any detail beyond the twentieth century to examine the relationships between international power and humanitarian intervention (Barnett 2011; Simms and Trim 2011; Everill and Kaplan 2013). However, as the end of the Cold War recedes in time and more intervention cases arise that reflect the new international situation, a broader context is needed to understand the development of the humanitarian paradigms that shape modern international norms. This type of analysis will aid in understanding the historic relationships that determine the paths of international interactions, and the historically informed ideas of sovereignty that allow interventions to occur.

A parallel can be drawn between the humanitarian intervention literature and the development economics literature in this regard. Since the era of decolonisation, critiques of development economics have been pointing to the underdevelopment of the 'third world' as a legacy of imperialism. This critique draws on a larger historical debate that sees the nineteenth century development of capitalism and imperialism as intertwined. Marxist historians and economists were quick to draw out connections between imperialism and capitalist expansion, and were therefore willing to see the 'development'/'underdevelopment' paradigm as historically contingent (Hobson 1902; Rhodes 1970; Rodney 1972; Dumett 1999; Cain and Hopkins 2001). The basis of global capitalism, in this reading, is the exploitation of resources (held in the 'Global South') by those in power (in the 'North'). This approach, and the more moderate structuralist critique, challenged older liberal ideas of economic development that held that 'underdevelopment' was a condition of 'traditional' economies that needed to be 'modernised' (Spero and Hart 2000).

There are significant problems with the framing of 'North–South' economic relations in terms of resources exploitation, or in terms of trade – most notably, that both historians and economists have shown that the contributions of the non-industrialised, resource-rich developing world to the industrialised economies in both trade and resource provision is nowhere near the levels that Marxist economists and historians believed it to be (Davis and Huttenback 1987; Porter 1988; Spero and Hart 2000). However, while trade was not as significant a factor, Cain and Hopkins have argued that the opportunities for investment in infrastructure, mining, railroads and other forms of industrial development in the colonial periphery (Foreign Direct Investment) were areas where growth rates were high, and therefore important to the early industrial economies, where growth rates – and returns on capital – had slowed (Hopkins and Cain 2001). The instability of these investments both yielded high returns and also required the help of the imperial government in order to protect investments through the use of 'supersanctions'.

In the economic history literature, 'supersanctions' have been invoked to understand the relationship between sanctions and 'external military pressure or political and financial control' (Mitchener and Weidenmier 2005: 1). The term is used primarily to discuss the options available to creditor nations hoping to prevent or punish sovereign debt defaults. However, the tools – gunboat diplomacy or the seizure of fiscal control of a country – were used effectively as 'supersanctions' for a variety of behaviours by imperial powers in the nineteenth and early twentieth century to alter the behaviour of other countries. The military blockade of Ouidah (in modern Benin) and bombardment of Lagos, Nigeria, in 1851, for instance, was intended to enforce an anti-slave trading treaty (Law 2004; Mann 2007).

The continuation of the slave trade after the Euro-American powers had outlawed it in the early nineteenth century was the focus of humanitarian efforts throughout the nineteenth century (Everill

2013a). The US, Britain, France, Spain and Portugal used a combination of economic and military interventions, as well as the development of refuges for freed slaves, in order to put an end to the traffic in people from Africa. The combined efforts of what would now be distinctly seen as 'humanitarian intervention' in the case of the military interventions against sovereign powers in West Africa, and the developmentalist and state-building policies (referred to at the time as the 'civilising mission') evolved in the early twentieth century as the colonial powers expanded their jurisdiction in Africa while justifying their presence with a rhetoric and policy of developmentalism (Cooper 2002).

State-level economic interventions

State-level economic interventions take place in a number of different ways. Money (and other forms of financial assistance) can be given to help in a military or developmental humanitarian crisis, or it can be withheld through a variety of forms of sanctions. At the state level, this form of economic intervention is used to exert pressure on other states to conform to international norms, usually determined and enforced by the wealthy states rather than those dependent on economic assistance.

There is a well-developed literature on the theory behind economic sanctions and on its success or failure as a tool of diplomacy (Pape 1977; Kaempfer and Lowenberg 1988; Martin 1992; Drudy 1998; Marinov 2005; Goldsmith 2008; Hufbauer et al. 2009). The focus of much of this has been isolating economic sanctions from other tools to determine its impact on a humanitarian scenario. While isolating this variable may be important for determining its effectiveness as a tool, this practice effectively removes the historical action from its context in order to create 'replicable' conditions. Thus, much of the critical analysis of sanctions becomes focused on measuring success, rather than assessing the wider context in which economic sanctions are deployed and the impact they have on violence, instability and humanitarian assistance.

Since 2000, economic sanctions have been used in more than fifteen interventions deemed to have been 'humanitarian' (Hufbauer et al. 2009: table 1A.2). The US has used sanctions unilaterally, but in the majority of these cases international organisations like NATO, the UN, the European Union and the African Union have also participated. Sudan, Syria and Burma (Myanmar) are currently under US economic sanctions explicitly for 'human rights abuses'. However, it would also be useful to consider economic tools used in humanitarian interventions during and prior to the Cold War in order to understand the historical context in which many on the receiving end of sanctions may see the imposition of sanctions. Since the early nineteenth century at least, international actors have used economic blockades, boycotts and other forms of sanctions to compel adherence to humanitarian norms determined by the world's hegemons. Although Hufbauer et al. point to economic sanctions as a tool deployed 'to force a target country to withdraw its troops from border skirmishes, to abandon plans of territorial acquisition, or to desist from other military adventures' (Hufbauer et al. 2009: 10), economic sanctions just as often led to the occupation of territory or the outbreak of military engagement by the country or empire imposing sanctions.

The impact of economic sanctions in the post-Cold War context reveals the interconnection between military force and economic force. In a case study by David Cortright et al. (2000), the economic sanctions imposed on Sierra Leone after the coup by the Armed Forces Revolutionary Council in 1997 led to almost no effect that is able to be disaggregated from the effects of the almost immediate military intervention by the Economic Community of West African States Military Observer Group (ECOMOG). These examples help to illustrate that to be effective, most economic sanctions have to be backed up or immediately followed by military interventions. Although some important empirical work on sanctions shows that economic coercion does not require military threat in order to be effective – particularly amongst allies – the practical effects of economic sanctions and even more importantly, the development of the humanitarian norms that they enforce, rests on unequal distributions of economic and military power (Drezner 1999; Hufbauer et al. 2009).

Financial sanctions, money laundering laws, freezing bank accounts and other means have also been connected with the campaign against terrorism. Attempts to prevent *hawala* money lenders from 'financing terrorists' has led to confusion and inefficient attempts to end a centuries-old banking system (Thompson 2011). As with, for instance, oil embargoes and trade embargoes, financial sanctions of this type can have a negative humanitarian consequence by reducing access to forms of credit or to goods required for daily life (Dashti-Gibson et al. 2000). A powerful, but controversial, critique of embargoes and sanctions argues that the population most affected by this form of intervention is usually the population most in need of humanitarian assistance.

Other forms of economic sanction, however, have been used in order to prevent countries or leaders from obtaining the means to inflict human rights abuses on their people or on neighbouring countries. For instance, sanctions have been imposed to prevent the spread of nuclear weapon technology, or arms embargoes have been used to attempt to end conflicts. The arms embargoes imposed by the UN and other international organisations in the conflicts in Somalia, Liberia and Rwanda revealed that in some cases, this form of economic sanction is intended as a limited but popular step that has been used to 'deflect criticism that the [UN Security] Council was ignoring the tragedy' (Cortright et al. 2000: 184). Notably, although arms embargoes may have ultimately had an effect on the outcome of the war, this particular form of sanction had no discernible impact on the humanitarian tragedy that inspired the action: the famine affecting Somalia's citizens (Cortright et al. 2000: 187).

Arms embargoes, too, have a long history in international humanitarian economic action. The Berlin Conference of 1884 and the Brussels Conference of 1890 are best known as the moments when European powers divided up the African continent amongst themselves. Part of the rationale for those conferences, however, was to establish a European consensus on the abolition of the slave trade and the abolition of the trade in arms to Africa. Preventing the sale of guns to Africans was intended as a means of effecting the abolition of the slave trade: it was widely believed that a 'gun–slave cycle' was in operation, whereby Africans would enslave others for sale in order to obtain guns to protect themselves from being enslaved. Outlawing the sale of guns on the continent would, therefore, eliminate one cause, as well as a means, of enslavement. The treaty passed at the Brussels Conference was entitled the 'Convention Relative to the Slave Trade and Importation into Africa of Firearms, Ammunition, and Spiritous Liquors'. Article I(7) contained the clause which allowed for the enforcement of 'Restriction of the importation of firearms, at least of those of modern pattern, and of ammunition throughout the entire extent of the territory in which the slave-trade is carried on'.

In practice, as might be expected from the clause that specified 'at least those of the modern pattern', sanctions on arms sales had a different effect: they created a vast and growing disparity in weapon technology between the European colonising powers and the African polities they encountered. In effect, European powers were thus able to support leaders who agreed to outlaw the slave trade by providing them with military assistance and economic aid, while denying it to those still engaging in the slave trade (or other behaviour outside of the established international norm). Sanctions were backed up by supersanctions.

The use of military supersanctions – the 'gunboat diplomacy' of the nineteenth century – suggest that economic interventions and military interventions are highly correlated, even if the literature debates how reliant one is on the other for success (Gardner 2015). Aid to one side in a conflict situation is an obvious form of intervention, and is the one most commonly discussed in the humanitarian intervention literature. This literature has largely been focused on defining interventions as 'humanitarian' or not, and on placing them within a new post-Cold War international context. Although some attempts have been made to contextualise the history of humanitarian intervention and complicate its definition, the emergence of the 'Responsibility to Protect' (R2P) doctrine has made careful definition important not only for scholars but for the wider international community (Hehir 2010).

Jennifer Welsh has debated the definitions of humanitarian intervention put forward by the international legal community, and which focus on determining the 'primary' motivation of an intervention, its legality and its unilateral or multilateral status (Welsh 2004; Welsh 2013). Moving beyond these narrow legal definitions, it is possible to see that intervention can have humanitarian, peacekeeping and security, as well as tactical, motivations, and that a situation and the rationale for intervening can evolve. Many of the military interventions in Africa during the Cold War era were framed in peacekeeping terms, but as Christopher Saunders (2013) has argued, the interventions undertaken by the UN, while not all justified on humanitarian grounds, usually had some form of humanitarian aspect in the mission or evolved into humanitarian missions once deployed.

As an economic intervention, wartime aid has had a much less ambiguously controversial history than 'humanitarian intervention' since aid to a warring faction is often construed in less humanitarian, and more tactical, terms. States and international organisations regularly offer help to re-establish regional stability during civil wars or international conflicts. However, in selling aid to domestic voters and international organisations, countries have, since the end of the Cold War, employed humanitarian language with increasing frequency. This happened in Libya in 2011, where the support of groups rebelling against Qaddafi was linked not only to their role in the democratic uprisings occurring throughout North Africa, but also to the violent suppression of those groups and 'human rights abuses' by the regime.

In the nineteenth century and early twentieth century, providing economic support to one side in a conflict was a classic strategy of the colonial powers as they came to control large territories in Africa. With limited manpower on the ground, British and French colonial governments largely relied on alternative means for establishing their effective occupation of a territory. While military conquest was an important tool, aid to already-warring parties was a more efficient use of scarce imperial resources and often resulted in the desired outcome without the loss of European lives. For instance, the policy of indirect rule favoured by Frederick Lugard (1922) allowed the Sokoto Caliphate to effectively rule in place of the British in Northern Nigeria.

At the moment of decolonisation and in the boundary and ethnic disputes that followed the creation of new nations in Africa (and elsewhere), the deployment of financial support, development aid and economic sanctions allowed the decolonising powers to back one side in a conflict. The Biafran War (1967–70), for instance, demonstrates that the financial and trade support that the Nigerian government received from France and Britain – despite the independent humanitarian aid being sent to Ojukwu's Biafran Republic – was the determining factor in the success of the Federal Government of Nigeria (Stremlau 1997; Aaronson 2013). Similarly, financial support prevented the secession of Katanga from Congo during its decolonisation by Belgium in the early 1960s (Saunders 2013). This form of humanitarian intervention is the most controversial when it includes the provision of troops, advisers, equipment and support, and the aftermath of the intervention in Somalia and the non-intervention in Rwanda shaped much of the debate over military humanitarian intervention. However, financial humanitarian assistance provided to one side or the other of a conflict happens with great frequency, either tacitly or explicitly, and is seen as a much less controversial form of support. In wars of attrition and in wars between parties with limited access to their own industrial base, external economic intervention in the form of wartime aid can be the determining factor.

The pressure of attrition can be especially acutely felt in places with an already low baseline of resources. The withholding of development aid can be as effective a tool for intervening as other forms of sanction or military aid. State-building aid has evolved since the nineteenth century, when it was first introduced in Africa as a means of mitigating the effects of the European slave trade. When the trade was legally abolished in 1807, European powers – especially Britain at the beginning – gave annual funds to established 'freed slave' colonies in West Africa, South Africa and eventually East Africa. The colonies were run by a combination of British officials, international missionary organisations and by the freed slaves themselves. Money went towards housing and feeding the resettled slaves for the first six months, providing them with education and paying for their apprenticeship. Funds were also required for infrastructure development, enforcement of laws and civil service development, and a military to defend against further enslavement (Everill 2013b).

Since then, developmental aid has been a regular form of intervention in African societies. A particularly important aspect of development aid as an intervention tool has been the US's ability to prevent or impose rules upon the World Bank and International Monetary Fund (IMF). Debt forgiveness is another way of rewarding states for correcting human rights violations (Spero and Hart 2000). Critiques have, however, been offered for this kind of intervention. Dambisa Moyo's *Dead Aid* (2010) argued that developmental aid was a form of handicap for developing economies, lining elite pockets and preventing the development of self-sufficient economies. Although controversial, the book contributed to a growing field of sceptical analysis of the aid industry and of state aid budgets. William Easterly (2006) similarly has drawn attention to the West's legacies of imperial interventionism in attacking state-building, humanitarian aid, and other interventions into the governance of developing countries. The creation of the 'microfinance' industry in response to the success of Muhammad Yunus's Grameen Bank (Yunus 1999; Scrase 2011) speaks to the West's general perception that development aid has been an unsuccessful intervention in developing countries. Donors and agencies rushed to embrace microfinance as a more sustainable strategy for economic self-improvement. It was believed that this model merely built on existing structures and therefore would be able to avoid the problems associated with external impositions and unforeseen consequences. The emphasis on the individual, on the private sector, and on micro-innovations has shifted the interventionist decision-making away from the state and down to local agents and private actors (Scrase 2011).

Individual economic interventions

Commercial interventions, while differing vastly from the magnitude of state-level interventions, also have a history tied up with the emergence of industrial capitalism and colonialism in the early nineteenth century. Commercial interventions – economic interventions undertaken by individuals or commercial agents – are the most 'voluntary' of the economic humanitarian interventions. In the eighteenth and nineteenth century, they centred on issues like the slave trade, with concerned consumers boycotting slave-produced goods or purchasing goods advertised to have been made with free labour (Sussman 2000; Glickman 2004; Trentmann 2007). The British slave sugar boycotts of the 1790s – reaching nearly 400,000 participants in 1792 – were widely believed at the time to have influenced later parliamentary decisions on the abolition of the slave trade (Midgley 1996; Katz-Hyman 2008).

In the late nineteenth and early twentieth century, boycotts of Cadbury for using enslaved labour in Sao Tome and Principe used similar tools (Grant 2005). As Grant writes, 'the general objective of British humanitarians in this period was to reform imperial labour policies in Africa to ensure that commercial development would simultaneously promote Africans' moral and material improvement and create a more efficient workforce to enhance European prosperity' (2005: 136). Additionally, in the 1980s, the anti-apartheid movement used boycotts as a means of protesting the South African regime. The variety of movements for 'divestment' by university organisations and state and local groups ultimately created a successful build-up of pressure on the US government to pass the Comprehensive Anti-Apartheid Act (Knight 1990). Divestment was a strategy promoted by those opposing the genocide in the Darfur region of Sudan in the early 2000s as well, marking the rise of 'socially responsible investing' as an important tool for humanitarian campaigns in the twenty-first century (Patey 2009; Soederberg 2009).

These examples all share a common tactic promoted by the activists: the most effective forms of consumer action were often aimed at domestic governments, businesses and agencies, rather than international governments or agencies. Boycotts organised at the individual level were historically most effective in compelling action by those closest to the consumer in the supply chain or political chain. Companies, for instance, have recently responded to this pressure by highlighting their own commercial interventions. Firestone Rubber, in Liberia, notorious during the early twentieth century for allegedly relying on enslaved labour, now points to its successes in promoting the eradication of the Ebola virus amongst its workers and their families in Harbel, Liberia, and the more general provision of healthcare and education for its employees (Beaubien 2014). Individual and corporate interventions in the Ebola crisis were, of course, supplemented by the aid of governments, national armies and groups like the World Health Organisation, *Médecins Sans Frontières* and the International Red Cross. But significant media attention during the crisis focused on individual stories and specific innovations that aligned with this preference for neoliberal approaches to development and humanitarian relief.

Other companies touting their corporate social responsibility (CSR) credentials include Cadbury, which uses Ghanaian fair trade chocolate in some of its products, and Tullow Oil, an exploratory oil company that promotes its approach to training local engineers in its concessions in Ghana and elsewhere in West Africa (Idowu and Towler 2004; Blowfield and Dolan 2010; Doherty et al. 2013). For these producers, corporate social responsibility is, amongst other things, a marketing tool, differentiating their product and their brand from other, less ethically responsible brands. Their emphasis is on 'ameliorating' the effects of a globalised commodity chain and appealing to the socially conscious consumer. While these practices undoubtedly have some positive effects, especially when put into place by corporations that are driven by a fundamentally different and socially responsible purpose, the effect of the rise of CSR has been critiqued as 'whitewashing' or 'greenwashing' (in the case of environmental sustainability). Littler (2011: 32) has argued that CSR is 'a discursive contest for control over the social'.

However, attempts to shorten the global supply chain or alter the relationship between the consumer and producer in ways that aim to reduce global poverty or intervene in a humanitarian crisis also have existed since the nineteenth century. The Free Produce movement, active in Britain and the US from the 1820s to the 1860s, attempted to replace slave-produced goods with goods produced by free labour (Nuermberger 1942; Faulkner 2007; Micheletti 2007). In the twenty-first century, consumer action has added this slightly different model of 'active purchasing' back into the arsenal of individual economic interventions. Fairtrade has offered consumers an option to intervene on behalf of producers in the developing world to increase their living standards (Sasson 2016). With all of these consumer movements, the idea of placing the responsibility for global inequality on the end-consumer has been problematic. The demand side of consumption is an important driving factor of decision-making, but so are fashion, cost and availability. This has had the tendency to relegate these movements to dealing in luxury goods, rather than staples, and in retaining the global networks of supply, rather than challenging their foundations (Scrase 2011).

However, interventions on the supply side also have precedent in the nineteenth century interventions in the slave trade. Activists attempted to replace the slave trade with 'legitimate' (non-slave) commerce from West Africa. Attempts to intervene in the production process included the establishment of commercial plantations, training schools for African labourers, aid to leaders who promoted legitimate production in their territories and the creation of new forms of credit and collateral to encourage independent producers (Law 2002; Lynn 2002). The attempt to intervene in the humanitarian crisis caused by the continuing slave trade gave rise to 'the West's first development program' in Africa (Hopkins 1980: 777).

The theory behind commercial interventions is twofold. On the consumer end, the rise of industrial capitalism fuelled a concern about the separation of consumers from the production process. The rise of classical liberal economic theory – most notably Adam Smith's contributions to ideas about the division of labour and the law of supply and demand – was part of a developing awareness of economic cause and effect in the early nineteenth century. Increasing access to exotic luxuries associated with the slave trade and enslaved labour further contributed to a sense of the consumer as the party ultimately responsible for directing production (Ashworth 1987; Larson 2015). Combined with the rise of popular democracy, consumption was increasingly seen as 'consumer voting' (Dickinson and Carsky 2005; Barnett et al. 2007).

Both forms of commercial intervention have been subjected to recent critiques, however. The shift to 'innovation' and entrepreneurial solutions to humanitarian crises and humanitarian development has aided in the promotion of individualised and corporate – rather than state-based – solutions. 'Disruption', a powerful term in corporate strategy and marketing, has been carried over into the language of humanitarian aid and intervention. The emergence of the Humanitarian Innovation Fund, the Oxford Humanitarian Innovation Project and corresponding efforts like the Humanitarian Innovation Conference aim to introduce change from the private sector, particularly the growing (in popularity, funds and influence) technology sector.[1]

In the modernist models that prevailed in the mid-twentieth century, the accountability for development largely rested on the state, and interventions at that level focused on infrastructure development, education and healthcare provision, and other measures for reducing poverty and human suffering (Spero and Hart 2000; Cooper 2002). With the Washington Consensus changing the targets of economic development in the 1990s, new, neoliberal models of development, which focus on entrepreneurialism, individual success, and financial instruments like microcredit have been widely critiqued for the ways in which they have imposed the responsibility for development on the poor (Scrase 2011).

The new model places the onus for humanitarian action on the individual, rather than the state. Although the state can still be the target of boycotts or political action to intervene in a humanitarian crisis, as with the Save Darfur campaign and the ill-fated Kony 2012 campaign by Invisible Children, 'ethical consumer citizens' are once again taking the burden of action (Lanz 2009; Drumbi 2012; von Engelhardt and Jansz 2014). Littler (2011: 33) writes that in this 'responsibilisation' narrative 'ethical consumption is a symptom of a profoundly individualistic society in which individuals are being presented with both the opportunity and responsibility for tackling a number of deep-rooted social problems . . . through their purchasing decisions'. Nonetheless, a historical look at the role of the consumer in economic interventions on behalf of suffering producers and casualties of humanitarian emergencies reveals that the 'responsibilisation' associated with individual economic interventions is more deeply connected to the development of industrial, global capitalism and the growth of popular democracy than a short-term focus on neoliberalism suggests. The forms of individual and collective humanitarian activism that emerged in the late eighteenth and nineteenth century have always relied on a combination of individual consumer responsibility; collective action to influence government and corporate interventions; and a strong relationship between economic aid, developmentalism, sanctions and military intervention.

As these different types of intervention were put into practice by a complement of states, international organisations, individual actors and companies, however, they were all attempting to impose a typically Western liberal humanitarian ideology. Using sanctions to discipline violent or 'rogue' regimes has been cast as a less invasive form of normalising state behaviour (Hufbauer et al. 2009). In a similar way, consumer action and economic humanitarian intervention in development has been deployed by agencies and entrepreneurs as a way to generate 'self-led' change (Yunus 1999; Ferguson 2015). Even those that have adapted to post-colonial critiques in their approaches to economic intervention have still largely used the new 'ground-up' or women-focused approaches to implement societal changes that will encourage a gender model more in line with Western norms, or a class model that removes the forms of personal patronage that have been important elsewhere, but which are seen as hampering the individual by Western organisations. As during the colonial period, then, these economic interventions are most measurably 'successful' according to Western standards in places where Western ideas and education have already made significant inroads, because the people who are the focus of the interventions are likely to understand, and possibly even buy into, the Western norms being promoted. Since economic relations form the heart of many social relations, though, attempts at economic intervention at a micro-level can be as violently disruptive to communities as state-level sanctions and military aid. While this may certainly be justified by agreed humanitarian and development norms, it is wise to bear in mind that those norms are almost uniformly based, as they have been since the late eighteenth century, on Western liberal standards. This makes them vulnerable to critique not only by anti-interventionists, but by the regimes and societies they are trying to 'reform'.

Conclusion

Economic tools of humanitarian intervention are often seen as a measure that helps to prevent violence and conflict. They are also strongly linked in the literature to the history of the Cold War, a period during which both the US and the West and the USSR and its allies used economic aid and sanctions to create allies and ostracise enemies. However, their association especially with the decolonisation of Africa and Asia, and the empire-building in Latin America, also reveals an earlier use of economic interventions in the form of imperial humanitarianism. By viewing economic interventions over the *longue durée* it is possible to see past their role in the realist calculations of the mid-twentieth century to their deeper connections to the liberal idealism of the nineteenth century. As this chapter has argued, this helps to explain how interventions are connected to the ideological battles of the post-Cold War era, as well as why they have had violent and contradictory affects on humanitarian projects.

Because of their associations with the kinds of imperial interventions during the pre-colonial and colonial periods, more recent attempts by states or international organisations to use sanctions to discipline 'rogue' regimes like Zimbabwe, Libya, North Korea and most recently Russia have had a mixed impact. While they do serve to marginalise elite actors in these states, politicians like Robert Mugabe and Muammar al-Qaddafi were able to turn the international sanctions to their own ends, by arguing that these interventions just demonstrated the continuing colonialist mentality of the US, Britain and France (Wroughton 2013). Although sanctions (and the possibility of their removal) have succeeded in moving some dialogues forward in the cases of Iran and Cuba, they have been undermined in places where the post-colonial critique has been able to galvanise the population in support of the regime.

Sanctions, supersanctions, military aid, development aid, boycotts and ethical consumption are all linked as tools that have been used to combat human rights abuses and promote humanitarian causes ranging from anti-slavery to anti-apartheid to anti-poverty campaigns. The fact that these tools have been used in combination since the emergence of international humanitarian campaigns in the late eighteenth century should alert practitioners to the historically constructed nature of their relationships with industrialisation, imperialism and globalisation. Fundamentally, economic tools of intervention are forms of power that punish and regulate individual, national or corporate behaviour. In order to be effective, they must have military and political power to enforce their implementation. The use of economic tools by both individuals and states reveals the continuities between development (state-building) and intervention, continuities which also highlight the power differentials between those who can be sanctioned or who rely on development aid, and those with the means to enforce their vision of human rights and dignity.

Note

1. See, for instance, www.oxhip.org and www.elrha.org.

References

Aaronson, M. (2013), 'The Nigerian Civil War and "Humanitarian Intervention"', in B. Everill and J. Kaplan (eds), *The History and Practice of Humanitarian Intervention and Aid in Africa*, Basingstoke: Palgrave, pp. 176–96.

Ashworth, J. (1987), 'The Relationship between Capitalism and Humanitarianism', *American Historical Review*, 92(4), pp. 813–28.

Barnett, C., N. Clark, P. Cloke and A. Malpass (2007), 'Globalising the Consumer: Doing Politics in an Ethical Register', *Political Geography*, 26(3), pp. 231–49.

Barnett, M. (2011), *Empire of Humanity: A History of Humanitarianism*, Ithaca, NY: Cornell University Press.

Beaubien, J. (2014), 'Firestone Did What Governments Have Not: Stopped Ebola in its Tracks', NPR.org, 6 October, available at: http://www.npr.org/sections/goatsandsoda/2014/10/06/354054915/firestone-did-what-governments-have-not-stopped-ebola-in-its-tracks, last accessed 23 December 2016.

Blowfield, M. E. and C. Dolan (2010), 'Fairtrade Facts and Fancies: What Kenyan Fairtrade Tea Tells us About Business' Role as Development Agent', *Journal of Business Ethics*, 93, pp. 143–62.

Cain, P. J. and A.G. Hopkins (2001), *British Imperialism, 1688–2000*, 2nd edn, London: Longman.

Convention Relative to the Slave Trade and Importation into Africa of Firearms, Ammunition, and Spiritous Liquors, 1890.

Cooper, F. (2002), *Africa since 1940*, Cambridge: Cambridge University Press.

Cortright, D., G. A. Lopez and R. W. Conroy (2000), *The Sanctions Decade: Assessing UN Strategies in the 1990s*, Boulder, CO: Lynne Rienner.

Dashti-Gibson, J., D. Cortright and G. Lopez (2000), 'Helping Haiti', in D. Cortright, G. A. Lopez and R. W. Conroy (eds), *The Sanctions Decade: Assessing UN Strategies in the 1990s*, Boulder, CO: Lynne Rienner, pp. 87–106.

Davis, L. E. and R. A. Huttenback (1987), *Mammon and the Pursuit of Empire*, Cambridge: Cambridge University Press.

Dickinson, R. A. and M. L. Carsky (2005), 'The Consumer as Economic Voter', in R. Harrison, T. Newholm and D. Shaw (eds), *The Ethical Consumer*, London: SAGE Publications, pp. 25–37.

Doherty, B., I. A. Davies and S. Tranchell (2013), 'Where Now for Fair Trade?', *Business History*, 55(2), pp. 161–89.

Dumett, R. E. (ed.) (1999), *Gentlemanly Capitalism and British Imperialism: the New Debate on Empire*, London: Routledge.

Drezner, D. W. (1999), *The Sanctions Paradox: Economic Statecraft and International Relations*, Cambridge: Cambridge University Press.

Drudy, A. C. (1998), 'Revisiting Economic Sanctions Reconsidered', *Journal of Peace Research*, 35(4), pp. 497–509.

Drumbi, M. A. (2012), 'Child Soldiers and Clicktivism: Justice, Myths, and Prevention', *Journal of Human Rights Practice*, 4(3), pp. 481–5.

Easterly, W. (2006), *The White Man's Burden: Why the West's Efforts to Aid the Rest Have Done So Much Ill and So Little Good*, New York: Penguin.

Everill, B. (2013a), *Abolition and Empire in Sierra Leone and Liberia*, Basingstoke: Palgrave.

Everill, B. (2013b), 'Freetown, Frere Town and the Kat River Settlement: Nineteenth Century Humanitarian Intervention and Precursors to Modern Refugee Camps', in B. Everill and J. Kaplan, *The History and Practice of Humanitarian Intervention and Aid in Africa*, Basingstoke: Palgrave, pp. 23–42.

Everill, B. and J. Kaplan (eds) (2013), *The History and Practice of Humanitarian Intervention and Aid in Africa*, Basingstoke: Palgrave.

Faulkner, C. (2007), 'The Root of the Evil: Free Produce and Radical Antislavery, 1820–1860', *Journal of the Early Republic*, 27(3), pp. 377–405.

Ferguson, J. (2015), *Give a Man a Fish: Reflections on the New Politics of Distribution*, Durham, NC: Duke University Press.

Gardner, L. (2015), 'Colonialism or Supersanctions: Managing Sovereign Risk in Sierra Leone and Liberia, 1871–1914', EHES Working Paper, available at: http://www.ehes.org/ehes2015/papers/Gardner.pdf, accessed 23 December 2016.

Glickman, L. B. (2004), '"Buy for the Sake of the Slave": Abolitionism and the Origins of American Consumer Activism', *American Quarterly*, 56(4), pp. 889–912.

Goldsmith, A. A. (2008), 'Making the World Safe for Partial Democracy? Questioning the Premises of Democracy Promotion', *International Security*, 33, pp. 2120–47.

Grant, K. (2005), *A Civilised Savagery: Britain and the New Slaveries in Africa*, London: Routledge.

Hehir, A. (2010), *Humanitarian Intervention: an Introduction*, Basingstoke: Palgrave.

Hobson, J. A. (1902), *Imperialism: A Study*, London: James Pott & Company.

Hopkins, A. G. (1980), 'Property Rights and Empire Building: Britain's Annexation of Lagos, 1861', *Journal of Economic History*, 40(4), pp. 777–98.

Hufbauer, G. C., J. J. Schott, K. A. Elliott and B. Oegg (2009), *Economic Sanctions Reconsidered: History and Current Policy*, 3rd edn, Washington, DC: Peterson Institute for International Economics.

Idowu, S. O. and B. A. Towler (2004), 'A Comparative Study of the

Contents of Corporate Social Responsibility Reports of UK Companies', *Management of Environmental Quality*, 15(4), pp. 420–37.

Kaempfer, W. H. and A. D. Lowenberg (1988), 'The Theory of International Economic Sanctions: A Public Choice Approach', *American Economic Review*, 78(4), pp. 786–93.

Katz-Hyman, M. (2008), 'Doing Good While Doing Well', *Slavery & Abolition*, 29(2), pp. 219–31.

Knight, R. (1990), *Sanctioning Apartheid*, Trenton, NJ: Africa World Press.

Lanz, D. (2009), 'Save Darfur: A Movement and Its Discontents', *African Affairs*, 108(433), pp. 669–77.

Larson, J. L. (2015), 'An Inquiry into the Nature and Causes of the Wealth of Nations', *Journal of the Early Republic*, 35(1), pp. 1–23.

Law, R. (ed.) (2002), *From Slave Trade to 'Legitimate' Commerce: The Commercial Transition in Nineteenth Century West Africa*, Cambridge: Cambridge University Press.

Law, R. (2004), *Ouidah: The Social History of a West African Slaving 'Port', 1727–1892*, London: James Currey.

Lynn, M. (2002), *Commerce and Economic Change in West Africa*, Cambridge: Cambridge University Press.

Littler, J. (2011), 'What's Wrong With Ethical Consumption?', in T. Lewis and E. Potter (eds), *Ethical Consumption: a Critical Introduction*, London: Routledge, pp. 27–39.

Lugard, F. (1922), *The Dual Mandate in British Tropical Africa*, London: W. Blackwood.

Mann, K. (2007), *Slavery and the Birth of an African City: Lagos, 1760–1900*, Bloomington: Indiana University Press.

Marinov, N. (2005), 'Do Economic Sanctions Destabilize Country Leaders?', *American Journal of Political Science*, 49, pp. 564–76.

Martin, L. L. (1992), *Coercive Cooperation: Explaining Multilateral Economic Sanctions*, Princeton: Princeton University Press.

Micheletti, M. (2007), 'The Moral Force of Consumption and Capitalism: Anti-slavery and Anti-sweatshop', in K. Soper and F. Trentmann (eds), *Citizenship and Consumption*, Basingstoke: Palgrave, pp. 121–36.

Midgley, C. (1996), 'Slave Sugar Boycotts, Female Activism and the Domestic Base of British anti-slavery culture', *Slavery & Abolition*, 17(3), pp. 137–62.

Mitchener, K. J. and M. D. Weidenmier (2005), 'Supersanctions and Sovereign Debt Repayment', National Bureau of Economic Research Working Paper 11472.

Moyo, D. (2010), *Dead Aid: Why Aid Is Not Working and How There Is a Better Way for Africa*, New York: Farrar, Straus and Giroux.

Nuermberger, R. K. (1942), *The Free Produce Movement: A Quaker Protest against Slavery*, Durham, NC: Duke University Press.

Pape, R. (1977), 'Why Economic Sanctions Do Not Work', *International Security*, 22(2), 90–136.

Patey, L. A. (2009), 'Against the Asian Tide: The Sudan Divestment Campaign', *Journal of Modern African Studies*, 47(4), pp. 551–73.

Porter, A. N. (1988), 'The Balance Sheet of Empire', *Historical Journal*, 31(3), pp. 685–99.

Rhodes, R. I. (ed.) (1970), *Imperialism and Underdevelopment: A Reader*, New York: Monthly Review Press.

Rodney, W. (1972), *How Europe Underdeveloped Africa*, London: Bogle-L'Ouverture Publications.

Sasson, T. (2016), 'Milking the Third World? Humanitarianism, Capitalism, and the Moral Economy of the Nestle Boycott', *American Historical Review*, 121(4), 1196–224.

Saunders, C. (2013), 'Interventions by the United Nations in Southern Africa', in B. Everill and J. Kaplan (eds), *The History and Practice of Humanitarian Intervention and Aid in Africa*, Basingstoke: Palgrave, pp. 158–75.

Scrase, T. J. (2011), 'Fair Trade in Cyberspace: the Commodification of Poverty and the Marketing of Handicrafts on the Internet', in T. Lewis and E. Potter (eds), *Ethical Consumption: a Critical Introduction*, London: Routledge, pp. 54–70.

Simms, B. and D. J. B. Trim (2011), *Humanitarian Intervention: A History*, Cambridge: Cambridge University Press.

Soederberg, S. (2009), 'The Marketisation of Social Justice: The Case of the Sudan Divestment Campaign', *New Political Economy*, 14(2), pp. 211–29.

Spero, J. E. and J. A. Hart (2000), *The Politics of International Economic Relations*, London: Routledge.

Stremlau, J. (1997), *The International Politics of the Nigerian Civil War 1967–70*, Princeton: Princeton University Press.

Sussman, C. (2000), *Consuming Anxieties: Consumer Protest, Gender & British Slavery, 1713–1833*, Stanford, CA: Stanford University Press.

Thompson, E. (2011), *Trust Is the Coin of the Realm: Lessons from the Money Men in Afghanistan*. Oxford: Oxford University Press.

Trentmann, F. (2007), 'Before "Fair Trade: Empire, Free Trade, and the Moral Economies of Food in the Modern World', *Environment and Planning D: Society and Space*, 25(6), pp. 1079–102.

von Engelhardt, J. and J. Jansz (2014), 'Challenging Humanitarian Communication: An Empirical Exploration of Kony 2012', *International Communication Gazette*, 76(6), pp. 464–84.

Welsh, J. (2004), *Humanitarian Intervention and International Relations*, Oxford: Oxford University Press.

Welsh, J. (2013), 'Foreword', in B. Everill and J. Kaplan (eds), *The History and Practice of Humanitarian Intervention and Aid in Africa*, Basingstoke: Palgrave, pp. vii–xii.

Wroughton, L. (2013), '"Shame, shame, shame" Mugabe tells U.S. and Britain', *Reuters*, 26 September, available at: http://www.reuters.com/article/us-un-assembly-mugabe-idUSBRE98P12A20130926#8Jzh5vk3fzs43z7i.97, last accessed 23 December 2016.

Yunus, M. (1999), *Banker to the Poor*. New York: Public Affairs.

4

Changing Patterns of Social Connection across Interventions: Unravelling Aberrant Globalisation

Paul Battersby

Introduction

International armed interventions in intrastate conflicts are planned with the expectation that order will be restored through the controlled application of limited military force. This persuasive orthodoxy endures despite the erratic course of foreign interventions in the Middle East over the past two decades. Notions of order, equilibrium or stasis imply systemic balances that, where disturbed, can be reconciled or restored through counteraction. Yet, while we can gather abundant conflict data, observe events from many different vantage points, correlate variables and calibrate possibilities, the calculation of future trajectories of conflict events remains an imprecise and hazardous exercise. Indeed, planned and coordinated international action to address selected strategic challenges, in the current global context, merely *manufactures* new uncertainties (Beck 1999; 2009). There is extensive evidence that armed interventions provoke protracted asymmetric retaliation on the part of those displaced by traumatic regime change. In the interconnected contemporary global system, the effects of these displacements have regional and global ramifications. 'Distant localities' (adapting James Rosenau's notion of 'distant proximities') are today intimately associated across political and geographical space (Rosenau 2003). Polarities between political interests and ideologies, geographical and societal inequalities in wealth and power broadly defined and the many and varied *complex* connections between people and peoples across space generate uncertainties that defy prediction. Thus, to anticipate only positive change from the rapid assertion of overwhelming military power into faraway places is to downplay the strings or threads of happenings, decisions, ideas and beliefs that shape the subjective realities of global security. Globalisation is aberrant in its complexity, and global dynamics do not yield simple choices between binary opposites of order and disorder, control or chaos. The search for a more nuanced and contextualised understanding of global security relations leads inescapably towards the analysis of global patterns of connection and organisation that generate and sustain *multiscalar* supply chains of violence. This chapter argues for a *global* and *adaptive* approach to the governance of private force.

Aberrant globalisation

Globalisation amplifies 'aberrant' tendencies in human affairs for which political decision-makers demand measured explanations and practical responses. However, there is no unfolding teleology of global integration or homogenisation that was once assumed to be globalisation's liberal promise, but rather a constant of multimodal and dynamic tensions (Battersby 2014). James Rosenau's ungainly but apt concept of *fragmegration* encapsulates the reality of coterminous patterns of integration and fragmentation in global affairs (Rosenau 2003). Globalisation's anomalies and perplexities are evident in parallel patterns of aggregation, disaggregation and re-aggregation, convergence, *concatenation*, divergence and reintegration at multiple levels and across multiple issue domains within the global system. Conventional approaches, to the study of international relations in particular, either struggle with or deny these aberrant tendencies, with major ramifications for national and global security practice (Kavalsky 2015). Robert Keohane and Joseph Nye accommodate some of this new reality in their analysis of complex interdependence by emphasising the 'connectivity, sensitivity and vulnerability' that increasingly shapes state foreign policies and interstate interactions (Keohane and Nye 2012: 231). Social theory brings us closer to appreciating the nature of this global complexity. Anthony Giddens stresses the 'runaway' nature of globalisation and the consequences of this for social relations in a globally and locally interconnected world (Giddens 1999). Control is elusive, trajectories unpredictable and risks incalculable, raising doubts that globalisation can be 'tamed' (Beck 1999; Koenig-Archibugi 2004). Systems of security governance today exist in a quantum universe subject to sudden, 'erratic [and] radical change', of a kind that cannot easily be countervailed through the application of overwhelming military force (Luhmann 2008: 233). Interventions framed by linear statist assumptions about, in the context of this paper, the nature of organ-ised and armed violence, invite disappointment, and worse.

An eclectic global approach is arguably the most appropriate strat-egy to guide empirical investigation in search of hidden or 'unseen' precursors to human insecurity (Rosenau 2003; Barkin 2010; Sil and Katzenstein 2010). To appreciate the intricacies of any given social context we need to map out patterns of relations spread across geographical space and analyse interactions over time, pursuing an open-ended inquiry equipped with more than one theoretical idea (Sil and Katzenstein 2010: 47). Barry Buzan's concept of the *security complex* provides one starting point from which to develop an analy-sis of the labyrinthine dynamics that connect subnational, transna-tional, regional and global actors, and also of the role of subjectivity is shaping official conceptions of security threat (Buzan 1983; Buzan and Waever 2007). Niklas Luhmann's social theory, through the deployment of biological metaphor, illuminates an organic dimen-sion to social change that captures the evolutionary nature of con-flict events and trajectories (Luhmann 2008; 2013). The sociological analysis of risk developed by Giddens and Beck helps to accentuate the *polymorphous* and *invented* nature of such events (Battersby 2014). Thinking about security relations in this expansive and reflex-ive mode is surely prerequisite for addressing insecurity in this more complex global age (Beck 2005).

'Transition' is a neutral technocratic term that implies orderly change from an undesired to a preferred set of political circumstances. Yet international armed interventions are inherently disruptive acts, and social disruption occurs at both a material and psychological level. Restoration of a semblance of peace and order does not mean that the rivalries or hatreds that gave cause for intervention are expunged. Revolutionary and terrorist 'movements' propound utopian imaginings driven by aspirations for the recovery of a golden age of authentic community, and sustained by a deeply felt sense of 'injustice-dishonor' suffered by the group at the hands of adversar-ies (Battersby et al. 2011; Midlarsky 2011: 56–67). 'Mortality sali-ence', contends Manus Midlarsky, strengthens extremist sentiment, which translates into a heightened danger or risk of armed extremism in societies with high rates of violent death (Midlarsky 2011: 57). The self-styled Islamic State of Iraq and Syria (ISIS) is perhaps the quintessential *viral* threat, a visible killer and an invisible contagion that exposes the vulnerability of complex systems. The terror entity draws from popular and widespread anti-US and anti-Western sentiment. Its ideology appeals to the frustrations and resentments of the psychologically vulnerable and socially marginalised, takes advantage of the traumas and uncertainties of life that are amplified by hyper-globalisation, and offers a utopian afterlife to which death is the only rite of passage. All societies have such fractures or gaps that are only papered over, not repaired, by increasingly draconian anti-terror laws. Divergent ideological constructions of the meanings of words, 'victory' especially, and divergent historical interpretations, can perpetuate grievance and violence across generations (Abizadeh 2011). As the bases of power are dismantled, however brutal or illegitimate that power might be, so the space for volatile disagreement is enlarged. The simple and logical inference to be drawn here is that the use of violence as a technique of control cannot alone negate the propensity of others the engage in violent acts.

Armed interventions, like any form of military action, are hostage to miscalculation and uncertainty, as demonstrated but unlearned through the US experience in Vietnam, and underlined by the collapse of the Iraqi army in the wake of the lightening advance by forces of ISIS in 2014–15. There is irony in the historical fact that this terror state emerged from wellsprings of resentment deepened during and after the US-led intervention, occupation and counterinsurgency in Iraq from 2003, and the accompanying regime of incarceration and punishment from which Abu Bakr al-Baghdadi, the leader of ISIS, emerged resolved and empowered (Stern and Berger 2015). ISIS provides yet another template for the imagination of future security threats, yet the inclination of orthodox security analysis is to seek to contain each new threat within a temporally limited threat perspective or horizon. There was nothing inevitable about the rise of ISIS, even if there is a known tendency for the illegitimate use of force to provoke violent asymmetric reactions, a factor that was not considered by US security strategists before or in the immediate aftermath of the Iraq intervention (Bowden 2005; Harnden 2013). Aberrant, untoward global events are linked to multilevel systemic failings as much as they are signals of localised societal dissonance. However, reflexive awareness of this is eminently missing in conventional security thinking.

Unintended deviations

'Compelling human need', one of the triggers of R2P-compliant intervention, must be balanced against 'reasonable prospects' for success

(GA 2005). The Libyan uprising of 2011 was meant to be controllable. With no evident sectarian frictions, the country was thought, mistakenly, to be defined by a single fault line, between an oppressed people and an oppressive state (Rudd 2011). The UN-sanctioned NATO intervention in Libya in May and June that year materially helped rebel forces topple the regime of Colonel Muammar al-Qaddafi. From a strategic security standpoint, and allowing for disagreements between NATO members over their respective roles in the air war against Qaddafi, tactics deployed by NATO demonstrated the effectiveness of what Pentagon strategists term 'light footprint' military operations, where air power is used in conjunction with local military forces to prosecute a ground war against an unpopular incumbent regime (Daadler and Stavridis 2012). Predicated on R2P, the actions of the international community reflected a persistent and alarmingly simplistic conviction that the removal of a reviled dictator would remove all impediments to a democratic future. It also reflected the statist assumptions upon which international security policies are normally based, being that the consequences of any military actions directed against one country will be contained within the targeted country and that any international diplomatic ramifications can be managed in the aftermath. If we adopt and adapt and contextualise Buzan's security complex idea, we can appreciate the alarming simplicities of national security doctrines writ as global strategic policy. States and peoples are connected by complex webs of relations that span nation-state border zones, and these organic networks can react violently to ill-conceived surgical applications of remedial force (Buzan 1983; Buzan and Waever 2007; Luhmann 2013).

The ramifications of foreign interventions are felt over a protracted period of time and across wide, and widening, geographic space. In the late 1990s, a body of expert opinion emerged endorsing unilateral intervention on humanitarian grounds, in certain circumstances. Vietnam's invasion of Cambodia in 1979, though contrary to international law, brought an end to a four-year reign of terror by the Khmer Rouge during which as many as 1.7 million Cambodians were killed or allowed to die. However, the disruption was followed by a decade of civil war between a Vietnam-backed government one the one hand and royalist forces and the Khmer Rouge on the other. Arms provided to rebel groups by foreign powers stimulated a regional illicit arms trade that persisted long after the transitional authority instituted by United Nations oversaw a general demobilisation of rebel forces. NATO intervention engineered Kosovo's 'peaceful' secession from Serbia in 1999. But while this was justified as a necessary step to prevent massive loss of civilian life at the hands of a notoriously brutal Serbian military, few recall the coterminous atrocities committed by the Kosovo Liberation Army (KLA), which received NATO support, or the subsequent regionally destabilising criminal activities of some senior KLA commanders and their armed confederates (Holzgrefe 2003; PACE 2010). The uncertainties confronting a remade Afghan state after 2014 bear distinct resemblance to conditions in the country following the Soviet withdrawal in 1989, when a weak government in Kabul faced a mounting Islamist insurgency. Guiding assumptions about the potential to force political redevelopment in both Afghanistan and Iraq to fit a liberal globalist template have proven mistaken. Post-intervention Libya too has not followed a linear liberal path towards stability and democracy. Events in Libya throughout 2013 gave little indication of stability or democratisation. Following the collapse of the Qaddafi regime, Libya was, regardless of the existence of an elected national government, *de facto* divided among rebel groups reluctant to disarm or submit to central authority. The intervention generated new supply chains of violence or replenished old ones through the filtering of small arms into conflict zones across the Sahel – and eastwards into Syria (Sullivan 2013). In short it created, unexceptionally, a permissive context within which new social formations could emerge to exploit the gaping fissures in the hastily reconstituted *de jure* Libyan state.

The implications of Western military aid to rebel forces fighting against the Syrian regime of Bashar al-Assad raise more perplexing permutations that confound simple binary constructions of 'good' and 'bad'. The civil conflict in Syria is the most traumatic consequence of the pressure for political change across North Africa and the Middle East from 2011. The conflict degenerated into a virtual proxy war between Sunni-majority Saudi Arabia supporting Syrian co-religionists against the Alawi-Shiite 'alliance' between Syria's governing elite and the Iranian state. Weapons transfers into Syria from all interested external parties to different elements within the country, both state and opposition, without UN authorisation, contributed to a murderous stalemate that precipitated the fragmentation of the National Coalition of Syrian Revolution and Opposition Forces. The limited and conflicted international response to the conflict-related deaths of over 200,000 people in Syria during 2011–15 demonstrates the limited reach of international law – and an enduring systemic tolerance for human suffering. The implication of elements from the Free Syrian Army in both transnational and war crimes coincided with the ideological and material disintegration of the opposition front to a point where no coherent alternative to the Assad regime existed by the end of 2013. Into this vacuum poured the hate-filled violence of ISIS, guided by the expert hands of displaced members of Saddam Hussein's military elite that US 'neocon' strategists calculated would melt away into obscurity (Bowden 2005; Fukuyama 2007; Harnden 2013).

One could switch to a more conventional reading of events and claim that the disintegration of Syria is yet more proof that international institutions and international laws are flawed and ineffectual. Up to the time of writing, the accumulated and concentrated imperatives of regional and global power politics negated all avenues for legal or UN Security Council-mandated solutions to this defining global crisis. Neither Russia nor China were prepared to authorise UN-sanctioned military intervention in Syria, and yet in September 2015 Russia escalated its support to the Assad regime by unilaterally launching air strikes against anti-Assad rebel groups and stationing Russian forces in Damascus. There is no denying that the Middle East is a 'theatre' for the projection of strategic capabilities by regional and global powers. Moscow's disruptive intervention is not unprecedented, and it is explicable according to traditionalist models of international relations. It was not however, publicly at least, on the table of options or possibilities to be addressed by NATO security planners when the Syrian civil war erupted. Power competition in part explains why Russian and Iranian strategic interests drive their interventionist policies in the direction of support for Assad. Yet traditional modes of thinking do not provide any answers to the complex of insecurities that connect global power relations to the struggle for control over crumbling outposts in the deserts of Syria and Iraq. It is possible to map out possible alliance permutations and suggest alternative scenarios for a durable resolution, but few are able to imagine 'what victory looks like' in Syria, or Iraq for that matter (Peter Leahy, cited in Kenny and Wroe 2015).

US–Russia strategic rivalry does not define Middle East politics, and neither does the rivalry between Iran and Saudi Arabia. Each constitutes but one layer of complexity and one element in the increasingly interconnected Eastern Europe–Middle East–North Africa crime-security complexes. Given the propensity for criminal violence to escalate into political violence, conceptual connections between licit/illicit cross-border trades in handguns and assault rifles need to be more forcefully asserted in global security debates (GIDS 2015). Military interventions, of any kind, merely assist in the transfer of weapons across the licit/illicit arms trade frontier and across physical state frontiers into new spheres of conflict, as borne out by the international interventions in Libya and Syria (Feinstein 2011a: 492–3; 2011b; Spencer 2011; Battersby 2014). The ISIS 'blitzkrieg' of 2014–15 netted stockpiles of legally transferred, rigorously coded and recorded modern armaments and other war-fighting materiel, including US-supplied M16 assault rifles and ammunition, heavy machine guns and grenade launchers, as well as Soviet-era tanks and armoured personnel carriers, all long-lasting legacies of earlier wars and foreign interventions. US manufactured and supplied weapons are being 'allocated' to Shiite militias drafted into the counteroffensive, and these militias have already garnered a reputation for summary violations of the Geneva Conventions in their operations against ISIS, and their impositions on Iraq's Sunni population (El-Hamed 2015). Regulating weapons transfers within chaotic conflict zones is an imperfect science but there are many points of vulnerability in international arms transfer chains that are more amenable to governance interventions.

Crime and security converge along multiple vectors in Syria through the subterranean underworld of arms traffickers, al-Qaeda sympathisers, and the violation of Syrian sovereignty and international law by states seeking to precipitate or prevent regime change (Mazzetti et al. 2013). Small arms and light weapons are responsible for more battle-related deaths than nuclear or chemical weapons combined, and there is a thriving global business in 'transitioning' legally traded and stolen armaments onto the illegal arms market. Governments engage lawfully in the distribution of armaments and war-fighting capabilities, with the US amongst the most active in military diplomacy, spending US$17.8 billion on foreign military aid in 2011, a substantial increase on the US$14.5 billion 'allocated' in 2010 (covered largely by a US$4 billion increase in expenditure in Afghanistan) (USAID 2013). The global conventional arms trade was estimated at US$43 billion in 2011, declining marginally in 2012, presumably because of ongoing contraction in the global economy. Obviously, the value of the illegal global arms trade is unknowable, but with major intrastate conflicts affecting countries in the Middle East, Central Asia, the Sahel and Latin America, and with significantly high rates of murder by firearm recorded in fifty-eight countries globally during the first decade of the twenty first century, the demand for illegal weapons is doubtless substantial (Feinstein 2011a; GDS 2011: 44; SIPRI 2013a; 2013b). Legal arms manufacturers and retailers both produce and distribute the small arms and light weapons that find their way into the hands of criminals and insurgents. Andrew Feinstein writes of a global 'shadow world' of arms trading that verges on trafficking by virtue of the clandestine, and often illicit, nature of many state-sanctioned transactions. There is a vast web of underground arms traders that connects indirectly with the legal arms trades of the US, EU countries, Russia and China, all of whom provided weapons to Libya under the Qaddafi regime, and then to rebel forces (Feinstein 2011a: 492–3). Through this web, armaments filter, directly or indirectly, into the Iraq-Syria complex. These irreconcilable entries in the ledger of Middle East conflict encapsulate the paradoxes and dangers of a new global political economy of violence in which privatised force is increasingly salient.

Systemic failures

The upsurge of violence across Syria and Iraq, and the fragmentation of political authority in Libya, are popularly represented as the foundering of democratic revolutionary sentiment – an Arab Winter following close on the heels of the Arab Spring – yet these 'reversals' are merely evidence of the non-linear nature of political and social change, marking new phases of transition that will lead in yet more divergent directions. Africa, long dismissed as a singular place of endemic internecine conflict, underdevelopment and HIV/AIDS, is changing rapidly, but rapid societal change brings new challenges and new risks on the 'upside' and the 'downside'. First is the limited remit of central authority – a consequence of colonial inheritance – and decades of economic hardship, and attendant long-running 'centre-periphery' tensions (Herbst 2000: loc. 352). Political struggles over the idea of the state in Sudan and Somalia especially have endured for decades and are not amenable to foreign interventions (Samatar 2011). So, too, are lesser-known and 'localised' territorial disputes encompassing northern Kenya, Somalia and Ethiopia. Topographies of conflict signal breakdowns in political relations attributable to a long list of interrelated factors. The illegal arms trade contributes to a complex feedback loop that aids the transference of organised violence from one regional hotspot to another. Trafficked arms – legally manufactured but illegally acquired – are available everywhere thanks to Western military support for anti- Qaddafi rebels in 2011, arms shipments from China, and the attentiveness of Russian arms dealers like Victor Bout. Simply put, the roots of effective, legitimate government run very shallow across this east–west belt, allowing political and criminal violence to escalate. Yet, while crime is integral to the supply chains that feed conflict, the coexistence of criminal networks alongside rebel groups does not necessarily signal convergence or 'threat solidification'.

The sudden collapse of order in Mali, once held up as an exemplar of African development, demonstrates the limited effects of strategic assistance to countries experiencing high levels of political dissonance. Substantial financial and military aid from the US during the presidency of George W. Bush did not shield against the southward and westward extension of vectors of insecurity. The 2012 Tuareg Rebellion in northern Mali was widely construed as incontrovertible proof of the spreading influence of al-Qaeda in the Islamic Maghreb (AQIM). Ethnic Tuareg rebels, fighting under the banner of the Azawad National Liberation Movement (ANLM), entered into tactical alliance with Islamist militants to prosecute its historical claims for an independent Tuareg state. What was in reality a three-cornered contest between ANLM and AQIM cadres who sought to 'merge' with and 'acquire' the Tuareg rebellion, and the Mali government backed by French troops, became yet one more 'site' in a spreading global struggle between 'good states', aligned to the West, and Islamist terrorists (Battersby 2014).

AQIM is at its core a gang of mainly Algerian Islamist fighters, numbering little more than five hundred active cadres, many of them the defeated and dishonoured remnants of the *Group Salafist pour la Predication et le Combat* (GSPC) which fought in the Algerian Civil War of the 1990s, and which includes Algerian volunteers who trained and fought in Afghanistan during the 1980s. Narcotics and people trafficking, kidnapping and theft provide financial resources necessary to sustain core group operations and, equally important, influence over affiliates and favour with the real al-Qaeda, to which it pays 'tax' (Mohamedou 2011; Masters 2013). While there are fears of a widening of the AQIM network in northern Africa, there is also evidence of rifts between its leadership and the central command of al-Qaeda. Volatility and disorder is evident both within this offshoot and its alliances of disparate, even mutually hostile, armed non-state groups. Government forces regained control over northern Mali in early 2013, and the Mali government then sought to engage the

ANLM in a dialogue to find a durable peace settlement. Even before this setback, AQIM was splintering into the Ansar al-Din and the Movement for Unity and Jihad in West Africa (MUJWA). Reports of ideological differences and internal friction point to weak institution-alisation and also frustration on the part of AQIM's central leader-ship with the opportunistic freelance terror operations of former core members turned affiliate, like the notorious Mokhtar Belmokhtar (Chivvis and Liepman 2013; Masters 2013; McElroy 2013). AQIM has the capacity to recruit and to mobilise, but not to bind people in sufficient numbers to be anything other than a destabilising militant entity.

Concerned that any visible increase in its military presence in North Africa could likely backfire by engendering further radicalisation and enhancing the appeal of the Islamists, the US quietly expanded its operations in East Africa, working with amenable governments to suppress Islamist activities through its Africa Regional Command (AFRICOM). AFRICOM's presence is both suspected and welcomed by African governments fearful of the appeal of radical Islamism. Framing of 'the problem' raises questions about the strategy and the tactics employed to arrest the spread of extremism, which is not, it must be repeatedly emphasised, purely Islamic extremism. A case in point, the Lord's Resistance Army (LRA) is a volatile amalgam of syncretic, fundamentalist Christian, 'anti-modern, anti-developmen-tal and anti-state' beliefs that originated in northern Uganda (Jackson 2010: 4). Despite AFRICOM's attention, and that of the whole inter-national community, temporarily, when LRA leader Joseph Kony became an overnight social media celebrity, the LRA has established footholds outside Uganda, in South Sudan and the Central African Republic. Al-Shabaab is *the* terror group of Western concern in East Africa, and yet the chaos upon which it thrives is informed by many conflicts, including those with little connection to radical Islam.

Future projections of global systemic transformation designate Nigeria as the African country most likely to rise to a position of regional leadership. Many structural factors contribute to Nigeria's current internal security challenges, not least rapid population growth and severe income inequality. The country's oil-dependent economy has seen rising levels of economic growth and aggregate prosperity, but these have not led to any appreciable reduction in the chronic prevalence of poverty (Battersby 2014). Armed sectarian violence persists in the predominantly Islamic north of the country. Jama'atu Ahlis Sunna Lidda'wati Wal-Jihad, the vaguely constituted Islamist group better known by its Hausa sobriquet, Boko Haram (variously translated as 'books are sinful' or 'Western education is sacrilege'), has graduated from robbing banks and kidnapping, its core business since its formation in 2002, to waging a guerrilla war against the Nigerian state from 2009. Whatever links there might be with elements of al-Qaeda or AQIM, Boko Haram is principally a collection of robber bands, and a reflection of the deeply-rooted sectarian rivalries dividing the north and the predominantly Christianised south (Bavier 2012; Campbell 2011; 2013; Jacinto 2013).

The idea that Nigeria should be an Islamic state is not a recent invention of Islamists, and political violence in Nigeria is not attributable solely to Boko Haram. Human rights violations by the Nigerian military against communities in the oil-rich Niger Delta are linked to armed struggles with militia groups, operating under the umbrella Movement for the Emancipation of the Niger Delta (MEND), for control over oil resources. MEND sustained its war economy through oil theft and maritime piracy. Nigeria's 'oil insurgency' is reportedly subsiding in the Delta following a government amnesty in 2009. It might be the case that the triggers for organised violence by and against the state in the south have been to some extent removed, but the structural conditions that sparked anti-state mobilisations have not. Noticeably, the incidence of piracy off the West Africa coast, linked to conflict and crime – in particular the trade in 'blood oil' – has not abated but doubled since 2006 (Batterbsy et al. 2011: 127; Battersby 2014).

Armed and coordinated al-Qaeda-linked terror groups operate in northern Africa and Asia, and there is ample evidence of global jihadi networks of varying levels of sophistication and violent intent across the globe (Chivvis and Liepman 2013). In this new state of flux, criminal actors merge with politically motivated rebel groups, rendering it increasingly difficult to distinguish between criminal entities and armed non-state actors. The alignment between Islamists and pirates is unclear, and there is evidently much antagonism between pirate clans and al-Shabaab. Crucially, however, and to reiterate the point made above, the politics of these new wars is local, as Kaldor foreshadowed, whatever the ideological fault lines exposed or chosen by belligerents and their criminal associates (Kaldor 2001). And this pattern is perhaps most in evidence in the aftermath of the collapse of Soviet power in Central Asia and the upsurge in drug-fuelled political violence where contests over state power are fed by the Afghanistan–Pakistan narco-terror complex (Cornell and Jonsson

2014). Transnational criminals and international terror entities are indeed cooperating for tactical gain and, in some instances, out of ideological affinity, but there are significant differences between those groups or entities lumped together as constituents of a convergent terror threat (Hanlon 2009). It is possible, using the quantitative tools of network analysis to quantify connections and nodes, the scale and expansion and the communication frequency of illicit networks of traffickers and terrorists. Care, however, is needed where horizontal data is used as a proxy for organisational 'depth' and intent. The presumption of an innate human tendency towards violence, combined with entrenched suspicion of peoples with differing value systems, can lead to the presumption that evidence of a network connection between declared or suspected adversaries necessarily translates into convergent action.

Criminal entities, revolutionaries and separatist groups, where they are converging, do so because the globalising dynamics present in the security complexes they inhabit encourage and facilitate more extensive interconnections. So, there are many subtle and less subtle links between crime and political violence but to reiterate, care must be taken not to detach these links from their socio-political and socio-economic contexts and conflate connections into the substance of empire. None of this is meant to imply that insurgencies or terror groups are trifling nuisances. Concerns that insurgency, Islamism and crime are closely connected are borne out in conflicts and political turmoil from Chechnya through to the Northwest Frontier (Cornell and Jonsson 2014). There is a danger inherent in dismissing the germ of genuine grievance, either against governments or the international system and its manifold flaws (Kilcullen 2010). As it unhinges established political orders and unleashes the criminally inclined, globalisation also provokes reaction from those most disadvantaged or 'disenfranchised' by the pace and direction of change. In many parts of the world, globalisation is not so much leading to the demise of the state as exacerbating conflicts over the very legitimacy of states that have smouldered for decades.

Aberrant globalities

States have never enjoyed a monopoly over the means and use of force, but state capacity to manage organised violence is steadily eroding with the proliferation of non-state armed actors. Arguably, the demand for irregular force is rising in the new global context of 'unending war' (Duffield 2007). From a critical standpoint, war is purely a mercantile venture that, through mutually supporting processes of organisation, destruction, recreation and reorganisation, establishes the preconditions for perpetual profit, provided that no side wins a decisive victory. This systemic dynamic connects directly and indirectly with localised conflicts through the supply of armaments and paramilitary personnel. We can imagine an emerging global ecology of organised and *privatised* force, aided materially by nation-state foreign policies, or surviving through independent means in a permissive globalised marketplace. Setting aside the flow of arms to governments in the Middle East and Africa, as stated, an increasing array of autonomous and state-sponsored armed actors access licit and illicit arms supply chains to pursue local and regional change agendas. Rather that recite this lengthening list of paramilitary or quasi-military forces, we can instead identify patterns of paramilitary formation and construct a taxonomy of armed entities. The term 'paramilitary' covers a vast category that includes militarised civil law-enforcement actors at one end of the scale and armed criminal gangs at the other. They are formed to advance (1) state security imperatives, (2) protect the interests of social groups against the state or against other non-state armed actors, (3) effect local regime change, (4) capture licit market opportunities and (5) protect and advance criminal self-interest (Battersby et al. 2011). Their use by states as instruments of strategic policy is not without historical precedent, but their proliferation should be subject to enhanced global scrutiny, not least because of their 'irregular' patterns of behaviour.

Conservative estimates are that India's paramilitary forces number over 1 million,[1] Russia's number 489,000, China 660,000, Thailand 93,000 and the Philippines 41,000 (IISS 2015: 484–9). Setting aside specially armed and trained police units that are a commonplace in modern societies, state-sponsored paramilitary forces undertake military-style operations at arm's length from established military chains of authority. Iranian paramilitaries are active in neighbouring conflicts, in Iraq, Yemen, and Syria, and are distinct from the Iranian-backed but autonomous Hezbollah which furthers Iranian strategic interests in Lebanon and Syria (Alfoneh 2010; IISS 2015: 487; Middle East Monitor 2015). These militarised formations expand or contract according to prevailing circumstances and are by their nature volatile. Indiscipline or brazen criminality by paramilitaries can be as much a catalyst for intrastate and interstate conflict as the depravations of regular soldiers. Private armies formed by wealthy landowners to protect property against rebel attack have in the Philippines engaged in the mass killing of civilians, while Columbia's right-wing paramilitaries are synonymous with international terrorism. In Thailand's fractious southern border provinces, civilians are caught between the guerrilla violence of Malay-Muslim separatists and state-sanctioned brutality at the hands of the military, police and local paramilitary forces. Reminiscent of the 1970s when villagers were mobilised to fight the Communist Party of Thailand (CPT), new 'volunteer' village defence units are recruited into the military campaign to eliminate or track down suspected insurgents and their sympathisers. Trained, equipped and paid by the Thai state, these paramilitaries are under the 'effective control' of the state and *de facto*, if not *de jure*, part of Thailand's state security apparatus (Ball and Mathieson 2007; Abuza 2014; Battersby 2014; Raymond 2014).

Private military security contractors (PMSCs) have attracted substantial public scrutiny because of the actions of armed operatives working for Blackwater (renamed Xe and, as of 2011, Academi) in Iraq during the US-directed counterinsurgency. In strict legal terms, PMSCs are not mercenaries, and yet the association persists, even in the minds of former security contractors who contribute to public debate about the growing phenomenon of military contracting (McFate 2014). Whatever assurances are given as to the professionalism of such private companies, frequent reports of irregularities give cause for, if not scepticism, then at least serious concern. Reports of the involvement of South African military contractors, STTEP and Pilgrims Africa, in the Nigerian government's fight against Boko Haram, offer further evidence that national regulations outlawing unsanctioned participation in foreign conflicts present little disincentive to the military 'fortune hunter'. STTEP, while recruiting mainly from the South African Army, is reportedly based in Lagos, brazenly beyond the reach of South African authorities (Campbell 2015; Fabricius 2015; Nossiter 2015). South African contractors in Nigeria become, by virtue of their presence and assistance, complicit in any breaches of international law by a Nigerian military with an abysmal human rights record. The risks posed by patterns of replication and diversification within this subcategory of private and under-regulated force should therefore be considered alongside those posed by battlefield-hardened former rebel fighters turned defence militia, or 'domestic' terrorists. And yet, each is treated separately in national security strategies, and this fragmentation contributes further to an already highly fragmented global regime of security governance.

Conclusion

Global strategic concern is focussed primarily on one element in a very broad spectrum of aberrant armed actors and this narrow frame of reference is troubling. The privatisation of force more broadly conceived is a hidden global security risk, because privatisation, in all its forms, multiplies already diverse and divergent global supply chains of violence. To put it another away, the privatisation of force magnifies the potential for indiscriminate killing and other forms of conflict-related violence. The global analysis adopted here is sufficiently expansive to accommodate the elusiveness and unpredictability of political and criminal trajectories that give rise to *distributed* and organised, but under- or unregulated, private force. Central to any viable governance response is the recognition by state security planners and decision-makers that *their* global securities are interlinked and increasingly interdependent. At a time when states everywhere are confronted by the ongoing socialisation of war and popularisation of the means to engage in combat, cast as righteous terrorism, commercial opportunity or masculine self-defence, there is space to debate the deep and complex systemic dynamics that threaten human security everywhere.

Note

1. This estimate encompasses state-controlled border security and armed police forces and reservists. Indian paramilitaries operating in Assam and Kashmir have been the subject of frequent reports of extrajudicial killing, torture and rape of suspected Islamist or Maoist insurgents, and of Rohingya refugees fleeing persecution in Bangladesh (Doherty 2012; DOS 2015).

References

Abizadeh, A. (2011), 'Hobbes on the Causes of War: A Disagreement Theory', *American Political Science Review*, 105(2), pp. 298–315.

Abuza, Z. (2014), 'Learning from Mindanao: Lessons for Thailand', *Indo-Pacific Review*, 30 October, available at: http://iag.org.ph/index.php/blog/798-learning-from-mindanao-lessons-for-thailand-abuza, last accessed 23 December 2016.

Alfoneh, A. (2010), 'The Basij Resistance Force: A Weak Link in the Iranian Regime?', Washington Institute, Policywatch 1627, available at: http://www.washingtoninstitute.org/policy-analysis/view/the-basij-resistance-force-a-weak-link-in-the-iranian-regime, last accessed 23 December 2016.

Ball, D. and S. Mathieson (2007), *Militia Redux: Or Sor and the Revival of Paramilitarism in Thailand*, Bangkok: White Lotus.

Barkin, J. S. (2010), *Realist Constructivism: Rethinking International Relations Theory*, Cambridge: Cambridge University Press.

Battersby, P. (2014), *The Unlawful Society: Global Crime and Security in a Complex World*, London: Palgrave Macmillan.

Battersby, P., J. M. Siracusa and S. Ripiloski (2011), *Crime Wars: the Global Intersection of Crime, Political Violence and International Law*. Santa Barbara, CA: Praeger.

Bavier, J. (2012), 'Who Are Boko Haram and Why Are They Terrorizing Nigerian Christians? *The Atlantic*, 24 January, available at: http:// www.theatlantic.com/international/archive/2012/01/whoarebokohara mandwhyaretheyterrorizingnigerianchristians/251729/, last accessed 23 December 2016.

Beck, U. (1999), *World Risk Society*. Cambridge: Polity Press.

Beck, U. (2005), *Power in the Global Age*. Cambridge: Polity Press.

Beck, U. (2009), 'World Risk Society and Manufactured Uncertainties', *Iris: European Journal of Philosophy and Public Debate*, 1(2), pp. 291–9.

Bowden, M. (2005), 'Wolfowitz: The Exit Interviews', *The Atlantic*, July/August, available at: http://www.theatlantic.com/magazine/ archive/2005/07/wolfowitz-the-exit-interviews/304078/, last accessed 23 December 2016.

Buzan, B. (1983), *People, States and Fear: The National Security Question in International Relations*. London: Wheatsheaf.

Buzan, B. and O. Waever (2007), *Regions and Powers: The Structure of International Security*. Cambridge: Cambridge University Press.

Campbell, J. (2011), *Nigeria: Dancing on the Brink*, Lanham, MD: Rowman & Littlefield.

Campbell, J. (2013), 'Should U.S. Fear Boko Haram?' CNN, available at: http://edition.cnn.com/2013/10/01/opinion/campbell-boko-haram/index. html, last accessed 23 December 2016.

Campbell, J. (2015), 'More on Nigeria's South African Mercenaries', *Africa in Transition*, Council on Foreign Relations (CFR), 13 May, available at: http://blogs.cfr.org/campbell/2015/05/13/more-on-nigerias-south-afri can-mercenaries, last accessed 23 December 2016.

Chivvis, C. S. and A. Liepman (2013), 'North Africa's Menace: AQIM's Evolution and the U.S. Policy Response', RAND Corporation, RR415, available at: http://www.rand.org/content/dam/rand/pubs/research_ reports/RR400/RR415/RAND_RR415.pdf, last accessed 5 January 2017.

Cornell, S. and M. Jonsson (2014), 'The Nexus of Crime and Conflict', in Cornell, S. and M. Jonsson (ed.), *Conflict, Crime and the State in*

Postcommunist Eurasia, Philadelphia: University of Pennsylvania Press, pp. 1–22.

Daadler, I. and J. Stavridis (2012), 'NATO's Triumph in Libya', *Foreign Affairs*, 91(2), pp. 2–7.

Doherty, B. (2012), 'India's Border Force Has Crossed the Line', *Sydney Morning Herald*, 21 April, available at: http://www.smh.com.au/world/indias-border-force-has-crossed-the-line-20120420-1xc5g.html, last accessed 23 December 2016.

Duffield, M. (2007), *Development, Security and Unending War: Governing the World of Peoples*, Cambridge: Polity Press.

El-Hamed, R. (2015), 'Ramadi and the Debate over Shia Militias in Anbar', Carnegie Endowment for International Peace: *Sada*, 21 May, available at: http://carnegieendowment.org/sada/60168, last accessed 23 December 2016.

Fabricius, P. (2015), 'SADF "Mercenaries" Turning Tide in Nigeria', *IOL*, 12 April, available at: http://www.iol.co.za/news/africa/sadf-mercenaries-turning-tide-in-nigeria-1.1843796, last accessed 23 December 2016.

Feinstein, A. (2011a), *The Shadow World: Inside the Global Arms Trade*, London: Hamish Hamilton.

Feinstein, A. (2011b), 'Where Is Gaddafi's Vast Arms Stockpile?' *The Guardian*, 26 October, available at: https://www.theguardian.com/world/2011/oct/26/gadaffis-arms-stockpile, last accessed 23 December 2016.

Fukuyama, F. (2007), *After the Neocons: America at the Crossroads*, London: Profile Books.

Geneva Declaration Secretariat (GDS) (2011), Global Burden of Armed Violence, 'the Geneva Declaration', available at: http://www.genevadeclaration.org/measurability/global-burden-of-armed-violence/global-burden-of-armed-violence-2011.html, last accessed 23 December 2016.

Giddens, A. (1999), *Runaway World: How Globalization Is Reshaping Our Lives*, London: Profile Books.

Graduate Institute of Development Studies (GIDS) (2015), *Small Arms Survey, 2015: Weapons of the World*, Cambridge: Cambridge University Press, available at: http://www.smallarmssurvey.org/fileadmin/docs/A-Yearbook/2015/eng/Small-Arms-Survey-2015-Chapter-04-EN.pdf, last accessed 23 December 2016.

Hanlon, Q. H. (2009), 'Globalization and the Transformation of Armed Groups', in J. H. Norwitz (ed.), *Pirates, Terrorists and Warlords: The History, Influence, and Future of Armed Groups Around the World*, New York: Skyhorse Publishing, pp. 124–34.

Harnden, T. (2013), '10 Years On, Paul Wolfowitz Admits US Bungled in Iraq', *Real Clear Politics*, 18 March, available at: http://www.realclearpolitics.com/articles/2013/03/18/10_years_on_paul_wolfowitz_admits_us_bungled_in_iraq_117492.html, last accessed 23 December 2016, last accessed 23 December 2016.

Herbst, J. (2000), *States and Power in Africa: Comparative Lessons in Authority and Control*. Princeton. NJ: Princeton University Press.

Holzgrefe, J. L. (2003), 'The Humanitarian Intervention Debate', in J. L. Holzgrefe and Robert Keohane (eds), *Humanitarian Intervention: Ethical, Legal and Political Dilemmas*, Cambridge: Cambridge University Press, pp. 15–52.

International Institute for Strategic Studies (IISS) (2015), 'Chapter Ten Country Comparisons – Commitments, Force Levels and Economics', *The Military Balance*, 115(1), pp. 481–92. doi: 10.1080/04597222.2015.996366.

Jacinto, L. (2013), 'What's in a Name? Boko Haram Gets a New Terror Title', France 24 International News, 11 November, available at: http://www.france24.com/en/20131115-nigeria-boko-haram-terrorist-group-usa-implications-designation, last accessed 5 January 2017.

Jackson, P. (2010), *Politics, Religion and the Lord's Resistance Army in Northern Uganda*, Religions and Development Programme, Working Paper 43–2010, University of Birmingham, available at: http://eprints.bham.ac.uk/974/1/Working_Paper_43_complete_for_web.pdf, last accessed 23 December 2016.

Kaldor, M. (2001), *New & Old Wars: Organized Violence in a Global Era*, Cambridge: Polity Press.

Kavalsky, E. (2015), 'Introduction: Inside/Outside and Around: Observing the Complexity of Global Life', in E. Kavalsky (ed.), *World Politics at the Edge of Chaos: Reflections on the Complexity of Global Life*, New York: SUNY Press, pp. 1–20.

Kenny, M. and D. Wroe (2015), 'Tony Abbott pushed for US request to join Syria air strikes', *Sydney Morning Herald*, 26 August, available at: http://www.smh.com.au/federal-politics/political-news/tony-abbott-pushed-for-us-request-to-join-syrian-air-strikes-20150825-gj7kfh#ixzz3qNrX18cv, last accessed 23 December 2016.

Keohane, R. O. and J. S. Nye, Jr. (2012), *Power and Interdependence*, 4th edn, London: Pearson.

Kilcullen, D. (2010), *Counter Insurgency*, Melbourne: Scribe.

Koenig-Archibugi, M. (2004), 'Introduction: Globalization and the Challenge to Governance', in D. Held and M. Koenig-Archibugi (eds), *Taming Globalization: Frontiers of Governance*, Cambridge: Polity Press, pp. 1–17.

Luhmann, N. (2008), *Law as a Social System*, trans. K. A. Ziegert, Oxford: Oxford University Press.

Luhmann, N. (2013), *Introduction to Systems Theory*, trans. P. Gilgen, Cambridge: Polity Press.

McElroy, D. (2013), 'Al Qaeda's Scathing Letter to Troublesome Employee Mokhtar Belmokhtar Reveals Inner Workings of Terrorist Group', *Daily Telegraph*, 29 May, available at: http://www.telegraph.co.uk/news/worldnews/al-qaeda/10085716/Al-Qaedasscathing-letter-to-trou blesome-employee-Mokhtar-Belmokhtar-reveals-innerworkings-of-terror ist-group.html, last accessed 5 January 2017.

McFate, S. (2014), *The Modern Mercenary: Private Armies and What They Mean for World Order*. Oxford: Oxford University Press.

Masters, J. (2013), 'Al Qaeda in the Islamic Maghreb', CFR Backgrounders, available at: http://www.cfr.org/terrorist-organizations-and-networks/al-qaeda-islamic-maghreb-aqim/p12717, last accessed 5 January 2017.

Mazzetti, M., C. J. Chivers and E. Schmitt (2013), 'Taking Outsize Role in Syria, Qatar Funnels Arms to Rebels', *The New York Times*, 29 June, available at: http://www.nytimes.com/2013/06/30/world/middleeast/send ing-missiles-to-syrian-rebels-qatar-muscles-in.html, last accessed 23 December 2016.

Middle East Monitor (2015), 'Iranian military commander: We have forces in Syria, Yemen and Iraq', Middle East Monitor, 1 January, available at: https://www.middleeastmonitor.com/news/middle-east/16115-iranian-military-commander-we-have-forces-in-syria-yemen-and-iraq, last accessed 23 December 2016.

Midlarsky, M. I. (2011), *Origins of Political Extremism: Mass Violence in the Twentieth Century and Beyond*, Cambridge: Cambridge University Press.

Mohamedou, M. O. (2011), *The Many Faces of Al Qaeda in the Islamic Maghreb*. GCSP Policy Paper No. 15, available at: http://www.gcsp.ch/ News-Knowledge/Publications/The-Many-Faces-of-Al-Qaeda-in-the-Islamic-Maghreb, last accessed 23 December 2016.

Nossiter, A. (2015), 'Mercenaries Join Nigeria's Military Campaign Against Boko Haram', *The New York Times*, 12 March, available at: http://blogs. cfr.org/campbell/2015/05/13/more-on-nigerias-south-african-mercenar-ies, last accessed 23 December 2016.

Parliamentary Assembly of the Council of Europe (PACE) (2010), 'Inhuman Treatment of People and Illicit Trafficking in Human Organs' (Draft Report). Committee on Legal Affairs and Human Rights, AS/ Jur (2010), 46, 12 December, available at: http://www.assembly.coe.int/ CommitteeDocs/2010/ajdoc462010prov.pdf, last accessed 23 December 2016.

Rama, A. and L. Diaz (2014), 'Violence Against Women "Pandemic" in Mexico', *Reuters*, 7 March, available at: http://www.reuters.com/ article/2014/03/07/us-mexico-violence-women-idUSBREA2608F2014 0307, last accessed 23 December 2016.

Raymond, G. (2014), 'Is Thailand Arming Civilians in the South? Not Quite', *The Interpreter*, 10 November, available at: https://www.lowyin-stitute.org/the-interpreter/thailand-arming-civilians-south-not-quite, last accessed 23 December 2016.

Rosenau, J. N. (2003), *Distant Proximities: Dynamics Beyond Globalization*, Princeton: Princeton University Press.

Rudd, K. (2011), 'Statement at the 3rd Contact Group Meeting on Libya', 9 June, available at: http://foreignminister.gov.au/speeches/Pages/2011/kr_sp_110609.aspx?ministerid=2, last accessed 23 December 2016.

Samatar, A. I. (2011), 'The Production of Somali Conflict and the Role of Internal and External Actors', in R. Bereketab (ed.), *The Horn of Africa: Intra-State and Inter-State Conflicts and Security*, London: Pluto Press, pp. 3119–528.

Sil, R. and P. J. Katzenstein (2010), *Beyond Paradigms: Analytic Eclecticism in the Study of World Politics*, London: Palgrave Macmillan.

Spencer, R. (2011), 'France Supplying Arms to Libyan Rebels', *Daily Telegraph*, 29 June, available at: http://www.telegraph.co.uk/news/world news/africaandindianocean/libya/8606541/France-supplying-weapons-to-Libyan-rebels.html, last accessed 23 December 2016.

Stern, J. and J. M. Berger (2015), *ISIS: The State of Terror*, London: William Collins.

Stockholm International Peace Research Institute (SIPRI) (2013a), *SIPRI Yearbook 2013*, available at: http://www.sipri.org/yearbook/2013/05, last accessed 23 December 2016.

Stockholm International Peace Research Institute (SIPRI) (2013b), 'Trends in International Arms Transfers, 2012', *SIPRI Fact Sheet*, March, available at: http://www.sipri.org/research/armaments/transfers/measuring/recent-trends-in-arms-transfers, last accessed 23 December 2016.

Sullivan, K. (2013), 'Two Years After Libya's Revolution, Government Struggles to Control Hundreds of Armed Militias', *The Washington Post*, 6 September, available at: https://www.washingtonpost.com/world/middle_east/two-years-after-libyas-revolution-government-struggles-to-control-hundreds-of-armed-militias/2013/09/06/6f32c4c0-13ae-11e3-880b-7503237cc69d_story.html?utm_term=.8f951521b796, last accessed 23 December 2016.

United Nations General Assembly (GA) (2005), *2005 World Summit Outcome*, Sixtieth Session, UN Document A/60/L.1, available at: http://www.un.org/womenwatch/ods/A-RES-60-1-E.pdf, last accessed 23 December 2016.

United States Agency for International Development (USAID) (2013), *U.S. Overseas Loans and Grants (Greenbook)*, https://catalog.data.gov/dataset/us-overseas-loans-and-grants-greenbook-usaid-1554, last accessed 23 December 2016.

United States Department of State (DOS) (2015), '2015 Human Rights Report: India', 13 April, available at: http://www.state.gov/j/drl/rls/hrrpt/2015/sca/252963.htm, last accessed 23 December 2016.

Part II

*The Limits of Sovereignty and
the Ethics of Interventions*

A Framework for Reimagining Order and Justice: Transitions in Violence and Interventions in a Global Era

Michaelene Cox

Introduction

At the cusp of a new millennium, the Secretary-General of the United Nations faced a throng of world leaders and boldly foretold a time in which their state-centric international system might be compromised – or at least reimagined. Kofi Annan essentially urged members of the General Assembly to embrace transformation because the future of the nation rested on the future of humanity, and as things stood, the needs of humanity were not being met. In his annual report he argued that any notions of order and justice, even within defined boundaries, cannot be promised by the state alone. In essence, the catharsis can only come from intervention:

> [f]irst, it is important to define intervention as broadly as possible, to include actions along a wide continuum from the most pacific to the most coercive . . . A global era requires global engagement. Indeed, in a growing number of challenges facing humanity, the collective interest is the national interest . . . Any such evolution in our understanding of State sovereignty and individual sovereignty will, in some quarters, be met with distrust, skepticism, even hostility. But it is an evolution that we should welcome. (Annan 1999)

A decade and a half into the twenty-first century, a new Secretary-General addressed the Assembly but on this occasion the message was less provocative. After enumerating escalating and horrific challenges to peace and security, Ban Ki-moon did not refer to the need for a redefinition of sovereignty or intervention. It could be argued that under his predecessor's guidance, the international community had already initiated that discussion during the 2005 World Summit by endorsing the 'Responsibility to Protect' (R2P). There subsequently appeared no need at this time to confront traditional concepts of territorial integrity and political independence. Ban called upon a collective recommitment to work towards conflict prevention and spoke benignly of building transnational partnerships to do so. Whereas Annan had found opportunity to incorporate a strong sense of moral authority into the groundbreaking R2P project, Ban drew upon mediation and bridge-building skills to shift the spotlight to its implementation. Primary responsibility for tackling their own problems would still reside with governments and their leaders, he stressed, or otherwise engagement in conflict situations would be perceived to 'undermine their sovereignty, internationalize a problem or legitimize an adversary' (Ban Ki-moon 2015).

In considering the perspectives of Annan and Ban, it appears that evolution in our understanding of state dominion remains at times ambiguous. As such, this chapter will focus on developments that extend beyond the state-centric model in the face of contemporary challenges to order and justice. The chapter first presents a brief view of systemic shifts precipitating the current era, and then considers transitions in violence and intervention. It concludes with an emphasis on the need for political adaptability during periods of flux, and argues that while we need to consider international, state and societal interests, the welfare and the participation of the human being is essential.

Reassessing security

Both UN Secretaries-General drew their assessment from a complex and in some cases deteriorating political and social environment following the end of the Cold War, and used their position to influence debate on a number of global matters. Kofi Annan assumed office in 1997 in the wake of several humanitarian crises, including Iraq after the Persian Gulf War, the Bosnian genocide, Somalian political catastrophes and Rwandan genocide. His annual report urged member states to welcome an 'evolution' in defining sovereignty and intervention, citing human rights abuses in Kosovo to justify air attacks on Serbia in 1999 without approval of the UN Security Council, and the multinational humanitarian and security intervention in East Timor in September of the said year. While it was clearly evident that the status quo would no longer be sufficient, Annan was also mindful of inadvertently advocating illicit engagement or reckless interference in the affairs of other states. In reconceptualising the parameters of autonomy in the new global era – a world order marked by an integrated system of diverse actors, structures and processes – Annan argued that it was imperative that vital state interests are firmly linked to those of its citizens, and international concerns are similarly connected to domestic concerns.

By the time Ban Ki-moon succeeded Annan in 2007, there appeared widespread use, if not acceptance, of military intervention aimed at mitigating internal conflicts in the name of humanitarian assistance and international security. At the same time, Ban cautioned member states about misuse of the Responsibility to Protect doctrine and the unwarranted contravention of its principles so as to disguise self-gain. The UN Security Council itself had authorised the use of force in circumstances where a more generous interpretation of threats to international peace had been applied. As such, Ban argued, state consent was vital to engagement and there remained 'limits to what outsiders can do when the political space to act is not there' (Ban Ki-moon 2015). He communicated an urgent need for the international community to pool its political will and resources with troubled states so as to curtail the insidious spread of turmoil and destruction by way of preventive measures; evident in the dramatic increase in the number of civil wars, transnational criminal activities, violent extremism, atrocities perpetuated against civilian populations and the number of traumatised and displaced persons. Ban's assertion was that consensus is the lynchpin to effectively and legitimately uphold the purposes and principles affirmed in the UN Charter and other international agreements. He carefully avoided reference to reactionary or *post facto* approaches to violence already in progress.

To some degree then, different tones about the appropriate rationale and nature of intervention are represented in remarks made by these two UN leaders. The overarching debate is still centred on evolving tensions between codified principles of non-interference and the growing international norm of R2P in face of threats to security. The human rights era of the 1990s had fueled growing awareness of the moral, legal and political imperatives, with a greater emphasis on human basic needs. A number of legal experts, for instance, found ample codified and normative universal agreement, as well as case law, in support of domestic jurisdiction conventionally defined as freedom from external coercion regarding its 'choice of a political, economic social or cultural system' (Wheatley 1993: 190). Nevertheless, they also acknowledged that there are occasions when state rights may be superseded by the rights of an individual human. In short, there developed a general consensus that the principle of non-intervention could be set aside when a government did not ensure fulfillment of certain basic human needs, and as such, forceful measures by the international community could be employed to remedy those shortcomings.

Another line of argument does not rest upon a hierarchy of rights and needs. It proposes that state and citizen interests are not mutually exclusive. An association with universal standards of human rights, manifested by assent and custom, lends a sense of political legitimacy beyond what moral justifications might contribute. Human rights rest on a legal positivist tradition in which states agree upon how rights are to be defined. Within this framework, social and economic rights are therefore socially-constructed with a view that they have added value. Rationalism is the intersection point between neoliberal and neorealist approaches to viewing human security, in which there are both internal and external incentives for states to comply (Cox 2009).

Thus, as restated generally by one scholar, rights-based development and security approaches can, among other things, enhance accountability; provide higher levels of citizens' empowerment, ownership and free, meaningful and active participation; offer greater normative clarity and detail, and so provide easier consensus and increased transparency in national development processes; and lastly, integrate safeguards against unintentional harm by intervention projects (Robinson 2006: 38). It remains for governments to gauge the costs and benefits of melding national security interests with provision of basic needs and human rights within the milieu of domestic and global politics. If the cost of compliance can be avoided or minimised – for example if state policies and practices are already consistent with international expectations – states are more likely to commit to binding treaty ratifications and adhere to various forms of soft law (Cox 2009).

Governments are vulnerable to both internal and external forces, and at no time is this more relevant than today when threats to international order chiefly emerge from conflict and chaos within individual states rather than between them. Provoked by human rights abuses and other attacks on the well-being of individuals, humanitarian crises jeopardise welfare at every level. More than a decade ago, a UN report anticipated that a sense of individual well-being was necessary for nations to obtain pacific goals; in other words, world order will not be secured by arms but by socio-economic development, the lack thereof prompting intervention:

For too long, the concept of security has been shaped by the potential for conflict between states. For too long, security has been equated with threats to a country's borders. For too long, nations have sought arms to protect their security. For most people today, a feeling of insecurity arises more from worries about daily life than from the dread of a cataclysmic world event. Job security, income security, health security, environmental security, security from crime, these are the emerging concerns of human security all over the world ... When the security of people is attacked in any corner of the world, all nations are likely to get involved. Famines, ethnic conflicts, social disintegration, terrorism, pollution and drug trafficking are no longer isolated events, confined within national borders. Their consequences travel the globe. (UNDP 1994: 3)

Security remains an overarching concern in the global era. The UNDP report coincided with the transition to a new international system after the end of the Cold War. It became evident that in this new era, security threats would be more opaque and would significantly test government capabilities and their willingness to peacefully manage them. It is striking, however, that foreknowledge about this latter sense of security was expressed even earlier in a report about the San Francisco meeting which inaugurated the United Nations. In his report to the president, the US secretary of state clearly made the connection between individual welfare and armed conflict by noting that '[n]o provisions that can be written into the Charter will enable the Security Council to make the world secure from war if men and women have no security in their homes and their jobs' (Stettinius 1945: 109). This placed basic human rights at the heart of discussions about global order, while also stirring debate about individual sovereignty and the role of the individual – and civil society – in interventions.

Inauguration of the global era

A proliferation of philosophical and theoretical discussions, arguments and prescriptions has created a virtual industry addressing relationships between governance and contemporary challenges to peace. What has changed, and what truly is the 'global era'? Answers abound and like answers to most big questions, many of them are contradictory or otherwise unsatisfactory. If we briefly look here at prevailing international relations theories for explanations about change from one era to the next, we still find it difficult to crystallise the vast, and growing, body of analyses. However, an especially succinct roadmap to navigating one strand of theoretical discourse comes from Andrew Moravcsik. He reminds us that there is a typical misunderstanding in viewing differences between two major competing paradigms; that is, we are incorrect in saying that liberal theories do not claim that states make foreign policy decisions based on security threats and balance of power, as do realists. On contrary, he says, threats and power considerations are of concern to both perspectives. The difference rests with the source(s) of security threats. Realists look to particular power structures as potential threats while liberals see challenges emerging from state preferences in regard to ideology, institutions and material concerns. Moravcsik gives weight to 'taking preferences seriously' but nevertheless argues for theoretical pluralism when looking to a more comprehensive and rigorous framework to explain state behaviour (1997: 548). While the summation herein teeters on oversimplification, it does provide room for us to organise some of our thoughts about the global era based on source(s) of current threats.

First, we can look to structural changes within the state system. It is commonplace for many observers to point to the power shift from that of bipolarity characterising the mid-to-late twentieth century to one of hegemony. This latter turn of events we generally agree occurred around 1992 and refer to as the post-Cold War era. There is disagreement, however, when speculating if the US continues to dominate the political, economic and cultural landscape now that we are well into the twenty-first century, or if there is currently a substantive diffusion of power among state and non-state actors. Despite its relatively narrow understanding, the nature of order and disorder rests in such a context. For the period when intense US–Soviet power struggles underscored the pre-eminence of geopolitics in foreign policy, and both military and non-military intervention were none too subtly motivated by vital state interests, a retrospective classification of the use of force purely for humanitarian reasons is difficult. While regional conflicts may have been restrained to some degree in order to maintain equilibrium between the two superpowers and their allies, atrocities associated with those outbreaks still occurred. They were simply relegated to the periphery of the world's attention and subsequently moved out of these shadows.

Second, we can look at institutions and state preferences during the Cold War period. Overall, non-governmental organisations were not in a position to temper armed aggression or adequately aid conflict victims. One observer writes that when privately funded charity groups did intervene, for example in liberation movements, 'there was disapproval not only on the part of Western governments but at the public level too. Politics was not a field for charities, and so fundraising stagnated' (Munro 1999). Attention, or lack thereof, remained state-centric in nature. Even the Security Council veto allowed circumvention of anything but state interest.

In the decade immediately following dissolution of the dual spheres of influence, rapid and profound changes in global relations began taking place and lively discussion continues to this very day. One perspective assumes a greater appreciation for the role of social forces in reshaping conceptions of power and structural configurations, as previously contended by critical theorists such as Robert Cox (1981). For instance, the millennium began with unprecedented integration. The International Monetary Fund points to four features of globalisation that have transformed dynamics of interaction at every level, and so requires rapid adaptability of institutions, processes and persons associated with it. Potential for both constructive and adverse outcomes are intertwined through changes in trade patterns, capital and investment, movement of peoples and spread of knowledge and technology (IMF 2000).

Phrasing challenges associated with this exceptional rate and extent of integration as 'threats', the IMF and other overseers are watchful for implications to national sovereignty, increased poverty and inequality, and regional or global financial crises. Additional related issues include implications for armed violence and external intervention. Academics have posited further arguments pertaining to how social forces, especially those connected with a market economy, are key to understanding global transformations. Buzan and Lawson (2014) place emphasis on modernisation itself, and the extent to which various kinds of capitalist governments compete and cooperate. A universal embrace of capitalism narrows political distance between countries so that interstate and intrastate relations are not dictated by hard geopolitics. The prospect of a unipolar system in which one state dominates the politico-economic landscape is therefore implausible, they maintain. It is far more likely that we will see great powers band together, building upon present international law and norms, to maintain economic order in what is now a decentred system (Buzan and Lawson 2014: 89).

Public consciousness about a new era might also be traced to the 2001 al-Qaeda terrorist attacks in the US. The ensuing invasion of Afghanistan by a US coalition to depose the militant Islamic group's

Taliban supporters has reprioritised threats for countless states. Initially under the banner of a Global War on Terrorism, an ongoing international campaign to ferret out and dismantle terrorist networks dominates many foreign policy agendas such as that regarding arms trade, military operations and other diplomatic efforts, as well as domestic issues such as anti-terrorism legislation. Subsequent interventions, linked or not to terrorist threats, an increase in public debate about avoiding or increasing international humanitarian operations and a heightened sense of vulnerability for populations even in non-combat zones present the international system as one of chaos. In remarking upon ongoing political unrest and lack of stability in such places as Syria, Israel and Gaza, Ukraine and Iraq, US President Barack Obama expressed this general perception of uncertainty:

> part of peoples' concern is just the sense that around the world the old order isn't holding and we're not quite yet to where we need to be in terms of a new order that's based on a different set of principles, that's based on a sense of common humanity, that's based on economies that work for all people. (Obama 2014)

The term 'new world order' has been bandied about by conspiracy theorists and commentators on the far ends of a conservative–liberal continuum to claim that there are designs among a powerful group of elites to control the world. However, the reference to a new order made by Obama and discussed in this chapter merely signals a transition from the post-Cold War period to one in which different challenges face the international system and its participants.

As noted previously, there is disagreement about the current structural nature of the modern system and where trends may develop, but it is fair to say that we are still in the midst of transition and there is considerable deliberation about how to harmonise relations within it. It is evident that in the first years of the post-Cold War world the international system was lacking in leadership, and so in that vacuum US dominance flourished. A number of researchers and political analysts staunchly argue that US hegemony would continue to remain unchallenged in the foreseeable future because of its economic and military staying power. Analysing US ability to command, or at the very least firmly steer the terms and conditions for global transactions in goods, services and finance even during periods of economic instability, applied economics scholar Gary Dymski finds that Wall Street, the dollar as a global reserve currency and a neoliberal era of open trade and deregulation of financial markets bolster its relative standing among other players such as Japan and the European Union. With muscle in both economic and military/political spheres, he says, the US remains hegemonic and 'unassailable' (2002: 253).

In contrast, there are just as many critics who note a decline in US soft power and an overall decline in US hegemony. The view of this author is that the period which concerns us now, the global era, is still a time in which interests and relative influence are evolving, but uncommon transnational challenges will preclude effective control by a single entity. Global politics have become far more decentralised. This reconfiguration can be defined as non-polar, maintains Richard Haass (2008). There remain a handful of major state powers, some of which may coalesce as regional partners, but the system cannot be considered multipolar either. It is populated by numerous influential IGOs and NGOs, and the interactions between the variety of state and non-state actors is complex and fluid. Thus globalisation and resulting cross-border capabilities is a major basis for attrition of the nation-state and loss of its 'gatekeeper rights', Haass adds, and suggests that a 'concerted nonpolitarity' among key governments and other actors is needed to avert new threats.

Transitions in structural and direct violence

It is evident that the international system was destabilised during this early phase of the global era in which there was not yet effective coordination of preferences and control of competing ideologies, institutions and processes. Such an environment serves to heighten risk and uncertainty for governments tackling both internal and external threats. Furthermore, the humanitarian consequences of those threats and responses remain paramount. The current UN Secretary-General, in an op-ed article following failure to obtain a treaty regulating the conventional arms trade, argues that military responses are not adequate to confront contemporary security concerns. The most critical threats to the global community are not diffused by defending borders but by focusing on human welfare dilemmas that he said arise from 'demographic trends, chronic poverty, economic inequality, environmental degradation, pandemic diseases, organised crime, repressive governance and other developments no state can control alone' (Ban Ki-moon 2012).

Although there is general consensus that governments have certain obligations to their citizens and to the wider community, adjustment in the 'architecture of global governance' is an ongoing mission (CFR 2008). International law, norms and practice are responding, some would say, far more slowly than expectations. Nevertheless, state self-interest is seen to be coupled with fostering human security. Over the past few decades, an evolving concept of human security takes a relatively generous turn to include subsistence needs and protections of human rights and dignity. Extensive literature, for instance, reflects upon the reduction of poverty as an essential component of national security in the contemporary era (Thomas 2001; Weber 2004; Chong 2006; Saith 2006; Cox 2009). With economic development and citizen welfare inextricably linked to political stability, we can see that violence against individuals and groups perpetuate threats to national and global order. In several contexts, the international community expands upon conventional notions of violence as intentional harm by use or threat of force to also include use of power in commission of harm. This is a significant development in accepting violence as a product of unequal power relations. The definition is further expanded in regards to the nature of intended harm(s) beyond physical and psychological injury and includes deprivation of liberty in public and/or private life (WHO n.d.; GA 1993).

Following trends in violence also begins with definitions and typologies, and here we have much scholarship. For instance, Johan Galtung, one of the earliest founders of peace and conflict studies as a discipline, observes that different social environments harbor various forms and degrees of institutionalised structural violence such as ethnocentrism, racism, socio-economic discrimination and nationalism. He distinguishes between physical and psychological violence, and between negative and positive approaches to responding to that violence (Galtung 1969). He adds that we should expect an increase in attention to or even commission of personal violence at home or in the community after political conflicts cease because structural sources of violence are not effectively addressed in the short term. One response to this predicament, Galtung suggests, is to consider vertical and decentralised partnerships in which participation and co-decision by all parties is expanded (1969: 186). We can envision this as a promising approach in some preventative or post-conflict situations at the state or global level, and will return to its potential later in the chapter.

Direct violence also receives considerable attention from researchers and policy makers, and from the public it receives perhaps even more attention than structural violence. After all, media headlines focus on a wide berth of current incidents and impacts of international and non-international armed conflicts. Depending on the indicators and databases used, not to mention the political agenda to be served, accounts may reveal somewhat dissimilar statistics. But overall, tracking contemporary global trends of direct violence offers both hope and pessimism. A top-ranked British think tank chronicles progressively declining numbers of all armed conflicts during the contemporary period, but at the same time reports a rise in levels of brutality and numbers of fatalities connected to those conflicts. For example, there were sixty-three international and non-international conflicts with 56,000 total fatalities in 2008, and forty-two ongoing conflicts in 2014 accompanied with 180,000 fatalities (IISS 2015).

Monitoring the intensity of those incidences goes beyond counting combat-related fatalities and injuries, of course. Far greater numbers of civilians are affected in a myriad of ways. According to the World Bank, more than 1.5 billion people, approximately one fifth of the world's population, live in countries affected by violent conflict. Further, roughly 40 per cent of post-conflict countries lapse back into conflict within ten years (World Bank 2011). A panorama of security concerns is also summarised in a recent annual report to the UN General Assembly. Atrocity crimes are on the increase and more frequently targeting civilians, sexual violence as a method of warfare persists and there are continuing flows of illicit arms. Finally, the largest recorded number of displaced persons as a result of armed conflict since the Second World War reached 60 million by the end of 2014 (Ban Ki-moon 2015).

A spotlight on the specific causes of these distressing human welfare conditions illustrate political and academic efforts to understand the phenomenon. Naturally there are as many thoughtful proposals about antecedents and triggers of violence as there are dissections of its nature. There is general agreement, though, that violence in the twenty-first century noticeably deviates from patterns of conflict preceding it. One senior fellow at the Brookings Institution first cautions that the worst of armed conflicts must be evaluated in their specific context. His perspective of trends, however, suggests four primary determinants of conflict in the global era. They include Islamic extremism among certain groups, resource competition between states, long-held animosities and efforts to control nuclear development (O'Hanlon 2014). We see other trends in key activities. In regards to the nature of intrastate violence, for instance, there appears to be a greater appreciation for the complex interplay between criminalisation of the state, transnational organised crime and regional/global terrorist networks. As noted earlier, we witness repeated cycles of violence. These 'new wars', characterised by Mary Kaldor (2015), are amalgamations of illegitimate and organised violence for political and/or private purposes and include civil or interstate armed conflicts, crime and violations of human rights. Contrasting the nature of organised violence in the global era with those in the last two centuries, she argues that they operate by a fundamentally different logic. At the risk of oversimplifying and purloining her judgement about basic differences between the old and the new, the following snippets point to widely shared neoteric assessments: old wars were contests of wills in which both sides wanted to win. These wars had beginnings and ends and were fought for territory or ideals. Tactics included battles in the countryside with forces pitted against one another.

Conversely, parties fighting in the new wars are more interested in the condition of war than in winning or losing. That is, territory is extended politically rather than merely by gaining territory; one of the main aims is displacement of unwanted peoples, and historical and cultural buildings. New wars are fought by a mix of state and non-state actors involving global networks of regular forces, militias, mercenaries and warlords. Fighting is in the name of ethnic or religious identity with a sense of entitlement to state access; in fact, war becomes a way of constructing identity or labels. New wars usually start with an authoritarian government which initiates neoliberal economic policies leading to drops in the economy and high unemployment. Financing of armed conflict thus comes from extortion, ransoms, smuggling drugs, antiquities and human beings. In this way, illicit activities become a self-perpetuating system in which weapons are needed to make money and money is needed to buy equipment. New wars are difficult to end, and like a social condition, they spread (Kaldor 2015). These observations present a contemporary landscape of violence in an especially alarming and overwhelming light.

Chaos at all levels has morphed. If we return to theoretical explanations for change at the international level, we might argue that stability and predictability are at risk because of increased numbers and differences in issues and interests among a multitude of state, non-state, and sub-state actors populating an increasingly interdependent system. As discussed earlier, for example, we have seen how conventional national security issues may be impacted by the weight given now to human security issues. Or, we might argue that a decline in US dominance and subsequent change in its relative standing with other major powers, along with exogenous changes such as universal capitalism – and new threats that such changes may pose – has replaced the previous post-Cold era with a rudderless structure. 'The takeaway is that when you have global instability of this kind, it's usually a signal that the existing order is beginning to break down. The things that kept hostilities in check for a long time, those rules, those stabilizing powers, aren't really there anymore. Things are changing', notes an official from the American Foreign Policy Council (Berman 2014). In sum, it indeed appears that the sources of threats will define the new era, and of course fashion responses to them.

Transitions in intervention and engagement

Decisions about those responses reflect current challenges to long-held state-centric perspectives. A Westphalian legacy, and wide adoption of R2P principles, placed national and international security – and human security – in the hands of states. However, recent transitions in the source and nature of armed violence reveal limitations and problems in guaranteeing protections under this arrangement. One difficulty faces weak states particularly. In fragile environments, even in the event a government is not corrupt and partner to illicit activities, upholding rules of law in the face of developmental challenges and organised domestic or transnational violence is virtually impossible. It is too easy for resourceful and malevolent non-state actors to embed themselves into the very fabric of society. In short, new threats can be stronger than the state itself. A second problem with state-centric approaches to security threats is that governments still tend to concentrate on the political and/or economic well-being of the state itself. Even threats to human welfare often provoke reaction only when there is an opportunity to pursue geopolitical goals or when there appears immediate harm to the state. For instance, governments often treat flows of political refugees in or out of their states as issues of population control. State-centric approaches may thus come at the expense of the well-being of individuals.

First we take a brief look at the logic of state-centred responses to the 'new wars', and then turn attention to alternative concepts of intervention and engagement. Nearly any primer on intervention in the context of international relations begins by tendering a typography; the objectives of the intervenor(s); the legal and moral frameworks within which it may be exercised; assessments of successful and less-than-successful missions; and because there is little agreement on any of these matters in light of contemporary events and evolving norms, concludes with calls for revisiting justifications, applications and implications. We summarise some of those aspects here, accepting a simple legal definition of foreign intervention as interference by one or more states in the affairs of another. It may take the form of coercive or non-coercive activities. The former includes absence of consent to use armed forces to trespass territorial jurisdiction in order to affect another government's structures, policies and actions, such as through violence or occupation. Non-aggressive intervention includes sanctions on the economy of a foreign country such as embargos and boycotts, and use of organised public protests or information warfare such as propaganda or computer hacking. Objectives for foreign intervention are varied, but can include national or international security, or ideological expansion. The focus of this chapter is on interventions purportedly conducted for humanitarian purposes, not as a result of natural disasters but for illegal organised violence. Trends now show that civil conflicts dominate the landscape of post-Cold War hostilities and the costs of those conflicts are overwhelmingly borne by non-combatants. Where does protection of basic needs and human rights come from if home states are unwilling or unable to act?

The human rights era of the 1990s is said to have given concurrent impetus to an era of humanitarian intervention. After all, a resolution adopted by the UN General Assembly in 1991 simply noted that state consent 'should' be given in advance of external responses to humanitarian crises, and so left room to argue the legitimacy of intervention when consent was not given (Arnison 1993). Further, with international attention paid to rampant abuse of human security in weak or failing states, the UN Charter was increasingly questioned about its ability to grant permission for states to undertake foreign intervention. Listing a string of current events around the globe characterised by bloodshed and human rights abuses, Secretary-General Annan argued that members needed to provide 'more than just words of sympathy' to suffering peoples. He defended the Charter as a living document and still applicable in spirit for meeting challenges to common interests. 'Nothing in the Charter precludes recognition that there are rights beyond borders', he said, and with that, he identified lessons for intervention in the future: broadly defining the nature of intervention to take into account unique situations, and yet applying that definition fairly and consistently; to understand that forceful intervention is a result of a failure for prevention; to define national interests more broadly; and to accept that actions for peace should continue after the conclusion of military missions (Annan 1999).

The post-Cold War era of rethinking interventions generated a number of new approaches and names for maintaining peace and security, including peacekeeping, strategic peace-making and peace enforcement (Pugh 2009). Security studies scholar Andrew Cottey (2008) examines changes from one generation of humanitarian interventions to the next. He notes that in the 1990s interventions began while armed conflict was in progress, without consent, used military force nearly exclusively and was generally carried out by Western powers. New trends are seen in the global era. Cottey observes that troops are deployed either during ongoing violence or post-conflict, with partial or no consent, use a combination of coercive and non-coercive measures, and unless Western interveners are motivated by strategic interests, most troops come from developing countries. Another shift we might argue finds that the number of unilateral interventions which augment UN-authorised missions and uneven rates of success and failure to address all human rights disasters, have fueled skepticism and more caution in interventionist foreign policies in the global era.

Critics complain more and more that ulterior motives of Western powers drive humanitarian interventions, particularly those of the US. Well-known pacifist theologian Stanley Hauerwas says '[i]f I were a person who was non-American, I would think humanitarian intervention is just another name for United States imperialism' (2013). They raise concerns that national self-interest is served by adopting R2P rhetoric to justify both intervention and non-intervention, thus political hegemony and neocolonial implications arguably steer foreign policy decisions. In addition, now that states are not facing the same geopolitical threats posed in a bipolar system, governments are reduced to other measures to justify increases in military spending (Falk 2006). Motives are not always easily spotted. It is especially curious as to why major powers undertake ventures far from home when it appears there is no threat to national interest. 'Why do powerful countries behave in a way that leads to entrapment in prolonged, expensive, and self-defeating conflicts?' asks Jeffrey Taliaferro (2004).

Political realism does not seem to support those decisions to engage unless we consider that senior leaders are driven to accept costly failed operations in order to avoid (perceived) losses in power and prestige. This 'balance-of-risk' theory proposed by Taliaferro can be useful in thinking about why intervention sometimes is not undertaken; states do not see benefits outweighing the costs to them. Another view is that states may claim ambiguity as to whether the criteria of R2P are met or not. Thresholds have been articulated as 'large scale loss life, actual or apprehended, with genocidal intent or not, which is the product either of deliberate state action, or state neglect or inability to act, or a failed state situation' and 'large scale ethnic-cleansing, actual or apprehended, whether carried out by killing, forced expulsion, acts of terror or rape' (ICISS 2001: 32). Regardless of motive, there is concern that interventions under the banner of R2P have not improved humanitarian crises in appreciable ways. Establishing order and justice is a long-term project that requires more than superficial attention (Parekh 1997; Hehir 2012).

Arguments that there is too much, or too little, foreign intervention today provide sharp debate. Points of contention revolve around questions of legitimacy, morality and feasibility. Some proponents see a dramatic increase in military engagement since the end of the Cold War and express unease only that there appear more frequent interventions in intractable conflicts (Hauss 2003). The US is looked to as providing leadership but the conviction is that efforts should be multilateral. Because states in trouble are those with limited military capabilities to curtail domestic violence, the UN and Western states particularly should participate more. Others agree that humanitarian grounds prompted more intervention in the early post-Cold War years and point to Operation Desert Storm as a step into a new era. A UN Secretary-General's special advisor on the R2P argues that now, however, '[f]ar from witnessing rampant interventionism, the period since (has been) marked more by non-intervention' (Welsh 2011: 1194). The issue is not only tied to questions of legitimacy and the need for new rules, one scholar adds, but also marshalling political will to act timely. The result is there are far too many cases of 'inhumanitarian non-intervention', says Chesterman (2012: 148).

For now, the War on Terror and questions raised about legitimacy of those related missions will dampen prospects to address true humanitarian crises. One might straddle both sides of the argument, as was proposed earlier, that state interests are tied to human welfare more than ever in the global era. Rights and duties may not be mutually exclusive. Rory Stewart and political economist Gerald Knaus are optimistic. 'We both believe that it is possible to walk the tight-rope between the horrors of over-intervention and non-intervention; that there is still a possibility of avoiding the horrors not only of Iraq but also Rwanda; and that there is a good way of approaching inter-vention that can be good for us and good for the country concerned' (Stewart and Knaus 2012: xvi). Prospects for order and justice, some would argue, may be enhanced by thinking beyond state and inter-national organisational frameworks such as the United Nations. We do not revisit here Hedley Bull's views of an international society as more than a system of states, and its role in bringing order to an 'anarchical society'. Still, we cannot resist pointing out his arguments in support of state sovereignty and principles of non-intervention. Sovereignty should not be seen as an obstruction to achieving world justice, however. If on occasion the two values needed to be priori-tised, rights of the individual should prevail over those of the state. To ensure minimum standards of human welfare and protections of human rights, a consensus of international society would allow for humanitarian intervention, he said (Bull [1977] 1995; 1984). This perspective leads us to look at alternatives in global governance.

Frameworks for future intervention

REGIONAL GOVERNANCE

Most observers are in agreement that humanitarian interventions should be in conformance with international laws and norms advanced by the United Nations, and be multilateral. Some, though, have suggested that leadership might fall on the shoulders of one or a few major actors due to their capabilities. But as noted above, critics contend that missions sanctioned by the UN Security Council or operationalised by the US and its allies maintain imperialistic under-tones. There remains ambiguity in which agents are best situated to undertake responsibility for preventing or alleviating human suffer-ing within the borders of state, particularly if that government has withheld or is unable to provide consent. Which body(ies) or state(s) respond to violations of human rights matters. Legitimacy of the intervention rests on numerous factors such as motives, resources, political will, internal and external support and ability to coordinate and strategise activities before, during and after conflict commences.

UN Secretary-General Ban Ki-moon reports a new age in interven-tion in which there is a multiplicity of diverse actors, especially those focusing on preventative measures, that are increasingly integrated into networks at all levels. For example, in some contexts organised regional state bodies already assume central roles, especially in peace negotiations and capacity-building. The future of UN peace operations, he says, rests on plans to strengthen global–regional partnerships, and in his view those cooperative arrangements are promising. He offers a litany of joint projects including the UNOWA and UNOCA collaboration with ECOWAS, ECCAS, the Gulf of Guinea Commission and the Group of Seven Plus Friends to address threats of piracy and armed robbery in the Gulf of Guinea; the UN Counter-Terrorism Centre working with the African Union in counterterrorism strategies; and the UNOWA and UNOCA partnership with ECOWAS, ECCAS and the Lake Chad Basin Commission to study insurgencies in the region. The UN has moved to institutionalise those partnerships by establishing liaison offices and regularly convening with regional organisational leaders during retreats. The activities and nature of the partnerships necessarily vary by need to respect differences among regions, he explained (Ban Ki-moon 2015). Although his report does not state so, it is understood – political unity and the support of regional governments is especially critical when there is no consent by the affected state for intervention and when financing and other resources are already strained and expected to increase further.

There is a somewhat different perspective on regionalism which challenges notions that global governance, constructed by Ban Ki-moon as partnerships between international and regional state actors, is a trend in the modern era. There are different theories and visions of this 'new regionalism', but we find that contrasts with the previous world order to be a helpful introduction. Hettne (2003) provides a number of fundamental distinctions. He explains that new regionalism is a spontaneous process of coordination among regional actors, which may be governments and/or non-state bodies, rather than being created from above. It operates within a multipolar system instead of a bipolar or hegemonic system, and is relatively open and integrated with the world economy instead of protectionist and inward-looking. Further, new regionalism entails shared objectives on many issues among the group instead of being fragmented into organisations that focus on security or the economy, for example; and that this multidimensional and comprehensive approach is carried over into international relations.

New regionalism goes beyond state-to-state relations and encompasses non-state actors at many levels in the system. Thus it is more than a geographical group of actors; it is a social system defined by unique actors, processes and issues that takes the shape of organised voluntary cooperation. Pooling sovereignty enables a region to tackle humanitarian crises in its neighbourhood as any collective security framework might do. Regional organisations might contribute something different to secure human rights and peace than other organisations, proposes Bruce Russett (1997). One thing they can do is to help shape community norms and require members to adhere to them. Those norms might be international in character but may also be specific to the region. In the event of outright violation of those norms, the regional body can employ mediation and other non-coercive methods, and can use coercive force that is consistent with international law to enforce compliance if necessary. An advantage that regional organisations may have over global institutions in this respect is that they are better positioned to 'generate the narratives of mutual identification across states and cultures' (Russett 1997: n.p.). In defence of regionalism, especially in regard to humanitarian intervention, some commentators find it a reasonable and more promising alternative to global responsibility. Reform of the UN Charter to include transfer of primary responsibility to regional organisations for authorizing military interventions would minimise the likelihood of non-intervention in the face of mass atrocities (Held and McNally 2014).

Nevertheless, political, economic and cultural diversity within a region may still be a challenge for coalescing around common goals. The European Union is often cited as a form of new regionalism that has had varying success in governing its neighbourhood. The prospect of a regional hegemon may also present dilemmas; in some cases, a greater burden may be borne by a bigger power and be welcomed. In others, a potentially unscrupulous, heavy-handed or imperialistic power may undermine a sense of community and shared governance. Despite the growing attention paid to this new framework as an alternative arrangement to international or state governance, it remains best to avoid generalising the promise or peril of regionalisation, and caution that choices about humanitarian intervention should be made on an ad hoc basis so as to reflect local circumstances and requirements. To glean what some of those special needs might be, we can look to the vantage point of civil society.

CIVIL SOCIETY

We are reminded, first, that there is no one definition of civil society and certainly no uniformity in civil society perspectives. The era of the 1990s was busy, bustling with discussions of state sovereignty and evolving human rights norms, and posing conundrums for intervention. During this decade, manifestations of civil society also gathered strength and assumed major roles in shaping the dynamics of human security discussions. The change was welcomed by policymakers who believed in pluralism and found hope in non-governmental contributions from this 'third' sector of democratic governance. Theoretically, individuals and NGOs had been thought to represent the private sphere and were considered separate from government and business, but this notion soon became antiquated. There is recognition now that funding and direction coming from those other agents can dissolve independence of thought and action.

A tightly integrated and competitive market economy, overlapping interests and objectives and ever-present reliance on public support and political will does not permit an ideal model of civil society. One of the realities is that corralling civil society by virtue of reciprocal linkages provides support to government and business actors for furthering certain ideologies (Mohan 2002). In some cases it is hard to separate interests. Civil society actors play different roles and at different times: they may complement or follow along with other civil society participants or with one or both of the other sectors, they may introduce new perspectives and strategies in collaborative arrangements, or they may directly challenge government or business policies and practices and attempt to reshape public attitudes.

In respect to humanitarian intervention, views of civil society may vary according to perceptions of the immediacy and extent of a crisis, trust that adequate political will and resources will be employed to correct the problem and belief that the intervention is justified (Falk 2006). A consensus by civil society participants might be reached if the UN Security Council were to endorse military intervention, but would likely be harder to come by without it. Falk provides an exception to the rule by recalling the 1999 NATO action in Kosovo to stop further violence and human rights violations. Despite lingering controversy about lack of UNSC authorisation, the mission was generally accepted by the public, in part because the gravity of humanitarian threat outweighed that consideration, but perhaps more importantly because there was significant UN follow-up during reconstruction.

On the other hand, most of civil society was not supportive of the Iraq War which was conducted purportedly for humanitarian reasons. Falk concludes that civil society is not resolved on the matter of humanitarian interventions without advance approval from the UN, and so takes its position(s) on a case-by-case basis. Although civil society actors generally have limited contributions directly in policymaking and implementation, he adds, their most significant work can be to reframe discussions about legal justifications for intervention. Keeping in mind the 'new wars', Kaldor argues that interventionist responses to conflict today still draw upon old war methods. A battle of wills in the past would be addressed by military intervention or talks of compromise between state parties, but that approach does not adequately deal with armed violence and continuation of human rights abuse today. Instead, the logic which mobilises rogue actors, for instance identity politics and a war economy, have to be confronted directly by a 'much more granular approach on the ground', she says, 'and it means supporting civil society groups on the ground from above' (2015).

Perspectives and actions taken by civil society also reflect the importance of regimes in fostering order and consensus. If we define regimes as social institutions that operate under a common framework of norms and regulatory principles, we clearly see that some civil society groups today operate across borders. They are interrelated with participants at the local, state and/or global levels and play a large role in the diffusion of – and subsequent cross-cultural negotiations of – norms over time (Zwingel 2012). Intervention by force for humanitarian cause rarely eradicates structural violence embedded in social structures. Civil society actors, however, through regimes built on consensus are in better positions to help transform cultures of violence before mass outbreaks of human rights violations and after external intervenors have left, all the while recognizing value in building partnerships with the affected groups. Ban Ki-moon expressed the needs of a sustainable future succinctly: 'it will need the engagement of all stakeholders – including the private sector and civil society, and especially the poor and marginalised (2013)'. Collective self-governance appears the way forward.

Conclusion

In view of an ongoing reconceptualisation of state autonomy, the emerging non-polar system and absence still of an international society, how might humanitarian interventions take shape in the global era? It depends in large part, of course, on transitions in violence. The pattern emerging is that armed conflict and its repercussions are not geographically bound. It may be foolhardy to assume there will remain zones of peace and zones of turmoil. The Arab Spring and Winter, for instance, illustrate the contagion effects of contemporary conflict. A wave of violent and non-violent protests quickly swept through the region following a revolutionary movement in Tunisia in 2010. While a rise in authoritarianism, ethnoreligious extremism and destabilisation continue to plague a number of countries, the nature and degree of intervention there has varied considerably.

For example, international consensus regarding the 2011 Libyan conflict was for military intervention and within a fairly short time its long-time leader was ousted by a foreign coalition. Renewed fighting soon broke out among rival domestic groups seeking control of the country, and at the time of writing the United Nations has facilitated several negotiation attempts to restore legitimate governance. On the other hand, continued violence in Syria has not yet garnered agreement for coordinated international or even regional military intervention; this, despite drastic destabilisation of the neighbourhood and the inordinate impact the civil war has had outside the region. Observers note that differing geopolitical situations of the two cases can help explain options that have or have not been taken to bring order to the failed states. But some also argue that greater public sensitivity to genocide in the global era, in large part enhanced by media coverage, calls for overriding traditional concepts of state sovereignty in light of R2P principles as much in Syria as in Libya. After all, the ongoing Syrian conflict has produced one of the world's worst humanitarian crises with about a quarter of a million Syrians killed to date, 6.5 million displaced within their country and more than 3 million fleeing as refugees. To what effect attempts by the Arab League for political settlement is under watch. Some military assistance to the Syrian government has been given, most notably from joint operations by Russia, Iran and Iraq, but might be seen as a proxy war with the US. A US-led coalition currently provides limited military support to a politically moderate Syrian opposition group. Complexity of the case, including what appear to be questionable motivations and unequal commitments by external actors, defies efforts to bring order.

On the whole, we might conclude that the particularities of conflicts, along with an apparent diffusion of power and decline in Western dominance, should direct greater responsibilities to regional organisations and civil society for tending to human security issues. This would include taking preventative measures as well as emergency responses to human rights violations. Collective action still remains fraught with challenges, and in the case of intervention, motives and abuse of power by regional or multilateral actors are not immune to suspicion. While pluralist approaches to global governance appear on the horizon, there is considerable support for envisioning the United Nations as a mediator. The international institution nevertheless needs to remedy perceptions of inefficiencies, ineffectiveness and inequities in managing international humanitarian interventions, and making further reforms to better position itself in a new era. Currently, there is no coherent rationale or consistent guidance provided for appropriate responses (Arnison 1993: 205).

Consistency does not mean, however, a one-size-fits-all approach to interventions or peace-building is workable. Criticism continues to be levied on operations that transfer frameworks from one initiative to the next even in dissimilar political, economic and cultural environments. Local ownership remains fundamental to success. Scholar Séverine Autesserre (2014) speaks from experience, having worked for humanitarian agencies in numerous countries including Afghanistan, Democratic Republic of Congo and Kosovo. She finds that strained everyday relationships between interveners and the local people are typical, and improving those relationships matter as much as national and international level institutions and diplomacy. The International Committee of the Red Cross (ICRC) is also adamant about the importance of civil society. There is a fixed link between armed interventions and international humanitarian law (IHL) (Ryniker 2001). IHL asserts that a right exists for impartial humanitarian intervention, regardless of national sovereignty, when grave breaches of human rights occur. Freedom to act must thus be preserved for humanitarian organisations, maintains the ICRC.

A convergence of norms, growing interdependencies and overlapping responsibilities characterise the path of intervention in the future. It is increasingly difficult to ignore mass atrocities, yet debate remains lively on the *who*, *what*, *when* and *how* of responding to them. Political realities answer those questions, but we can be optimistic. The global era has not yet matured and so there is room for rethinking our frameworks for building order and justice.

References

Annan, K. (1999), 'Secretary-General Presents His Annual Report to General Assembly', *United Nations Meetings Coverage and Press Releases*, 20 September, available at: http://www.un.org/press/en/1999/19990920.sgsm7136.html, last accessed 26 December 2016.

Arnison, N. D. (1993), 'International Law and Non-Intervention: When Do Humanitarian Concerns Supersede Sovereignty?', *Fletcher Forum of World Affairs*, 17(2), pp. 199–211, available at: http://dl.tufts.edu/catalog/tufts:UP149.001.00034.00016, last accessed 26 December 2016.

Autesserre, S. (2014), *Peaceland: Conflict Resolution and the Everyday Politics of International Intervention*, Cambridge: Cambridge University Press.

Axelrod, R. and R. O. Keohane (1985), 'Achieving Cooperation under Anarchy: Strategies and Institutions', *World Politics*, 48(1), pp. 226–54.

Ban Ki-moon (2012), 'The World is Over-Armed and Peace is Under-Funded', United Nations, 30 August, available at: https://www.un.org/disarmament/update/20120830/, last accessed 26 December 2016.

Ban Ki-moon (2013), 'Remarks at "Sustainable Cities Days"', United Nations News Centre, 12 December, available at: http://www.un.org/apps/news/infocus/sgspeeches/statments_full.asp?statID=2088#.VjAE8CvigZM, last accessed 26 December 2016.

Ban Ki-moon (2015), 'Report of the Secretary-General on the United Nations and Conflict Prevention: A Collective Recommitment', United Nations, 25 September, available at: http://www.un.org/en/ga/search/view_doc.asp?symbol=S/2015/730, last accessed 26 December 2016.

Berman, I. (2014), 'Why Is There So Much Turmoil Right Now? Understanding the Outbreak of Conflicts', interview by Colleen Curry, ABC News, 18 July, available at: http://abcnews.go.com/International/turmoil-now-understanding-outbreak-conflicts/story?id=24617406, last accessed 26 December 2016.

Bull, H. ([1977] 1995), *The Anarchical Society: A Study of Order in World Politics*, 2nd edn, London: Macmillan.

Bull, H. (1984), *Justice in International Relations*, Hagey Lectures, 1983–4, Waterloo, Ontario: University of Waterloo.

Buzan, B. and G. Lawson (2014), 'Capitalism and the Emergent World Order', *International Affairs*, 90(1), pp. 71–91.

Chesterman, S. (2012), 'Violence in the Name of Human Rights', in C. Gearty and C. Douzinas (eds), *The Cambridge Companion to Human Rights Law*, Cambridge: Cambridge University Press, pp. 134–9.

Chong, D. P. L. (2006), 'The Right to Subsistence: Strategic Implications of the US Social Justice Movement's Adoption of Human Rights', The Annual Conference of the American Political Science Association, Philadelphia, PA, 31 August–3 September.

Cottey, A. (2008), 'Beyond Humanitarian Intervention: The New Politics of Peacekeeping and Intervention', *Contemporary Politics*, 14(4), pp. 429–46.

Council on Foreign Relations (CFR) (2008), 'Program on International Institutions and Global Governance. World Order in the 21st Century: A New Initiative, 2008', available at: http://www.cfr.org/content/think-tank/CFR_Global%20_Governance_%20Program.pdf, last accessed 26 December 2016.

Cox, M. (2009), 'Viewing the Millennium Development Goals through Prisms of IR Theory', in N. Shawki and M. Cox (eds), *Negotiating Sovereignty and Human Rights: Actors and Issues in Contemporary Human Rights Politics*, London: Ashgate, pp. 159–79.

Cox, R. W. (1981), 'Social Forces, States and World Orders: Beyond International Relations Theory', *Millennium: Journal of International Studies*, 10(2), pp. 126–55.

Dymski, G. A. (2002), 'Post-Hegemonic US Economic Hegemony: Minskian and Kaleckian Dynamics in the Neoliberal Era', *Journal of the Japanese Society for Political Economy*, 39, pp. 247–64.

Falk, R. (2006), 'Civil Society Perspectives on Humanitarian Intervention: Governance and Accountability in International NGOs', Orfalea Center for International and Global Studies, University of California Santa Barbara, 10–11 November, available at: http://www.orfaleacenter.ucsb.edu/sites/secure.lsit.ucsb.edu.gisp.d7_orfalea-2/files/sitefiles/publications/Falk_OBii.pdf, last accessed 26 December 2016.

Galtung, J. (1969), 'Violence, Peace, and Peace Research', *Journal of Peace Research*, 6(3), pp. 167–91.

Haass, R. N. (2008), 'The Age of Nonpolarity: What Will Follow US Dominance', *Foreign Affairs*, May/June, available at: https://www.foreignaffairs.com/articles/united-states/2008-05-03/age-nonpolarity, last accessed 26 December 2016.

Hauerwas, S. (2013), 'What Makes America So Prone to Intervention?', interview by Noah Berlatsky, *The Atlantic*, 5 September, available at: http://www.theatlantic.com/national/archive/2013/09/what-makes-america-so-prone-to-intervention/279393, last accessed 26 December 2016.

Hauss, C. (2003), 'Military Intervention', in G. Burgess and H. Burgess (eds), *Beyond Intractability*, Conflict Information Consortium, University of Colorado, Boulder, August, available at: http://www.beyondintractability.org/essay/military-intervention, last accessed 26 December 2016.

Hehir, A. (2012), *The Responsibility to Protect: Rhetoric, Reality and the Future of Humanitarian Intervention*. London: Palgrave Macmillan.

Held, D. and K. McNally (eds) (2014), *Intervention in the 21st Century: Legality, Legitimacy, and Feasibility – A Global Policy E-Book*, available at: http://www.globalpolicyjournal.com/blog/author/lessons-from-intervention-in-the-21st-century, last accessed 26 December 2016.

Hettne, B. (2003), 'The New Regionalism Revisited', in F. Soderbaum and T. M. Shaw (eds), *Theories of New Regionalism: A Palgrave Reader*, London: Palgrave Macmillan, pp. 22–42.

International Commission on Intervention and State Sovereignty (ICISS) (2001), 'The Responsibility to Protect', Ottawa: International Development Research Centre, available at: http://responsibilitytopro tect.org/ICISS%20Report.pdf, last accessed 26 December 2016.

International Institute for Strategic Studies (IISS) (2015), 'Armed Conflict Survey', Press Statement, 19 May, available at: https://www.iiss.org/en/abo ut%20us/press%20room/press%20releases/press%20releases/archive/ 2015-4fe9/may-6219/armed-conflict-survey-2015-press-statement-a0be, last accessed 6 January 2017.

International Monetary Fund (IMF) (2000), 'Globalization: Threat or Opportunity?', available at: http://www.imf.org/external/np/exr/ ib/2000/041200to.htm, last accessed 26 December 2016.

Kaldor, M. (2015), 'New Wars and Old', interview by Metta Spencer, *Peace Magazine*, 31(4), available at: http://peacemagazine.org/archive/ v31n4p08.htm, last accessed 26 December 2016.

O'Hanlon, M. (2014), 'Why Is There So Much Turmoil Right Now? Understanding the Outbreak of Conflicts', interview by Colleen Curry, ABC News, 18 July, available at: http://abcnews.go.com/International/ turmoil-now-understanding-outbreak-conflicts/story?id=24617406, last accessed 26 December 2016.

Obama, B. (2014), 'Remarks by the President at a DNC Event – Seattle, WA.', Office of the Press Secretary, The White House, 22 July, available at: https://www.whitehouse.gov/the-press-office/2014/07/22/remarks-pre sident-dnc-event-seattle-wa, last accessed 26 December 2016.

Mohan, G. (2002), 'The Disappointments of Civil Society: The Politics of NGO Intervention in Northern Ghana', *Political Geography*, 21(1), pp. 125–54.

Moravcsik, A. (1997), 'Taking Preferences Seriously: A Liberal Theory of International Politics', *International Organization*, 51(4), pp. 513–53.

Munro, Sir A. (1999), 'Humanitarianism and Conflict in a Post-Cold War World', *International Committee of the Red Cross*, 30 September, available at: https://www.icrc.org/eng/resources/documents/article/ other/57jq2s.htm, last accessed 26 December 2016.

Parekh, B. (1997), 'Rethinking Humanitarian Intervention', *International Political Science Review*, 18(1), pp. 49–69.

Pugh, M. C. (2009), 'International Intervention', in J. Wiener and R. A. Schrire (eds), *International Relations*, vol. 2, pp. 218–38, available at: http://www.eolss.net/sample-chapters/c14/e1-35-04-03.pdf, last accessed 26 December 2016.

Robinson, M. (2006), 'What Rights Can Add to Good Development Practice', in P. Alston and M. Robinson (eds), *Human Rights and Development:*

Towards Mutual Reinforcement, Oxford: Oxford University Press, pp. 25–41.

Russett, B. (1997), 'Global or Regional: What Can International Organizations Do?' in T. Tanaka and T. Inoguchi (eds), *Globalism and Regionalism*, Tokyo: United Nations University Press, available at: http://archive.unu.edu/unupress/globalism.html, last accessed 26 December 2016.

Ryniker, A. (2001), The ICRC's Position on 'Humanitarian Intervention', *International Review of the Red Cross* 83(842), pp. 527–32, available at: https://www.icrc.org/eng/assets/files/other/527-532_ryniker-ang.pdf , last accessed 26 December 2016.

Saith, A (2006), 'From Universal Values to Millennium Development Goals: Lost in Translation', *Development and Change*, 37(6), pp. 1167–99.

Stettinius, E. R., Jr. (1945), 'Report to the President on the Results of the San Francisco Conference', United States Department of State, Publication 2343, available at: http://babel.hathitrust.org/cgi/pt?id=uiug.30112046487697;view=1up;seq=4, last accessed 26 December 2016.

Stewart, R. and G. Knaus (2012), *Can Intervention Work?*, New York: Norton & Company.

Taliaferro, J. W. (2004), *Balancing Risks: Great Power Intervention in the Periphery*. Ithaca, NY: Cornell University Press, 2004.

Thomas, C. (2001), 'Global Governance, Development and Human Security: Exploring the Links', *Third World Quarterly*, 22(2), pp. 159–75.

United Nations Development Programme (UNDP) (1994), *Human Development Report 1994: New Dimensions of Human Security*, Oxford: Oxford University Press, available at: http://hdr.undp.org/sites/default/files/reports/255/hdr_1994_en_complete_nostats.pdf, last accessed 26 December 2016.

United Nations General Assembly (GA) (1993), 'Declaration on the Elimination of Violence Against Women', UN Document A/RES/48/104, 20 December, available at: http://www.un.org/documents/ga/res/48/a48r104.htm, last accessed 26 December 2016.

Weber, H. (2004), 'Reconstituting the "Third World"? Poverty Reduction and Territoriality in the Global Politics of Development', *Third World Quarterly*, 25(1), pp. 187–206.

Welsh, J. M. (2011), 'A Normative Case for Pluralism: Reassessing Vincent's Views on Humanitarian Intervention', *International Affairs*, 87(5), pp. 1193–204.

Wheatley, S. (1993), 'The Non-Intervention Doctrine and the Protection of the Basic Needs of the Human Person in Contemporary International Law', *Liverpool Law Review*, 15(2), pp. 189–99.

World Bank (2011), 'Conflict, Security, and Development Report 2011', available at https://openknowledge.worldbank.org/bitstream/handle/10986/4389/9780821384398_overview.pdf, last accessed 26 December 2016.

World Health Organization (WHO) (n.d.), 'Definition and Typology of Violence', Violence Prevention Alliance, available at: http://www.who.int/ violenceprevention/approach/definition/en/, last accessed 26 December 2016.

Zwingel, S (2012), 'How Do Norms Travel? Theorizing International Women's Rights in Transnational Perspective', *International Studies Quarterly*, 56, pp. 115–29.

6

Humanitarian Intervention?
Responding Ethically to Globalising Violence in
the Age of Mediated Violence

Paul James

Introduction

There are dozens and dozens of examples used in the literature to
develop lessons-learned surveys of the difficulties of external humanitarian interventions. Here the normal concept of 'interventions' means
external, state-based, usually military interventions into places and
events that entail activities generating violent consequences across
jurisdictional borders. These interventions usually occur without the
explicit agreement of the relevant territorial polity in question. There
is a canonical list of key examples upon which everybody draws. And
notwithstanding fierce debate about what 'success' actually means,
there is relative implicit agreement about the consequences of the
cases.

The 1992 United Nations intervention in Somalia worked initially,
but failed in the end because early successes were undermined by a
misconceived military campaign against local militia culminating in
the Black Hawk Down fiasco (Evans 2008). The 1994 responses to
the Rwandan crisis – withdrawal, delayed deployment or refusal to
intervene based on learning from Somalia – allowed a furious genocide to unfold, leading to approximately 800,000 deaths (Adelman
2003: 357–74). The 1995 military intervention in Bosnia came too
late, worked in the immediate sense of stopping the war, and left the
country tense, partitioned into ethnic enclaves, managed by an external power and unreconciled (Belloni 2007). The 1999 NATO intervention in Kosovo against the Federal Republic of Yugoslavia learned
the 'lessons' of Bosnia, won the war, but then struggled politically
and economically because it left behind a wasteland of corruption,
ethnic tension, poverty and collapsed infrastructure (Zolo 2002). The
2007 UN intervention into the Ituri region of the Congo succeeded in

producing a fragile peace, but also instituted a damaging politics of indirect rule characteristic of its colonial and post-colonial predecessors, including the use of arbitrary state violence (Veit 2010). The 2011 intervention in Libya won the military invasion but left behind an inoperable state and a reverberating backlash across the region, including Syria (Kuperman 2015: 66–77). The 2015 intervention in Syria learned the 'lessons' of effecting unplanned regime change in Libya, but despite supplying the Free Syrian Army and Syrian Kurdish forces with arms, using drones and conducting thousands of air strikes, the situation remains chaotic and dangerous – worse, if that is possible.

The overt lessons are clear. Intervention is complicated, mostly is prone to failures or setbacks, often gives rise to counterproductive and unintended consequences, does not lend itself to clear guidelines for good practice and (paradoxically) sometimes needs to happen. If recent history is indicative, learning the 'lessons' of the last intervention, at least in the narrow instrumental and strategy-to-strategy manner in which the outcomes of the last intervention tend to be understood, has dangerous rather than illuminating effects. The dominant and largely misguided popular media understanding is that well-directed technology kills baddies, saves our troops from the danger of putting their boots on the ground and is often successful so long as it is part of a sustained campaign. The problems arise in the aftermath of intervention, so it is said, because we do not follow up with sufficient consistency.

The Hollywood biopic *Charlie Wilson's War* is an exemplar of this belief. Based on the 'true story' of a minor US congressman from Texas, it narrates the backstory to the US covert intervention in Afghanistan during the Reagan period. Charlie Wilson, played by incongruous American everyman Tom Hanks, is an affable, sexist, hard-drinking politician who sits on the House Appropriations Committee. According to the film, through stealth, luck and unlikely negotiation, Congressman Wilson manages to increase the military aid to the Mujahedeen from US$20 million per year in 1980 to over half a billion dollars in 1989. This was the year that the last Soviets left Afghanistan. Through Charlie Wilson's vision, an otherwise unlikely set of partnerships with Israel and Pakistan, and a lot of ground-to-air Stinger missiles (as well as many other anti-Soviet Reagan initiatives that don't appear in the film, including the NSDD-166 directive in 1985), the tribal Mujahedeen managed to defeat Soviet imperialism in Afghanistan. Just as the British Empire had faltered in the Third Anglo-Afghan War, the Soviet Empire is said to have been brought down by local resistance aided by good intervention and technological modernism.

For Hollywood, this is a good-news story of positive sustained intervention. It delivers victory while minimising risk to our troops. The popular story parallels the dominant Kosovo story: we stopped the evil Milosevic from ethnic cleansing by targeted bombing. We forget that the Kosovo intervention took the form of 38,000 bombing sorties, including the first non-stop missions by Stealth Bombers from Whiteman Air Force Base on the other side of the world. Liberal commentators as well informed as Gareth Evans gloss over the fact that NATO's three-month-long bombing of the former Yugoslavia killed between 500 and 1,800 civilians, and inflicted an estimated US$4 billion damage on public infrastructure such as bridges, factories and electrical plants, not only exacerbating the ethnic cleansing for the period of the bombing, but destroying much of the life-world of the country (Cohn 2003). The liberal commentators (and it almost goes without saying, the right-wing advocates of intervention) gloss over the consequentialist question that military intervention may have made things worse in the short, intermediate and long term. Should NATO have intervened? Yes. Was a military response called for? Possibly. Was this an ethical or productive way of intervening? No.

The screenplay of *Charlie Wilson's War* is by Aaron Sorkin, creator of *The West Wing*, and his liberal politics are exemplars of the mainstream left (and largely of the right) in the United States. As the film concludes: '[t]hese things happened. They were glorious and they changed the world, and then we fouled up the end game'. These words, 'we fouled up the end game', scroll across the credits confirming mainstream understandings, as if international relations was a football game where we make a few simple coaching mistakes at the end. Cinema audiences never meet the Mujahedeen in the film – they are shown second-person-shooter images filmed from an abstract and safe distance. Missiles are fired, a helicopter is shot down, and the Mujahedeen cheer. And as an audience we also rejoice that Russian imperialism has taken another blow at the hands of locals. These local jihadists were romanticised in Doris Lessing's book *The Wind Blows Away Their Words*:

> In the face of sophisticated weapons of destruction and more than 100,000 Russian troops, the warriors of the Afghan Resistance – the Muhjahadin – continue their fight for freedom, although there are Western journalists who seem anxious to claim that the war is over. Some of the most

extraordinary battles of our time have been fought between armies of
tanks and gunships, and ragged men, women and children armed with
home-made grenades, catapults and ancient rifles. (Lessing 1987: cover)

These cover words on the book leave out the detail that the US
war machine had provided sophisticated Stinger missiles. However,
apart from that, sentiments of Lessing's book fit into a messy dominant refrain: intervention should happen[1] (Müller and Wolff 2014:
280–90), but it should be either mediated by working with chosen
locals or mediated through technology. Then we should clean up the
mess properly, usually through a state-controlled aid and reconstruction programme where the intervener guides (dominates) the political
and economic reconstruction until *good* locals can again take over.

The problem with this mainstream argument, including the most
detailed and sophisticated renditions of humanitarian interventions
such as the Responsibility to Protect doctrine (R2P), is that the
compounding imperial restructurings, colonisations, resentments,
humanitarian interventions, uneven globalising pressures, withdraw-
als, guided reconstructions, reinterventions, neo-traditional back-
lashes and interventions-from-a-distance have produced a world of
such complexity that is now impossible to 'do the right thing'. There
are no innocent political factions to protect. There is no moment that
marks the winning of interventionary war. There is no adequate end-
plan other than withdrawal after having restored semi-chaos.

In order to begin the task of establishing an alternative framework for intervention – not necessarily to argue against or replace
the R2P doctrine, but to reframe it – this chapter will firstly set out
some definitional claims. It will begin with an argument for returning to encompassing definitions based on the idea of humanity as
historically constituted and made up of persons-in-relation. Second,
the chapter will argue that the nature of contemporary conditions
makes conventional interventions unviable. Intervention requires a
different grounding process. For example, part of the problem of
learning lessons is that each act of intervening is judged as a separate
act in a modernist timeline of separate events and separable spatial
zones. Third, the chapter will argue for a more synthetic ethics of
intervention, suggesting that the different forms of ethics need to be
brought into interrelation: a *code-based ethics*, including an ethics of
rights; a *consequentialist ethics* based on assessing outcomes, and a
virtue-based ethics based on arguing for a grounded sense of human
values about what is good.

My overall argument is that intervention is currently framed by increasingly material and ideational abstraction in such a way as to inevitably undermine humanitarian intervention efforts, however well intentioned (see Damian Grenfell's chapter in this volume). Materially, for example, we now live in the age of drones and guided missiles, commanded by communications technologies that abstract time and space, that disembody the war machine, and which blur the boundaries between combat and assassination (Dunn 2013). Ideationally, we now pick selectively through the enumerated sections of abstract codes of conduct (such as R2P) while emptying out virtue-based ethics through passionate speeches in parliament or congress about the need to act in the name of 'humanity'. This does not mean intervention should not occur, but it does suggest that the terms of intervention have to be fundamentally changed.

Redefining the meaning of humanitarian intervention

What is meant by humanitarian intervention? This apparently simple question is beset by discussions that now mostly use the concept either to defend or critically leave behind 'humanitarian intervention'. In both cases the focus is on those external military interventions that occurred in response to state-sponsored or state-sanctioned violence against civilian populations in the 1990s and 2000s. On the 'critically leave behind' side, one writer devotes a book to saying that the discourse of humanitarian intervention has been so subsumed by a self-serving ethics of rights that it now allows for the justification of anything, therefore humanitarian intervention by implication is bad (Chandler 2006). That discourse leaves at least this reader in despair. A second writer, ostensibly on the same side, spends a volume wanting 'to sideline the humanitarian intervention terminology' in favour of a different doctrine that for all intents and purposes is much the same as humanitarian intervention, except that it is based on R2P principles rather than the need to intervene (Evans 2008). That argument leaves this reader a little incredulous (Thakur and Weiss 2009).[2] It is unclear, given the complexity of the world, that a top-down codified set of suggestions for action will result in *Ending Mass Atrocity Crimes Once and For All* – the subtitle of the second book. Both of these authors use the term 'humanitarian intervention' as the concept that names a particular form of military intervention that they do not like or want to circumvent. Using the first author against the second, it is sadly the case that:

the bombing of Libya was the first success for military intervention *without responsibility*. The current bombing of Syria and Iraq should be seen as the culmination of a process through which the R2P doctrine fully achieved the goal of enabling military intervention to escape the legal and normative concerns of sovereignty and intervention. (Chandler 2015: 4, emphasis added)

However much I agree with those bleak conclusions, it is still a historically narrow critique that elaborates no way forward. We can, and should, also ask questions in the opposite direction. Is it necessarily the case that humanitarian intervention should essentially consist of military action by an external state or organisation that directly challenges the sovereignty of the state in which that action occurs (Weiss 2012)? If we stay inside the writing on international relations it seems to be so. Some definitions within the field of international relations are stunningly narrow in their historicising precision: '[h]umanitarian intervention is the use of military force by one or more states within the jurisdiction of another, without its permission, to protect innocent people from violence by the target state's government' (Pape 2012). This definition is so specific that it even turns on the meaning of 'innocent people' – that is, 'people who are themselves not engaged in unjust violence' (Pape 2012: 44). This definition of innocence is unsustainable, both philosophically and practically. How are we to judge innocence? Does localised *domestic* violence constitute 'unjust violence'? And so on. The broader definition is also problematic. It starts by assuming that the pointy end of humanitarian intervention resides in cutting through the dominance of the convention in international relations that states cannot legitimately interfere in matters across state borders except during times of emergency. Questions arise here too. For example, what about consensual intervention given by local people where 'the people' are defined as not the same as 'the state'?

What about arms embargos, economic sanctions, global media campaigns, military aid or cyber-attacks? Are they not also interventions, even though they do not fit the dominant definition? They do not necessarily cross state borders. They do not necessarily involve agents of an outside power actually entering the sovereign territory of another state, and yet they can clearly be directed as interventions. The proponents of such reductive definitions of intervention are still working with a methodologically statist framework that assumes that crossing a territorial boundary, and therefore infringing state sovereignty, entails physical embodied movement across a border. In a world of intensifying globalisation, and where the dominant forms of power are increasingly abstracted – that is, materially abstracted and conducted through material processes from a distance – intervention cannot no longer be so narrowly defined (Nairn and James 2005).

The narrowing of the meaning of both *humanitarian* and *intervention* is as reductive as saying that *class* should be defined as a group of students in a university who regularly attend a particular teaching event – namely, a *class* of students – because that is the dominant convention in the field of activity in which the writer happens to be framing the definition: in this case, education studies. In other words, the dominant definition of 'humanitarian' today succumbs to the problem of field-specific codification, based on international relations conventions, and methodological reductionism, based on a reductive *realpolitik* understanding of the contemporary nation-state.

If we go back to the basics the confusions can be cleared up in a couple of paragraphs. *Intervention* involves an act of interposition that enters into a situation with the intention of changing that situation in some way. Simple. Thereafter the complex adjectives and qualifiers in front of the concept of 'intervention' do the work. For example, an intervention can be a *cross-border* state intervention, a cross-border *civil* intervention or an *internal* state intervention conducted within a nation-state into a local situation, and so on. The classic example of an internal state intervention is the Northern Territory National Emergency Response (2007–11), a damaging intervention by the Australian military and medical officers into local Aboriginal communities to address child sexual abuse. As this example also suggests, the concept of 'intervention' often includes but extends beyond *military* intervention. Forms of intervention include state-building, peace-building and nation-building processes, sustainable development projects, civil aid projects, disaster-mitigation responses and so on.

When the adjective *humanitarian* goes in front of intervention it should mean one thing, albeit as an essentially contested concept: the intervention is done in the name of humanity. That is, the intervention is initiated, conducted and followed-up according to principles that derive from an ethical claim about the human condition. How then does this relate to the R2P doctrine? It simply means, all obfuscation aside, that R2P is a form of humanitarian intervention based a set of principles that go beyond the usual one-stage military intervention with a bit of reconstruction work in the aftermath. What does this mean for some of the interventions that called themselves 'humanitarian interventions'? It means that the extent to which they are humanitarian can be analytically taken apart and judged accordingly on a series of basic issues: intention, support, conduct and consequence. This would require spelling out, debating at a global and local level and constantly refining through ongoing debate, both in general and in relation to each specific instance.

This issue has all that same consequences as going back to basics when attempting to understand the meaning of *human security*. As I argued in another place, human security in its fullest sense, including relative security from extreme natural events, needs to be understood as a variable condition of *the human* or what the 1994 *Human Development Report* called the 'universalism of life claims' or 'human life for itself' (UNDP 1994). In other words, if these things called 'human security' or 'humanitarian intervention' have the concept of 'the human' embedded at the heart of them, then let us address the question of the human condition directly. Thus understood, human security would no longer be the vague amorphous add-on to harder-edged areas of security such as military security or state security. Neither would it be reduced to a few complementary factors such as food security, economic security and personal security, linked by the notion of 'freedom from want'. It would become the centre of all discussions of security. It would become the basis of thinking about all security – including military security and disaster management (James 2014). Similarly, humanitarian intervention would not be defined in terms of military intervention or state-defined territories, as if these are the only ways of defining the human condition today.

Understanding the spaces into which interventions sometimes need to occur

What then is the dominant nature of contemporary interventions, and what does this mean in relation to their failures and mixed successes? For all the talk of 'local mediation' in the case of military interventions, or 'community engagement' in the case of sustainable development interventions, interventions in the contemporary world tend to be made as decisions from on high and commanded from great distances away. Knowledge about local conditions is usually either limited or deeply qualified by *modernist* understandings and presumed definitions of what constitutes the good: progress, development, freedom and happiness. Tellingly, one of the few areas in which internal and self-critique goes on – with the interveners publicly addressing their own failures or counterproductive practices, as they should – is in the area of humanitarian aid intervention. Fiona Terry, Director of Research for *Médecins Sans Frontières*, has for example written a searching account of the global aid industry. The title of the book gives a sense of what she is saying: *Condemned to Repeat? The Paradox of Humanitarian Action* (Terry 2002). The problem here is that right-wing critiques of international aid have stepped into this space to suggest that humanitarian aid is always a failure and neoliberal market principles should rule.

Intervention is not inevitably bad. Nevertheless, we need to be clear about its limits and probable failures. Across the twentieth century and into the present we have seen a series of changes that make humanitarian intervention increasingly vexatious or at least increasingly complicated. This is a structural issue, not a given. It goes back to a proposition that underlies my core argument. Under conditions of the increasing abstraction of human relations, humanitarian intervention is bound to be deeply problematic – sometimes badly counterproductive and occasionally disastrous, even if *sometimes necessary*. Here the key phrase is 'increasing abstraction of human relations', where continuing embodied relations – sometimes of mutuality, other times of conflict (the level of antagonism is not the key issue here) – are overlaid by an intensifying and dominant level of mediated, extended relations characterised by processes of automation, codification, rationalisation and objectification.

In military terms, the other important phrase is what could be called the 'sometimes necessary proviso': the Rwandan Tutsi genocide or Jewish Holocaust principle. Moreover, in civil and disaster-relief terms, climate-change intensifications of weather events will sometimes necessitate short-term interventions. But overall the emphasis needs to move towards cooperative mutuality, not intervention. I will return to the question of principles for intervention in the last part of the chapter, but for the moment the argument requires a brief excursion into the changing nature of the local–global conditions that makes intervention so problematic.

The intensification of globalisation has been part of some extraordinary changes in social relations across the twentieth century into the present. Every part of the world is more present to every other part of the world, albeit mediated by abstracting structures of power and divided by cleavages of inequity. The lines of exploitation, dependency and post-dependency are deeply entangled. Within this

simultaneous process of interconnection and mediation, one significant empirical change is that war is no longer primarily an *interstate*
phenomenon. While there are standoffs and confrontations, such as
between India and Pakistan, or as mediated by a globalising nuclear
machine, *direct* inter-state military conflict has declined in recent
decades. This apparently direct point is however not so simple.

First, while many commentators have come to this factually accurate point, it is usually part of an unsustainable argument linked to
the decline of the nation-state argument. Changes are actually occurring at all levels, stretching from the global to the local and back
again. Globalised interconnection – ranging from globalising media
reporting to the massive global movement of small arms – means that
once-local conflicts bear back upon state legitimacy and spill over
borders with transnational (if not global) consequences. This means
that while it seems obvious that the phenomenon of major armed
conflict is increasingly characterised by intrastate violence, even the
meaning of *intrastate* no longer works. That kind of violence is better
called 'localised transnational violence'. Internally directed responses
to such violence by local states seeking to maintain their own limited
legitimacy and fragile sovereignty act to intensify the consequence of
this violence, just as it sets up the conditions for other states to consider humanitarian intervention. And the violence spirals.

Second, it is also relatively well known that these localised transnational conflicts are in a statistical sense lasting longer than previous
wars and usually have no clear winners. Charlie Wilson's war is still
ongoing a decade after the film, albeit in a different guise. However,
there is no developed and generalising literature that explores the
meaning of this change and its consequences for intervention. What
such an exploration would need to do is analyse the intersecting
forms of political authority and the contradictions between them.
Over large regions of the Global South, with Iraq-Syria being the
latest focus of the world's attention, there is a fracturing (though not
necessarily a decline) of modern state authority, together with an
undermining of localised customary authority and a reconstitution
of traditional authority by neo-traditional (modern-skewed) funda-
mentalists. These three ontological forms of authority – modern,
traditional and customary – and their complex intersections need to
be brought to the fore in an analysis of violence and intervention.[3]
Processes of destructive contradiction between these forms underpin a refiguring of political competition at all levels: local, national,
regional and global.

Into the spaces opened by massive change step a variety of polities and authority figures described too easily in the literature and media as 'rogue states', 'failed states', 'death cults', 'warlords' and 'terrorists'. There is a lot of work to be done here to understand the nature of localised transnational complexities. These dramatically named entities exist in a local–global context of imperially ravaged and post-colonial zones, characterised by territories where ethnic, religious and/or class-divided entities project a strategy that emphasises the control of sources of wealth and power. They respond to a world of rapacious capitalism and militarism, itself in flux, in which states in both the Global North and South have become instruments of market enhancement and divided enrichment. These entities are a historical consequence of a worldwide process of colonisation/decolonialisation, restructured by capitalism and dominated by contradictory modern ontologies of meaning and practice, where internal and external lines of power have continued to exploit the political fragmentation of the regions that gave birth to them.

Rethinking the principles of intervention

Under such conditions, ethics needs to be less formulaic and instrumental. It needs to be more dialogical and reflexive, bringing together global protocols with local differences. Let us begin with one example of a seemingly plausible claim about the principles that should underpin military humanitarian intervention. Robert Pape argues for replacing the complex claims of the R2P with a pragmatic version that has three basic requirements:

1. an ongoing campaign of mass homicide sponsored by the local government in which thousands have died and thousands more are likely to die;
2. a viable plan for intervention with reasonable estimates of casualties not significantly higher than in peacetime operations and near zero for the intervening forces during the main phase of the operation; and
3. a workable strategy for creating lasting local security, so that saving lives in the short term does not lead to open-ended chaos in which many more are killed in the long term (Pape 2002).

How many thousands? We may well ask. And Robert Pape has a relatively precise answer:

A government can be assumed to have crossed the threshold for mass homicide when it has killed several thousand of its citizens (i.e., 2,000 to 5,000 unarmed protesters, bystanders, or those commonly called 'civilians') in a concentrated period of time (i.e., one to two months), and it is likely to kill many times that number (i.e., 20,000 to 50,000) in the near future, an often credible likelihood when hundreds of thousands or more are fleeing for their lives. (Pape 2002)

And here his attempt to bring simple sureties against the complexity of R2P principles becomes a *reductio ad absurdum* of the problem. Should we intervene if 5,000 people are killed (it is over the numbers threshold) but the murders occur slowly across the course of a year (it is under the temporality threshold)? Pape's false precision provides an illustration of exactly what we should not be advocating. For example, seeking to accommodate current sensibilities, he suggests a near-zero mortality rate for intervening forces. What this means in practice is a form of intervention that involves either dropping bombs from three kilometres in the sky or deploying drones in a way that renders spatial distance meaningless.

It is hard to think of a war machine that causes more unintended and long-term adverse consequences than the drone-and-guided-missile complex, defended as saving the lives of intervening combatants. When I said earlier that drones abstract time and space, blurring the boundaries between military intervention and assassination, I could have been much more concrete and damning. Imagine living under local circumstances where Predator MQ1 killing machines are guided to your place from a distant office in Langley, Virginia, arriving quietly, regularly and precisely to kill someone you know or destroy part of your neighbourhood. Abstracted, risk-calculated death by robotic stealth is still the death of a family member, a civilian neighbour or a militant sheltering in your community. Current calculations of civilian drone casualties vary from three civilians for every ten militants to fifty civilians to one militant (McDonnell 2012). However, the issue that unethical collateral murder occurs is not the point to which I am drawing attention, as important as it is. The central point is that drones set up a culture of abstracted judgement over life and death, they fracture communities and they reproduce the conditions for producing more terrorists. Moreover, even without any civilian casualties they, like nuclear weapons, undermine the meaning of *jus in bello*. In short, principles of *just action in war* are stretched to breaking point by abstracted killing, however well targeted.

The same critique could be brought to bear against to other attempts to answer ethical questions with reductive or problem-solving sets of principles. James Pattison, for example, devotes a volume to answering the question 'who should intervene?' (Pattison 2010) In the end his so-called 'moderate instrumentalist approach' works on surface issues of current international conventions while the world changes around us. The same could be also said in relation to Jean Pictet's Seven Fundamental Principles developed in the 1960s to guide the International Committee of the Red Cross in making their decisions about aid interventions: humanitarianism, impartiality, neutrality, independence, voluntary service, unity, and universality.[4] Principles are important. However, dominated by a culture of modernist accounting and without a broader framing ethics, they become black-letter propaganda points. In Pictet's list it is only the concept of 'humanitarianism' that continues to lend itself to being elaborated in terms of questions of positive relationality – perhaps also 'voluntary service' in the broadest sense of that concept – that is, the belief in being there as a service to others.[5] Single-level modernist principles such as impartiality or neutrality have in the age of the drone come to be part of the problem. This is linked to Alasdair MacIntyre's claim that ethics and social structure tend to be inextricably bound up with each other (MacIntyre 1985). What this means in the context of our increasingly abstracted dominant formations of practice – mediated, extended, codified, rationalised, commodified and objectified[6] – is that ethical moves which mirror this abstracting process, including proclamations of impartiality, neutrality and universality, become complicit in reproducing the world that produces the problems in the first place. To the contrary, in Fiona Terry's words:

> Humanitarian action is more than a technical exercise aimed at nourishing or healing a population defined as 'in need'; it is a moral endeavour based on solidarity with other members of humanity. If reduced to a technical act it can be employed in the service of any kind of abuse. Thus the consequences of humanitarian action must be given equal weight with the intention if an ethic of responsibility is be to more than an ethic of response. (Terry 2002: 244)

Developing humanitarian intervention as more than an 'ethic of response' requires, in other words, a grounding of *code-based ethics*, including an ethics of rights based on setting out rules or protocols for action, through a *consequentialist ethics* based on assessing outcomes, and based in a *virtue-based ethics*, arguing for a grounded sense of human values about what is good and virtuous (including an ethics of care). Instead of Jean Pictet's Seven Fundamental Principles we can in conclusion suggest seven alternative principles or virtues under the heading of *human relationality*. For relationality to be meaningful it requires that we have the capacity to establish *ongoing* regimes of mutual care, affinity, reciprocity and so on. At the same time it is important to recognise the complexities of social difference. Therefore, positive relationality also requires capacities for reconciliation and negotiation across the boundaries of that difference. Proceeding on this basis, the following seven sets of capacities are taken to be provisionally fundamental:

1. *Communication and dialogue* are basic to all questions of relationality. This includes the capacity on the one hand to share ideas with others in a way that is understandable and expressive, and, on the other hand, to listen, take in the ideas of others, and respond. While there are some writers who make communications *the* basis of social life (Luhmann 1995), here, while it is treated as basic, it is not a master category. Nevertheless, without dialogue about intervention with key constituents and stakeholders, including those most affected – people on the ground – an intervention is at best just a bundle of good intentions. This entails, as with all the other principles, already being on the ground in some fashion, working in partnership.

2. A second basic set of principles for relating is *affinity and reciprocity*. There is a vast literature on this area, with *affinity* naming the capacity to develop ongoing affiliations as families, friends, groups and communities. Practices of embodied reciprocity are associated with the dominant form of exchange in customary communities, but also in the more abstract form of generalised cooperation they are also necessary to well-functioning modern social systems.[7] As one important way of relating, *reciprocity* is a difficult concept. It cannot be reduced to compensation or the process of exacting *quid pro quo* through mutual self-interest (a reductive form of modern understanding). And it means more than equal giving and taking. In relation to intervention, *reciprocity* is defined broadly as exchange relations of negotiated mutuality that emphasises relations based upon circles of return. The importance of the principle of reciprocity therefore cannot be reduced to liberal considerations of balance or fairness. Interventions in these terms entail and build social relationships

158

that require prior and ongoing negotiation of the possible consequences of any humanitarian action.

3. The cluster of principles for *care* and *trust* in and for others
involves a stronger claim about a social interrelation than the
acceptance of others or tolerance of difference. This cluster brings
in Carol Gilligan's embodied notion of an 'ethics of care' developed by others including Joan Tronto (Gilligan 1993; Tronto
1993), but it also includes more abstract notions of trust in cooperative activities from communal relations to market-based and
bureaucratic-based exchange processes (Fukuyama 1995; Misztal
1996). Care in intervention entails consideration not only of consequences but also of whether good is being done. This means
that interventions need to be more than reactive. They ideally
need to be based on a history of already being on the ground,
with the intervention managed as an extension of already existing
programmes of mutually negotiated care.

4. Capacities for *justice and truth* also need to be included as a set
of principles that are basic to good relationality and, therefore,
to good intervention. It is interesting that Martha Nussbaum's
list of fundamental capabilities does not include this cluster
directly even though the capabilities approach is directed towards
developing a theory of justice (Nussbaum 2006). This cluster
has already received significant discussion in the literature on
intervention, but the question of truth does not seem to apply to
the usual self-legitimating *post facto* assessments by our political
leaders in considering the role of their states in intervention situations.

5. The capacity to reconcile potentially destructive or negative
differences across social and natural boundaries of continuing
and flourishing positive differences, including through positive
friction, is named under the fifth principle of *reconciliation and
negotiation*. The concept of 'social friction' is important here. A
flourishing world is not one in which all differences have dissolved
into empty harmony. It highlights the need to reconcile across
the *continuing* (and positively tension-producing) boundaries of
difference beyond human encounter. *Continuing* boundaries of
difference are emphasised here because there is a postmodern tendency to argue for the dissolution of boundaries into differences
that, in our terms, do not make a difference.

6. The cluster of capacities concerning *faith and love* includes the
capacity to have faith in others, to love them. This suggests a

capacity for an understanding of the limits of human rationality. To have faith includes the capacity to step beyond modern scientific reasoning, whatever that faith may be directed towards. To have the capacity for love ranges from the capacity for interpersonal intimacy to the capacity for relating to others beyond one's neighbours. Good intervention does not occur for reasons of guilt or image management, but for reasons of love of the other, however tense those relations might be. This principle is perhaps the most awkward to express. Nevertheless, we need to address this directly, including its cutting paradoxes. Christianity and Islam, two religions that include love as central to their theologies, are currently the most violence-creating civilisations of our time. Their war machines do not operate according to their own central principles.

7. Principles of *conviviality and hospitality* express another important set of capacities for relating to others. The concept of *conviviality* comes from the Latin *con* and *vivium*, meaning to come together in live-affirming ways: to eat, to celebrate or to enjoy social engagement. *Hospitality* in relation to others can include both hospitality to intimate others and to strangers, including the needs of migrants and refugees. In the case of external intervention this means, for example, that the bombing of Afghanistan to force the Taliban to end their hosting of Osama bin Laden was illegitimate – not to mention counterproductive in a consequentialist sense. This would have been more ethically conducted as a negotiated bringing to justice of a global criminal between two states in dialogue, reconciled to debating difference over the long term.

None of these principles are primary. None of them are absolute. They are principles for thinking with, intended to slow down the dominance of humanitarian accounting that seems to overwhelm current considerations of what should be done.

Notes

1. This legitimation of humanitarian intervention is often based on the Rwandan genocide. See Harald Müller and Jonas Wolff (2014).
2. As does the shamelessly self-promoting academic industry that pays homage to R2P. For example, in a journal devoted to the doctrine, Ramesh Thakur, one of the original developers of the doctrine, describes that doctrine as 'the most dramatic normative development of our time' (Thakur and Weiss 2009: cited from the abstract).

3. I have attempted to explore this in a limited way in James (2015).
4. See the excellent discussion in the introductory chapter to Barnett and Weiss (2015).
5. *Positive relationality* is a term that I do not have the space to elaborate here, but for relationality to be positive it requires that we have the capacity to establish regimes of mutual care, affinity, reciprocity and so on. At the same time it is important to recognise the complexities of social difference. Therefore, positive relationality also requires capacities for reconciliation and negotiation across the boundaries of that difference.
6. This abstraction of social relations is paradoxically and contradictorily co-extensive with, and defended by a constant ideological struggle to reclaim, the concrete, embodied and face-to-face (that is, invoke and appropriate for reasons primarily of legitimation, effect or rhetorical influence; not for itself). For example, newsreaders who read nightly of crises around the world and how 'we' are intervening or not, will invoke the embodied pain of those in need while maintaining an abstract distance from those situations in such a way as to allow them to move comfortably on at the end of the news story. Politicians will give speeches and express deep feelings for those in need, while at the same time their positions demand an abstract distance from that embodied need impinging upon their own lives.
7. Sennett (2012) is instructive on this capacity, except in relation to his treatment of tribalism as internally directed affinity essentially involving aggression to those who are different. This ontological insensitivity is all too common in the non-anthropological literature, and mars an otherwise searching book.

References

Adelman, H. (2003) 'Bystanders to Genocide in Rwanda', *International History Review*, 25(2), pp. 357–74.

Barnett, M. and T. G. Weiss (eds) (2015), *Humanitarianism in Question: Politics, Power, Ethics*, Ithaca, NY: Cornell University Press.

Belloni, R. (2007), *State Building and International Intervention in Bosnia*, London: Routledge.

Chandler, D. (2006), *From Kosovo to Kabul and Beyond: Human Rights and International Intervention*, 2nd edn, London: Pluto Press.

Chandler, D. (2015), 'The R2P Is Dead, Long Live the R2P: The Successful Separation of Military Intervention from the Responsibility to Protect', *International Peacekeeping*, 22(1), pp. 1–5.

Cohn, M. (2003), 'The Myth of Humanitarian Intervention in Kosovo', in A. Jokic (ed.), *Lessons of Kosovo: The Dangers of Humanitarian Intervention*, Peterborough: Broadview Press.

Dunn, D. H. (2013), 'Drones: Disembodied Aerial Warfare and the Unarticulated Threat', *International Affairs*, 9(5), pp. 1237–46.

Evans, G. (2008) *The Responsibility to Protect: Ending Mass Atrocity Crimes Once and For All*, Washington, DC: Brookings Institution Press.

Fukuyama, F. (1995), *Trust: The Social Virtues and the Creation of Prosperity*, London: Hamish Hamilton.

Gilligan, C. (1993) *Psychological Theory and Women's Development*, 2nd edn, Cambridge, MA: Harvard University Press.

James, P. (2014) 'Human Security as a Left-Over of Military Security, or as Integral to the Human Condition', in P. Bacon and C. Hobson (eds), *Human Security and Japan's Triple Disaster*, London: Routledge.

James, P. (2015), 'Despite the Terrors of Typologies: The Importance of Understanding Categories of Difference and Identity', *Interventions: International Journal of Postcolonial Studies*, 17(2), pp. 174–95.

Kuperman, A. J. (2015), 'Obama's Libya Debacle: How a Well-Meaning Intervention Ended in Failure', *Foreign Affairs*, 94(2), pp. 66–77.

Lessing, D. (1987), *The Wind Blows Away Our Words*, London: Picador.

Luhmann, N. (1995), *Social Systems*, Stanford, CA: Stanford University Press.

McDonnell, T. M. (2012), 'Sow What You Reap? Using Predator and Reaper Drones to Carry Out Assassinations or Targeted Killings of Suspected Islamic Terrorists', *George Washington International Law Review*, 44, pp. 243–316.

MacIntyre, A. (1985), *After Virtue: A Study in Moral Theory*, London: Duckworth.

Misztal, B. A. (1996), *Trust in Modern Societies*, Cambridge: Polity Press.

Müller, H. and J. Wolff (2014), 'The Dual Use of an Historical Event: "Rwanda 1994," the Justification and Critique of Liberal Interventionism', *Journal of Intervention and Statebuilding*, 8(4), pp. 280–90.

Nairn, T. and P. James (2005), 'Control and the Projection of a Totalizing War-Machine', in T. Nairn and P. James (eds), *Global Matrix: Nationalism, Globalism and State-Terrorism*, London: Pluto Press.

Nussbaum, M. C. (2006), *Frontiers of Justice: Disability, Nationality, Species Membership*, Cambridge, MA: Harvard University Press.

Pape, R. A. (2012), 'When Duty Calls: A Pragmatic Standard of Humanitarian Intervention', *International Security*, 37(1), pp. 41–80.

Pattison, J. (2010), *Humanitarian Intervention and the Responsibility To Protect: Who Should Intervene?* Oxford: Oxford University Press.

Sennett, R. (2012), *Together: The Rituals, Pleasures and Politics of Cooperation*, New Haven, CT: Yale University Press.

Terry, F. (2002), *Condemned to Repeat? The Paradox of Humanitarian Action*, Ithaca, NY: Cornell University Press.

Thakur, R. and T. G. Weiss (2009), 'R2P: From Idea to Norm – and Action', *Global Responsibility to Protect*, 1(1), pp. 23–53.

Tronto, J. C. (1993), *Moral Boundaries: A Political Argument for an Ethic of Care*, London: Routledge.

United Nations Development Programme (UNDP) (1994), *Human Development Report 1994: New Dimensions of Human Security*, Oxford: Oxford University Press, available at: http://hdr.undp.org/sites/default/files/reports/255/hdr_1994_en_complete_nostats.pdf, last accessed 26 December 2016.

Veit, A. (2010), *Intervention as Direct Rule: Civil War and Statebuilding in the Democratic Republic of Congo*, Frankfurt: Campus Verlag.

Weiss, T. G. (2012), *Humanitarian Intervention*, Cambridge: Polity Press.

Zolo, D. (2002), *Invoking Humanity: War, Law and Global Order*, London: Continuum.

7

'Manifestly Failing' and 'Unwilling or Unable' as Intervention Formulas: A Critical Assessment

Ingvild Bode

Introduction

After 2001, states have increasingly invoked the 'unwilling or unable' formula when justifying military intervention against non-state or terrorist targets. Moreover, the closely related term 'manifestly failing' has served as a key determinant triggering the international community's responsibility for protecting vulnerable populations following the third pillar of the Responsibility to Protect (R2P) doctrine. Since 2014, the 'unwilling or unable' formula has also served to justify US-led air strikes against the so-called Islamic State in Iraq and al-Sham (ISIS) in Syria. Given the formula's apparent rising prominence, this chapter will critically assess the legal foundations and policy practice of the 'unwilling or unable' formula and evaluate what this means for the evolution of intervention standards.

The inclusion of R2P in the United Nations World Summit Outcome of 2005 marked a decisive shift in the evolution of interventions for humanitarian purposes. A key trigger of shifting R2P to the level of the international community, and thereby moving towards intervention, is determining that 'national authorities *manifestly fail* to protect their populations from genocide, war crimes, ethnic cleansing and crimes against humanity' (GA 2005: para. 139, emphasis added). The phrase 'manifest failure' corresponds to the 'unwilling or unable' formula previously used in this context by the R2P-defining International Commission on Intervention and State Sovereignty (ICISS) (ICISS 2001: xi).[1] Apart from this connection, the 'unable or unwilling' formula has also been used to justify military intervention in a counterterrorism context. In September 2014, a US-led international coalition has therefore commenced airstrikes on Islamic State in Iraq and al-Sham (ISIS) targets in Syria because 'the government of the State where the threat is located is *unwilling or unable* to prevent the use of its territory for such attacks' (UNSC 2014d, emphasis added). This is the latest prominent example of a state using the 'unwilling or unable' formula as a legal justification for military intervention serving the purpose of self-defence against terrorist or non-state actors on the sovereign territory of 'host' states. Because this marks a departure from the three conventional legal theories regulating the use of force in self-defence against terrorist actors in 'host' states – proof of established links of support or state sponsorship of terrorist actors (the attribution standard), explicit state consent or a Security Council authorisation – this practice may indicate a shift in how interventions are justified.[2]

The rising prominence and, arguably, relevance of the 'unwilling or unable' formula warrants a more thorough examination of its legal foundations and policy practice. Adding to existing literature which considers either the counterterrorism (Reinold 2011; Deeks 2012; Williams 2012; Ahmed 2013; Scharf 2013: 183–210) or the R2P context only (Rosenberg and Strauss 2012; Ramos 2013; Gallagher 2014a; 2014b), this chapter offers a critical examination of its usage *across* both contexts. I will proceed in three steps: first, I discuss how the 'unwilling or unable' formula relates to the fulfilment of both internal and external responsibilities (increasingly) tied to state sovereignty. Second, I examine and compare the development of the formula in relation to first, R2P and second, counterterrorism. This will entail accounting for its legal bases, state and policy practice, *opinio juris*, as well as inherent problems of the formulas. These parts also consider the application of the formulas across two situations: the international intervention in Libya (R2P) and the ongoing interventions against ISIS targets in Syria. This latter case will be discussed in a more detailed exploratory case study. I conclude with a summary of what these developments might indicate in terms of evolving intervention standards.

Sovereignty and internal/external responsibilities

The character of the state as the legitimate sovereign authority constitutes (disputably) the very cornerstone of international law and international order. State sovereignty has both internal and external aspects: internally, it refers to the principal authority over its own affairs within a particular territory and externally, that authority is acknowledged by others as expressed by the UN Charter's principle of non-intervention (Biersteker and Weber 1996: 2). As the International Court of Justice has found, the state 'is subject to no other state, and has full and exclusive powers within its jurisdiction' (quoted in Hoffman 1966: 164).

Despite its supposed pride of place, sovereignty has often been recognised as a (convenient) fiction across both aspects.[3] Internally, there are many examples of states that either do not exert effective control over their territorial space or are unable to fulfil international commitments. Externally, breaches of the non-intervention principle have been a repeated and deliberate characteristic of international relations (Krasner 1999), not least because that principle has stood in dichotomous contrast with UN Charter commitments to human rights.

Since the 1990s, these challenges have given rise to understanding 'sovereignty as responsibility' (Deng et al. 1996), tied to specific responsibilities both vis-à-vis its own population and the international community. It is disputed whether this responsibility-based understanding is part of a longer tradition dating back to the seventeenth century or the latest in a series of changes constituting sovereignty as a social product (Barkin and Cronin 1994; Glanville 2014). Notwithstanding its genealogy, the responsibility dimension has a distinct effect on how sovereignty, and therefore the nature of states themselves, is understood. Internally, sovereignty as responsibility requires states to provide at least a minimum amount of goods and services, in particular security, and to ensure the protection and well-being of their citizens. As articulated by the UN General Assembly, should states fail on this account:

> we [the international community] are prepared to take collective action, in a timely and decisive manner, through the Security Council, in accordance with the Charter, including Chapter VII, on a case-by-case basis and in cooperation with relevant regional organizations as appropriate, should peaceful means be inadequate and national authorities are manifestly failing to protect their populations from genocide, war crimes, ethnic cleansing and crimes against humanity. (GA 2005: para. 139)

In other words, if a state 'manifestly fails', it becomes the international community's – ultimately the Security Council's – responsibility to react and protect its citizens as agreed upon unanimously by the UN membership in 2005. The Security Council is therefore set up as the principal organ to determine whether a state has failed in fulfilling its responsibilities and may even authorise the use of force to protect the state's population.

Externally, sovereignty as responsibility requires states to adhere to the international community's basic standards and fundamental principles. After 9/11, fulfilling international counterterrorism obligations, as for example outlined in Security Council Resolution (SCR) 1373, has become a key responsibility. In contrast to the provisions on R2P, these obligations neither designate who has the clear authority to determine their fulfilment or failure, nor what should be done if their failure has been ascertained. There is likewise no clear path towards authorising the use of force in the case of failure.

Despite these differences, both scenarios share a similar formula that helps in deciding whether state responsibility has been fulfilled: the 'unwilling or unable' test, which the chapter turns towards examining in more detail now. Although the 'unwilling or unable' terminology has only appeared comparatively recently on the international plain, it has already been used in a variety of contexts, as will be shown in the following sections.

'Unwilling or unable', 'manifestly failing' and the Responsibility to Protect

The 'unwilling or unable' formula made several prominent appearances in the ICISS's report entitled *The Responsibility to Protect*. In particular, it was used as a 'test' to judge state behaviour in pillar three, in cases where the international community takes collective action to protect vulnerable populations. However, when the inclusion of R2P was discussed at the World Summit in 2005, the resolution's drafters decided on a last-minute change. Instead of using the term 'unwilling or unable', they chose to qualify state behaviour as having 'manifestly failed' in order to trigger the international community's response. Some sources suggest that the latter may have been introduced to make the respective paragraph more acceptable to the wider UN membership, as the former 'was perceived to have a more subjective quality' (Garwood-Gowers 2013: 84; Gallagher 2014b: 432).

Despite this attempt to reduce subjectivity, determining whether a state is 'manifestly failing' to protect its population from the four major crimes (genocide, war crimes, crimes against humanity and ethnic cleansing) falling within the scope of R2P remains linked to uncertain criteria. It may therefore still be criticised precisely for the subjective judgement it invariably relies on. While the Security Council is clearly designated as the authority evaluating manifest failure, how precisely this evaluation happens and which criteria it applies remain unspecified. Indeed, more than ten years after the World Summit, the application of manifest failure in the context of R2P is characterised by unresolved issues, ambiguities and inconsistencies (Rosenberg and Strauss 2012; Gallagher 2014b: 433–4). Security Council practice in the years since 2005 has been inconsistent in applying R2P: the international community has not taken responsibility for local populations even after state authorities have demonstrably and manifestly failed to protect their populations. In this regard, for every case of successful R2P application, such as in Libya and Côte d'Ivoire, there have been at least as many cases of inaction, such as in Darfur and Syria.

Inconsistencies are also related to R2P discourse: major countries continue to use the 'unwilling or unable' formula in the R2P context and some key R2P scholars either use 'manifest failing' and 'unwilling or unable' interchangeably or merge both terms.[4] ICISS co-chair Ramesh Thakur noted that the two formulas are really only 'different wording to say the same thing' (Thakur 2015). Both the US' and the UK's official endorsements of R2P therefore refer to 'unwilling or unable' rather than manifestly failing, as stated in the US National Security Strategy of 2010:

> The United States and all member states of the UN have endorsed the concept of the 'Responsibility to Protect.' In so doing, we have recognised that the primary responsibility for preventing genocide and mass atrocity rests with sovereign governments, but that this responsibility passes to the broader international community when sovereign governments themselves commit genocide or mass atrocities, or when they prove *unable or unwilling* to take necessary action to prevent or respond to such crimes inside their borders. (Obama 2010: 48, emphasis added)

In order to ascertain how the Security Council has determined a state to be 'manifestly failing' in practice, the chapter briefly considers its response to the Libyan crisis in 2011 as arguably the most prominent example of R2P application.

THE LIBYA INTERVENTION AND THE CRITERIA OF 'MANIFESTLY FAILING'

In the spring of 2011, the Libyan government began to use force against its population following popular protests against the Qaddafi rule. This situation escalated quickly as the government lost control over many eastern cities and territories and ordered air and ground strikes. These actions were met with condemnation by the international community, who set up a sanctions regime against members of the Qaddafi family and an arms embargo through SCR 1970 on 26 February (UNSC 2011b). The same resolution also referred the situation in Libya unanimously to the International Criminal Court. Undeterred, governmental troops continued to advance on opposition-held areas in eastern Libya. In March 2011, Qaddafi moreover made a series of hate speeches in the course of which he announced his intent of committing atrocities on civilians in Benghazi (Karam and Heneghan 2011; Williams and Bellamy 2012: 288). In response, the Security Council adopted SCR 1973, declaring a no-fly zone across Libyan territory and authorising member states 'to take all necessary measures . . . to protect civilians and civilian populated areas under threat of attack in the Libyan Arab Jamahiriya' (UNSC 2011d). When the non-negotiable demands on the Qaddafi government to end the violence against Libyan civilians were not met, NATO Operation Unified Protector, acting with regional support, began conducting airstrikes against military targets and infrastructure.

Based on this brief summary of events leading up to the R2P-based intervention, the Security Council clearly had determined the Libyan government's 'manifest failure' to protect its own population. But how? It is sometimes (critically) noted that only three weeks passed between the first Council Resolution 1970 and SCR 1973 authorising the use of military force (O'Connell 2011: 16). However, determining Libya's manifest failure had already started in the context of SCR 1970: the resolution 'recall[s] the Libyan authorities' responsibility to protect its population' and in 'considering that the widespread and systematic attacks . . . against the civilian population may amount to crimes against humanity' prompted the applicability of R2P (Popovski 2011; UNSC 2011b: 1–2). This determination is not only clear from the text of SCR 1970 but also from its included referral to the ICC, whose jurisdiction only applies to the four atrocities also falling within the scope of R2P.

This type of reasoning can also be underlined by considering the Council meeting records in the lead-up to SCR 1970. UN Secretary-General Ban Ki-moon as well as a range of member states kept alluding to the 'manifest failure' of Libya and what this meant for the responsibility of the international community (UNSC 2011a; UNSC 2011c: 4–5). The strongest of these statements came from the Permanent Representative of Libya to the UN himself, who addressed the Council and then resigned from his position, closing his speech with an emotive 'please, United Nations, save Libya. No to bloodshed. No to the killing of innocents' (UNSC 2011a: 5).

In the time that passed between SCR 1970 and SCR 1973, Libya not only failed to abide by the earlier resolution but violence against civilians also escalated. Qaddafi even broadcast his intention and willingness to manifestly fail in fulfilling his government's responsibilities. In the Council deliberations that preceded the vote on SCR 1973, members therefore seemed to confirm what SCR 1970 had assumed, namely that Qaddafi was committing atrocities on Libyan civilians. Determining manifest failure therefore seems to have followed a dual approach, but was mostly already judged at the time of SCR 1970.

Although it is demonstrably clear that Libya had manifestly failed to protect its own population, the above discussion of events also shows that the international community's determination of 'manifest failure' did not seem to follow a set of established criteria. Given the situation's clarity, especially as atrocity intentions were frankly expressed by the Libyan president, this has not been very problematic in the Libyan case, often cited as a success for R2P (see, for example, Bellamy 2011; Popovski 2011; Weiss 2011b; Welsh 2011). Still, a tighter set of criteria would be needed in order to make Security Council decision-making on R2P scenarios transparent, consistent and clear. Gallagher has attempted to ascertain what 'manifestly failing' means in practice by coming up with five criteria: (1) government intentions, (2) weapons of choice, (3) death toll, (4) number of people displaced, and (5) the international targeting of civilians, especially women, children and the elderly (2014a: 6–12). Lists such as these are clearly a step forward in clarifying assessments on 'manifestly failing' and therefore also increasing the accountability of decision-makers. They however remain, for the time being and as I will also show in relation to counterterrorist determinations of 'unwilling or unable', purely aspirational.

'Unwilling or unable' states in the context of counterterrorism

The international community has recognised terrorist attacks as a key threat to international peace and security since the 1970s. However, it was only after the 9/11 attacks that its response to terrorism took on a new sense of urgency, which led to substantive changes in (customary) international law. In an international order defined by a society of states, the non-state nature of terrorists creates substantial challenges as to how 'victim' states should be able to respond to terrorist attacks in self-defence, in particular because these are invariably planned and staged on the territory of 'host' states. When considering military intervention in these scenarios, there are three legal theories to account for: the attribution standard, consent of the 'host' state and an authorisation of the Security Council.

Starting with the attribution standard, Alexandrov stated in the mid-1990s that '[a]ccording to the [International Law] Commission, an armed intervention into a state in order to attack terrorists cannot be regarded as self-defense when the State itself has not been guilty of an armed attack and has not directed or controlled the terrorists in question' (Alexandrov 1996: 183). As indicated by SCR 1373 and 1378 related to Afghanistan (UNSC 2001a; UNSC 2001b), customary law and state practice have changed decisively after the 9/11 attacks. Although the Taliban were not in direct control of al-Qaeda, they had allowed its presence and had not cooperated with the international community when it had demanded al-Qaeda's removal (UNSC 1999). This highlights that the attribution standard now appears to be broader in scope, although it still requires the establishment of some sort of link, be it tolerance of or tacit support for terrorist actors by state authorities, in order to justify military intervention. Second, interventions by external actors on 'host' state territory can also be legal if the 'host' state of terrorist actors consents (ICJ 2005; Visser 2015). This argument has a straightforward connection to sovereignty understandings giving national authorities the authority over decisions within their territories. Third, the Security Council may determine that a situation constitutes a threat to international peace and security, allowing it to authorise interventions and the use of force across various contexts. In this case, a clear Security Council resolution either 'deciding' or 'authorising' the intervention under Chapter VII of the UN Charter – or in Security Council terms, the use of 'all necessary measures' – would be needed to clearly determine an intervention's legality (Akande and Milanovic 2015). Additionally, any use of force in the form of military interventions, also against non-state actors, has to be necessary and proportionate. Therefore, it should be used as a last resort once reasonable non-peaceful means have been exhausted ('necessary'), be commensurate with the attack and limited to the amount needed to prevent further attacks ('proportionate').

The 'unable and unwilling' formula enters considerations both in relation to the attribution standard, but in particular with regard to the necessity criterion. In brief, the formula refers to the 'right of a victim state to engage in extra-territorial self-defense when the host is either unwilling or unable to take measures to mitigate the threat posed by domestic non-state actors' (Williams 2012: 625). Potential legal sources of the test can be found in international law both prior to and after 9/11, especially in documents related to the various obligations of states not to assist or condone terrorists. Key examples are SCR 1373 of 2001, the International Court of Justice's Corfu Channel case of 1949 and the 1970 Friendly Relations Declaration, which noted that:

> Every State has the duty to refrain from organizing, instigating, assisting or participating in acts of civil strife or terrorist acts in another State or acquiescing in organized activities within its territory directed towards the commission of such acts, when the acts referred to in the present paragraph involve a threat or use of force. (GA 1970)

However, none of these explicitly link the permissibility of using force to a non-compliant state – and only SCR 1373 represents a legally binding commitment under Chapter VII of the UN Charter.

More scholars have therefore argued for a connection between the 'unwilling and unable' test and the necessity criterion of self-defence (Dinstein 2001: 275; Deeks 2012: 495; Williams 2012: 630–1). Judging a host state to be 'unwilling or unable' to take measures against terrorist actors therefore becomes part of determining whether the extraterritorial use of force is necessary. As Williams summarises, 'if the host is willing and able, then the use of force will be illegal and unnecessary' (2012: 630). Although this appears to be a reasonable connection, it encounters difficulties because neither the criteria of the 'unwilling or unable' assessment nor who is entitled to make it are clearly defined.

Having also identified this 'substantive indeterminacy', Deeks examines past 'victim' state practice and *opinio juris* in the pre- and post-Charter era, deriving a set of six substantive and procedural factors for the test, such as prioritisation of consent and cooperation and request to address the threat and time to respond (2012: 503, 516). Despite Deeks offering the first substantial and practice-oriented analysis of criteria that could or should inform the 'unwilling or unable' test, it remains purely aspirational and, moreover, restricted to the *opinio juris* of intervening states. While she acknowledges this bias, her methodological choice therefore does not allow for a comprehensive picture of customary international law, with the lacking host state *opinio juris* representing a key impediment. Moreover, Deeks fails to designate a clear authority to verify the intervening state's 'unwilling or unable' judgement – something that, following the current set-up of the international system, should fall within the Security Council's authority (Ahmed 2013: 21–6).

Practical impediments of the 'unwilling or unable' formula

There are at least two further practical impediments to the 'unwilling or unable' test as a justification for military interventions: first, although unwillingness and inability appear to be used interchangeably so as to generally imply a state's ineffectiveness in meeting its obligations, there are valid differences between the terms (Ahmed 2013: 8–9). Comparing their meanings, the Oxford English Dictionary defines unable as 'not having ability or power, to do or perform . . . something specified' and unwilling as 'not intending, purposing, or desiring (to do a particular thing); . . . averse, reluctant' (2015a; 2015b). 'Unable' therefore appears to be the more objective criterion, while 'unwilling' requires an accurate value judgement about another state's intentions, something that has long been a problem for international policymakers and scholars alike (for a summary, see Holmes 2013: 831–3). Additionally, the two terms imply different levels of responsibility relating to state inaction. That is, while a state's inability to fulfil its obligations may be due to inadequate resources or capacities and therefore may present a legitimate reason for inaction, unwillingness presumes a purposeful decision to refrain from fulfilling these obligations either by choice or perhaps by economic necessity as it prioritises other policy areas.

Seen in this light, it becomes apparent why some studies have therefore identified 'unwillingness' as the central determinant of the 'unwilling or unable' formula: '[a] state that is willing but unable to deal with domestic non-state actors will inevitably provide its consent for the victim state to use force in its territory' (Williams 2012: 627). Providing this consent puts the intervening state's use of force on safe legal grounds. However, when considering prominent applications of the 'unwilling or unable' test, such as US targeted killing operations against terrorist targets in Pakistan, Yemen and Somalia, things are not as easy as they seem (Warren and Bode 2014: 122–3). Yemen is often cited as an example of open consent based on President Hadi's official statements to this point (Al-Shamahi 2013). However, not only has the Yemeni parliament issued diverging statements, but drone strikes have also continued after Hadi's forced resignation in January 2015 amid unclear sovereign control, highlighting the tenuous nature of consent (Ackermann 2015).

The Pakistani case is more complicated as sources simultaneously outline tacit consent to drone strikes by the country's military leaders and open condemnation by its political leaders (Aslam 2011: 318; Zaidi 2011; McNeal 2014: 697–8). Pakistan's trajectory illustrates an important observation: it may be opportune for a state to protest in public, while the use of force is consented to behind closed doors. The status of consent is even more difficult to ascertain in Somalia, a state that has been lacking a central government since the early 1990s. Although there are only few reliable sources to be found, some suggest that Somali government authorities and parliamentarians have occasionally issued statements of support on the matter, while members of civil society have expressed concern about potential civilian casualties (Pelton 2011). As US practice indicates, 'host' state consent and the connected determination whether the host state is 'unable' to exert control over its territory provides for murky instead of clear-cut legal grounds.

In terms of the second practical impediment of the 'unwilling or unable' test: how is it possible to determine if a state is 'unwilling or unable' in the face of state disintegration? Are state authorities that are not in full control of their state's territory to be automatically counted as unable? Does it matter whether they purposely did not fulfil their responsibilities? And if there are several parties with contested authority claims, who should be considered as the main party whose unwillingness or inability has to be determined to justify the potential use of force? All of these open questions point to a wide grey area inhibiting the practical utility of the 'unwilling or unable' test. I will come back to these questions and demonstrate their problematic answers in my subsequent case study of interventions against the ISIS in Syria.

The 'unable and unwilling' formula in state and policy practice

Despite these challenges, the 'unwilling or unable' test predates post-9/11 practice, although it has since gained traction. The most prominent cases of intervening states to have referred to the test are Turkey against the PKK in northern Iraq (repeatedly since the mid-1990s), Israel against Hezbollah in Lebanon (late 1970s–early 1980s, 2006), the United States against al-Qaeda in Afghanistan, Pakistan, Yemen and Somalia (ongoing since 2001), the Russian Federation against Chechen rebels in Georgia (summer 2002), and Kenya against al-Shabaab in Somalia (2011) (Reinold 2011: 252–84; Deeks 2012: 549–50; Ahmed 2013: 3; Scharf 2013: 204–5). A brief comparison of these usages reveals that they only triggered limited and restrained reactions by the international community. In the case of Russia's 2002 air strikes in Georgia (UNSC 2002), for example, only three actors – Georgia itself, the US and the Council of Europe – issued statements opposing the use of force, while the vast majority of states remained silent (Council of Europe, Parliamentary Assembly 2002; GA-UNSC 2002; Myers 2002; Ruys 2010: 465–6). Similar observations can be made with regard to other state usages of the test, leading some studies to suggest that 'in the area of self-defense, many incidents fail to elicit much of an international response, which could be interpreted as an indicator of legal uncertainty or as tacit acquiescence' (Reinold 2011: 257). Presuming that these state non-reactions count as consent still represents too early a conclusion as 'true' acquiescence depends above all on how *long* states maintain their silence (MacGibbon 1954: 144; Peters 2015).

The 'unwilling or unable' formula has gained traction through being put into regular practice by both the Bush and the Obama administrations. John B. Bellinger and Harold Koh, legal advisers of the Bush and the Obama administrations, respectively, have explicitly referred to the 'unwilling or unable' reasoning in prominent speeches (Bellinger 2006; Koh 2010). During President Obama's tenure, the test has consistently been used as a legal justification for the administration's policy of interventions in the form of targeted killings outside established theatres of conflict; in other words, when the US has used military force on the territories of states with whom it is not at war (Brennan 2012; DOJ 2013: 2). Moreover, in September 2014, the US also provided official endorsement of the test through referencing it in relation to the expansion of airstrikes against IS targets in Syria in official correspondence (UNSC 2014d), something I will turn to in more detail now.

Intervention against ISIS in Syria: 'unwilling or unable'?

Since August 2014, a variety of states acting as part of a US-led coalition or independently have intervened militarily in the form of airstrikes against ISIS on both Iraqi and Syrian territory. Interventions on Iraqi territory have been uncontroversial on legal grounds as the country formally requested military assistance of the UN membership in late June 2014 (UNSC 2014a: 2). The US-led international coalition against ISIS has conducted air strikes on Iraqi territory since August 2014 and has since reached a certain level of formalisation comprising approximately sixty states with varying contributions.

On Syrian territory, interventions against ISIS targets led by the US, actively cooperating with Bahrain, Jordan, Saudi Arabia, the United Arab Emirates and with Qatari support, started on 22 September 2014. These air strikes have been framed as collective self-defence on behalf of Iraq, which requested that the United States strike ISIS sites and military strongholds 'outside Iraq's borders' without explicitly mentioning that strikes were supposed to occur on Syrian territory (UNSC 2014c). The US has explicitly referred to Syria and the 'unwilling or unable' formula in this context (UNSC 2014d).

Across the second half of 2015, military interventions of individual states against non-state targets in Syria have multiplied. As of October 2016, seven further states have conducted air strikes on Syrian territory as part of the US-led coalition (Turkey, France, Australia, Canada, the United Kingdom, Belgium and the Netherlands),[5] while the Russian Federation has intervened militarily after having received a request by Syrian authorities (UNSC 2015d: 4). After the November 2015 terrorist attacks in Paris linked to ISIS, France, the UK and Germany have put forward additional broad individual/collective (pre-emptive) self-defence arguments to justify their interventions (Deutscher Bundestag 2015; House of Commons 2015; Peters 2015).[6]

The UK and Germany were also able to refer to unanimous SCR 2249 of 20 November 2015 to legitimise actions. SCR 2249 does not, however, authorise interventions against ISIS in Syria with reference to Chapter VII of the UN Charter. The key Operative Clause 5 reads:

> *Calls upon* Member States that have the capacity to do so to take all necessary measures, in compliance with international law, in particular with the United Nations Charter, as well as international human rights, refugee and humanitarian law, on the territory under control of ISIL also known as Da'esh . . . (UNSC 2015f: Operative Clause 5, emphasis added)

By referring to standing international law and using 'calls upon' rather than 'authorises' or 'decides', the resolution remains ambiguous as to whether it provides a legal basis for intervention against ISIS targets on Syrian territory. While the UK and Germany have construed it as such, legal scholars are doubtful on this matter (Akande and Milanovic 2015).

In the following section, I summarise arguments provided by intervening states as well as other states' reactions to these interventions, paying special attention to whether these explicitly or implicitly evoked the 'unwilling or unable' formula or in how far they referred to other legal theories, in particular 'host' state consent and the attribution standard. I mainly study state arguments in the context of debates at the Security Council from September 2014 to December 2015. This exploratory case can therefore help in ascertaining the current discursive standing of the 'unwilling or unable' test, although developments in 2015 have clearly shown that this is a moving target.

Debates about ISIS in Syria and interventions on Syrian territory at the Security Council: September 2014 to December 2015

In late August 2014, the US authorised surveillance flights over Syria, with a particular focus on the Iraqi border, which were seen as a step towards military intervention against ISIS targets in Syria (Security Council Report 2014c). The first Security Council debate to include substantial references to the possibility of intervening military against ISIS in Syria was held on 19 September 2014 on 'the situation concerning Iraq' at a ministerial level. Although the topic was Iraq, more than half of the forty states on the speakers' list also referred to the Syrian conflict.[7] Up until mid-December 2015, there was one further ministerial debate dealing with the issue of ISIS at the Security Council (UNSC 2015d), while some states also made statements after the vote on S/RES/2249 (UNSC 2015e). I will consider these two debates in chronological order.

September 2014

At the ministerial-level debate on 19 September 2014, there was much discussion about whether treating Iraq and Syria as separate situations in the fight against ISIS was still feasible (Security Council

Report 2014a; UNSC 2014b: 24). On 8 September, US President Obama had already announced that his government's strategy to 'degrade and destroy' ISIS may include an expansion of the air campaign to Syria (Obama 2014). The gist of this statement was underlined by US Secretary of State John Kerry, who, speaking at debate, stated: 'in the face of this sort of evil, we have only one option to confront it with a holistic, global campaign that is committed and capable of degrading and destroying this terrorist threat and ensuring that ISIL cannot find safe haven in Iraq, Syria or elsewhere' (UNSC 2014b: 7). This point was echoed in similar terms by several foreign ministers, including the Iranian, French, Iraqi, Turkish and Saudi officials (UNSC 2014b). On 22 September, the US expanded its airstrikes to targets in Syria. This course of action, described as 'necessary and proportionate actions in Syria' after having determined that 'the government of the state where the threat is located is *unwilling or unable* to prevent the use of its territory for such attacks' was reported to the Security Council on 23 September (UNSC 2014d, emphasis added).

This intervention was not discussed at the Council. This is remarkable because the US had invited the Council membership and interested states for an open debate on the topic of foreign terrorist fighters on 24 September 2014. Given the close temporal proximity to the start of airstrikes against targets in Syria, one could have expected states to use this opportunity for some sort of statement on the occasion. But only two states, Australia and Estonia, referred to the ongoing strikes against ISIS in Syria and both references can be characterised as supportive, albeit brief. Apart from an oblique remark by Russian foreign minister Sergey Lavrov, not even Syria addressed the intervention on its territory directly (UNSC 2014e: 40).

A number of public statements were offered outside the Council. The United Kingdom spoke in firm support of US action, while the US regional partners issued statements noting their involvement that, however, did not explicitly cite the US. Speaking against the legal viability of the 'unwilling or unable' test, Russia 'note[d] that such actions can be carried out only within the framework of international law. This implies not a formal unilateral notification of the strikes, but the existence of explicit consent of the Syrian government or a relevant decision by the UN Security Council' (Russian Ministry of Foreign Affairs 2014).

From September 2014 to June 2015, many states remained silent on the matter. Some legal scholars, such as Deeks, interpret this as a 'silent acquiescence' of the legality of air strikes and therefore, by association, a silent condonement of the 'unwilling or unable' formula (2014), while sceptical scholars such as Heller instead point to the continued lack of public state approval (2014).

As of June 2015, a total of eight states had participated in the air campaign on Syrian territory, compared to eight states in Iraq (Drennan 2014; Mullen 2014). Moreover, the make-up of these coalitions was almost entirely different with the US being the only joining factor: while the Syrian campaign was composed of regional partners, Western states dominated the campaign in Iraq. These participation differences illustrated a certain level of discomfort when it comes to the legality of the 'unwilling or unable' formula.

Still, a June 2015 summary of state practice on the matter, for example, outlined the position of the Dutch government whose foreign minister states: 'it is now sufficiently established in fact that there are continuous attacks from Syria against Iraq, directed by the ISIS headquarters in Raqqah, Syria . . . It is also evident that Syrian authorities are *incapable* of stopping these armed attacks' (Ruys et al. 2015: 26, emphasis added). Canada had likewise referred to the 'unwilling or unable' formula upon joining the US-led coalition in March 2015, becoming the first Western state apart from the US to extend its operations into Syria:

> In accordance with the inherent rights of individual and collective self-defense reflected in Article 51 of the United Nations Charter, States must be able to act in self-defense when the Government of the State where a threat is located in *unwilling or unable* to prevent attacks emanating from its territory. (UNSC 2015a, emphasis added)

However, from February 2016, Canada ended its participation in air strikes both in Iraq and Syria following the election of Liberal Prime Minister Justin Trudeau. This move can be associated with a lack of belief both in their effectiveness and, potentially, overall legitimacy.

July to December 2015

As noted in the introduction to this section, by December 2015, Australia, France, Canada, Turkey and the United Kingdom had joined the US-led coalition against ISIS in Syria and communicated this intent in letters to the Security Council. In addition to Canada, Australia and Turkey confirmed that Syria has been 'unwilling or unable' to counter the threat posed by ISIS (UNSC 2015b; UNSC 2015c). France and the UK, instead, referred to individual and collective self-defence under Article 51 of the UN Charter, only, to justify their participation in military intervention, without any reference to the attribution standard or even the 'unwilling or unable' formula. In analysing statements at the September 2015 ministerial level debate, I will therefore pay particular attention to how the Syrian national authorities figure in state reasoning.

With sixty-six member states on the speaker's list, as well as remarks by four regional organisations, this provides a good overview on how state perspectives may have changed (UNSC 2015d). It is important to note that not a single state mentioned the 'unwilling or unable' formula explicitly at the debate. In order to assess how far the formula is supported, I paid attention to whether a state spoke in favour or opposed to military intervention against ISIS targets in Syria. Support of this intervention or of using military means in Syria would signal an at least implicit approval of arguments as to its legal standing.

Out of sixty-six states, fourteen spoke favourably and mentioned the US-led coalition as an important means in the fight against ISIS, while many countries in this group also took some part in the coalition themselves (e.g. Australia in UNSC 2015d: 69). A further twelve states spoke in favour of military means in counterterrorism in more general terms, frequently however highlighting how these can and should only ever be part of the international solution (e.g. Uruguay in UNSC 2015d: 58). Thirteen speakers included critical remarks about atrocities committed by the Assad regime in their remarks (e.g. Luxembourg in UNSC 2015d: 44). In the majority of cases, however, these were not connected to the potential of military intervention to counter terrorist threats. Moreover, two sets of seven states either voiced their opposition to military solutions to what they perceived as political problems or highlighted non-interference and respect for national sovereignty (e.g. Venezuela in UNSC 2015d: 16). Twenty-three statements did not include any reference to military intervention or the use of force. Overall, state statements, compared to those made in 2014, indicated a growing basis of support for military intervention against terrorist targets in Syria and therefore, at least some more implicit consent to the 'unwilling or unable' formula. As more states have intervened on Syrian territory and these states have either used the 'unwilling or unable' formula explicitly in their notifications or have implicitly condoned its reasoning by participating in US-led interventions, the fact that many states still remain silent on the matter potentially gives more weight to 'tacit acquiescence' arguments.

Considering the content of arguments provided by France, the UK and Germany, moreover, speaks for a broad interpretation of individual and collective self-defence under Article 51 of the UN Charter. Although their interventions still happen on Syrian territory, they do not concern themselves with the attribution standard or the response undertaken by the Syrian authorities at all. For some parliamentarians at the German Parliament's debate, debating the legality of the intervention was even construed as a 'nitpicking' matter in the face of the ISIS threat (Peters 2015). If these interpretations of Article 51 hold, its scope would be decidedly broader than in previous practice.

Moreover, ignoring the Syrian authorities, in these cases, is also clearly connected to them being deemed illegitimate rather than unwilling or unable. I consider these questions and the Syrian response in some detail in the next section.

Syria under Assad: willing but unable?

A key weakness of Deeks's study on the 'unwilling or unable' formula has been her lack of attention paid to the 'target' state. This section will therefore consider Syria's reaction, as well as how it was assessed according to the 'unwilling or unable' formula.

Initially, Syria had stated that it would consider US attacks on targets in Syria as an act of aggression (Security Council Report 2014c). However, when US strikes started in September 2014, it did not protest formally and instead referred to having received prior notice of the strikes (Security Council Report 2014d). Even that simple statement contains some uncertainty as Syria held that it was notified by the US delegation to the UN, while other sources point to prior notice being given by the Iraqi government (AP 2014; Security Council Report 2014d;). In light of applying the 'unwilling or unable' formula, it is noticeable that the US contradicted giving any official notification to the Syrian regime so as to avoid the semblance of 'formal' coordination, arguing that 'they had provided only a general warning about the possibility of military action' (Morello and Gearan 2014). Was Syria arguably willing to cooperate and could therefore only have been found to be unable? Syria has contradicted this latter assessment at the Security Council, speaking in late September 2014:

My country's Government is an active participant in combatting the terrorist groups ISIL and Jabhat al-Nusra. We have undertaken those activities unilaterally within Syria over the past three years. We always emphasise the importance of counter-terrorism efforts, putting an end to terrorist financing and combating terrorists who come to our country from other countries. (UNSC 2014b: 43)

Of course, the Assad regime has worked with a broad and untenable definition of terrorism since the Syrian conflict started, which encompasses not only those groups that appear on the Security Council's sanctions lists but also all groups opposed to the regime. While Assad and the members of the Syrian delegation therefore like to portray themselves as 'a bulwark against the rise of terrorism', actual confrontations between government forces and ISIS have been scarce (Security Council Report 2014b). Rather than being 'unwilling or unable', the Syrian government appears to have been deemed a bit of both.

Syria may not have protested at the time as air strikes against ISIS are opportune for the Assad government, while it could not openly consent to such strikes given the overall political situation (Goodman 2014). At the second Security Council ministerial-level debate, Syria characterised the interventions as 'a flagrant violation of Syria's national sovereignty' and instead hailed Russian intervention, to which it had consented, as the best way forward (UNSC 2015d: 30). This, therefore, constitutes a clear dismissal of the 'unwilling or unable' formula from a 'target' state.

Conclusion: similarities and differences across the 'unwilling or unable' and 'manifestly failing' formulas

This chapter aimed at comparing the 'unwilling or unable' formula across two contexts of its application: the responsibility to protect and counterterrorism. Although the growing international support for military intervention against ISIS in Syria appears to indicate implicit consent to the 'unwilling or unable' formula, this remains disputed, especially in light of 'target state' opinion. Given this development, this chapter aimed at providing more clarity on the formula itself, its legal standing and how relevant it has been in state practice across R2P and counterterrorist contexts.

Although there are clear differences in terms of how force is used and the terms employed, this analysis has identified four open questions that are similar across the two contexts. These questions are significant as they highlight the problematic nature of the 'unwilling or unable' formula as a test to inform intervention decisions.

First, determinations of 'unwilling or unable' and 'manifestly failing' states both work with uncertain criteria. This is the major and most problematic similarity. Without such clear criteria, it is not only impossible to verify how states or the Security Council have come to their assessments, thereby making this type of assessment reproducible under other circumstances, but it also makes their decision-making incomprehensible and therefore unaccountable. Given the gravity with which use-of-force decisions should be attributed, this increased intransparency is concerning, especially in the context of use-of-force decisions in response to non-state threats. Here, not only are the criteria for 'unwilling or unable' decision-making unclear, there has also been no designated authority making these decisions as they are argued to fall within the scope of the right to self-defence. As a consequence, determinations have invariably been made by the intervening state, which is unlikely to be positioned in an information environment ideal for making them.

Second, although there are clear differences between the terms 'unwilling' and 'unable' as well as between the potential reasons that have led to a state 'manifestly failing', both scenarios have been worked with interchangeably in practice. This is problematic because 'unwilling' and 'unable' point to very different contexts that require an equally different response in order to lead to a situation in which the state can sustainably meet its responsibilities and obligations. Third, although the 'unwilling or unable' formula was ostensibly changed to 'manifestly failing' in the World Summit Outcome on account of the subjective judgement the former entailed, it appears as if that subjectivity is shared by both terms – at least, it remains practically unclear how 'manifestly failing' is anything other than determining a state's inability and unwillingness in disguise. Lastly, neither 'manifestly failing' nor 'unwilling or unable' has been applied consistently across the UN membership. While it is at least clear in the case of R2P *who* can use these terms inconsistently, the 'unwilling or unable' formula has served to justify a growing number of unilateral uses of force outside the Security Council framework (Bode 2016). This latter development is not only threatening to the general prohibition on the use of force as enshrined in Article 2(4) of the UN Charter but also to even a 'thin' understanding of the international rule of law.

Notes

1. Interestingly, the ICISS report also refers to the 'unwilling or unable' formula in the context of the counterterrorist use of force (ICISS 2001: 12).
2. Further, Article 17 of the Rome Statute on the International Criminal Court (ICC) authorises the ICC to conduct investigations falling under its jurisdiction if a state has been unwilling or unable to prosecute itself (ICC 2002: 12–13). Articles 17(2) and (3) outline criteria for the Court to conduct such an examination, which makes this case distinct from the 'unwilling or unable' formula in both contexts discussed in this chapter. Not only has an independent third party, the ICC, been charged with conducting the examination, but comparatively clear criteria have also been formulated.
3. Today's sovereign states have long lost the 'full' control and authority over what happens inside their borders, in particular in the contexts of (economic) globalisation, the growing recognition of 'transsovereign' problems and processes of regional integration, such as in the European Union (e.g. Sassen 1996; Strange 1996; Cusimano 2000).
4. Thomas Weiss, for example, speaks about the responsibility of the international community in situations '[w]hen a state is unable or manifestly unwilling to protect the rights of its population' (Weiss 2011a: 9).
5. Germany also participates in the US-led coalition, but does not fly airstrikes.
6. Both the UK and German parliaments voted on participating in the military interventions against ISIS targets in Syria, acting upon requests by France and the French invocation of the EU Treaty clause on mutual defence.
7. This choice did not escape the notice of the Syrian delegation: 'Some speakers today have gone beyond the agenda item under consideration, which is the situation in Iraq. That is what is on the agenda' (quoted in Security Council 2014b: 43).

References

Ackermann, S. (2015) 'White House Says Drone Strikes in Yemen Continue Despite Houthi Coup', *The Guardian*, 24 January, available at: http://www.theguardian.com/world/2015/jan/24/white-house-drone-strikes-yemen-houthi-coup, last accessed 27 December 2016.

Ahmed, D. I. (2013), 'Defending Weak States Against the "Unwilling or Unable" Doctrine of Self-Defense', *Journal of International Law and International Relations*, 9(1), pp. 1–37.

Akande, D. and M. Milanovic (2015), 'The Constructive Ambiguity of the Security Council's ISIS Resolution', *EJIL: Talk!*, 21 November, available at: http://www.ejiltalk.org/the-constructive-ambiguity-of-the-security-co uncils-isis-resolution/, last accessed 27 December 2016.

Alexandrov, S. A. (1996) *Self-Defense against the Use of Force in International Law*, Developments in International Law, The Hague: Kluwer Law International.

Al-Shamahi, A. (2013), 'US Drones Strain on Yemeni's Dual Loyalties', BBC News, 30 April, available at: http://www.bbc.co.uk/news/world-middle-east-22340837, last accessed 27 December 2016.

AP (2014), 'U.S. Notified Bashar Assad's Government Before Syria Airstrikes', NBC News, 23 September, available at: http://www.nbcnews.com/news/world/u-s-notified-bashar-assads-government-syria-airstrikes-n209436, last accessed 27 December 2016.

Aslam, M.W. (2011), 'A Critical Evaluation of American Drone Strikes in Pakistan: Legality, Legitimacy and Prudence', *Critical Studies on Terrorism*, 4(3), pp. 313–29.

Barkin, J. S. and B. Cronin (1994), 'The State and the Nation: Changing Norms and the Rules of Sovereignty in International Relations', *International Organization*, 48(1), pp. 107–30.

Bellamy, A. J. (2011) 'Libya and the Responsibility to Protect: The Exception and the Norm', *Ethics & International Affairs*, 25(3), pp. 263–69.

Bellinger, J. B. (2006), 'Legal Adviser Bellinger Speech, "Legal Issues in the War on Terrorism"', United States Department of State, 31 October, available at: http://www.state.gov/s/l/2006/98861.htm, last accessed 27 December 2016.

Biersteker, T. J. and C. Weber. (1996) 'The Social Construction of State Sovereignty', in T. J. Biersteker and C. Weber (eds), *State Sovereignty as Social Construct*, Cambridge Studies in International Relations 46, Cambridge: Cambridge University Press, pp. 1–21.

Bode, I. (2016), 'How the World's Interventions in Syria Have Normalized the Use of Force', *The Conversation*, 17 February, available at: http://theconversation.com/how-the-worlds-interventions-in-syria-have-nor malised-the-use-of-force-54505, last accessed 27 December 2016.

Brennan, J. O. (2012), 'The Efficacy and Ethics of US Counterterrorism Strategy', Wilson Center, 30 April, available at: http://www.wilson-center.org/event/the-efficacy-and-ethics-us-counterterrorism-strategy, last accessed 27 December 2016.

Council of Europe, Parliamentary Assembly (2002), 'Recommendation 1580. The Situation in Georgia and Its Consequences for the Stability of the Caucasus Region', available at: http://assembly.coe.int/nw/xml/XRef/Xref-XML2HTML-en.asp?fileid=17043&lang=en, last accessed 27 December 2016.

Cusimano, M. K (ed.) (2000), *Beyond Sovereignty: Issues for a Global Agenda*, New York: St. Martin's Press.

Deeks, A. (2012), '"Unwilling or Unable": Toward an Normative Framework for Extra-Territorial Self-Defense', *Virginia Journal of International Law*, 52(3), pp. 481–550.

Deeks, A. (2014), 'The UK's Article 51 Letter on Use of Force in Syria', *Lawfare*, 12 December, available at: http://www.lawfareblog.com/2014/12/the-uks-article-51-letter-on-use-of-force-in-syria/, last accessed 27 December 2016.

Deng, F. M., S. Kimaro, T. Lyons, D. Rothchild and I. W. Zartman (1996), *Sovereignty as Responsibility: Conflict Management in Africa*, Washington, DC: Brookings Institution Press.

Deutscher Bundestag (2015), 'Bundestag billigt Einsatz der Bundeswehr gegen IS', *Deutscher Bundestag*, 4 December, available at: https://www.bundestag.de/dokumente/textarchiv/2015/kw49-de-bundeswehreinsatz-isis-freitag/397884, last accessed 27 December 2016.

Dinstein, Y. (2001), *War, Aggression, and Self-Defense*, 3rd edn, Cambridge: Cambridge University Press.

Drennan, J. (2014), 'Who Has Contributed What in the Coalition Against the Islamic State?', *Foreign Policy*, 12 November, available at: http://foreignpolicy.com/2014/11/12/who-has-contributed-what-in-the-coalition-against-the-islamic-state/, last accessed 27 December 2016.

Gallagher, A. (2014a), 'Syria and the Indicators of a "Manifest Failing"', *International Journal of Human Rights*, 18(1), pp. 1–19.

Gallagher, A. (2014b), 'What Constitutes a "Manifest Failing"? Ambiguous and Inconsistent Terminology and the Responsibility to Protect', *International Relations*, 28(4), pp. 428–44.

Garwood-Gowers, A. (2013), 'The BRICS and the Responsibility to Protect in Libya and Syria', in R. Maguire, B. Lewis and C. Sampford (eds), *Shifting Global Powers and International Law: Challenges and Opportunities*, London: Routledge, pp. 81–99.

Glanville, L. (2014), *Sovereignty and the Responsibility to Protect: A New History*, Chicago: University of Chicago Press.

Goodman, R. (2014), 'Taking the Weight off of International Law: Has Syria Consented to US Airstrikes?', *Just Security*, 23 December, available at: http://justsecurity.org/18665/weight-international-law-syria-consented-airstrikes, last accessed 27 December 2016.

Heller, K. J. (2014), 'Do Attacks on ISIS in Syria Justify the "Unwilling or Unable" Test?', *Opinio Juris*, 13 December, available at: http://opiniojuris.org/2014/12/13/attacks-isis-syria-justify-unwilling-unable-test/, last accessed 27 December 2016.

Hoffman, S. (1966), 'International Systems and International Law', in R. A. Falk and S. H. Mendlovitz (eds) *The Strategy of World Order*, New York: World Law Fund, pp. 134–66.

Holmes, M. (2013), 'The Force of Face-to-Face Diplomacy: Mirror Neurons and the Problem of Intentions', *International Organization*, 67(4), pp. 829–61.

House of Commons (2015), 'House of Commons Debate', Parliament. uk, 2 December, available at: http://www.publications.parliament.uk/ pa/cm201516/cmhansrd/cm151202/debtext/151202-0001.htm#151202 54000002, last accessed 27 December 2016.

International Commission on Intervention and State Sovereignty (ICISS) (2001), 'The Responsibility to Protect', Ottawa: International Development Research Centre, available at: http://responsibilitytopro tect.org/ICISS%20Report.pdf, last accessed 27 December 2016.

International Court of Justice (ICJ) (2005), *Case Concerning Armed Activities on the Territory of the Congo (Democratic Republic of the Congo v. Uganda)*, judgment of 19 December 2005.

International Criminal Court (ICC) (2002), Rome Statute of the International Criminal Court.

Karam, S., and T. Heneghan (2011), 'Gaddafi Tells Rebel City, Benghazi, "We Will Show No Mercy"', *The Huffington Post, Reuters*, 17 March, available at: http://www.huffingtonpost.com/2011/03/17/gaddafi-beng hazi-libya-news_n_837245.html, last accessed 27 December 2016.

Koh, H. (2010), 'The Obama Administration and International Law', United States Department of State, 25 March, available at: http://www.state. gov/s/l/releases/remarks/139119.htm, last accessed 27 December 2016.

Krasner, S. D. (1999), *Sovereignty: Organized Hypocrisy*, Princeton: Princeton University Press.

MacGibbon, I. C. (1954), 'The Scope of Acquiescence in International Law', *British Yearbook of International Law*, 31, pp. 143–86.

McNeal, G. S. (2014), 'Targeted Killing and Accountability', *The Georgetown Law Journal* 102(3), pp. 681–794.

Morello, C. and A. Gearan (2014), 'Around World, Mixed Reactions to US-led Airstrikes in Syria', *The Washington Post*, 23 September, available at: http://www.washingtonpost.com/world/national-security/around-world- mixed-reaction-to-us-led-airstrikes-in-syria/2014/09/23/16985bb6-4352- 11e4-9a15-137aa0153527_story.html, last accessed 27 December 2016.

Mullen, J. (2014), 'Airstrikes on ISIS in Syria: Who's In, Who's Not', CNN, 2 October, available at: http://www.cnn.com/2014/09/23/world/meast/ syria-airstrikes-countries-involved/index.html, last accessed 27 December 2016.

Myers, S. L. (2002) 'Echoing Bush, Putin Asks UN to Back Georgia Attack', *The New York Times*, 13 September, available at: http://www.nytimes. com/2002/09/13/world/echoing-bush-putin-asks-un-to-back-georgia- attack.html, last accessed 27 December 2016.

Obama, B. (2010), 'The National Security Strategy of the United States of America 2010', The White House, May, available at: http://www. whitehouse.gov/sites/default/files/rss_viewer/national_security_strategy. pdf, last accessed 27 December 2016.

Obama, B. (2014), 'Statement by the President on ISIL', The White House,

10 September, available at: http://www.whitehouse.gov/the-press-offi
ce/2014/09/10/statement-president-isil-1, last accessed 27 December 2016.

O'Connell, M. E. (2011), 'How to Lose a Revolution', in A. Stark (ed.),
*The Responsibility to Protect: Challenges & Opportunities in Light of
the Libyan Intervention*, e-International Relations, pp. 15–17, available
at: http://www.e-ir.info/wp-content/uploads/R2P.pdf, last accessed 27
December 2016.

Oxford English Dictionary (2015a), 'Unable, Adj.', *Oxford English
Dictionary*, Oxford: Oxford University Press.

Oxford English Dictionary (2015b), 'Unwilling, Adj.', *Oxford English
Dictionary*, Oxford: Oxford University Press.

Pelton, R. Y. (2011), 'Enter the Drones: An In-Depth Look at Drones,
Somali Reactions, and How the War Might Change', *Somalia Report*, 7
June, available at: http://www.somaliareport.com/index.php/post/1096,
last accessed 27 December 2016.

Peters, A. (2015), 'German Parliament Decides to Send Troops to Combat ISIS
– Based on Collective Self-Defense "in Conjunction With" SC Res. 2249',
EJIL: Talk!, 8 December, available at: http://www.ejiltalk.org/german-
parlament-decides-to-send-troops-to-combat-isis-%e2%88%92-based-on-
collective-self-defense-in-conjunction-with-sc-res-2249/, last accessed 27
December 2016.

Popovski, V. (2011), 'Siblings, but Not Twins: POC and R2P – United
Nations University', *United Nations University*, 1 November, available at:
http://unu.edu/publications/articles/siblings-but-not-twins-poc-and-r2p.
html, last accessed 27 December 2016.

Ramos, J. M. (2013), *Changing Norms Through Actions: The Evolution of
Sovereignty*, Oxford: Oxford University Press.

Reinold, T. (2011) 'State Weakness, Irregular Warfare, and the Right to
Self-Defense Post-9/11', *American Journal of International Law*, 105(2),
pp. 244–86.

Rosenberg, S. and E. Strauss (2012), 'A Common Approach to the
Application of the Responsibility to Protect', in D. Fiott, R. Zuber
and J. Koops (eds), *Operationalizing the Responsibility to Protect: A
Contribution to the Third Pillar Approach*, Brussels: Madariaga – College
of Europe Foundation, pp. 55–72.

Russian Ministry of Foreign Affairs (2014), 'Statement by the Russian
Ministry of Foreign Affairs Regarding the Strikes on the Syrian Territory',
Embassy of the Russian Federation, Washington, DC, 23 September,
available at: http://www.russianembassy.org/article/statement-by-the-
russian-ministry-of-foreign-affairs-regarding-the-strikes-on-the-syrian-
ter, last accessed 27 December 2016.

Ruys, T. (2010), *'Armed Attack' and Article 51 of the UN Charter:
Evolutions in Customary Law and Practice*, Cambridge: Cambridge
University Press.

Ruys, T., N. Verlinden and L. Ferro (2015), 'Digest of State Practice', *Journal on the Use of Force and International Law*, 2(2), pp. 257–98, doi: 10.1080/20531702.2015.1101202, available at: http://www.tandf online.com, last accessed 27 December 2016.

Sassen, S. (1996), *Losing Control? Sovereignty in an Age of Globalization*. University Seminars/Leonard Hastings Schoff Memorial Lectures. New York: Columbia University Press.

Scharf, M. P. (2013) *Customary International Law in Times of Fundamental Change: Recognizing Grotian Moments*, Cambridge: Cambridge University Press.

Security Council Report (2014a), 'July 2014 Monthly Forecast: Iraq', Security Council Report, 30 June, available at: http://www.securitycoun-cilreport.org/monthly-forecast/2014-07/iraq_6.php, last accessed 27 December 2016.

Security Council Report (2014b), 'August 2014 Monthly Forecast: Syria', Security Council Report, 1 August, available at: http://www.security councilreport.org/monthly-forecast/2014-08/syria_10.php, last accessed 27 December 2016.

Security Council Report (2014c), 'September 2014 Monthly Forecast: Syria', Security Council Report, 29 August, available at: http://www. securitycouncilreport.org/monthly-forecast/2014-09/syria_11.php, last accessed 27 December 2016.

Security Council Report (2014d), 'October 2014 Monthly Forecast: Syria', Security Council Report, 30 September, available at: http://www.security councilreport.org/monthly-forecast/2014-10/syria_12.php, last accessed 27 December 2016.

Strange, S. (1996), *The Retreat of the State: The Diffusion of Power in the World Economy*. Cambridge Studies in International Relations 49, Cambridge: Cambridge University Press.

Thakur, R. C. (2015), 'Responsibility to Protect: Ten Years on', United Nations University, 8 June.

United Nations General Assembly (GA) (1970), 'Declaration on Principles of International Law Concerning Friendly Relations and Co-Operation among States in Accordance with the Charter of the United Nations', UN Document A/RES/25/2625, available at: http://www.un-documents.net/ a25r2625.htm, last accessed 27 December 2016.

United Nations General Assembly (GA) (2005), 'World Summit Outcome Document', UN Document A/RES/60/1, available at: http://www. un.org/womenwatch/ods/A-RES-60-1-E.pdf, last accessed 27 December 2016.

United Nations General Assembly and Security Council (GA-UNSC) (2002), 'Identical Letters Dated 15 September 2002 from the Permanent Representative of Georgia to the United Nations Addressed to the Secretary-General and the President of the Security Council', UN

Document A/57/408–S/2002/1033, available at: https://documents-dds-ny.un.org/doc/UNDOC/GEN/N02/591/96/PDF/N0259196.pdf, last accessed 27 December 2016.

United Nations Security Council (UNSC) (1999), 'Resolution 1267'.

United Nations Security Council (UNSC) (2001a), 'Resolution 1373'.

United Nations Security Council (UNSC) (2001b), 'Resolution 1378'.

United Nations Security Council (UNSC) (2002), 'Statement by Russian Federation President V. V. Putin. Annex to the Letter Dated 11 September 2002 from the Permanent Representative of the Russian Federation to the United Nations Addressed to the Secretary-General', UN Document S/2002/1012.

United Nations Security Council (UNSC) (2011a), 'Sixty-Sixth Year. 6490th Meeting', UN Document S/PV.6490.

United Nations Security Council (UNSC) (2011b), 'Security Council Resolution 1970'. UN Document S/RES/1970.

United Nations Security Council (UNSC) (2011c), 'Sixty-Sixth Year. 6491st Meeting', UN Document S/PV.6491.

United Nations Security Council (UNSC) (2011d), 'Resolution 1973. The Situation in Libya', United Nations.

United Nations Security Council (UNSC) (2014a), 'Letter Dated 25 June 2014 from the Permanent Representative of Iraq to the United Nations Addressed to the Secretary-General', UN Document S/2014/440.

United Nations Security Council (UNSC) (2014b), 'Sixty-Ninth Year, 7271st Meeting', UN Document S/PV.7271.

United Nations Security Council (UNSC) (2014c), 'Letter Dated 20 September 2014 from the Permanent Representative of Iraq to the United Nations Addressed to the President of the Security Council', UN Document S/2014/691.

United Nations Security Council (UNSC) (2014d), 'Letter Dated 23 September 2014 from the Permanent Representative of the United States of America to the United Nations Addressed to the Secretary-General', UN Document S/2014/695.

United Nations Security Council (UNSC) (2014e), '69th Year. 7272nd Meeting', UN Document S/PV.7272.

United Nations Security Council (UNSC) (2015a), 'Letter Dated 31 March 2015 from the Chargé d'Affaires A. I. of the Permanent Mission of Canada to the United Nations Addressed to the President of the Security Council', UN Document S/2015/221.

United Nations Security Council (UNSC) (2015b), 'Letter Dated 24 July 2015 from the Chargé d'Affaires A. I. of the Permanent Mission of Turkey to the United Nations Addressed to the President of the Security Council', UN Document S/2015/563.

United Nations Security Council (UNSC) (2015c), 'Letter Dated 9 September 2015 from the Permanent Representative of Australia to the

United Nations Addressed to the President of the Security Council', UN Document S/2015/693.

United Nations Security Council (UNSC) (2015d), 'Provisional Verbatim Record of the 7527th Meeting', UN Document S/PV.7527.

United Nations Security Council (UNSC) (2015e), 'Provisional Verbatim Record of the 7565th Meeting', UN Document S/PV.7565.

United Nations Security Council (UNSC) (2015f), 'Resolution 2249', UN Document S/RES/2249.

United States Department of Justice (DOJ) (2013), 'Department of Justice White Paper. Lawfulness of a Lethal Operation Directed Against a US Citizen Who Is a Senior Operational Leader of Al-Qa'ida or An Associated Force', available at: http://msnbcmedia.msn.com/i/msnbc/sections/news/020413_DOJ_White_Paper.pdf, last accessed 27 December 2016.

Visser, L. 2015, 'Russia's Intervention in Syria', *EJIL: Talk!*, 25 November, available at: http://www.ejiltalk.org/russias-intervention-in-syria/, last accessed 27 December 2016.

Warren, A. and I. Bode (2014), *Governing the Use-of-Force in International Relations. The Post-9/11 US Challenge on International Law*, London: Palgrave Macmillan.

Weiss, T. G. (2011a), 'Whither R2P?', in A. Stark (ed.), *The Responsibility to Protect: Challenges & Opportunities in Light of the Libyan Intervention*, e-International Relations, pp. 7–11, available at: http://www.e-ir.info/wp-content/uploads/R2P.pdf, last accessed 27 December 2016.

Weiss, T. G. (2011b), 'RtoP Alive and Well after Libya', *Ethics & International Affairs*, 25(3), pp. 287–92.

Welsh, J. (2011), 'Civilian Protection in Libya: Putting Coercion and Controversy Back into RtoP', *Ethics & International Affairs*, 25(3), pp. 255–62, doi: 10.1017/S0892679411000207.

Williams, G. D. (2012), 'Piercing the Shield of Sovereignty: An Assessment of the Legal Status of the "Unwilling or Unable" Test', *University of New South Wales Law Journal*, 36(2), pp. 619–41.

Williams, P. D. and A. J. Bellamy (2012), 'Principles, Politics, and Prudence: Libya, the Responsibility to Protect, and the Use of Military Force', *Global Governance*, 18(3), pp. 273–97.

Zaidi, H. (2011), 'Army Chief Wanted More Drone Support', *Dawn*, 19 May, available at: http://www.dawn.com/news/630057, last accessed 27 December 2016.

8

Interventions and the
Limits of the Responsibility to Protect:
Regional Organisations and the Global South

Joseph Hongoh

Introduction

Contemporary discourses and practices of humanitarianism have increasingly sought to transcend the politically contentious debate between perspectives that embrace and legitimise external intervention as necessary to prevent human rights violations, and those that view it as a version of paternalistic liberal internationalism and liberal imperialism. To mediate this split, the doctrine of the Responsibility to Protect (R2P) has gained considerable prominence in theory, analysis and policy. Unanimously adopted by United Nations member states at the 2005 World Summit, R2P is premised on the moral advocacy that prevention of mass atrocities is a shared responsibility and a matter of collaboration between states and the international community. Further, the mechanism for executing this shared responsibility necessitates that some constraints are placed upon the meaning and practice of sovereignty.

Thus, under the principle of sovereignty as responsibility, it is argued that states have a primary duty to protect their citizens from war crimes, crimes against humanity, genocide and ethnic cleansing. However, if states are unable or unwilling to protect their citizens from such atrocities, the responsibility is transferred to the international community. On this account, R2P emerges as a doctrine that seeks to transform how we conceive of humanitarianism in relation to state sovereignty. Responses to gross and systematic violations of human rights will henceforth begin by an articulation of state sovereignty as responsibility. This, it was argued, represented a departure from humanitarian intervention that was condemned as an affront to sovereignty (ICISS 2001; Evans 2006; Cramer-Flood 2008). A decade has passed since the idea of R2P was introduced to the world of humanitarianism. Over that period, R2P has done exceedingly well in mobilising global public interest and concern about human rights violations and, in the process, has helped establish the principles of civilian protection. However, its emergence and international presence has been accompanied by the persistence of the very dilemma it was expected to resolve: how to justify intervention on the basis of principle rather than political expediency (Hopgood 2014: 182). In other words, how can the international community enforce the responsibility to protect victims of mass atrocities, without taking away their sovereignty by embracing the contentious language of humanitarian intervention?

This chapter examines the activities of regional organisations (ROs) in the Global South as practices of unmaking and remaking the idea of sovereignty as responsibility. It suggests that the struggle to navigate the tension surrounding sovereignty as the responsibility to protect obscures, rather than enables, productive engagements with the concept and practice of intervention. It argues that the focus on the capacities of the territorial state and its inhabitants, as the locus for articulating sovereignty and responsibility, has resulted in a thinner, and historically contested, understanding of sovereignty and mechanisms for exercising responsibility. Drawing on examples from Africa, this chapter suggests that integrating ROs within the international–regional–national axes of R2P potentially restricts the broader conception of sovereignty as responsibility and the practice of intervention. This is because for many of these organisations, the idea of sovereignty, and the practices for exercising responsibility, are both transnational and transhistorical.

The outcome of this differential conception of sovereignty as responsibility, the chapter suggests, is a recharacterisation of both sovereignty and the R2P. On the one hand, sovereignty as responsibility manifests as an expansive national, cross-border and regional undertaking that is also attuned to cultural, economic and political imperatives and interests. On the other hand, the universality of the R2P is rendered conditional, context specific and a component of bilateral and regional relational interests. This chapter therefore suggests that, in the contemporary context, where conflicts and crises are complex and interconnected, ROs are better placed to offer a broader integrative approach to intervention in ways that combine the protection of human rights with broader goals of regional peace, stability and economic development. In this way, the chapter argues, concepts such as sovereignty and responsibility are expressed in broader political transnational categories beyond R2P, to include struggles for realisation of social and economic rights, transnational human solidarity and international justice and equality.

The chapter develops in three sections. It begins by engaging with the discourse of sovereignty as responsibility as an operational framework for the R2P. It shows how the knitting of both concepts together allows for continued reproduction of floating ideas that, at times, appear removed from the context they claim to represent. The incorporation of regional organisations into the R2P framework has an implicit effect of undermining some of their struggles against particular forms of framing sovereignty and responsibility. Section two gives an alternative reading of sovereignty as responsibility, which invests in broader and enduring conceptions of intervention. It demonstrates how regional organisations in Africa have perennially engaged with the questions of sovereignty, responsibility, protection and human solidarity within the broader frames of political and economic empowerment and emancipation. In the final section, this chapter shows how broader conceptions of intervention have the potential effect of producing transnational sovereignty, in ways that are not imagined within R2P. The result, this chapter argues, may lead to implementation of R2P within the conditions of sovereignty that are determined by ROs. Rather than a conditional sovereignty, there is potential for a conditional R2P.

Responsibility to Protect and the reconceptualisation of sovereignty

For many advocates of the R2P, the relationship between the founding principles of the doctrine and the claim to sovereignty ought to be understood as mutually reinforcing rather than antagonistic. Paradigmatically, R2P is framed as a doctrine of human protection that sits between, and necessarily combines, the liberal state-centred conception of sovereignty with the post-liberal international conception of responsibility. Thus, in unanimously adopting the R2P principles at the 2005 World Summit, UN member states made a distinction between two frames of sovereignty as responsibility: the local and planetary.

Locally, states exercise their sovereignty to act responsibly to protect their population from war crimes, genocide, ethnic cleansing and crimes against humanity. Conventionally, this reproduces the liberal order, where provision of security and protection rests on sovereign power within the confines of the prevailing social contract. Where sovereign states are deemed to be unable or unwilling to uphold their obligation in the liberal sense, they become subject to post-liberal order through the residual responsibility of the international community. As noted in the International Commission on Intervention and State Sovereignty (ICISS) report, 'where a population is suffering serious harm, as a result of internal war, insurgency, repression or state failure, and the state in question is unwilling or unable to halt or avert it, the principle of non-intervention yields to the international responsibility to protect' (ICISS 2001: xi). This double conception of responsibility has ensured that the concept and practice of sovereignty is an obligation and not a right. Further, as an obligation, the exercise of sovereignty for the purpose of enforcing the civilian protection principle is a shared duty between national and international actors.

It has been argued that this conception of responsibility and the need to protect vulnerable populations clears any lingering doubt about the mutually reinforcing relationship between the concept of sovereignty and the R2P doctrine. Proceeding from that understanding, proponents of R2P have continued to make the case that ideas embedded in the doctrine correspond to and complement the practice of sovereignty. Edward Luck, the UN special adviser on the Responsibility to Protect has, for example, maintained that R2P has deep roots in the very notion of sovereignty. According to Luck, the doctrine reinforces the four sources of sovereignty identified by Stephen Krasner, namely domestic sovereignty, interdependence sovereignty, international legal sovereignty and Westphalian sovereignty (Luck 2009: 12; see also Krasner 1999: 9). In contrast to those who have argued that the R2P doctrine would be used as a new tool for imperial domination and to control smaller and weaker states, Luck makes the clarification that R2P 'would not impinge on interdependence sovereignty and might even bolster it when the state lacks capacity or is under siege by armed groups ready to ignore their own protection responsibilities' (2009: 15).

The perspective that weaker and smaller states should embrace rather than reject R2P is further amplified by the argument that the R2P is anti-political and apolitical and, therefore, should be excluded from the toxic and politically charged conventional modes of categorising intervention. Here, the shared analytical ground is that R2P reflects the international community's will and capacity to rise above politics in the protection of vulnerable populations (Brown

2013). This is seen in the way that the ICISS report sought to replace the notion of the 'right to intervene' with that of a 'responsibility to protect' (ICISS 2001). In the process, the R2P drafters took 'the issue of dealing with mass atrocity crimes out of the realm of world politics and placed it in a more elevated context where political considerations will no longer apply' (Brown 2013: 441). The understanding here is that in the pursuit of transnational solidarity, R2P-type interventions would easily wade into the 'toxic politics of international humanitarianism' in ways that 'would not constitute an assault on sovereignty' (Brown 2013: 441).

Beyond these arguments, other R2P scholars have sought to show how, far from signaling a new language of imperial domination in the already unequal and uneven distribution of power in the modern world order, sovereignty has historically been contingent and conditional. Luke Glenville (forthcoming) for example, makes the case that the enjoyment of rights to sovereignty comes with the obligation 'that the behaviours of sovereigns be reconciled to the justifications for sovereignty'. Likewise, Francis Deng (2010: 354) makes a similar point, arguing that for states to make claims about sovereign rights, and in the process qualify as legitimate and respected members of international society, they must honor the obligation to protect their population. Deng further argues that the conditional nature of sovereignty is based on the notion that states are expected to be accountable to the international community in terms of how they discharge their responsibility for the welfare of their citizens (2010: 355). Contained in these arguments is the view that states are recognised not as free agents, but rather as part of an international community of states who 'are expected to adhere to that community's evolving norms regarding what is legitimate and permissible' (Etzioni 2006: 72). The implication here is that the practice of sovereignty should be understood as the exercise of equality of representation by states in achieving their obligation as responsible global governors.

In drawing proximate linkages between R2P and sovereignty, these scholars mobilise repertoires of justifications that place regional organisations at the intermediary point between the demands of the international community, and the activities of individual states as far as the conduct of sovereignty as responsibility is concerned. According to the report of the UN Secretary-General on '[t]he role of regional and sub-regional arrangements in implementing the responsibility to protect' (UNSG 2011: 1), regional and global actors are partners in civilian protection. In a time of crisis, therefore, regional and subregional bodies 'can play a critical facilitating role as political and operational bridges between global standards and local and national action' (2011: 4). Further, it is argued that proximity to the contexts of crisis make regional actors reliable partners in detecting failures to the realisation of full and peaceful expression of sovereignty within the UN Charter and the principles of international law. Accordingly, ROs can serve as 'conduits for the two-way flow of information, ideas, and insights between stakeholders at the local and national levels and those at the global level' (UNSG 2011: 8).

This implies that global–regional linkages situate ROs in some role as local enforcers of global terms of sovereignty and responsibility. They accomplish that on the two accounts suggested by Deng above. Firstly, they pass judgement on who in the region qualifies as a legitimate and respected member of the international community. Secondly, they identify those who have failed in achieving sovereign accountability and, therefore, register them as subjects of international intervention. From the operational imperatives of R2P, the responsibility and 'duty of care' enjoyed by regional organisations as agents of peoples' security interests is an asset that can be leveraged by the international community in building consensus and gaining legitimacy and consent for intervention (Newman 2015: 125). As evidenced in the case of Libya, UN–RO cooperation further ensures greater convergence in flagging the notion that sovereignty is responsibility. From that logic, the mode of intervention and the agencies that intervene are seen as benevolent actors implementing the humanitarian duty of care within the spirit and practice of global governance. What emerges here is an assumption that sovereignty and responsibility are floating concepts that can easily be reproduced without necessarily subjecting their meanings to the historical and contemporary contexts in which they emerge.

Challenging the practice of sovereignty as responsibility

For critics of how sovereignty is conceived within the frames of the R2P, there are problematic issues that are glossed over when sovereignty is reproduced as a floating concept. To borrow from Homi K. Bhabha, one is confronted with discourses 'that attempt to give a hegemonic 'normality' to the uneven development and differential, often disadvantaged, histories of nations, races, communities, peoples' (1994: 171). Indeed, in his analysis of modern conceptions of sovereignty, international relations scholar Siba Grovogui has challenged the idea that modern sovereignty obtains from the Peace of Westphalia and that it has thus led to 'an international order of relatively autonomous states' (Grovogui 2002: 315–16). He contends that this 'Westphalian commonsense' reproduces a 'particular conception of the world to effect a specific understanding of international reality' (2002: 316). There is, he notes, a need for re-examination of the idea of sovereignty, state, and security. Grovogui challenges the popular view that the notion of a 'uniform international system of sovereignty' has been in existence 'across time and space' (p. 316). Instead, he argues that the practice of sovereignty has operated on the spectrum of 'concurrent but parallel coordinates that prescribe and legitimise specific patterns of actions in each region of the world' (p. 316). Accordingly, he observes, the current regimes of sovereignty have consistently 'produced modulations of power, interests and identities that favour European entities at the expense of African ones' (p. 316). As a result, any comparison of states based on their exercise of sovereignty and responsibility will produce the image of a resilient European state on the one hand, and a weak and failing African state on the other.

Giving the example of Switzerland and Belgium on the one hand, and today's Democratic Republic of the Congo on the other, Grovogui argues that Westphalian common sense gives rise to theoretical modulations that favourably compare Belgium as a successful 'quasi-state' against a 'failed quasi-state' of Congo (2002: 317). This is despite the fact that it is on the very question of colonial conquest, exploitation and post-colonial destabilisation of the Congo that Belgium attained a modicum of sovereignty.

The implication here is that the international system that has continued to dominate since the end of the Second World War has always been unequal. Where notions such as rights, citizenship and sovereignty were upheld as constitutive frames for membership in the international system, the reality of international inequality embedded in the system denied rights, citizenship, and sovereignty to much of the colonised society (Mamdani 2010; Hobson 2012). Such inequality was further sustained by modes of theorising international relations that hardly question the absence of a level playing field of juridically equal sovereign states (Hobson 2012). In effect, Hobson argues, Eurocentric international relations entrenched a system of hierarchy that 'awards hyper-sovereignty to Western states' and grants Eastern states 'conditional sovereignty that can be withdrawn if civilised conditions are not met' (2012: 19). When the assumed universality and equality of sovereignty in an anarchic international system is not attuned to the conditions it claims to speak about, and when such assumptions produce a bifurcated international system under the frames of sovereignty as responsibility, it risks misrepresenting the very idea of responsibility and the attendant goal of protecting human life.

Indeed, a major element of that misrepresentation of responsibility resides in how sources of threats to human life are conceived, and the particular errors and omissions that are concealed within such conceptions. Many of these relate to how the doctrine of responsibility to protect embraces the post-Cold War moment of international order in defining the contours of the new international humanitarianism, while at the same time relying on ideas of progress, civilisation and emancipation and their roots in 'Western international society' (Gruffydd Jones 2006: 7). According to this language, what it means to speak about responsibility entails the determination of the performance of the sovereign nation-state against the international standards of humanitarianism. In applying the principle of sovereignty as responsibility, the language of R2P endeavors to make a distinction between the national and the international, differentiating politics within the domestic sphere of the state from those that occur as part of interstate relations. The nation emerges as the sole agent of its own fate, the principle source of, and antidote against, potential threats to human life.

More fundamentally, as a new humanitarian order, R2P retains the prerogative of determining the boundaries of what constitutes vulnerability and the means of response. As has been argued by Mamdani (2010: 54), R2P 'describes as "human" the population to be protected, and as humanitarian the crisis they suffer from, the intervention that promises to rescue them, and the agencies that seek to carry out intervention'. The result is a conception and practice of responsibility as politics, which entrenches difference and separation. Rather than embodying the articulation of transnational and transcontinental relations of struggle and solidarity, responsibility is localised, bounded and internalised as a problem within the territorial borders of the state, through successive reproduction of its weaknesses and failures. Paradoxically, it is also through the same system of distinguishing the state from the system of states, and the national from the international, that the foundational elements of interstate law such as 'the rights of sovereignty' and territorial integrity are suspended in the pursuit of the protection of human life (Doucet and de

Larrinaga 2011: 130). Separated from the national on one end, the international re-emerges as the avatar of emancipation and salvation that creates the conditions of possibility for the realisation of human life and dignity.

While these may appear obvious in the context of responding to threats against civilian populations, they are equally disquieting and, in some contexts, invite skepticism about the moral imperatives of the R2P (see, for example, De Waal 2007; Çubukçu 2013). In particular, they elicit debates about what it means to speak about intervention, as well as global human solidarity and equality. Granted, R2P's idea of knitting together sovereignty and responsibility makes its case by clarifying what it has been assumed to be: 'just another name for humanitarian intervention' (Evans 2008: 56). The aim here, it is argued, is to eliminate the right of Western nations to militarily intervene and instead focus on responsibility of 'failing states' (Chandler 2009) to protect their populations.

It is surprising that the application of such a shared goal appears to have expanded the right of intervention by external actors in two senses. First, the right has been devolved to 'failing states' within the terms, and under the watchful eye, of the international community and the international human rights regime. Second, it has suspended the terms of devolution and replaced it with an international order for human solidarity in the face of an unable or unwilling state. In other words, both shared and contested practices of intervention are joined together in implementing R2P. But, as has been argued, the history of international humanitarian order, international morality and ethics is also a history characterised by gradated sovereignty, hollowed-out responsibility and uninterrupted articulation of hierarchy and difference in the international system. It follows that it is also essential that R2P ought to re-examine the terms of intervention to prevent mass atrocity crimes, and the need to recover equality of sovereignty and responsibility in the international system. The premise under which such recovery takes place is not to be found in how R2P navigates and expands its normative ideals: responsibility to prevent, responsibility to react and responsibility to rebuild. Rather, it resides in the implications of processing those ideals as warrants to deploy international power and morality in the non-Western world where questions about, and the meaning of, responsibility, global human equality, and solidarity have remained contested, both historically and in contemporary contexts.

Here, it is important to draw attention to the often-missed realities of intervention when the subject, object and context of intervention are bound up in promises of global human solidarity, and emancipation by way of a thin definition of what impedes the realisation of such promises. It is worth remembering that in contemporary contexts of conflict and crises, the 'extreme, conscience-shocking' cases of mass atrocities that Gareth Evans (2008: 294) spoke about and which are the subject of the R2P doctrine – and, therefore, invite international condemnation and a sense of obligation to act – are not isolated problems of human barbarism and irrationality in territorially and temporally defined contexts.

Rather, mass atrocity crimes are, at once, enmeshed in contested claims of historical and contemporary injustices – social, political and economic – that take place within and beyond the territorial spheres of the state. While they are powerful in alerting humanity's conscience, they are not analytically removed from other forms of mass violence such as counterinsurgency and the war on terror that are argued to be legitimately sanctioned. In fact, there is no shortage of evidence to suggest the existence of complex connectedness and blurred distinctions between mass atrocity crimes and other forms of violence that are tolerable under international law and the international humanitarian order (Mamdani 2010: 57). When advocates of the R2P doctrine confine their attention to the problem of mass atrocity crimes rather than the broader contexts of conflicts and crises, under which bare life is rendered vulnerable, they partake in the reproduction of international responsibility as an international system of human inequality. Their positions are seen to show little departure from the language of imperial power that promised civilisation and emancipation through colonial intervention, systems of trusteeship and post-colonial tutelage (Mamdani 2010; Grovogui 2011a; 2011b).

Accordingly, when the 9/11 Commission Report (2004: 362) claims 'that the American homeland is the planet', and proceeds to wage war on terror as a form of intervention that is unhinged from any spatial or temporal grounding, there is a need to question the claims about national, international and global security under which such intervention becomes justified. The reality that the protection of certain categories of vulnerable (and innocent) populations takes place by a simultaneous process of rendering other populations vulnerable but not protectable must also be questioned. At the very least, R2P advocates the need to reconcile the conflicting responsibilities of protecting civilian populations at the risk of crimes against humanity, and claims about the responsibility to protect the world from the risk of failed states or the terrorist organisations that thrive in them.

A thin conception of atrocity crimes raises questions about what it means to speak about the responsibility to rebuild. The drafters of the R2P doctrine envisaged a world where the responsibilities to prevent, react and rebuild could be read as at once interconnected concepts and practices, while at the same time being delinked from humanitarian imperialism. Accordingly, much as R2P advocates continue to show how the R2P differs from Western conceptions of the right to intervene, implementation practices continue to reproduce similarities. On the contrary, implementation of R2P and 'the right to intervene' appear to share common ground in the principal view that 'international peace and individual rights are best advanced through cosmopolitan frameworks whereby democratic and peaceful states take a leading responsibility for ensuring the interests of common humanity' (Chandler 2004: 60). Two problems arise when R2P's implementation practices emerge as a carbon copy of the right to intervene. Firstly, the responsibility to protect vulnerable populations is also the responsibility to advance the intervener's political and economic interests. In most cases, the economic and political interests of the international community often trump arguments for alternative approaches to ending crimes against humanity. In the case of Libya, for example, the African Union's call for dialogue and a negotiated framework went unheeded by the international community.

Soon after the intervention, foreign companies were queuing for a slice of Libyan wealth. British Defence Secretary Phillip Hammond, for instance, urged British firms to head to Libya, as it was, as he put it, 'open for business' (cited in Adetunji 2011). Underlining the significance of the dispensation to British interests, Hammond said he expected 'British companies, even British sales directors, [to be] packing their suitcases and looking to get out to Libya and take part in the reconstruction of that country as soon as they can' (cited in Adetunji 2011). When, as ICISS (2001: 12) states, 'changing the language of the debate does not of course change the substantive issues which have to be addressed', the argument that the R2P departs from that of the 'right to intervene' does not inspire confidence among states in the Global South. Secondly, as with many instances of liberal peace-building, implementing the R2P in ways that reproduce images of rights to intervene risks undermining opportunities for structural transformation and meaningful democratic reforms. This is because the choices of intervention largely privilege ending of mass violence and emergence of conditions of negative peace.

We see glimpses of this in, for example, the case of Libya, where the international community's focus on ending violence between and saving the people of Benghazi overlooked the complexities of historical and contemporary dynamics of politics and social relations. While proponents of R2P concluded that Libya reflected 'a new politics of protection' (Bellamy and Williams 2011: 825), such politics of protection were written on planes of global democratic deficits. The promise of protection, liberation and ultimately emancipatory democracy to the people of Benghazi was contingent on denial of the same to the people of Libya, including those in Benghazi. The lesson that is missed here is how some of these historical and contemporary complexities of identities and relations, including religion, ethnicity and clan structures, 'hold more promise for creating sustainable reciprocity-based and socially reinforced norms that reduce suffering, even if they fail to deliver on the promise of global liberal norms' (Hopgood 2013: 21).

Regional organisations and transnational sovereignty

These discussions on the concept and practice of the R2P demonstrate why the principle of sovereignty as responsibility is a hotly contested issue. In thinking about the role of regional organisations in implementing R2P, perhaps it is important to pay attention to how regional organisations in areas of weak states respond to gaps left by how R2P conceives of humanitarian intervention. As discussed in the section below, an emboldened conception of crimes against humanity, global human solidarity and equality, as well as mechanisms of implementing responsibilities to react and rebuild, offer a different lens for conceiving sovereignty as responsibility. To borrow from Mustapha Kamal Pasha's conception of the subject of human security, the subject of the responsibility to protect doctrine is 'not preconfigured as in conventional accounts but exposed to mutation and transformation in the very act of encountering threats to survival' (2013: 4). A thicker conception places the subject of the R2P not as a mere recipient of bundles of protection defined in advance, but rather as a constitutive part of a broader definition of the threats to human life and the existence of different locally generated and contextually informed possibilities for responding to the threats. Three ways in which states in the Global South have imagined and practiced transnational solidarity illuminate how we may begin to imagine sovereignty as responsibility.

Firstly, contrary to anti-political and apolitical beliefs that underpin the R2P, regional organisations in the Global South have internalised intervention as inherently political, both historically and in contemporary contexts. The idea of responsibility to self and to others has been part of the Global South's collective struggle for the moral transformation of the international order (Grovogui 2013). It defined the trajectories of North–South relations in terms of contestations around sovereignty and a struggle for a different international order. Responsibility and human solidarity set the pace for debates within the Pan-African and Pan-Asian movements, the Bandung Conference and later Non-Aligned Movements (Burton 2010; Carment et al. 2016). It is also worth remembering that the Global South's argument for a collective conception of sovereignty and responsibility was lost when the sovereign territorial state was identified as the logical context for shaping international relations and the politics of human solidarity. What followed such a loss was the successive weakening of the state, unrealised self-determination and the demise of regional solidarity under the weight of Cold War imperatives, European neocolonialism and American globalism. The post-Cold War period presented conditions of possibility for recovering responsibility and sovereignty.

Such recovery of responsibility, it can be argued, has emerged through steady consolidation of solidarity through regional organisations as an exercise in self-making and self-determination. Such recovery of solidarity has enabled the Global South to reorient their political claims within what David Scott has called 'new problem-space[s], new context questions that define our present' (1999: 224). We see, for example, how the African Union (AU) challenged the invocation of R2P in Libya. Despite the UNSC and NATO's commitment to military intervention and regime change, the AU suggested negotiated mediation and new constitutional dispensation as ways to democratically reconstitute Libyan politics. Jean Ping, the AU Commission Chairperson, reminded the international community that the African Charter on Democracy, Governance and Election adopted in 2007 commits member states 'towards a regional and collective approach to democracy building and consolidation' (Ping 2011). The AU's approach to non-indifference, he argued, seeks to reconstitute 'African politics from being a zero sum to a positive sum game, characterised by reciprocal behaviour and legitimate relations between the governors and the governed' (2011). He concluded that 'Africa's destiny will be shaped by how much Africa constructs a sense of common identity based, not on the narrow lenses of state, race or religion, but constructed on Africa's belief in democracy, good governance and unity as the most viable option to mediate, reconcile and accommodate our individual and collective interests' (2011).

Three years later, the Inter-Governmental Authority on Development (IGAD), a subregional organisation that covers East Africa and the Horn of Africa, undertook a negotiated mediation process when South Sudan descended into political crisis. IGAD's mediation process was accompanied by a Commission of Inquiry established by the AU to look into the causes of the crisis and make 'recommendations on how to move the country forward in terms of unity, cooperation and sustainable development' (AUCISS 2015: 3). The Commission noted that a sustainable solution rested upon understanding the context of the crisis and articulating it as 'an outcome of multiple causes: historical, political, moral, and economic' (AUCISS 2015: 54). It noted that the 'peace and reconciliation agenda' in South Sudan should 'proceed from the position that a genuine national dialogue must involve various stakeholders, build from the grassroots, and recognise the significance of traditional conflict resolution mechanisms that are appropriately linked with a national institution that drives the peace and reconciliation agenda' (AUCISS 2015: 275). A common characteristic shared by both AUCISS and IGAD is the embrace of the crisis's complexity, especially the social and political relations that transcend spatiotemporal identities associated with South Sudan as a state. Rather than isolate the affected state as failing on responsibility duties and therefore subject to international intervention, both initiatives embrace it as an integral part of the geopolitical dynamics of the region.

Secondly, the fact that regional organisations in the Global South are the vanguards of practices that would later result in the doctrine of the R2P does not necessarily compel them to implement the principles as framed. Mechanisms for exercising responsibility are largely dictated by geopolitical dynamics and relations within the region, and not just by the desire to be seen as good citizens of international society. Accordingly, there is potential for a diversity of debates and decisions about what constitutes crimes against humanity and determination of criminal responsibilities. Even though they have been challenged as being inconsistent with the international community's terms of responsibility, these debates and decisions have emerged as avenues for communicating the diversities of the languages of sovereignty as responsibility.

Here, it is important to draw attention to the various protocols that originated from subregional organisations in Great Lakes region and West Africa, but have since been adopted as an amendment to the Statute of the African Court of Justice and Human Rights. As noted by Siba Grovogui, one particular protocol 'that has drawn most attention is the association of illicit exploitation of natural resources with crimes against humanity' (2013: 89). Under Article 28L bis,

> [i]llicit exploitation of natural resources means any of the following acts if they are of a serious nature affecting the stability of a state, region or the Union: a) Concluding an agreement to exploit resources, in violation of the principle of peoples sovereignty over their natural resources; b) Concluding with state authorities an agreement to exploit natural resources, in violation of the legal and regulatory procedures of the State concerned; c) Concluding an agreement to exploit natural resources through corrupt practices; d) Concluding an agreement to exploit natural resources that is clearly one-sided; e) Exploiting natural resources without any agreement with the State concerned; f) Exploiting natural resources without complying with norms relating to the protection of the environment and the security of the people and the staff; and g) Violating the norms and standards established by the relevant natural resource certification mechanism. (African Union 2012: 26)

Clearly, there are reasons to believe that such a list goes beyond a mere depiction of 'white criminality and retaliation against the West' (Grovogui 2013: 89). The underlying logic here is to focus not on observable outcomes of state failure and state irresponsibility, but rather, to shift attention to the larger vexed context of sources and causes of failure, the challenges they pose to the stability and exercise of sovereign responsibility and the need to articulate them within the language of international law and human solidarity. More than that, they signal how eradication of threats to sovereign power is key to guaranteeing protection of vulnerable populations. In articulating these issues at regional and subregional levels rather than just the national, African states are making a case for a transnational conception of sovereignty as responsibility, especially in instances where the national sphere has been hollowed out of any form of sovereignty and international equality. Such transnational conceptions and recovery of sovereignty are, in turn, avenues for pursuing meaningful responsibility, engaging in emancipatory politics and consolidation of regional security.

Thirdly, in much of Africa, the struggle for transnational sovereignty – and therefore transnational solidarity – has been, in part, aimed at fashioning legal and political frameworks that recognise the history of interdependence between states, and the realisation that the threats to the 'good human life' need to be framed in transnational and transcontinental terms. Conceptually, such awakening begins with a no confidence vote against methodological nationalism's naturalisation of the territorial state as the locus of human emancipation. Here, one is reminded of the changing historical conditions that at once seem to erode and affirm the relevance of the nation-state under the weight of globalisation and the emergence of post-national politics. Evident here is the reality that what Gary Wilder (2015: 4) calls 'the presumptive unity of culture, nationality, and citizenship' has generated an ill-fitting garment that undermines, rather than enables, the realisation of human emancipation and political freedom. We see, for example, where the 'North–South partnerships are typically restricted either to neo-colonial patron–client relations or neoliberal free-trade zones' (Wilder 2015: 252). Rather than focus on the performance of each state in averting threats to the 'good life' and ensuring political freedom, states in Africa are engaging in forms of interventions that recreate the politics of democratic participation and political solidarity by recasting relations between people and their sovereign power beyond the national sphere.

For example, the International Conference on the Great Lakes Region (ICGLR) recognises the challenging task of state-centric approaches to peace and security. Under the Protocol on Development of Border Zones and the Promotion of Human Security, the ICGLR underscores the transnationality of threats to human security, which include poverty, smuggling, organised crime, terrorism, drug trafficking and the flow of small arms and light weapons (ICGLR 2007). A notable feature of their analysis is that 'conflicts in the GLR revolve around contestation over the idea of the state (ideologies around which state politics are organised), physical base (population and resources) and institutional framework of the states' (ICGLR 2007: 1). The artificiality of borders, the ICGLR protocol notes, has led to splits in communities, 'making it impossible for them to move their goods and services across especially when conflicts emerge' (2007: 1). In addressing these threats, the Protocol provided for a border security and development framework that operates from the premise that transformation of conflicts and crisis should start with investing in 'security generating variables for state, regional and community socio-economic and political reproduction' (2007: 2). Such a process, the Protocol notes, can only take place through a regional approach to development. Accordingly, the Protocol recognises, among others, that:

1. The first core beneficiaries are communities living across frontiers. It will allow them to cooperate and add value to their common resources while ignoring artificial divisive borderlines;
2. The states will benefit through increased community-based security generating economic activities. It will also increase its tax base, while reducing the costs of insecurity;
3. International development partners will be able to participate in regional activities such as supranational environmental protection that benefit groups across frontiers. (ICGLR 2007: 2)

What these efforts reveal is that at the local level, the idea of intervention has often acquired a complex and multifaceted meaning beyond that imagined in classical international humanitarianism. While the language of R2P identifies its object of protection as humans in their individual capacity, many regional organisations in the Global South have intervened in ways that recognise the protractedness of social and political relations and the need for alternative approaches to sovereignty and responsibility. Rather than being a relational concept that is 'at the centre rather than periphery of governance' and aligned with 'the duty of care' and accountability to international regimes, sovereignty here is imagined as the capacity to imagine the exceptional. It includes a post-national democratic participation that appreciates the limits of the modern territorial state and the role of local communities in complementing security provision.

Implications for the Responsibility to Protect

The United Nations Security Council Resolution 1973 on the situation in Libya contains a contradiction. On the one hand, the Council determined that Libya had lost its sovereignty by breaching its conditions and, therefore, was subject to international intervention to protect its civilian population. The imposition of a no-fly zone and the authorisation of member states 'to take all necessary measures to protect civilians and civilian populated areas under threat of attack in Libyan Arab Jamahiriya' (UNSC 2011) were interpreted as an endorsement of military intervention in Libya. This is despite the fact that the National Transitional Council of Libya had requested the same international community 'to fulfill its obligations to protect the Libyan people from any further genocide and crimes against humanity without any direct military intervention on Libya soil' (INTC 2011). Such intervention proceeded even after the African Union, the international organisation that represented African states, including Libya, had proposed and even laid the groundwork for a mediated (and peaceful) settlement out of the political crisis.

On the other hand, the Council, through the same resolution, reaffirmed 'its strong commitment to the sovereignty, independence, territorial integrity and national unity of the Libyan Arab Jamahiriya' (UNSC 2011). If, as has been argued elsewhere, Libya was an example of implementing the R2P doctrine (see, for example, Bellamy and Williams 2011; Evans 2013), then the contradiction contained in this resolution and the events that followed say much about how intervention is conceived of within the R2P doctrine. It may also explain why regional organisations in the Global South may be skeptical about supporting the implementation of the sovereignty as responsibility principle, despite generally accepting its basic tenets.

Protecting vulnerable populations from mass atrocities is a key plank in intervention and transnational humanitarian solidarity. States have generally accepted their responsibility in protecting their citizens. Furthermore, there is currently a universal consensus on the importance of R2P norms in supporting states to protect their population. But just as it is important to reiterate the commitment to 'end mass atrocities once and for all' (ICISS 2001), so too it is important to articulate the problem of mass violence and political crisis in broader terms if intervention is to be accepted as compatible with sovereignty. Transnational solidarity within the language of R2P is tilted towards putting out fires when they break out, rather than challenging particular norms of international politics and neoliberal ways of war (Rosow and George 2015: 124) that continue to define the tangents of mass violence, human precarity and destabilisation of peace.

Consequently, R2P appears to have less appetite for engaging with the local structures of transnational solidarities and human emancipation that are part of everyday practices of responsibility in the Global South. As we have seen in the case of the ICGLR above, these local structures not only draw from enduring social relations, local capacities, cultural values and indigenous practices, but also frame their solidarities within the continuous struggles against global political and economic forces. Tellingly, and contrary to the R2P framework, these local transnational solidarities begin by integrating, rather than isolating, the state in defining threats to humanity. Many regional organisations in Africa are now moving towards integrated economic zones, where strategies for the protection of populations promote social and economic programmes, rather than expansive military spending and reduced state resources. The result is a thicker conception of sovereignty as responsibility, grounded in concrete political realities and everyday challenges of governance.

Apart from the failure to fashion the language of responsibility within thicker and locally attentive forms of transnational sociopolitical solidarities, R2P is yet to find an answer to the problem of divided sovereignty, and therefore, the problem of responsibility as an expression of the interests of global powers. Clearly, the problem of mass violence and atrocities call for genuine responsibility for, and moral solidarity with, the struggles to promote human rights. And yet, in implementing R2P's pillars of reacting and rebuilding, the international community has shown little departure from Eurocentric ideas of civilisation and transformation of social order. Here, the interests of Western powers appear to precede their commitment to solidarity with the suffering. In Libya for example, the intervention to protect the civilian population turned into a project of regime change and an opportunity for foreign companies to 'pack their bags' and head to Libya for business. In Côte d'Ivoire, the interest of France as a former colonial power and a major shareholder in the Ivorian economy could not be divorced from the level of military power deployed to restore order. To some, such a thin conception of intervention invariably persists as an exemplifier of the West's commitment to international solidarity and emancipatory politics through regimes of human rights, freedom and democracy. To others, it exemplifies how the regime of global governance isolates weaker states and ignores their values and contributions to the global responsibility to protect. In the case of Libya, the African Union was sidelined within the global R2P civilian population. The regional body's call for a negotiated settlement was understood as different from, and in opposition to, that of the international community. Right now, Libya is seen as a toxic situation that no one wants to fully engage with in terms of the policy reforms that are required as part of the responsibility to rebuild. Four years after the fall of Qaddafi, a functioning state, political stability and democracy remain a long way away.

Conclusion

As Hofmann and Jütersonke have stated, 'the capacity of regional organisations to resolve crises (both within their own region and elsewhere) varies considerably, as do their respective interests, ambitions and agendas. As a result, they add a further layer of complexity to UN negotiations playing themselves out in the Security Council and General Assembly' (2012: 134). As discussed in this chapter, attempts to resolve the tension that surrounds the principle of sovereignty as responsibility remains a contested idea in respect of intervention. For many regional organisations in the Global South, the idea of responsibility to self and to others had always been at the heart of decolonialisation, self-determination and the moral transformation of the international order. Such a conception of responsibility has, conceptually and geographically, broadly engaged with what constitutes threats to the good life as well as transnational mechanisms for addressing these threats. In doing so, sovereignty as responsibility has, in many ways, assumed a transnational turn. The processes that produce such transnational approaches have been less about implementing international norms and more about responding to local economic, political and social solidarities and realities. Articulated as such, intervention has been an ongoing process of human solidarity and emancipation.

Such a conception and practice of sovereignty as responsibility challenges one of the founding principles of R2P – that states have primary responsibility for the protection of civilian populations. If regional organisations in the Global South are to be local partners in implementing R2P, there has to be a way out of the contestation between thin and thick conceptions of responsibility, and what that means for sovereignty. The lessons from Libya and South Sudan show that the gap between R2P and regional organisations needs further narrowing. While the former showed the limitations of state-centric conceptions of sovereignty as responsibility, the latter offers promise as to how a transnational conception of sovereignty presents an opportunity for broader and thicker articulation of intervention. The post-Cold War world offered conditional possibilities for greater transnational solidarity and articulation of emancipatory politics beyond the nation-state. The effect is a more expansive and transnational conception of sovereignty as responsibility, and in the process, intervention for human solidarity. Such an expansion has the possibility of rendering R2P's conception of sovereignty more conditional.

References

Adetunji, J. (2011) 'British firms urged to "pack suitcases" in rush for Libya business', *The Guardian*, 21 October, available at: http://www.theguard ian.com/world/2011/oct/21/british-firms-libya-business, last accessed 27 December 2016.

African Union (2012), 'Protocol on the Amendments of the Protocol on the Statute of the African Court of Justice and Human Rights', available at: https://africlaw.files.wordpress.com/2012/05/au-final-court-protocol-as-adopted-by-the-ministers-17-may.pdf, last accessed 27 December 2016.

African Union Commission of Inquiry on South Sudan (AUCISS) (2015), 'Final Report of the African Union Commission of Inquiry on South Sudan', available at: http://www.peaceau.org/en/article/final-report-of-the-african-union-commission-of-inquiry-on-south-sudan, last accessed 27 December 2016.

Bellamy, A. J. (2015), 'R2P at 10: From Iraq to South Sudan, does it make a difference?' OpenCanada.org, available at: https://www.opencanada.org/features/r2p-at-10-from-iraq-to-south-sudan-does-it-make-a-difference/, last accessed 27 December 2016.

Bellamy, A. J. and P. D. Williams (2011), 'The New Politics of Protection: Libya, Côte d'Ivoire and Responsibility to Protect', *International Affairs*, 87(4), pp. 825–50.

Bhabha, H. K. (1994), *The Location of Culture*, London: Routledge.

Brown, C. (2013), 'The Antipolitical Theory of Responsibility to Protect', *Global Responsibility to Protect*, 5, pp. 423–42.

Burton, A. (2010), 'The Solidarities of Bandung: Toward a Critical 21st Century History', in C. Lee (ed.), *Making a World after Empire: The Bandung Moment and Its Political Afterlives*, Athens, OH: Ohio University Press, pp. 351–62.

Carment, D., J. Landry and S. Winchester (2016). 'The Role of Regional Organizations: A Responsibility Gap?', in A. J. Bellamy and T. Dunne (eds), *The Oxford Handbook of the Responsibility to Protect*, Oxford: Oxford University Press.

Chandler, D. (2004), 'The Responsibility to Protect? Imposing the "Liberal Peace"', *International Peacekeeping*, 11(1), pp. 59–81.

Chandler, D. (2009), 'Unraveling the Paradox of Responsibility to Protect', *Irish Studies in International Affairs*, 20, pp. 27–39.

Cramer-Flood, E. (2008), 'The "Responsibility to Protect" and Unilateral

Humanitarian Interventions: An Emerging Legal Doctrine?', *Minerva*, 33, pp. 35–40.

Çubukçu, A. (2013), 'The Responsibility to Protect: Libya and the Problem of Transnational Solidarity', *Journal of Human Rights*, 12(1), pp. 40–58.

Deng, F. M. (2010), 'From Sovereignty as Responsibility to Responsibility to Protect', *Global Responsibility to Protect*, 2(4), pp. 353–70.

De Waal, A. (2007), 'Darfur and the Failure of the Responsibility to Protect', *International Affairs*, 83(6), pp. 1039–54.

Doucet, M. G. and M. de Larrinaga (2011), 'Human Security and Human Life: Tracing Global Sovereign and Biopolitical Rule', in D. Chandler and N. Hynek (eds), *Critical Perspectives on Human Security: Rethinking Emancipation and Power in International Relations*, London: Routledge, pp. 129–43.

Etzioni, A. (2006), 'Sovereignty as Responsibility', *Foreign Policy Research Institute*, 1, pp. 71–85.

Evans, G. (2006), 'From Humanitarian Intervention to the Responsibility to Protect', *Wisconsin International Law Journal*, 24, pp. 703–22.

Evans, G. (2008), 'The Responsibility to Protect: An Idea Whose Time Has Come . . . and Gone?', *International Relations*, 22(3), pp. 283–98.

Evans, G. (2013), 'Mass Atrocity Crimes After Syria: The Future of the Responsibility to Protect', public lecture at the University of Queensland, 6 November.

Glenville, L. (forthcoming), 'Sovereignty', in A. J. Bellamy and T. Dunne (eds), *The Oxford Handbook of the Responsibility to Protect*, Oxford: Oxford University Press.

Grovogui, S. (2002) 'Regimes of Sovereignty: International Morality and the African Condition', *European Journal of International Relations*, 8(3), pp. 315–38.

Grovogui, S. (2011a), 'A Revolution Nonetheless: The Global South in International Relations', *The Global South and World Dis/Order: The Global South*, 5(1), pp. 175–90.

Grovogui, S. (2011b), 'Looking Beyond Spring for the Season: An African Perspective on the World Order after the Arab Revolt', *Globalizations*, 8(5), pp. 567–72.

Grovogui, S. (2013), 'The Missing Human Intervention, Human Security, and Empire', in K. Pasha (ed.), *Globalization, Difference, and Human Security*, London: Routledge, pp. 79–90.

Gruffydd Jones, B. (2006), 'Introduction: International Relations, Eurocentrism, and Imperialism', in B. Gruffydd Jones (ed.), *Decolonizing International Relations*, London: Rowman & Littlefield, pp. 1–19.

Hobson, J. (2012) *The Eurocentric Conception of World Politics: Western International Theory, 1760–2010*, Cambridge: Cambridge University Press.

Hofmann, S. C. and O. Jütersonke (2012), 'Regional Organizations and the

Responsibility to Protect in the Context of Arab Spring', *Swiss Political Science Review*, 18(1), pp. 132–5.

Hopgood, S. (2013), 'The Last Rights of Humanitarian Intervention: Darfur, Sri Lanka and R2P', *Global Responsibility to Protect*, 6, pp. 181–205.

Hopgood, S. (2014), *The Endtimes of Human Rights*, Ithaca, NY: Cornell University Press.

International Commission on Intervention and State Sovereignty (ICISS) (2001) 'The Responsibility to Protect: Research, Bibliography, Background', Ottawa: International Development Research Centre.

International Conference on the Great Lakes Region (ICGLR) (2007), 'Program of Action for Joint Security and Development of Common Borders, African Union'.

Interim National Transitional Council of the Libyan Republic (INTC) (2011), 'Founding Statement of the Interim National Transitional Council', 5 March, available at: http://archive.is/QXW2, last accessed 27 December 2016.

Krasner, S. (2009), *Sovereignty: Organized Hypocrisy*, Princeton: Princeton University Press.

Luck, E. (2009) 'Sovereignty, Choice, and the Responsibility to Protect', *Global Responsibility to Protect*, 1, pp. 10–21.

Mamdani, M. (2010), 'Responsibility to Protect or Right to Punish?' *Journal of Intervention and Statebuilding*, 4(1), pp. 53–67.

National Commission on Terrorist Attacks Upon the United States (The 9/11 Commission Report) (2004), *The 9/11 Commission Report: Final Report of the National Commission on Terrorist Attacks Upon the United States*. Washington, DC: National Commission on Terrorist Attacks Upon the United States.

Newman, E. (2015), 'The Responsibility to Protect, Multilateralism and International Legitimacy', in R. Thakur and W. Maley (eds), *Theorizing the Responsibility to Protect*, Cambridge: Cambridge University Press, pp. 125–43.

Pasha, K. M. (2013), 'Introduction', in K. Pasha (ed.), *Globalization, Difference, and Human Security*, London: Routledge, pp. 1–14.

Piiparinen, T. (2012), 'Norm Compliance by Proximity: Explaining the Surge of Regional Actors in Responsibility to Protect', *Conflict, Security & Development*, 12(4), pp. 387–415.

Ping, J. (2011) 'Challenges and Future of Democracy in Africa', Presentation at the 44th Lecture of the Americas, Washington, DC, April 14–15.

Rosow, S. and J. George (2015), *Globalization and Democracy*, Lanham, MD: Rowman & Littlefield.

Scott, D. (1999), *Refashioning Futures: Criticism after Postcoloniality*, Princeton: Princeton University Press.

United Nations Secretary-General (UNSG) (2011), 'The Role of Regional and Sub-Regional Arrangements in Implementing the Responsibility to

Protect', UN Document A/65/877–S/2011/393, Report of the Secretary-General, 27 June.

United Nations Security Council (UNSC) (2011), 'Security Council Resolution 1970', UN Document S/RES/1970.

Wilder, G. (2015), *Freedom Time: Negritude, Decolonization, and the Future of the World*, Durham, NC: Duke University Press.

9

Regulating the Abstraction of Violence: Interventions and the Deployment of New Technologies Globally

Aiden Warren

Introduction

The dichotomous interpretations pertaining to the ethics and politics of armed humanitarian intervention have proven to be arguably some of the most theoretically and logistically challenging issues facing the international community over the last twenty years. At the end of the twentieth century the examples of Rwanda, Somalia, Bosnia, Kosovo, Chechnya and Timor-Leste illustrated that past actions would deeply impact future complexities, opportunities and anxieties for the twenty-first century, with clearly no sign of interventions 'becoming more manageable' (Coady 2002). Of course, since 9/11, military interventions for motives divergent from the humanitarian kind have come to dominate the discourse, evident in the US incursions in Iraq and Afghanistan. Additionally, with the volatile position of the Arab Spring states such as Egypt, Libya and Syria, in which 250,000 people have perished, many analysts and policy-makers have remained firmly critical of the reluctance to use force for humanitarian purposes. It is unlikely that this discontent will dissipate (evident in the calls in 2013 to intervene in the Syrian crisis), or that humanitarian crises will be consigned to history (as illustrated by the refugee flows generated by the conflict in Syria). Notwithstanding the apparent limitation of powerful states to *effectively* intervene in the post-Arab Spring states, there still remains an 'impetus to urge and support such armed intervention among many of those sincerely concerned with continuing human rights violations' (Coady 2002: 9).

However, as this chapter will argue, the continual advancement of new technologies in theatres of conflict – and more specifically, in the context of interventions – poses some very distinct challenges, particularly in regard to their regulation, the ethical and legal debates that surround them, and of course their impact on logistics. As the most topical form of new technology, a significant portion of the chapter will focus on the advent and use of drones in war, and the extent to which the evolution of these devices has spurred debate on their capacity to resolve security issues. The chapter will begin by looking at the key debates associated with their increasing use after 9/11, including what can be referred to as the 'threshold enticement'. It will then consider the moral and ethical discourse surrounding their use and the 'dehumanisation of death', including those who are complicit in their science and construction. In the context of humanitarian interventions, the chapter interrogates the debates pertaining to the potential of drone usage and the security dilemmas that could arise should they continue to become a significant option in a state's intervening repertoire. Lastly, the chapter examines the additional complexities that may arise in future security scenarios as technology rapidly advances and drones become wholly 'off the loop' in the form of 'killer robots', as well as the sort of regulations that need to be considered.

New technologies, drones and the infancy of the conversation

In considering where new forms of technology (particularly drones) sit in the context of interventions, it is imperative to understand the varying layers pertaining to their evolution and different uses which this section addresses.

It is evident over the course of history that human beings have come up with creative and varying ways to kill each other. Over the last hundred years or so, combatants have become increasingly detached from the act of killing as new inventions – including planes, cruise missiles and, in recent times, unmanned aerial weapons – have allowed them to engage enemy targets from ever-increasing distances. Controlled remotely from virtually anywhere on the planet, these devices have come to the fore in the military arsenal and contributed significantly to what has been termed as the further 'dehumanisation of death' (Strawser 2013: 3). Indeed, these new forms of technology – referred to as unmanned aerial vehicles (UAVs), remotely piloted vehicles (RPVs), unmanned military systems (UMS) or simply 'drones' – illustrate that 'we are currently in the midst of an epochal transformation' of violence (Lathan and Christiansen 2014: 767) in response to what has been deemed a 'new species of war' (Mundy 2011: 280).

It is important to acknowledge that the use of drones in war extends back to the Second World War and rose to prominence during the second half of the twentieth century.[1] While the first generation of military drones were used predominantly for aerial reconnaissance, their use has progressively expanded into areas such as communications systems relay, search and rescue, suppression of hostile air defence and direct attacks against designated targets (DOD 2011: 46). Over the course of the last decade or so, there has been an exponential increase in the use of armed drones, beginning with the Second Intifada in the Palestinian Territories (since 2000), continuing in the second Iraq War (2003–11), and attaining its recent status in the US war against al-Qaeda and affiliate groups in Afghanistan, Pakistan, Yemen and Somalia since 2001, and against the Islamic State of Iraq and Syria (ISIS) since 2014. The trajectory that the drone form of operation has obtained in comparison to other means and methods of warfare is quite remarkable; particularly their systematic use for the targeting of preselected persons in the territory of other states. By 2012, the US Department of Defense was in possession of approximately 7,000 drones (Stanford-NYU 2011: 8) that performed 20,000 missions per year, with a total of 1 million combat hours achieved already in 2010 (DOD 2011: 22). Additionally, it is estimated that between 2004 and 2012 drones operated by the CIA carried out approximately 350 attacks in Pakistan alone, killing somewhere in the vicinity of 2,000 to 3,000 individuals (Melzer 2013: 7). The number of drone strikes in Pakistan reached an astonishing 122 in 2010, although they have since decreased (twenty-two drone strikes in 2014) as the administration broadened its strike to other theatres. The same period has seen an increasing number of drone strikes in Yemen, peaking at forty-seven in 2012, as well as a limited number in Somalia (New America Foundation 2015a; 2015b).

Of course, the expansion of drone use, principally under the Obama administration, has been accompanied by the emergence of deep divides in the discourse about their legality, strategic utility and proportionality. In particular, the continued use of drones by the US in Afghanistan, Yemen, the Federally Administered Tribal Areas (FATA) of Pakistan, and in response to ISIS in Syria and Iraq, have presented some moral implications (Strawser 2013: 9). One of the main concerns pertains to the practice known as 'targeted killing', a tactic that should otherwise be referred to as an assassination as it is practically identical to an extrajudicial execution. The moral and legal debates deriving from this form of killing are extensive and remain markedly complex, particularly as theatres of conflict continue to become more asymmetrical and newer actors enter the scene – the evolving Iraq–Syria conflict being a case in point. Notwithstanding the widespread use of drones in war and the moral questions surrounding the practice, however, the perceived efficiency of targeted killing via drone strikes has evidently become permissible in the public domain in the United States. Indeed, despite the 'association of drones and targeted killing [being] inseparable', their acceptance to a war-weary and war-wary America has evidently been embraced by the 'popular imagination' (Strawser 2013: 12). A February 2013 Washington Post-ABC poll showed that a little more than eight in ten Americans (83 per cent) approved of the administration's use of unmanned drones against suspected terrorists overseas, with 59 per cent strongly approving of the tactic. And in a rare example of bipartisan agreement, support for the drone attacks comprised 76 per cent of Republicans and 58 per cent of Democrats (Cillizza 2013).

In the face of this apparent approval, there is ample data to suggest that the use of drones is exceedingly problematic, particularly as their ability to discriminate between what can be termed appropriately liable targets and non-liable people is not accurate *enough*. While many proponents extol their precision, the targeting capabilities of their use in many instances actually elicits a disproportionate 'collateral harm' (i.e. unintended death) to civilians and non-combatants, and thereby does not adequately comply with the rules of *jus in bello*. The concerns posited here are often in comparison to other forms of weapon platforms (such as manned aircraft) or alternate means in executing a given mission (such as as the use of ground force troops on land to engage a specific target rather than from the air). As indicated, the main point of contention is that drones are not as discriminate or proportionate, or on par, with other 'more reliable' options. (Strawser 2013: 13). In terms of their speed, agility, military capability and their ability to act autonomously, the current generation of operational drones are still limited when compared to manned military jets and, consequently, are not yet in a position to wholly supplant them in conventional warfare between sophisticated armed forces. However, with the rise in asymmetrical conflicts and loosely organised, transnational 'low-tech' enemies, the advantages drones offer to policy-makers in their weight, cost and risk reduction have seen them become the 'weapon of choice, particularly in permissive airspace outside the territorial control of the operating state' (Melzer 2013: 7).

Not surprisingly, the effectiveness of drone-based warfare is a contentious subject. The Obama administration's *jus in bello* arguments for instance have reflected this uncertainty in what has been termed the 'drone myth' (Brunstetter and Braun 2011: 347) – that drones can lower the risk of civilian casualties '[b]y loiter[ing] and gather[ing] intelligence for long periods of time before a strike, coupled with the use of precision-guided munition' (GA 2014: 7). However, determining the accuracy here is dependent on information provided by informants in the field, who may or may not be reliable, signals of intelligence or intelligence officers on the ground. In other words, 'the strikes are only as accurate as the intelligence that goes into them' (Mayer 2009). As Sarah Kreps and John Kaag state, '[s]ome observers wrongly conflate increasingly sophisticated technology with increasingly sophisticated individual judgment' (Kreps and Kaag 2012: 2). Additionally, as noted by UN Special Rapporteur Philip Alston, these accuracy claims are 'impossible for outsiders to verify' (Human Rights Council 2010). Simply put, the data that could be considered as the most applicable for evaluating the extent to which particular strikes or a policy of strikes is morally justifiable (that is, the specifics of who is killed and whether such people were morally liable to be killed) is the type of data that is most lacking, uncertain, non-conclusive or contradictory (Strawser 2013: 13).

Asymmetry between actors in a conflict

Further criticism of drones pertains to the argument that remote-control killing creates a degree of asymmetry between actors in a conflict. Here, the conflict not only becomes a newer form of warfare, but transcends a threshold that, while not discounting the method's acceptability in principle, spurs morally insuperable concerns in a real context. Some analysts claim that this asymmetry does not necessarily make drones inherently 'bad', nor they argue, is asymmetry morally applicable if the killing is concise and most importantly, justified. However, there are concerns associated with the marked disparity in risk of harm between the *killed* and the *killer*, brought about by the operators of drones themselves who are not in physical proximity to the vulnerability of combat in which they partake. Philip Alston argues that drones represent a significant change in the conduct of warfare because they 'mak[e] it easier to kill targets, with fewer risks to the targeting state' (Human Rights Council 2014). Similarly, Peter Singer argues that the remoteness of the person pulling the trigger may make the act of killing easier as it dehumanises victims, impersonalises the battle and reduces personal accountability (Singer 2009a). In expanding on this sentiment, Air Force Major General James Poss has described it thus:

> the overwhelming advantage we get is that if you want to go and talk to a world expert on Iraq or Afghanistan, maybe you don't need to go to Iraq or Afghanistan. Maybe you need to talk to that young captain down at Creech [Air Force Base, Nevada], because they've been staring at that ground for the past nine years. (Poss 2011)

In this regard therefore, targeting actions are executed by people who are not, and never have been, in close physical proximity to their targets and in most instances have no 'real-life' experience of the war zones they only encounter on-screen (Warren and Bode 2014: 114). But while many maintain the view that drones make war more likely by making it 'too easy', there is an emerging literature by scholars, such as Julian Savulescu and Zack Beauchamp (2013), who see their use as potentially providing an actual net gain by permitting states to engage in humanitarian military intervention without the risk aversion, and thereby removing the 'threshold' objection against drone employment altogether (Galliott 2015).

Aside from the debates associated with asymmetry itself and the extent this can be justified if the 'appropriate' target is killed, the continued expansion of drone usage in theatres of conflict establishes the potential long-term conditions for contraventions of justice and an international power relationship that ultimately undermines peace (Strawser 2013: 13). The main worry is that if combatants can take part in conflicts with no corporeal risk to themselves, then notions that are significant to the very fabric of what it means to be a 'death-defying warrior' are essentially lost. In simple terms, because of this loss and the stripping away of the morally preventive components of the 'warrior ethos', the penchant to undertake warfare becomes more likely (Altman 2012: 12). Indeed, the extent to which fighting a remote-control war morally impacts the 'combatants' who operate drones and, in particular, how it influences our moral rationale on issues such as the significance of courage and other 'soldierly virtues' has been an emerging, albeit somewhat limited, point of contention for some scholars (Strawser 2013: 13).[2]

Remotely piloted versus autonomous weapon systems

Aside from the debates surrounding the 'easy threshold' in using drones, there are other ethical arguments relating to the development and future use of what have been defined as 'autonomous weapons;' weapons that have an advanced artificial intelligence (AI) that can discern their own specific mission actions and, specifically, can make lethal decisions on their own accord (Strawser 2013: 16). In fact, according to the US Delegation Opening Statement at the CCW Meeting in 2014, 'too often, the phrase "lethal autonomous weapons system" appears still to evoke the idea of a humanoid machine independently selecting targets for engagement in operating in a dynamic and complex urban environment. But this is a far cry from what we should be focusing on, which is the likely trajectory of technological development, not images from popular culture' (US Mission to the UN 2014). Indeed, much of the extensive discourse has focused on the projections for – and ethics of – autonomous weapons systems (AWSs), which, as the name signifies, are systems that are capable of performing a role in combat without any human control.

However, practically *all* of the robotic weapon systems that are being developed and deployed in the present context necessitate a human operative to make strategic judgements; simply put, they are remotely operated or unmanned military systems (UMS) rather than actual autonomous systems. The latter devices comprise unmanned aerial vehicles (UAVs) such as the Predator, Reaper and Global Hawk, which have been used widely in Afghanistan and Iraq. They are robots insofar as they are unmanned and do not have a pilot onboard, typically possess the capacity to undertake autonomous movements (e.g. the Reaper is capable of flying between waypoints without a human operator) and because the prevalent view of robots often does not differentiate clearly between autonomous systems and remote-control machines (Whetham 2013: 83). To clarify, it should be noted that the spectrum of human–machine autonomy has three levels: a human-controlled system that can operate on autopilot for simple tasks but requires a human to make major decisions is often referred to as having a 'man *in* the loop', while a human-supervised system that can perform all tasks autonomously but is subject to human override is said to have a man 'man *on* the loop'. Finally, an unsupervised system capable of full autonomy acts with a 'man *out of* the loop'. The gender-neutral term is to replace 'man' with 'human', for example, 'human on the loop', though this is less common in the discussion surrounding lethal autonomous weapons systems (LAWS) (Melzer 2013: 6).

Notwithstanding the varying delineations in the discourse, it is evident that as such weapons continue to evolve *out of* present-day UAVs to the truly autonomous kind, debates about the morals and ethics of war-fighting and interventions will increasingly become more complex (Strawser 2013: 16). Certainly, the advent and deployment of autonomous weapons systems that have the capacity to wield deadly force without the involvement of a human actor creates a distinct set of ethical concerns. Some of these concerns pertain to: the extent to which they may further lower the threshold for military action; the accountability for deaths produced by these devices; and the prospect that autonomous weapons could – as farfetched as this may sound now – turn against those who have designed them (Sparrow 2007: 62–77; Asaro 2008: 50–64; Sharkey 2008: 4–17; Merchant et al. 2011: 272–315). An array of contemporary security theatres signify that such weapons will continue to play an increasingly important role in future conflicts, particularly given that many states in the context of the wars of choice-rather-than-necessity are concerned by casualties and subsequent political fallout. In this light, unmanned systems provide the scope in which states may conduct military campaigns and minimise the risk of their citizens perishing, for example by providing real-time video of the terrain they review, thereby allowing force to be used more accurately.

An additional appeal to states pertains to the economic aspect. Many militaries are under budgetary pressure and unmanned systems are viewed to be more cost-efficient than those they replace. While these can be considered as the political merits of UMS, there are a number of important military-strategic benefits (as mentioned in the above) that 'greatly reduce the fog of war' in enabling strategic operations, accelerating the tempo of battle, and which subsequently places pressure on adversarial militaries to adapt to these systems and new forms of conflict (Adams 2001: 57–71; Sparrow 2013: 87). Overall, the prevailing view from proponents is that unmanned systems can actually help keep war-fighters out of harm's way and thus enable decision-makers to embolden the strength of their forces while fulfilling the responsibility to protect the lives of those under their command. It is this rationale that will see a 'greatly increased role for unmanned systems in the future of the armed services' (Singer 2009a; Sparrow 2013: 88).

Dehumanising death and the division of labour

While states and their governments are increasingly vying for the political leverage that drones provide, the orchestrated division of labour that conspicuously attempts to absolve contractors of their individual or organisational responsibilities for the death and destruction that UAVs cause poses major ethical questions. For many analysts and commentators, it is the state and its political leadership, and *not* its defence industries, scientists or contractors that determine whether and how it undertakes its conflicts, and thus determine the military or non-military strategy to do so. However, there is an emergence of senior-level managers and directors of private military contractors and defence contracting firms that are inextricably linked with the defence of the state, to the extent that the boundaries between what or who *is* military or non-military, public or private, is ambiguous at best. Chief executive officers as well as crucial scientists, engineers and employees of such industries are also citizens of the state, and thereby need to be concerned of either the risk or the occurrence of war that their efforts actually engender (even if they work to mitigate war's most damaging effects through their innovations). Indeed, their dual responsibilities as both citizens and experts in military technology necessitates their responsibility to 'offer faithful advice, grounded in their professional experience, on the prospects and problems inherent in political policies regarding preparation for or engagement in military conflict' (Lucas 2013). In building upon this statement, Peter W. Singer argues that those involved at *all* levels of the development and manufacture of military robots and unmanned systems – scientists, engineers and leaders of industry – must take it upon themselves to be active in ensuring the wise and lawful use of new and emerging technologies (Singer 2009b; Singer 2010).

Of course, concern deriving from machine autonomy is the very reality that those involved in the process *do not* take into account. There seemingly appears to be an unreflective and unbridled drive from scientists and engineers, as well as the aforementioned military and political leaders, to accelerate the development of autonomous weapons systems 'ranging from reckless endangerment to outright criminal negligence' regardless of the objections raised by critics.[3] Singer goes as far as describing this as an 'ethical illiteracy' among engineers, who are all too willing to proceed with their scientific and technological work while passing on any moral considerations to others outside of their 'domain' (Singer 2009b; Singer 2010). In this regard, there is marked compromising of professional ethics that is nothing short of indefensible when practitioners in the field of military robotics engineering continue to remain selectively uninformed, unconcerned and uninvolved in this area of scientific research. This deliberate negligence of this crucial dimension of the overall robotics engineering project establishes what is understood in law and morality as 'culpable ignorance'. Practitioners who continue to divorce themselves from the unpalatable consequences of their involvement in the practice could find themselves legally culpable and quite possibly criminally accountable in maintaining their current lines of research while ignoring the ramifications of their key engineering designs (Lucas 2013).

Understanding the dichotomy between proponents and critics of enhanced machine autonomy is further hindered through an almost desperate kind of conceptual misperception and linguistic prevarication. That is, proponents complicate the debate through their inclusion of terms such as 'machine morality', or by describing their proposals for an 'ethical governor' for lethally armed autonomous robots (Arkin et al. 2012: 571–89). They deceptively point to autonomous combat weapon systems that would have the capacity to make 'moral decisions and judgments', and that would also experience the machine equivalent of 'guilt' from incursions that had 'gone wrong', and 'learn' from such involvements. In this regard, they argue, lethally armed autonomous military robots would be 'more ethical' and even 'more humane' than their human equivalents. For Noel Sharkey, the use of this type of terminology is decidedly deceptive and wholly unnecessary – for what is being proposed is legal acquiescence attained through machine and software program design – and certainly not something analogous to human moral judgement (Lucas 2013). In response, critics also embellish their own assessments, where cyborgs akin to those portrayed in the *Terminator* film franchise or some form of 'killer robots' (Asaro 2008: 50–64; Krishnan 2009) are on the loose, in command of nuclear weaponry, roaming the mountainous southern Afghanistan, but unable to distinguish (without human supervision) between an enemy insurgent and a local inhabitant. While this may appear somewhat exaggerated, a more tempered account would suggest that there is clearly a moral inappropriateness of machines 'making decisions to kill humans', as well as a distinct lack of meaningful accountability for resulting 'war crimes' that will likely be committed as newer technologies of this form continue to rise.[4]

Drones, the use of force and interventions

As discussed above, the most common criticism of the proliferation of drones in warfare is the argument that by removing humans from the combat equation, the costs of going to war are reduced, and thereby the instigation of war by states that possess drones will become more likely. While there is minimal evidence that the use of drones have actually lowered the threshold to war – any more than, say, cruise missiles or regular aircraft – it is plausible to argue that as the technology progresses and as drones increasingly take the place of humans in combat roles, this critique may gain traction. Notwithstanding this common viewpoint, a contrasting argument has suggested that lowering the threshold is *not* necessarily a bad thing; and that drones have the potential to actually advance the practice of humanitarian intervention, that is, the use of military force to protect citizens from mass violence such as genocide or ethnic cleansing (Beauchamp and Savulescu 2013: 106). Much of this view stems from the fact that states have had a poor track record in intervening in states when there was a very strong justification. While the most defining cases of genocide – Rwanda in 1994 and Darfur from 2003 to 2007 – were not met with international intervention,[5] there are persistent and contemporary conflicts involving extraordinary suffering that have also not resulted in intervention. Even in instances where intervention has taken place, mass atrocities have been allowed to go on for an extensive period of time (such as in Kosovo and Timor-Leste, both in 1999).[6]

The Obama administration's failure to intervene in Syria is a further case in point. Over the course of the Syrian conflict, many commentators have supported intervention on humanitarian grounds in line with the emerging norm of the responsibility to protect (R2P). Although the Obama administration regularly declared that force should be used as a last option in Syria after 'exhausting a host of other measures' (Rice 2013), it was only the revelation that Asaad had used chemical weapons on innocents that an intervention was seriously considered in the conflict that up until that point had seen 100,000 people perish. The humanitarian rationale for an intervention continued to be present well after the Obama administration decided to vie for political resolution in September and October 2013 (BBC News 2013). Neither the indiscriminate bombing of Aleppo by the Syrian regime in mid-December of the said year (Eddy and Cottrell 2014), nor any subsequent reports on grave human rights violations and crimes against humanity coming from Syria (Human Rights Council 2014), shifted the positions of both Democrats or Republicans. This raises questions about the subjectivity of intervention conditions, in particular Obama's so-called 'red line' on chemical weapons (Kessler 2013). Moreover, because the US would not endorse these unilateral use-of-force considerations if undertaken by other member states, it appeared as though it was supporting an exception to the rules applicable only to *itself* and *its* own vested interests.

Clearly there is a disinclination on the part of industrialised democracies – the only states with the capacity to undertake a successful intervention – to risk their own soldiers for foreign lives. There are a myriad of reasons for this aversion, ranging from what is perceived to be the moral responsibilities to the interests of their own soldiers and the nation, to the political inhibition posed by the predominance of differing beliefs among their respective domestic public or political factions (Beauchamp and Savulescu 2013: 109). If casualty aversion has been deemed to be a significant constraint, then by removing combat roles away from humans, drones may enable military decision-makers, generals and policymakers to actually execute strategies gauged towards minimising civilian deaths *rather* than their own casualties. So while drones significantly lower the threshold in going to war, it is argued by some proponents that their significance in reducing the need for humans in risky combat roles can thereby ameliorate the effect of casualty aversion in the consideration of intervention and mitigate genocide.

In this light, if drones can be effective enough in conflict that states are prepared to use them in lieu of humans, then they can be effectively deployed in humanitarian interventions, and enable the development of a strategy for protecting civilians with fewer impediments presented by the prospect of human casualties. UAVs currently in use, such as the Predator and Reaper, have illustrated their utility for humanitarian intervention in Libya (Beauchamp and Savulescu 2013: 119). As stated by Tom Ricks:

> [w]e have seen Qaddafi's forces adapting to the presence of NATO aircraft overhead, for example, moving from tanks to pickup trucks. So closer observation is needed before striking. That requires getting down low, but that can sucker a NATO aircraft into getting hit. Drones are a good answer to this tactical problem. Likewise, they can get down under clouds in bad weather, taking away from Qaddafi's goods [sic] the advantage of attacking under overcasts. Plus, drones can 'loiter' over a target, which helps both with observation and deterrence. (Ricks 2011)

Based on this viewpoint, UAVs are able to differentiate between adversaries and non-combatants and can engage ground troops in ways that would be limited through the use of a manned aircraft. Additionally, surveillance drones can provide important advantages to peacekeepers in the context of information-gathering activities near populations at risk; identify potential arms smugglers and embargo breakers that could have thwarted their efforts; and provide overall situational awareness and therefore the capacity to respond promptly when people were at risk, evident in Chad in 2009 (Whetham 2015: 199–200). Likewise, in 2013 the UN Security Council granted the Department of Peacekeeping Operations (DPKO) permission to bring in surveillance drones to support the United Nations Organization Stabilization Mission in the Democratic Republic of the Congo (MONUSCO) (Whetham 2015: 199–200). According to Colum Lynch, these drones were 'equipped with infrared technology that could detect troops hidden beneath forest canopy or operating at night, allowing them to track movements of armed militias, assist patrols heading into hostile territory, and document atrocities' (Lynch 2013). While signifying to adversarial actors that they *can be seen wherever they are* cuts against standard surveillance practice (where the idea is generally to watch without the actor being aware), it does provide a form of deterrence insofar that if they can be seen, they can be caught, and they can also be killed (Whetham 2015: 199–200).[7] In highlighting some further potential positives of drones in interventions, Alyoscia D'Onofrio states:

> [t]herein lies a major dilemma around the emerging use of UAVs (unmanned or unwomanned aerial vehicles) in humanitarian response situations: We don't think of tracking the movements of displaced civilians in Congo or carrying out building damage assessments in Haiti – we think of military strikes. Yet aid agencies are exploring the use of UAVs to carry out assessments, track populations of concern and deliver supplies. (D'Onofrio 2014)

As has been well documented, the discourse surrounding drone usage is often focused on the violations of international law or excessive collateral damage, particularly regarding their role in perpetrating various types of alleged atrocities in the form of Central Intelligence Agency (CIA) targeted killing operations. Indeed, the system of compiling 'kill lists', comprising of suspected militant leaders, for drone strikes is problematic to say the least. Reportedly, there is a weekly routine where officials from several US agencies review a group of preselected terrorist leader suspects on the basis of their threat potential (Klaidman 2012: 209–23). Both the selection criteria of this group as well as the preselection criteria remain unclear, as does the extent to which imminence and other standards of the laws of war are considered in the equation (CLSHRC 2012). Additionally, the criteria is also vague on who specifically assembles these 'kill lists'. To Just War theorist Michael Walzer, the issue is compounded by the fact that the CIA – and not the military – is in charge of putting this compilation together, rendering the procedure entirely covert and evidently not subject to any legal code or judicial mechanisms (Mayer 2009). The elusive approach has been linked to an attempt to 'shield officials involved against possible court challenge' (Entous et al. 2012). Most of the valid information senior officials posit on the review process is an attempt to sway the (American) public into putting their 'trust' in the 'moral' standards that go into targeting decisions by the administration, and particularly Obama himself (Warren and Bode 125–6). As Brennan states:

[t]here is absolutely nothing casual about the extraordinary care we take in making the decision to pursue an al-Qa'ida terrorist, and the lengths to which we go to ensure precision and avoid the loss of innocent life. . . . To ensure that our counterterrorism operations involving the use of lethal force are legal, ethical and wise, President Obama has demanded that we hold ourselves to the highest possible standards and processes. (Brennan 2012)

The justification articulated in this statement highlights some noteworthy concerns regarding its actual authenticity. Given the number of drone strikes that have been authorised during Obama's presidency it appears unlikely that he would actually have the time to *personally* assess the plausibility of each strike. Additionally, it should be noted that the most explicit speeches articulating the Obama administration's legal rationale on drone strikes only came in the spring of 2012 when the midterm election campaign was in full swing. This illustrates the moral authority President Obama has attempted to convey on the administration's drone target decision-making process; as long as *he* is deciding, it is 'acceptable' to *not* conform to international law or any other form of rules and norms (Warren and Bode 2014: 126). Despite Obama's apparent penchant for expanding the use of drones in theatres of war, there is not enough substantive analysis in the discourse about their potential use in preventing violations of human rights. April 2014 signified the twentieth anniversary of the beginning of the genocide in Rwanda that claimed the lives more than 800,000 innocent people. The genocide has been described by United Nations Secretary-General Ban Ki-moon as 'an epic failure' of the international community. Some twenty years on, mass atrocities continue unabated in Syria, and, notwithstanding US congressional debates in September 2013, there has been little in the way of response. As of August 2016, an estimated 250,000 plus people have perished over the course of the five-year civil war and according to the UN, approximately 9 million people have been forced to evacuate and over 3 million refugees have fled into nearby states (Whetham 2015: 199–200).

Despite some of the potential advantages of using technology in humanitarian interventions mentioned here, the key objection to the efficacy of humanitarian intervention remains problematic. Again referring to Singer, an important concern is that drone-driven wars or interventions undermine democratic legitimacy. On this note, wars executed by democratic states are morally justified only if they have been endorsed by legitimate legal channels and with substantive public input. Otherwise, 'the already tenuous link between the public and its foreign and defence policy, the whole idea of a democratic process and citizenship is perverted' (Singer 2009a: 323). Simply put, by removing the public's crucial role in considering the security issue at hand and then consenting to the decision to start a war, in essence, renders the war necessarily unjust. In relying on the standard 'right authority' *ad bellum* principle, even the most just interventions for Singer are illegitimate if they are executed principally with drones that eliminate the costs to the intervening state (Beauchamp and Savulescu 2013: 109).

A further argument suggests that even if the state acts on a just cause, such as the desire to impede genocide, the use of force can be considered to be a form of 'selfish charity'. On the one hand there is the clear capital advantage that enables the more powerful state to use sophisticated technologies, which clearly the recipient state does not have. The only message of 'moral character' a state conveys is that it alone has the right to mitigate human insecurity, but only at the time and location that it deems appropriate, and most impor- tantly, where associated costs are viewed to be at the requisite low level. While the people in the conflict zone are protected and may well be thankful, they may also see a rudimentary calculation that to some extent denigrates their lives (Singer 2009a: 323). And while this line of thinking clearly questions the motivations behind a drone intervention, there is still a level of 'selfish charity' intervention that is undertaken for altruistic reasons. An additional point of consternation in the use of drones in interventions pertains to the extent that any use of force can be undertaken without significant unintended ramifications for the very people it is ostensibly protecting from harm. Given that the most advanced drone technologies are yet to be developed, discourse surrounding their consequences, moral or otherwise, is still open to speculation, particularly when considering the astonishing pace at which this form of technology is expanding and the parties developing it (Beauchamp and Savulescu 2013: 122–3).

Indeed, while concerns have been expressed in the context of China's acquisition of drone technology, other states have also been active in their push. On 7 September 2015, Pakistan officially became the world's ninth state to successfully develop its own unmanned combat aerial vehicle, used in an incursion against the Taliban in the northwestern tribal area near its border with Afghanistan. Aside from furthering Pakistan's advance against the Taliban, in which three militants perished, the drone strike pointed to a potential shift in the theatre's equation, where the era of Washington's own drone actions within Pakistani sovereignty may be drawing to a close (Fazl-e-Haider 2015). Moreover, the fleet of armed drones has emboldened the Pakistani state's military strength against both internal and external threats. Apart from the internal Taliban-led insurgency in its northwest, and a separatist insurgency in its southwest, Pakistan faces an external volatile situation on both its eastern border with India and its western border with war-torn Afghanistan. With both armed and unarmed UAVs, it can better monitor the security developments on its borders and undertake missions including intelligence gathering and target detection and destruction. Not surprisingly, any justification endorsing the use of drones in a humanitarian intervention will only be further complicated as states like Pakistan join the 'drone club'. It is already evident that Pakistan's participation has spurred a race in South Asia, with India recently accelerating the production of its own unmanned aerial vehicle development programme, the Rustom-2. It has purportedly accelerated its work on weaponising the Rustom-1 medium-altitude long-endurance UAV, which it tested in 2016. Additionally, New Delhi has reportedly endorsed the acquisition of ten armed UAVs from Israel Aerospace Industries under a US$400 million deal (Fazl-e-Haider 2015).

In response to the growing demand for drones among an increasing number of states, Buchanan and Keohane have proposed the establishment of a Drone Accountability Regime to ensure better compliance with existing laws and to prevent the rules being undermined through an apparent lack of accountability. For a plethora of reasons, states have been disinclined to publicise the specific details of their actions when using lethal drones, 'especially extraterritorially' (Whetham 2015: 204). However, this can understandably create the view that the rules are being contravened and the law ignored. Even if the action has been undertaken with the best of intentions and a justification based on a clear self-defence requirement in the face of an imminent threat, with the absence of a credible explanation it might as well be considered an assassination or murder – there is no way for the rest of the world to tell the difference. Buchanan and Keohane's intention, therefore, is to build towards a position in which an impartial ombudsman can review the legal justification for an attack and has the right to hold actors to a standard in meeting their responsibilities. While conceived for a different context, such a regime, if expanded to cover observer missions of the type, might address many of the political problems with deploying drones to monitor and prevent human rights abuses in the case of an intervention (Whetham 2015: 204).

However, at this point in time the lack of a distinct regulatory unit poses many security concerns, particularly in regard to the clearly evolving and apparently ad hoc approach to when and where UAVs can be used, if at all. Not surprisingly, this will only become further complicated as more sophisticated and affordable vehicles become available, and civilian use continues to expand and increase – which could translate into more regular use in civil protection and disaster responses. The pressure for humanitarians to utilise this technology, or to articulate their principled rationale for why they do not, will also need to be factored in. In terms of the technical side, humanitarian organisations are more likely to continue to rely on small, agile UAVs, specifically gauged towards disaster responses. Notwithstanding the limited range and air time of these devices, they are likely to have the fewest legal and moral concerns (as conveyed earlier on), and may cause humanitarians to engage more closely with the communities they are surveying rather than remotely from afar. Of course, until UAVs are much more established in general civilian use, and there are clearer regulatory mechanisms pertaining to their use in humanitarian-military contexts, the risks associated with their use in one's conflict-zone calculi will continue to outweigh the benefits (Gilman 2014). As such, the emphasis should therefore be on defining and orchestrating 'best practices and guidelines for their use in natural disasters, slow-onset emergencies and early recovery'. In this context, humanitarian organisations will need to specify the extent to which they will use UAVs 'belonging to peacekeeping missions and military and intelligence actors, as well as human rights organizations'. This would encompass at a state level a 'common humanitarian position on the use of UAVs', and where possible, be endorsed via the Humanitarian Country Team (HCT) so as to foster 'consistent messaging and practices' (Gilman 2014).

New(er) and evolving technologies and interventions

Further complexities regarding humanitarian interventions and the role new technology may play is evident with the emergence of lethal autonomous robotics. As this chapter has indicated, the speed of drone development and the marked increase in their usage has been clearly on display after 9/11. When the US invaded Iraq in March 2003, it possessed only a limited range of drones. Since then the stockpile has increased markedly to approximately 7,000, including the now-famous Predator and Reaper and the Navy's new MQ-8 Fire Scout, a helicopter drone that recently completed autonomous tests via a guided-missile destroyer (Singer 2015). In terms of actual execution, while the US programme's largely secretive stance have made accurate numbers difficult to attain, it is clearly evident that drone strikes targeting 'confirmed terrorist targets at the highest level' (Kerry 2013) have become a core fixture during Obama's tenure in office. In the state of Pakistan, the number of drone strikes authorised in Obama's first year in office surpassed the number endorsed by Bush during his entire two terms in office.[8]

Notwithstanding such concerning figures, the reality is that existing armed unmanned aerial vehicles are only the precursors to what is termed 'autonomous robotics': devices that could choose targets without further human intervention once they are programmed and activated. While this may appear somewhat exaggerated, the Pentagon is already planning for them, 'envisioning a gradual reduction by 2036 of the degree of human control over such unmanned weapons and systems, until humans are completely out of the loop' (Garcia 2015). The former UN High Commissioner for Human Rights, Navi Pillay, has said that these 'so-called "killer robots" – autonomous weapons systems that can select and hit a target without human intervention, also known as 'lethal autonomous robots'

(LARs), 'lethal autonomous weapons systems' (LAWS) and 'fully autonomous weapons systems' (FAWS) (Wegmann 2014: 7–8) – are no longer science fiction, but a reality' (Pilay 2013). Unlike drones, fully autonomous robots would make their own decisions and act independently from humans. The term 'human out of the loop' (Melzer 2013: 6) has proven uncomfortable for both policy-makers and analysts alike (Belarusian Mission to the UN 2014). While no one is exactly sure how these robots of the future will evolve, or what actions they might be able to perform, roboticists, soldiers, politicians, lawyers and philosophers must ask some very complex and interdisciplinary questions regarding the future use of LAWS, particularly if considered to be a device used in a humanitarian context.

Indeed, the pace of development is clearly moving at a level that policy or law makers are struggling to keep up with. On the ground, the inventory numbers are in the vicinity of 12,000, extending across a spectrum encompassing iRobot's PackBots (utilised as a means to locate roadside bombs in Afghanistan), through to the US Marine Corps Warfighting Lab's tests with Qinetiq's Modular Advanced Armed Robotic System (a tracked robot that holds cameras and small weaponry). While the United States is a key player in this technology drive, there are approximately eighty-seven other states, including the UK and China, that have used various types of military robotics (Singer 2015). Most concerning is the revelation that there have been non-state actors who have added robots to their military suites, including both sides of the Syrian conflict and ISIS, while in the Ukraine conflict both sides were also using them. As robots' intelligence and autonomy continues to expand and advance so too will the intensification of multifaceted and (in)secure scenarios. One only has to look at the transition from Predator-class systems that were originally 'unmanned'; their function and movements were remotely guided by human operators on the ground. The recent designs now have greater autonomy, where they can fly to different mission waypoints, take off and land, carry sensors that make sense of what they are seeing – and all on their own accord without human involvement (Singer 2015).

In trying to put a balancing restraint on such developments, in April 2015, US Navy Secretary Ray Mabus announced that he would work to unify the navy's efforts to keep up with advances in unmanned technology by appointing a new Deputy Assistant Secretary of the Navy for Unmanned Systems, bringing 'together all the many stakeholders and operators who are currently working on this technology' (Gady 2015). This would encompass a new office for unmanned vehicles in the context of the N-9 and the N-Code for Warfare Systems, so that all domains of the 'unmanned' – 'over, on and under the sea and coming from the sea to operate on land' – will be streamlined. Ultimately this will contribute to the US military's push to obtain *real* autonomously operating weapon systems (Gady 2015). As Sydney Freedberg put it:

> Imagine a swarm of buzzing, scuttling or swimming robots that are smaller but smarter. While a human has to fly the Predator by remote control, these systems would make decisions and coordinate themselves without constant human supervision – perhaps without any contact at all. (Freedberg 2015)

Indeed, Heather M. Roff has argued that systems will progressively be tasked to do more complex activities and less 'vaguer tasks'. So while humans will certainly be coordinating combat from 'somewhere', the degree of what they know and how much they delegate to these rapidly developing weapons systems will continue to evolve. In echoing Freedberg's imagery, Roff states, 'depending upon the task, depending upon the required payload capacity, we could see a menagerie of systems compiled and reconfigured in a variety of ways' (Roff 2016). She does, however, point to what she sees as an evolving trend in autonomy that has less to do with the hardware and more to do with the areas of communications and target identification. In simple but somewhat alarming terms, this trend would entail better war-fighting capabilities that encompass sounder and more sophisticated 'target identification capabilities, identification friend or foe (IFF), as well as learning' (Roff 2016).

Of course, the almost revolutionary advancement in new technologies – particularly as they become *truly* autonomous and 'off the loop' – will pose immense quandaries in the context of humanitarian interventions. For instance, the forerunner to the Unmanned Carrier-Launched Airborne Surveillance and Strike (UCLASS) programme, the Northrop X-47 test aircraft, already has the capability to take off and land from an aircraft carrier, and is now being equipped with the capacity to perform air-to-air refueling and partnering up with manned planes. As the next stage, the UCLASS looks to refine the jet-powered and stealthy system to the extent that drones will become a regular feature of a carrier's repertoire, involving reconnaissance and eventually bombing and strike missions. Other states such as Britain are also testing an unmanned system called Taranis that is jet-powered and stealthy, and also trying out new forms of target selection software. While advancements are not yet at the stage where machines and robots are completely 'off the loop' and make their own decisions on when and where to go to war, the current Iraq War 3.0 has multiple actors – the US, ISIS, Iran and Iraqi government forces – who are using various forms of drones with some autonomous capabilities (Singer 2015).

Conclusion

As the predecessor to such robots, concerns deriving from the expanding use of UAVs in the context of legalities, ethical procurement, privacy and data protection, collateral damage, transparency and informed consent will continue to be subject to extensive debate, particularly in regard to humanitarian interventions (D'Onofrio 2014). Indeed, for UAVs to be used in a humanitarian response, perhaps, for now, their use should be limited to natural disasters as it is still too complex to separate them from their military uses. The multifarious nature of humanitarian environments already means that it is very difficult to construct a well-ordered division of labour between humanitarian and military entities. NGOs and militaries may find themselves in shared space in diverse environments, yet they may not fully understand each other's role and goals. In considering the rampant advancement of military technology in the equation, any sort of coexistence between both perhaps requires the development of a robust legal and regulatory framework, encompassing standard procedures, guidelines and certification programmes, so as to ensure that humanitarian uses for UAVs are recognised as an established practice. This would also require an additional push for national regulatory agencies to recognise humanitarian uses of UAVs, or to provide exemptions in an emergency. Beyond these measures, there needs to be greater transparency and community engagement, including the development of best practices in UAV programme design, codes of conduct and data security guidelines. Lastly, there needs to be a principled partnership between states, humanitarian organisations and other stakeholders that ensures all actors – including those of a commercial-military nature – adhere to humanitarian principles (Gilman 2014).

As technology continues to expand and as the human role moves from being 'in the loop' of the decision-making process (with such devices making all the key calls), to 'on the loop' of the decision-making process (where the role pertains to overseeing operations rather than actually directing), complexities and debate will continue to emerge as the human role moves ultimately 'out of the loop' (Gilman 2014). Additionally, as cyber-conflict, artificial intelligence and software algorithms that increasingly make most of the decisions at digital speed continue to expand, the question of where this will fit in the context of current and future conflicts, humanitarian interventions, international law and considerations regarding the further dehumanisation of death remains problematic to say the least. The issue has already drawn the attention of the international community, underlined with three expert meetings on LAWS held by state parties of the Convention on Certain Conventional Weapons (CCW) at the UN office in Geneva in 2014 and 2015. While international humanitarian law mandates that the use of force must be proportional and avoid indiscriminate damage and death, 'killer robots' lack the knowledge and heuristical skills that allow them to consistently recognise what constitutes proportional force or discriminate between legitimate and illegitimate targets (Garcia 2015). Given that international law is ill-equipped to deal with the myriad of advances in such weapons technology (by the time law is adjusted for one set of technologies, a new set emerges), the regulation of drones, let alone 'killer robots' in the context of complex humanitarian interventions, will clearly remain an ongoing security challenge deep into the twenty-first century.

Notes

1. States having employed drones for military purposes during that period include, for example, the United States in the Vietnam War (1965–75), the First Gulf War (1991) and the wars in Bosnia (1995) and Kosovo (1999), Israel in the Lebanon War (1982) and Iran in its war with Iraq (1980–8).
2. These 'virtues' of drones also make it more likely that governments will resort to violence. The assessment of the overall impact of the development and use of drones on levels of casualties, both civilian and military, is therefore more complex than first appears and must take account of casualties in incidents that would not have occurred were it not for the capacity drones provide for governments to wield force across national borders with little risk of casualties in their own armed services.
3. See Bekey (2005) and Bekey et al.(2008).
4. This lack of accountability was first posited by Sparrow (2007) and Asaro (2008), and has subsequently led to the creation of the International

Committee for Robot Arms Control (ICRAC) with Noel Sharkey (Lucas 2013: 217).

5. This cut-off point of 1990 is non-arbitrary because (1) 1990–2000 saw more humanitarian interventions than any other ten-year period in history and (2) modern understandings of humanitarian intervention have shifted considerably in the post-Cold War period. See Finnemore (2003).

6. Libya in 2011 is a rare exception where intervention was premised on the imminent risk of mass atrocities rather than evidence of ongoing atrocities. For evidence that views of the morality of intervention are shifting, see Weiss (1995) and ICISS (2001).

7. This may be part of the political calculation in the publicity surrounding the deployment of observation drones to the Ukraine by the Organization for Security and Co-operation in Europe. See Hovet and Lopatka (2014).

8. The majority of drone strikes under Bush's leadership, a total of thirty-six, took place during his last year in office in 2008. This indicates the beginning of an emerging trend (New America Foundation 2015a).

References

Adams, T. K. (2001), 'Future Warfare and the Decline of Human Decision-making', *Parameters: US Army War College Quarterly*, Winter, pp. 57–71.

Altman, A. (2012), 'Introduction', in C. Finkelstein, J. D. Ohlin and A. Altman (eds), *Targeted Killings: Law and Morality in an Asymmetrical World*, Oxford: Oxford University Press, pp. 1–29.

Arkin, R. C., P. Ulam and A. R. Wagner (2012) 'Moral Decision-making in Autonomous Systems: Enforcement, Moral Emotions, Dignity, Trust, and Deception', *Proceedings of the IEEE*, 100(3), pp. 571–89.

Asaro, P. (2008), 'How Just Could a Robot War Be?', in P. Brey, A. Briggle and K. Waelbers (eds), *Current Issues in Computing and Philosophy*, Amsterdam: IOS Press, pp. 50–64.

BBC News (2013), 'Syria Death Toll Rises above 100,000', BBC News, 25 July, available at: http://www.bbc.co.uk/news/world-middle-east-23 455760, last accessed 27 December 2016.

Beauchamp, Z. and J. Savulescu (2013) 'Robot Guardians: Teleoperated Combat Vehicles in Humanitarian Military Action', in B. J. Strawser (ed.), *Killing by Remote Control: The Ethics of an Unmanned Military*, Oxford: Oxford University Press.

Bekey, G. (2005), *Autonomous Robots: From Biological Inspiration to Implementation and Control*, Cambridge, MA: MIT Press.

Bekey, G., P. Lin and K. Abney (2008), *Autonomous Military Robotics:*

Risk, Ethics, and Design, Washington, DC: US Department of the Navy, Office of Naval Research.

Belarusian Mission to the UN (2014) 'CCW Closing Statement', *UN Office at Geneva: 2014 Meeting of States Parties to CCW*, 14 November, available at: http://www.unog.ch/__80256ee600585943.nsf/(httpPages)/700b d7373a1fe2bcc12573cf005afc00?OpenDocument&ExpandSection=21, last accessed 27 December 2016.

Brennan, J. O. (2012), 'The Efficacy and Ethics of US Counterterrorism Strategy', Wilson Center, 30 April, available at: http://www.wilson-center.org/event/the-efficacy-and-ethics-us-counterterrorism-strategy, last accessed 28 December 2016.

Brunstetter, D. and M. Braun (2011), 'The Implications of Drones on the Just War Tradition', *Ethics & International Affairs*, 25(3), pp. 337–58.

Cillizza, C. (2013), 'The American Public Love Drones', *The Washington Post*, 6 February, available at: http://www.washingtonpost.com/news/the-fix/wp/2013/02/06/the-american-public-loves-drones/, last accessed 28 December 2016.

Coady, C. A. J. (2002) 'The Ethics of Armed Humanitarian Intervention', Peaceworks No. 45, Washington, DC: The United States Institute of Peace.

Columbia Law School Human Rights Clinic and the Center for Civilians in Conflict (CLSHRC) (2012), *The Civilian Impact of Drones: Unexamined Costs, Unanswered Questions*, available at: http://civiliansinconflict.org/resources/pub/the-civilian-impact-of-drones, last accessed 28 December 2016.

Cronin, A. K. (2013), 'Why Drones Fail: When Tactics Drive Strategy', *Foreign Affairs*, July/August, pp. 44–54, available at: https://www.for eignaffairs.com/articles/somalia/2013-06-11/why-drones-fail, last accessed 28 December 2016.

D'Onofrio, A. (2014), 'Drones 'R' Us? Reflections on the use of UAVs in humanitarian interventions', International Rescue Committee, 4 September.

Eddy, M. and C. Cottrell (2014), '"Human Rights Watch Criticizes Inaction on Syria"', *The New York Times*, 21 January, available at: http://www.nytimes.com/2014/01/22/world/middleeast/rights-group-assails-inaction-on-syria.html, last accessed 28 December 2016.

Entous, A., S. Gorman and E. Perez (2012), 'U.S. Unease Over Drone Strikes', *The Wall Street Journal*, 26 September, available at: http://www.wsj.com/articles/SB10000872396390444100404577641520858011452, last accessed 28 December 2016.

Fazl-e-Haider, S. (2015), 'Pakistan's Own Drones', *Foreign Affairs*, 4 October, available at: https://www.foreignaffairs.com/articles/paki stan/2015-10-04/pakistans-own-drones, last accessed 28 December 2016.

Finnemore, M. (2003), *The Purpose of Humanitarian Intervention:*

Changing Beliefs about the Use of Force, Ithaca, NY: Cornell University Press.

Freedberg, S. J., Jr. (2015), 'Learning From Termites: Navy, Marines Seek New Breed Of Drones', *Breaking Defense*, 15 April, available at: http://breakingdefense.com/tag/swarm/, last accessed 28 December 2016.

Gady, F.-S. (2015), 'Unmanned "Killer Robots": A New Weapon in the US Navy's Future Arsenal?' *The Diplomat*, 17 April, available at: http://thediplomat.com/2015/04/unmanned-killer-robots-a-new-weapon-in-the-us-navys-future-arsenal, last accessed 28 December 2016.

Galliott, J. (2015), *Military Robots: Mapping the Moral Landscape*, London: Ashgate.

Garcia, D. (2015), 'The Case Against Killer Robots. Why the United States Should Ban Them', *Foreign Affairs*, 10 May, available at: http://www.foreignaffairs.com/articles/141407/denise-garcia/the-case-against-killer-robots, last accessed 28 December 2016.

Gilman, D. (2014) 'Unmanned Aerial Vehicles in Humanitarian Response', Geneva: United Nations Office for the Coordination of Humanitarian Affairs (OCHA), available at: https://docs.unocha.org/sites/dms/Documents/Unmanned%20Aerial%20Vehicles%20in%20Humanitarian%20Response%20OCHA%20July%202014.pdf, last accessed 28 December 2016.

Hovet, J. and J. Lopatka (2014), 'OSCE Says Will Use Drones for Ceasefire Monitoring in Ukraine', *Reuters*, 10 September, available at: http://www.reuters.com/article/2014/09/10/usukraine-crisis-osce-idUSKBN0H50Q920140910, last accessed 28 December 2016.

Human Rights Council (2014), 'Report of the Independent International Commission of Inquiry on the Syrian Arab Republic', UN Document A/HRC/27/6013, August.

Human Rights Council (2010), 'Report of the Special Rapporteur on Extrajudicial, Summary or Arbitrary Executions, Philip Alston. Addendum: Study on Targeted Killings'. UN Document A/HRC/14/24/Add.6, 28 March, available at: http://www2.ohchr.org/english/bodies/hrcouncil/docs/14session/A.HRC.14.24.Add6.pdf, last accessed 28 December 2016.

International Commission on Intervention and State Sovereignty (ICISS) (2001), 'The Responsibility to Protect', Ottawa: International Development Research Centre, available at: http://responsibilitytoprotect.org/ICISS%20Report.pdf, last accessed 28 December 2016.

Kerry, J. F. (2013), 'Remarks at Youth Connect: Addis Ababa Featured by BBC's Hardtalk', 26 May, available at: http://www.state.gov/secretary/remarks/2013/05/210012.htm, last accessed 28 December 2016.

Kessler, G. (2013), 'President Obama and the "Red Line" on Syria's Chemical Weapons', *The Washington Post*, 6 September, available at: http://www.washingtonpost.com/blogs/fact-checker/wp/2013/09/06/

president-obama-and-the-red-line-on-syrias-chemical-weapons/, last accessed 28 December 2016.

Klaidman, D. (2012), *Kill Or Capture: The War on Terror and the Soul of the Obama Presidency*, New York: Houghton Mifflin Harcourt.

Kreps, S. and J. Kaag (2012), 'The Use of Unmanned Aerial Vehicles in Contemporary Conflict: A Legal and Ethical Analysis', *Polity*, 44(1), pp. 1–26.

Krishnan, A. (2009), *Killer Robots: Legality and Ethicality of Autonomous Weapons*, London: Ashgate.

Latham, A. and J. Christensen (2014), 'Historicizing the "New Wars": The case of Jihad in the early years of Islam', *European Journal of International Relations*, 20(3), pp. 766–86.

Lucas, G. R., Jr. (2013), 'Engineering, Ethics, and Industry: The Moral Challenges of Lethal Autonomy', in B. J. Strawser (ed.), *Killing by Remote Control: The Ethics of an Unmanned Military*, Oxford: Oxford University Press.

Lynch, C. (2013), 'U.N. Wants to Use Drones for Peacekeeping Missions', *The Washington Post*, 8 January, available at: http://www.washington post.com/world/national-security/un-seeks-drones-for-peacekeeping-mis sions/2013/01/08/39575660-599e-11e2-88d0-c4cf65c3ad15_story.html, last accessed 28 December 2016.

Mayer, J. (2009), 'The Predator War: What are the Risks of the CIA's Covert Drone Program?', *The New Yorker*, 26 October, available at: http:// www.newyorker.com/reporting/2009/10/26/091026fa_fact_mayer, last accessed 28 December 2016.

Melzer, N. (2013), 'Human Rights Implications of the Usage of Drones and Unmanned Robots in Warfare', EU Document EXPO/B/DROI/2012/12, Brussels: Directorate-General for External Policies of the Union, Directorate B, Policy Department, May, available at: http://www.euro parl.europa.eu/RegData/etudes/etudes/join/2013/410220/EXPO-DROI_ ET(2013)410220_EN.pdf, last accessed 28 December 2016.

Merchant, G. E., B. Allenby, R. Arkin, E. T. Barrett, J. Borenstein, L. M. Gaudet, O. Kittrie, P. Lin, G. R. Lucas, R. O'Meara and J. Silberman (2011), 'International Governance of Autonomous Military Robots', *Columbia Science and Technology Law Review*, 12, pp. 272–315.

Mundy, J. (2011), 'Deconstructing Civil Wars: Beyond the New Wars Debate', *Security Dialogue*, 42(3), pp. 219–37

New America Foundation (2015a), 'Drone Wars Pakistan: Analysis', New America Foundation, 12 April, available at: http://securitydata.newamer ica.net/drones/pakistan-analysis.html, last accessed 28 December 2016.

New America Foundation (2015b), 'Drone Wars Yemen: Analysis', New America Foundation, 22 April, available at: http://securitydata.newamer-ica.net/drones/yemen-analysis.html, last accessed 28 December 2016.

Permanent Mission of the United States of America to the United Nations and Other International Organizations in Geneva (US Mission to the UN) (2014), 'U.S. Delegation Opening Statement at CCW Informal Experts Meeting on Lethal Autonomous Weapons Systems', 13 May, available at: https://geneva.usmission.gov/2014/05/13/u-s-delegation-opening-state ment-at-ccw-informal-experts-meeting-on-lethal-autonomous-weapons-systems/, last accessed 28 December 2016.

Pillay, N. (2013), 'A 20-20 Human Rights Vision Statement by the UN High Commissioner for Human Rights Navi Pillay for Human Rights Day', 10 December, available at: http://www.ohchr.org/EN/NewsEvents/Pages/DisplayNews.aspx?NewsID=14074, last accessed 28 December 2016.

Rice, S. E. (2013), 'Remarks as Delivered by National Security Advisor', The White House, 9 September, available at: http://www.whitehouse.gov/the-press-office/2013/09/09/remarks-prepared-delivery-national-security-advisor-susan-e-rice, last accessed 28 December 2016.

Ricks, T. E. (2011), 'A Rare Disagreement with Ignatius, on the Deployment of Armed Predators to Libya', *Best Defense*, 22 April, available at: http://foreignpolicy.com/2011/04/22/a-rare-disagreement-with-ignatius-on-the-deployment-of-armed-predators-to-libya/.

Roff, H. M. (2016), 'Weapons Autonomy is Rocketing', *Foreign Policy*, 28 September, available at: http://foreignpolicy.com/2016/09/28/weapons-autonomy-is-rocketing/, last accessed 28 December 2016.

Sharkey, N. (2008), 'Cassandra or False Prophet of Doom: AI Robots and War', *IEEE Intelligent Systems* 23(4), pp. 4–17.

Singer, P. W. (2009a), *Wired for War: The Robotics Revolution and Conflict in the 21st Century*, New York: Penguin.

Singer, P. W. (2009b), 'Military Robots and the Laws of War', Brookings Institution, 11 February, available at: http://www.brookings.edu/research/articles/2009/02/winter-robots-singer, last accessed 28 December 2016.

Singer, P. W. (2010), 'The Ethics of Killer Applications: Why Is It So Hard to Talk About Morality When It Comes to New Military Technology?' *Journal of Military Ethics*, 9 (4), pp. 299–312.

Singer, P. W. (2015), 'The Future of War Will Be Robotic', CNN, 23 February, available at: http://edition.cnn.com/2015/02/23/opinion/singer-future-of-war-robotic/index.html, last accessed 28 December 2016.

Sparrow, R. (2007), 'Killer Robots', *Journal of Applied Philosophy*, 24(1), 62–77.

Sparrow, R. (2013), 'War without Virtue', in B. J. Strawser (ed.), *Killing by Remote Control: The Ethics of an Unmanned Military*, Oxford: Oxford University Press.

Stanford Law School (International Human Rights and Conflict Resolution Clinic) and NYU School of Law (Global Justice Clinic) (Stanford-NYU) (2011), 'Living under Drones: Death, Injury, and Trauma to Civilians from US Drone Practices in Pakistan', available at: http://chrgj.org/wp-content/uploads/2012/10/Living-Under-Drones.pdf, last accessed 28 December 2016.

Strawser, B. J. (2013), 'Introduction: The Moral Landscape of Unmanned Weapons', in B. J. Strawser (ed.), *Killing by Remote Control: The Ethics of an Unmanned Military*, Oxford: Oxford University Press.

United Nations General Assembly (GA) (2014), 'Report of the Special Rapporteur on the Promotion and Protection of Human Rights and Fundamental Freedoms While Countering Terrorism', UN Document A/68/389.

US Department of Defense (DOD) (2011) *The Unmanned Systems Integrated Roadmap FY2011–2036*, Washington, DC: Department of Defense, available at: http://www.acq.osd.mil/sts/docs/Unmanned%20 Systems%20Integrated%20Roadmap%20FY2011-2036.pdf, last accessed 10 January 2017.

Warren, A. and I. Bode (2014), *Governing the Use-of-Force in International Relations: The Post 9/11 US Challenge on International Law*, London: Palgrave McMillan.

Wegmann, F. (2014), *Autonomie unbemannter Waffensysteme. Das CCW-Expertentreffen zum Thema 'Lethal Autonomous Weapons Systems' und der gegenwärtige Stand der Technik*, IFAR Working Paper, Hamburg: Institute for Peace Research and Security Policy at the University of Hamburg, June, pp. 7–8.

Weiss, T. G. (1995), 'Overcoming the Somalia Syndrome-Operation Rekindle Hope?' *Global Governance*, 1, pp. 289–98.

Whetham, D. (2013), 'Drone and Targeted Killing: Angels or Assassins?', in B. J. Strawser (ed.), *Killing by Remote Control: The Ethics of an Unmanned Military*, Oxford: Oxford University Press.

Whetham, D. (2015), 'Legal and Ethical Implications of Drone Warfare', *The International Journal of Human Rights*, 19(2), pp. 105–26.

Part III

*The Politics of Post-intervention (Re-)Building
and Humanitarian Engagement*

10

(Re-)Building the World:
Local Agency and Human Security
in the New Millennium

Trudy Fraser

Introduction

The 'building', or 'rebuilding' – '(re-)building'[1] – of a society in the aftermath of conflict or mass violence often subsumes the dynamic requirements of human security into a technical task that belies or fails to fully comprehend the needs of the community being 'built'. Indeed, critics have suggested that 'building' in the aftermath of conflict or mass violence merely serves to impose externally configured normative benchmarks as a panacea for peace, privileging the goals of international actors at the expense of the needs, goals and norms of local actors (see Richmond and Mitchell 2011: 326). One of the main problems is that externally configured normative benchmarks do not necessarily conform to local models of peace and security, and even when these benchmarks conform to notions of 'liberal peace' they often remain at odds with local logic (see Tom 2015).

A decade ago, the statistics on successful state-, peace- and nation-building[2] could not be viewed with much optimism. Despite the huge amounts of financial and human capital spent on 'building' enterprises it was reported that almost half of all countries receiving assistance returned to conflict within five years, and that 72 per cent of peace-building operations conclude with an authoritarian regime in place (Bassu 2005: 13; Barnett et al. 2007: 35). Despite a massive upsurge on the part of the international community towards supporting countries out of conflict-created insecurity and fragility, contemporary 'building' enterprises continue to 'incline towards pessimism' (Haken 2014) and continue to be called to account in terms of demonstrable, long-term impact.

This chapter will draw on case studies including the UN Peacebuilding Commission (PBC), Burundi and Afghanistan, to

247

establish that the busy future of peace operations – defined here as any attempt to 'rebuild' or 'build' from scratch a society in the aftermath of conflict or mass violence – must seek to engage with a revitalised and dynamic understanding and application of human security and that the blueprints for such must strive to be resilient to externally imposed notions of failure or success.

Crucially, this process of dynamic, human-security-based 'building' must be performed in conjunction with local agents and stakeholders to allow for local agency and ownership by the community being 'built' – even if that ownership is at odds with the 'builders'' notions of what local peace and security might look like. 'Building' cannot exist in technical or normative isolation from the original community of the intervened. If the purpose of 'building' is to establish community security and sovereignty, the building tools must be capable of delivering more than fractured Westphalian concepts of stability and structure. Ideally, the 'building' must be part of a consent-based, locally relevant and resilient engagement by both the intervening parties and the intervened.

In order for the 'building' to be reflective of the dynamic requirements of human security, this chapter asserts that it must be responsive to the following questions: (1) who is doing the building?; (2) what is being built?; and (3) for whom is it being built? These three questions speak to separate but interrelated issues in the context of modern state-, peace- and nation-building, and highlights the ambiguity that currently exists between the initial (state-security-centric) and subsequent (human-security-centric) phases of intervention and '(re-)building'. The question of 'who?' speaks to the origins of the intervention, in which the intervening parties deal primarily with agents of the state in their endeavours to resolve a conflict or situation of mass violence. The question of 'what?' speaks to both the intent of the intervener, and to the receptiveness of the intervened to the building project. The question 'for whom?' speaks to the long-term viability of the intervention, in which local actors are the physical and normative vanguards for the peace, security and stability that has been delivered by the intervention.

It is absolutely necessary that the answers to the questions of *who, what,* and *for whom* are expressed and understood in such a way as that they do not favour, or seek to establish, any particular party as the definitive and singular authority on behalf of the intervened. Rather, this chapter is concerned with two key issues:

1. How can parties to a formally agreed intervention do more to support, or work in conjunction with, evolving normative standards for a human-security-centric peace in post-conflict and post-violence communities?
2. How can modern expressions of state-, peace- and nation-building be reflective of the inherent dynamism of human security to engender better working practices across all stages of an intervention?

In essence, this chapter will seek to interrogate and analyse the *who, what,* and *for whom* in the context of contemporary human security in order to assess how state-, peace- and nation-building can be better executed by both the intervening parties and the intervened, for the better establishment and maintenance of long-term peace and security.

The UN's problematised human security/peace-building nexus

During the early 1990s, the interdependence between traditional and human security started to become recognised in dominant security discourses (see ul-Haq 1995) and 'in order to achieve this [new pathway], a peace-building industry [emerged]: donors, international organisations, international financial institutions, and NGOs ... developed a dizzying array of definitions and 'toolboxes' ... as well as a plethora of networks and institutions' (Turner et al. 2010: 85). Nowhere did this peace-building industry become more embedded than at the UN. Although he did not explicitly use human security in his language, UN Secretary-General Boutros Boutros-Ghali, writing in his 'Agenda for Peace' in 1992, argued for the need for UN peacekeepers to be more than the arbiters of traditional military security, that peacekeepers should become active participants in building social and economic security as part of their mandate (UN 1992).

The emergent doctrine of 'human security' upon which UN peace-building was established is articulated in the United Nations Development Programme's (UNDP) 1994 *Human Development Report* as a twofold concept encompassing freedom from fear and freedom from want. Crucially, the document espouses, 'human security is not a concern with weapons – it is a concern with human life and dignity' (UNDP 1994: 22). The report identified seven areas of threat to human security that peace-builders should be cognisant of, encompassing:

1. Economic
2. Food
3. Health
4. Environment
5. Personal
6. Community
7. Political

Upon its release, the UNDP's attempts to elevate these seven threats to human security into actionable policy agendas was met with a mixed international response, and the human security concept proved too broad to operationalise on a general policy level (see Axworthy 1999). Instead, various UN agencies and individual UN member states adopted specific human security issues and individual human-security-based policy projects that could be pursued on a case-by-case basis (see Fraser 2015: 153).

In 2001, the Commission on Human Security was established by the UN and the government of Japan in response to the call by UN Secretary-General Kofi Annan in his 2000 Millennium Report that '[there are two] founding aims of the United Nations whose achievement eludes us still: freedom from want, and freedom from fear' (UNSG 2000: 17). According to Turner et al. (2010: 91), the Commission 'was tasked with mobilizing public opinion and operationalizing the concept'. The Commission's 2003 report, entitled 'Human Security Now: Protecting and Empowering People', defined human security as the 'vital core of all human lives . . . It means creating political, social, environmental, economic, military and cultural systems that together give people the building blocks of survival, livelihood and dignity' (UNCHS 2003: 4).

The report ultimately proposed a new security framework to address human security and suggested that although the state remains the primary source of security, it often fails to fulfil its security obligations and can even become a threat to its own people. To this end, the report urged for a new paradigm of security that moved *away* from being exclusively state-based and included 'upholding human rights, pursuing inclusive and equitable development and respecting human dignity and diversity . . . [and developing] the capability of individuals and communities to make informed choices and to act on their own behalf' (UNCHS 2003: 2, 5). Notwithstanding these arguments, however, human-security-based peace-building once again failed to gain traction as an implementable and multilateral security policy.

The inclusion of a distinct human security voice in the UN's 2004 Report of the Secretary-General's High-level Panel on Threats, Challenges and Change, entitled 'A More Secure World: Our Shared Responsibility', initiated a movement towards a more expansive notion of international peace and security across the entire UN system. An implicit theme of the panel's findings was that the concept of human security – an individual's ability to access sustainable material, legal and political resources – plays a fundamental role in local, national and international security issues: 'threats are from non-State actors as well as States, and to human security as well as State security' (UN 2004: synopsis).

By 2005, in large part due to Boutros-Ghali's Agenda for Peace initiative, there were already significant elements of human security being introduced to UN peace operation mandates, however, it was the 2005 creation of the UN's Peacebuilding Commission (PBC) that saw a direct attempt to integrate traditional and human security in the UN's peace operations. The primary mandate of the PBC is to improve conflict prevention and recovery efforts, but it works towards this goal from a uniquely created space within the UN system. The PBC was created as the result of two parallel resolutions in the Security Council (SC Resolution 1645, 20 December 2005) and the General Assembly (GA Resolution 60/180, 20 December 2005), making it the first subsidiary body that is responsible to two main organs – the first institutionalised relationship between the Security Council and the General Assembly in the name of human security.

Drawing upon what peace scholar pioneer Johan Galtung referred to as 'positive peace' (1964: 2) – or the conceptualisation of peace in positive terminology based on future-positive societies, moving away from the standard 'peace is the absence of war' definition – the PBC is intended to centralise the UN's institutional knowledge from both traditional and human security perspectives in its peace operations. The existence of the PBC signifies the UN's position that the triggers of conflict (and post-conflict violence) can include human security threats such as poverty, environmental degradation, disease and ethnic hostility, to name a few, and that these triggers should be positively addressed to prevent the onset or recurrence of violence or conflict.

Specifically, the PBC's mission is threefold. First, it convenes all relevant actors to marshal resources and proposes integrated strategies for post-conflict peace-building and recovery. Second, it focuses attention on the reconstruction and institution-building efforts necessary for recovery from conflict and supports the development of integrated strategies to lay the foundation for sustainable development. Finally, it provides recommendations and information to improve the coordination of relevant actors, to develop best practices, to ensure predictable financing for early recovery activities and to extend the period of attention given by the international community to post-conflict recovery. Despite these viable alternatives and options, human security, according to Taylor Owen, failed to gain substantive traction as an implementable and multilateral security policy (Owen 2008).

At its core, human security elevates the security of individual human beings to be of equal or higher priority than the security of states, and 'although definitions of human security vary, most formulations emphasize the welfare of ordinary people' (Paris 2001: 87). Indeed, the concepts of human life and human dignity are fundamental to human security insomuch as it 'takes humans as its object of analysis – as opposed to the state – and it can be applied to all people' (Bacon et al. 2014: 10). As noted by David Chandler, human security securitises *everything* (2008). Subsequently, the potential for every aspect of human life to be an issue of security means that the concept is both fixed (everything comes down to survival) and malleable (security is a moveable concept that can be applied in degrees), and therein lies both its strength and its weakness when we consider how human security is applied to technical 'building' projects, and the decision-making process that determines what aspects of a community's security are prioritised and which are determined to be less important to the community's survival.

As far as the UN is concerned, the integration of human security concepts into its peace operations is an attempt to institutionalise a malleable normative concept. While there have been recognised successes in specific PBC field cases, there remains criticism that the UN, and the PBC, has required human security to operate at its lowest common denominator in its attempts to institutionalise human security into a series of technical or material accomplishments.

The point of this critique is not to say that peace-building, as conceptualised by the UN or the PBC in particular, has universally failed. Instead, it is to suggest that the PBC does itself and its constituents a disservice when it fails to see beyond the institutionalised pass/fail rubric that is presented when human security is reduced to a series of material benchmarks. For instance, the PBC mandate in Burundi is both a success (it met several of its human security benchmarks) and a failure (those benchmarks do not fully encapsulate the notion that existential security requires more than meeting a society's material needs). From the granting of independence in 1961 to the signing of the Arusha Peace and Reconciliation Agreement in 2000, Burundi suffered through three decades of civil war and ethnic violence. On 21 May 2004, the UN Security Council passed Resolution 1545 to establish the UN Operation in Burundi (ONUB) to restore lasting peace and to bring about national reconciliation and on 26 October 2006, the Security Council passed Resolution 1719 to establish the UN Integrated Office in Burundi (BINUB) following the completion of ONUB's mandate.

On 20 June 2007, Burundi became the subject of the PBC's first country-specific mandate that included six major objectives for building long-term peace in Burundi:

1. The promotion of good governance, including anti-corruption measures, strengthening the capacity of the public administration, the preparation of future elections through the establishment of an independent national electoral commission;
2. The completion of the implementation of the ceasefire agreement;
3. The completion of the reform of the security sector and of the disarmament of the civilian population;
4. Equitable access to justice, the promotion of human rights, the fight against impunity as well as reaching a consensus on the modalities of the implementation and functioning of transitional justice mechanisms;
5. Finding sustainable solutions to the land issue and to socioeconomic recovery of populations affected by the war and conflicts;
6. Mainstreaming gender in the implementation of these priorities and in the entire process of peace-building (PBC 2007).

Addressing the PBC in April 2011, Burundian Minister for Foreign Affairs Augustin Nsanze identified that several key areas of the PBC mandate had been achieved, including the creation of an electoral commission and an electoral code; a countrywide strategic framework to combat poverty; an awareness-raising campaign against government and private-sector corruption; a wide-ranging programme for the defence corps and national police; a civilian disarmament programme that led to the collection of 83,287 weapons; a legal framework aimed at securing weapons from public agents; an improvement in the rule of law that led to the government carrying out arrests for crimes committed during wartime; the creation of a programme to build the capacity of magistrates; the modification of the penal code to introduce serious penalties for violence against women; the creation of the National Independent Commission of Human Rights; the adoption of a new land code for coordinating institutions, technical and financial partners and civil society organisations; and the development of reinsertion kits for repatriated people (UN 2011).

The PBC mandate in Burundi is generally recognised as a success by the UN insomuch as Burundi has not descended once again into armed civil conflict. It is undeniable that Burundi is materially safer, and its citizens ostensibly more secure, than was the case during the conflict and its immediate aftermath. However, Devon Curtis (2013) argues that the Burundian experience illuminates the inherent problem when human security is reduced to a series of externally imposed material benchmarks, suggesting that the introduction of these externally imposed benchmarks left the society vulnerable to local renegotiation and reinterpretation of those benchmarks, resulting in a situation in which the prevailing 'order' is one in which violence, coercion and militarism remain central.

The UN's 2010 'Review of Peacebuilding Architecture' similarly recognised this paradox, suggesting that peace-building 'does not lend itself to compartmentalization or "boots on the ground" measurement' and that the UN 'can find it inherently difficult to deal with this complexity and interrelatedness. There is inevitably a gravitational pull, for organizations and donors, towards the concrete and more readily measurable ... There is impatience for the Commission to construct its narrative, to find its success stories, to define precisely its added value' (UN 2010). This gravitational pull towards readily measurable positive outcomes is the result of both individual and institutional psychology that wants to be able to complete tasks, and in many instances provide demonstrable positive outcomes to political/institutional leadership to whom individuals are accountable and to donors to whom various projects are indebted: '[sponsors] ... are looking for concrete, measurable impact. They seem to understand the value of peace-building as a full-spectrum affair, involving efforts to prevent mass violence, the collapse of states, etc., but are generally unwilling to fund the capacity to make this possible' (Zuber 2015).

The problem with measurable outcomes is that individual peace-building tasks, in and of themselves, cannot bring about peace: '[p]

eace processes of intractable conflicts have ups and downs, are not linear, and need a long-term commitment of the peace-builders rather than momentary conjectural optimism or opportunism' (Adwan and Bar-On 2004: 514). Being able to say 'mission accomplished' to peace-building tasks might be useful (career-wise, or financially) to the individual and institutional drivers responsible for peace-building, but it does not necessarily mean 'mission accomplished' to the constituents of the communities being 'built'.

Human security, and the PBC, were conceived at the UN as a means of mitigating human suffering and providing a platform upon which to build a better future for populations emerging from conflict, but as with most projects where there is an uneven balance of power between the intervener and the intervened, the institutionalisation and application of these normative ideals has been weighted more towards the interests of the interveners than the intervened. The 2010 review was cognisant of this dissonance, suggesting that: '[p]ut simply, people must own their own peace: it has to begin, grow and become embedded in people's minds' (UN 2010). The positive implementation of such local ownership, however, is a complicated project that requires substantive interrogation of how the material and normative priorities of both the intervening and the intervened can positively intersect to result in consent-based, locally-relevant and resilient building projects.

Human security, institutionalisation and the surviving versus thriving debate

As noted at the beginning of this chapter, it is the belief of this author that the 'building' of a society in the aftermath of conflict or mass violence requires a specifically dynamic understanding and application of 'human security'. Indeed, 'it has become inexplicably rare for the obvious semantic core of the concept [of human security] to be examined. To do so would be to begin to interrogate the meaning of "the human" in ways that would challenge dominant paradigms', and we are urged to 'take a couple of steps into the task of redefining human security by treating security and risk as part of the contingent and negotiated condition of human living' (James 2014: 72).

In other words, it is necessary to emancipate human security from dominant security discourses in which it is subsumed as a separate and unequal partner to traditional state-based security. But to use Paul James's language, 'the Emperor has only one set of clothes' and 'despite the active and engaged attempts by the proponents of a human security paradigm to get beyond the overwhelming emphasis in this world on military and economic issues, they tend to bring an emphasis on such issues back into contention by using the very same frameworks which are used by those who actively elevate economic and military concerns to the pinnacle of human interest' (James 2014: 74).

As a result, there are those who would argue that 'human security cannot be rescued because it has been institutionalised and co-opted to work in the interests of global capitalism, militarism, and neo-liberal governance' (Turner et al. 2010: 83), or, as David Chandler (2008) admonishes, the idea of human security has been relegated to the 'dog that didn't bark'. Indeed, if the foundational ingredient to 'building' – human security – is an unsuitably imported house of cards then it is indeed true that any building project using its tools will suffer long-term consequences of instability and ultimately failure. However, the rootedness of the 'human security' concept in Western ideologies is not as necessarily fixed as its critics might insist. If human security *can* be reconceptualised so that it *is* contextual, as opposed to being framed by economic, military or political absolutes (or the pass/fail dichotomy that is available when human security is measured by the Human Development Report's absence of threat to economic, food, health, environment, personal, community and political freedoms), then there is still an opportunity for a dynamic and locally relevant human security to be implemented in 'building' projects.

A dynamic human security can be reconstructed from the fact that its etymology is not as fixed at its record of usage and application in 'building' policy. The application of a dynamic human security requires a re-interrogation of the UN-centric application of what human security means on a technical policy level – in other words, a recognition of its contextual malleability over its institutional fixedness. In this context, a dynamic human security requires its application to be dependent on criteria for what it means to be safe and secure, one which is measured locally in the 'built' community, and for the benchmarks for security to be based on a locally derived conception of survival. To ask 'what does it mean for this community to survive?', and to acknowledge that surviving (the meeting of a community's basic material needs) is not the same as thriving. To that end, we return to the initial questions required for 'building' to be reflective of the dynamic requirements of human security: (1) *who is doing the building?*, (2) *what is being built?*, and (3) *for whom is it being built?*

WHO ARE THE (RE-)BUILDERS?

The '(re-)builders' are most often an extension of the parties responsible for the intervention, and their legitimacy as 'builders' stems from their investment and acquiescence to the formally agreed rules of intervention under international humanitarian law.

In the case of the UN, the 'building' process has been institutionalised via the PBC to be part of a wider conception and operationalisation of their peace operations. However, 'builders' generally represented a variety of intervening parties who are making a territorial or political claim upon the community, or who are assisting domestic parties whose territorial or political claim parallels their own interests in the community. In some cases, the 'building' is a necessary accommodation resulting from the military and political violence imposed upon communities by the intervening parties and is undertaken primarily by the intervening parties (i.e. if you break it, you buy it.) Other times, the opportunity to 'build' is a formative consideration in an intervening parties' decision to take action against a particular state and is a direct extension of the intervening parties' interests in the '(re-)built' community (i.e. the introduction of democratic rule after the removal of a despotic leader or non-democratic regime). In other circumstances, the 'building' is conducted by existing local actors within the intervened community, or by external opportunists, who utilise post-conflict instability to create opportunities for the advancement of their interests that do not bear a direct relationship to the interests of the original interveners.

In all cases, the identity of the 'builders' is reflected in their core normative values. Too often, however, and especially at the UN, there is confusion about who the 'builders' are (and by extension, what their values are), resulting in the PBC being urged to positively reposition their 'brand' away from dysfunctionality towards determination and resolve (UN 2010). Again, this speaks to the UN's gravitational pull towards readily measurable positive outcomes and that 'building' projects are often principally answerable to institutional drivers before constituent communities.

WHAT IS BEING (RE-)BUILT?

The diversity of technical blueprints for '(re-)building' are as diverse as the intervened communities and speak directly to the distribution of decision-making between the intervener and the intervened, and the 'what?' is directly related to the 'who?'

For instance, 'different agencies tend to prioritise different activities. These alternative priorities are shaped not only by their knowledge of how to reduce the risk of conflict but also by a consideration of how they might best and most easily extend their existing mandates and expertise into the post-conflict arena' (Barnett et al. 2007: 45). For example, if the 'building' is being conducted as a necessary (but secondary) accommodation resulting from the military and political violence imposed upon communities by the intervening parties, it is likely that the 'building' process will represent a continuum of the vested interests of the intervening parties only for as long as such endeavours continue to benefit their position in the community. In such circumstances, 'building' efforts will most likely prioritise the material 'building' of specific physical infrastructures.

If the opportunity to 'build' is a formative consideration in an intervening parties' decision to take action within a particular community and is a direct extension of the intervening parties' long-term interests in the community, it is more likely that the 'building' will extend beyond physical infrastructures. As such, the 'building' efforts will encompass both the '(re-)building' of physical infrastructures and the creation of political and social systems that will positively align or ally the community with that of the intervening party. If the 'building' is conducted by existing local actors within the intervened community, or by external opportunists who utilise post-conflict instability to create opportunities for the advancement of their own interests that do not bear a direct relationship to the interests of the original interveners, it is probable that the focus will be on the creation of political and social systems that will maximise benefit to the 'builders'. In such circumstances, the rebuilding of physical infrastructure is a secondary consideration conducted to generate popular support for the new political and social systems being established.

Of course, there is no common material ingredient capable of institutionalising a 'built' peace in the aftermath of conflict or mass violence. As outlined above, 'building' projects encompass a diverse range of tasks, ranging from the rebuilding of physical infrastructure (roads, housing, schools, and so on) to the establishment of political and social systems that can institutionalise wider normative progress in issues such as governance, democracy, justice and the rule of law. Additionally, 'building' projects might seek to specifically build material or normative foundations against the underlying causes of the original conflict in order to avoid a return to conflict.

Whilst there is no common material ingredient, 'there is widespread agreement, as well, that peace-building means more than stability promotion; it is designed to create a positive peace, to eliminate the root causes of conflict, to allow states and societies to develop stable expectations of peaceful change' (Barnett et al. 2007: 44). However, even within this acknowledged diversity, specific 'building' tasks are generally born of liberal articulations of what it means to be safe and secure in contemporary society, or 'the ingrained belief by wealthy countries that liberalisation, largely defined as the movement toward democracy, markets and the rule of law, is the best way to develop a positive peace in poor ones' (Barnett et al. 2007: 36). The prioritisation of some 'building' outcomes over others is critically important. For example, security sector reform (SSR) is often listed as a human security operational benchmark for 'building', as it was in the PBC mandate in Burundi; however, 'creating huge military capacities with limited democratic oversight is a recipe for state repression, human rights abuses, and military coups' (Turner et al. 2010: 87).

FOR WHOM IS THE COMMUNITY BEING (RE-)BUILT?

Arguably, one of the most vital considerations in state-, peace- and nation-building concerns the question '*for whom* is the community being (re-)built?'. To consider this question requires us to interrogate the critical agency of the intervening parties and the intervened, and to interrogate the nature of the relationship between the two parties. Most often, it is expected that this power dynamic is represented in an easily recognisable distinction between the power of the intervening party and the powerlessness of the intervened. For example, despite claims that the human security agenda has never directly informed a country's foreign policy, or manifested in a direct application of traditional military power, there is clear evidence that policymakers have found fertile opportunity in the human security concept to relocate otherwise non-actionable threats into an actionable security discourse that, in turn, allows for greater justification for their intervention (see Duffield and Waddell 2006; Turner et al.

2010). However, the complex interrelatedness of the two parties means that the power dynamic is not always as easily recognisable as might be expected.

Critically, 'the existence of *popular support* and *legitimacy* for any ['building'] transformation is fundamentally important, whether it be registered at the moment of change or years later, at first election. A democratic transformation in which the people are not invested and where the people seek something else entirely is hardly self-sustaining ... [it] should *require* the people's support to earn the sacred space' (Hamoudi 2012: 723). Indeed, the need for national ownership as part of any 'building' process is something that the PBC is fundamentally aware of:

> '[n]ational ownership' is not something that is merely desirable or politically correct; it is an imperative, an absolute essential, if peace-building is to take root ... The international community must understand the limits of its role as midwife to a national birthing process ... ownership cannot be approached as a right wrested from the international community: what people need and require of their Governments is that they exercise the responsibilities conferred by ownership. (UN 2010)

National ownership is about the agency of the intervened and speaks directly to the question of '*for whom* is the community being (re-)built?'. However, the practice of national ownership is not as easy as merely passing the reins. That is, while allowing the intervened to exercise critical agency over the 'building' process has proven to do more to improve 'impact on the conditions and substance of peace-building than is often assumed even if they only operate as a form of subsistence peace-building' (Richmond and Mitchell 2011: 339), too often attempts to foster national ownership are little more than a semantic agreement for 'partnerships' and 'interim governance' that leaves most of the decision-making with the intervening 'builders'. As a result, the PBC has been encouraged to work towards a definition of national ownership 'that fully embraces all stakeholders – it must go beyond mantra to substance' (UN 2010: 10), but any significant shift towards establishing real agency for the intervened would require more than the sequenced acquiescence of the local community; rather, the building project must have its roots – equally semantic and operational – *in* the local community.

The problems that can occur when neoliberal policies are introduced into reticent societies came to the fore following the 2001 US intervention into Afghanistan, when 'transnational feminism' (see

Abu-Lughod 2002) was introduced to the country as a universal human rights norm by post-conflict 'builders'. However, there were significant debates about whether or not transnational feminism was merely colonial feminism in disguise:

> Can we only free Afghan women to be like us or might we have to recognise that even after 'liberation' from the Taliban, they might want different things than we would want for them? What do we do about that? Second, we need to be vigilant about the rhetoric of saving people because of what it implies about our attitudes. (Abu-Lughod 2002: 787)

As Deniz Kandiyoti points out:

> The processes of state-building and peace-consolidation are themselves subject to blueprints that are laid out by international players, and which the internal political constituencies respond to with varying degrees of enthusiasm ... The so-called 'failed states' that emerge from conflict situations with weakened or vestigial institutions of governance present very specific challenges. These have to be taken fully on board before contemplating any meaningful discussion of how women's rights may be promoted or safeguarded in the process of post-conflict reconstruction. (2005: 2)

The 2001 *Agreement on Provision Arrangements in Afghanistan Pending the Re-establishment of Permanent Government Institutions* (a UN-brokered agreement between four Afghan tribal factions, signed in Bonn, Germany, and known as the Bonn Agreement) established a number of criteria for post-conflict governance, including the long-term establishment of 'a broad-based, gender-sensitive, multi-ethnic and fully representative government' and 'the participation of women as well as the equitable representation of all ethnic and religious communities in the Interim Administration and the Emergency *Loya Jirga* ["grand council" in Pashto]' (UN 2001).

However, 'at the same time as women's increased participation in formal decision-making was being celebrated, the majority of women in Afghanistan continued to feel powerless and insecure' (Otto 2010: 268). Indeed, as Otto argues, the negotiated participation of women in post-conflict Afghanistan constitutes nothing more than the 'formal performance of inclusivity' (2010: 274) that can be more damaging, and ultimately marginalising, than if such conditions were never negotiated on behalf of Afghan women. For example, the Emergency *Loya Jirga* was comprised of 1,501 delegates, with 160 seats reserved for women, 'however, the [Emergency *Loya Jirga*] did not set a good precedent for women's participation: there were widespread reports of intimidation of women delegates and their supporters, and many women delegates pointed out that they were not able to speak during the plenary session as their microphones were cut off, in clear violation of their right to freedom of expression' (Kandiyoti 2005: 18). Additionally, there were reports that attempts to recruit qualified women delegates from rural areas of the country resulted in illiterate women being used by their male relations as political proxies and served merely to reinforce existent hierarchies of power and did nothing to allow women's voices to be heard in Kabul.

Reporting for the BBC in 2010, Quentin Sommerville stated that there remains a 'risky climate for women candidates in Afghan elections' and that 'some women have received death threats from the Taliban. A number of candidates, and campaign workers, have been murdered' (Sommerville 2010). The underlying problem with the 'builders'' presence in post-conflict Afghanistan was that the multitudes of 'builders' – comprised of international and local agents – sought a diverse and not always mutually compatible series of interests and outcomes. As such, the very notion of a 'transnational feminism' was not sufficiently rooted in Afghani culture or politics to provide local uptake of the norm, and 'given the factious nature of politics in Afghanistan, there [was] little *a priori* ground for making simplistic assumptions about women's primary commitment to subscribing to a common agenda' (Kandiyoti 2005: 22).

Conclusion

State-, peace- and nation-building in the aftermath of conflict or mass violence has historically assumed ownership of the human security paradigm, and in doing so has subsumed such into a technical task that belies, or fails to fully comprehend, the needs of the community being 'built'. Peace-building and human security have become conjoined twins, and the UN and the PBC in particular have singularly developed human security as benchmark-driven practice in their peace operations. However, when interrogated against questions of *who, what, and for whom*, the dominant human security discourses that prioritise the HDR's seven threats (economic, food, health, environment, personal, community, political) are found generally to pay only lip service to the unique identities of the intervened and their autonomy to discern and deliver their own political future. As a result, the human-security-derived priorities of contemporary building projects often reinforce the powerlessness of the intervened, albeit under the cloak of empowerment. A dynamic human security requires that the concept be emancipated from the dominant narratives of the intervening parties over the intervened.

The technical task of mitigating threats to human security must, of course, emanate from a fixed point. It is the position of this author, however, that this fixed point is context dependent and should not necessarily be rooted on the banks of the East River in New York City. The fixed technicalities of delivering a positive peace must not be singularly determined by intervening agents on behalf of the intervened, but must rather be discerned by local agents, based on a locally derived conception of what it means for the local community to thrive, and not merely to survive.

The difference between external *determination* on behalf of the intervened and local *discernment* amounts to the difference between the delivery of material and political benchmarks and the positive utilisation of these gains in the local context. There is an old adage that proposes that if you give a man a fish you will feed him for a day, but if you teach a man to fish you can feed him for a lifetime. A consent-based, locally-relevant and resilient version of dynamic human security asks instead how local populations feed themselves in time of need and recognises that negotiating a positive future does not require that externally imposed short-term survival mechanisms usurp locally established conditions under which the community has historically thrived. As this chapter has argued, whether or not the UN's commitment to ensuring an 'integrated, coherent, and holistic approach to post-conflict peace-building' (UN 2014) can be developed in line with a dynamic application of human security remains to be seen, and in the context of twenty-first century interventions, remains very much contested.

Notes

1. Hereafter referred to as 'building'.
2. The concepts of state-, peace- and nation-building are understood and articulated in a variety of different ways by a variety of different actors and authors, and have sometimes been described as having a conflicted and/or competitive relationship with one another. However, the tensions between state-, peace- and nation-building are merely representative of the different historical and political contexts in which each has evolved, and the different agendas and 'entry-points' that accompany each process. Whilst each can be defined separately for analytical purposes

(i.e. state-building does not tend to engage in civil society very much, whereas peace building often does, and so on) they each employ a shared commitment to building an enduring peace. For the purposes of this chapter, state-, peace- and nation-building are generally understood as congruous terms that can be generally defined as the process of external intervention in the aftermath of conflict or mass violence for the purpose of rebuilding, or building from scratch, the physical and normative infrastructures necessary to support an enduring peace, and are referred to generally in this chapter using only the 'building' suffix (unless referring to a specific project or using the preferred terminology of a specific actor or institution).

References

Abu-Lughod, L. (2002), 'Do Muslim Women Really Need Saving? Anthropological Reflections on Cultural Relativism and Its Others', *American Anthropologist*, 104(3), pp. 783–90.

Adwan, S. and D. Bar-On (2004), 'Shared History Project: A PRIME Example of Peace-Building Under Fire', *International Journal of Politics, Culture and Society*, 17(3), pp. 514–21.

Axworthy, L. (1999), 'Address by the Canadian Minister of Foreign Affairs to the G8, "An Address On Human Security"', 9 June.

Bacon, P., R. Cameron and C. Hobson (eds) (2014), *Human Security and Natural Disasters*, Tokyo: UNU Press.

Barnett, M., H. Kim, M. O'Donnell and L. Sitea (2007), 'Peace-building: What's in a Name?', *Global Governance*, 13(1), pp. 35–58.

Bassu, G. (2005), 'Fixing Failure', *The World Today*, 61(8/9), pp. 13–14.

Chandler, D. (2008), 'Human Security: The Dog that Didn't Bark', *Security Dialogue* 39(4), pp. 427–38.

Chandler, D. and N. Hynek (eds) (2010), *Critical Perspectives on Human Security: Rethinking Emancipation and Power in International Relations*, London: Routledge.

Curtis, D. (2013), 'The International Peace-building Paradox: Power Sharing and Post-Conflict Governance in Burundi', *African Affairs*, 112(446), pp. 72–91.

Duffield, M. and N. Waddell (2006), 'Securing Humans in a Dangerous World', *International Politics*, 43(1), pp. 1–23.

Fraser, T. (2015), *Maintaining Peace and Security? The United Nations in a Changing World*, London: Palgrave Macmillan.

Galtung, J. (1964), 'Editorial', *Journal of Peace Research*, 1(1), pp. 1–4.

Haken, N. (2014), 'It Takes a Generation: West African Success Stories', *Fragile States Index 2014*, available at: http://library.fundforpeace.org/fsi14-sierraleone, last accessed 28 December 2016.

Hamoudi, H. A. (2012), 'Arab Spring, Libyan Liberation and the Externally Imposed Democratic Revolution', *Denver University Law Review*, 89(3), pp. 699–734.

James, P. (2014), 'Human Security as a Military Security Leftover, Or as Part of the Human Condition?', in P. Bacon and C. Hobson (eds), *Human Security and Japan's Triple Disaster: Responding to the 2011 Earthquake, Tsunami and Fukushima Nuclear Crisis*. London: Routledge.

Kandiyoti, D. (2005), 'The Politics of Gender and Reconstruction in Afghanistan', *United Nations Research Institute for Social Development Occasional Paper No. 4*, February.

Otto, D. (2010), 'The Security Council's Alliance of Gender Legitimacy: The Symbolic Capital of Resolution 1325', in H. Charlesworth and J-M. Coicaud (eds), *Fault Lines of International Legitimacy*, Cambridge: Cambridge University Press.

Owen, T. (2008), 'The Critique the Doesn't Bite: A Response to David Chandler's "Human Security: The Dog that Didn't Bark"', *Security Dialogue*, 39(4), pp. 445–53.

Paris, R. (2001), 'Human Security: Paradigm Shift or Hot Air?', *International Security*, 26(2), pp. 87–102.

Richmond, O. P. and A. Mitchell (2011), 'Peace-building and Critical Forms of Agency: From Resistance to Subsistence', *Alternatives: Global, Local, Political*, 36(4), pp. 326–44.

Sommerville, Q. (2010), 'Risky Climate for Women Candidates in Afghan Elections', BBC News, 16 September, available at: http://www.bbc.com/news/world-south-asia-11334475, last accessed 28 December 2016.

Tom, P. (2015) 'A "Post-Liberal Peace" Via Ubuntu?' *Peace-building*, May, pp. 1–15.

Turner, M., N. Cooper and M. Pugh (2010), 'Institutionalised and Co-opted: Why Human Security Has Lost Its Way', in D. Chandler and N. Hynek (eds), *Critical Perspectives on Human Security: Rethinking Emancipation and Power in International Relations*, London: Routledge.

Ul-Haq, M. (1995), *Reflections on Human Development* Oxford: Oxford University Press.

United Nations (UN) (1992), *An Agenda for Peace: Preventative Diplomacy, Peacemaking, and Peacekeeping*, UN Document A/47/277-S/24111, 17 June, available at: http://www.un-documents.net/a47-277.htm, last accessed 28 December 2016.

United Nations (UN) (2001), 'Agreement on Provision Arrangements in Afghanistan Pending the Re-establishment of Permanent Government Institutions', 5 November, available at: http://www.un.org/News/dh/latest/afghan/afghan-agree.htm, last accessed 28 December 2016.

United Nations (UN) (2004), 'Report of the Secretary-General's High-level Panel on Threats, Challenges and Change: A More Secure World: Our Shared Responsibility', UN Document A/59/565, 2 December, available at: http://www.un.org/en/ga/search/view_doc.asp?symbol=A/59/565, last accessed 28 December 2016.

United Nations (UN) (2010), *Review of the United Nations Peacebuilding Architecture*, UN Document A/64/868-S/2010/393, 19 July, available at: http://www.un.org/ga/search/view_doc.asp?symbol=A/64/868, last accessed 28 December 2016.

United Nations (UN) (2011), *General Assembly Press Statement*, UN Document PBC/80, 21 April, available at: https://www.un.org/press/en/2011/pbc80.doc.htm, last accessed 28 December 2016.

United Nations (UN) (2014), *Report of the Special Committee on Peacekeeping Operations, 2014 Substantive Session*, UN Document A/68/19, 1 April, available at: http://www.securitycouncilreport.org/atf/cf/%7B65BFCF9B-6D27-4E9C-8CD3-CF6E4FF96FF9%7D/a_68_19.pdf, last accessed 28 December 2016.

United Nations Commission on Human Security (UNCHS) (2003), 'Human Security Now: Protecting and Empowering People', available at: http://www.un.org/humansecurity/sites/www.un.org.humansecurity/files/chs_final_report_-_english.pdf, last accessed 28 December 2016.

United Nations Development Programme (UNDP) (1994), *Human Development Report 1994: New Dimensions of Human Security*, Oxford: Oxford University Press, available at: http://hdr.undp.org/sites/default/files/reports/255/hdr_1994_en_complete_nostats.pdf, last accessed 28 December 2016.

United Nations Peacebuilding Commission (PBC) (2007), *Monitoring and Tracking Mechanism of the Strategic Framework for Peacebuilding in Burundi*, UN Document PBC/2/BDI/4, 27 November, available at: http://www.un.org/ga/search/view_doc.asp?symbol=PBC/2/BDI/4, last accessed 28 December 2016.

United Nations Secretary-General (UNSG) (2000), *We The Peoples: The Role of the United Nations in the 21st Century*, New York: United Nations Department of Public Information, available at: http://www.un.org/en/events/pastevents/pdfs/We_The_Peoples.pdf, last accessed 28 December 2016.

Zuber, R. (2015), personal interview with Robert Zuber, Executive Director of UN-based Global Action to Prevent War, 28 December.

11

Who Rebuilds?
Local Roles in Rebuilding Shattered Societies

Susan H. Allen[1]

Introduction

Though many descriptions of peace-building focus on institutions and external interventions, it is local people, not governments or organisations or external interveners, who rebuild their own social ties in the aftermath of destruction. We human beings are social animals. We learn our roles socially (Bandura 1977). When our communities are torn apart, we seek to rebuild them together, socially. When healthy resilient people experience trauma and lose the societal support patterns we rely on, we reimagine and reinvent new ways of engaging with each other. As societies develop over time, and change rapidly during times of extreme disruption, it is clear we cannot return to or recreate the past, rebuilding exactly the same social structures that preceded a crisis. We co-construct our new relationships together in conversation with each other, making meaning together (Harre 1983). Rooted in these understandings of human nature and social relationships, this chapter focuses on the people and partnerships that rebuild shattered societies, and the actions through which they do so, as the local meets the global.

The understandings presented here differ from a state-centric or international-law-based understanding of the process of recovery from war. Societies that have been shattered must rebuild in multi-faceted ways, including rebuilding electoral, economic, civil society and the range of social institutions (Paris 2004). Our focus is not on external people, organisations or states intervening to support that rebuilding; others in this book have focused on a variety of forms of external interventions. We focus instead in this chapter on local roles in recovery from disaster, and on local-international partnerships. This is not to discount the roles that external actors can usefully play. Rather, it is to highlight the opportunities for local actors to intervene in their own societies. As such, we ask the fundamental question, 'who rebuilds?'

In addressing this question, we first look at a case study of rebuilding Georgian–South Ossetian relationships so as to provide both relevant and substantive experiences. By considering *who* rebuilds shattered societies, we see there is an ongoing process of rebuilding even as minor breakdowns occur. Indeed, the skills and abilities that come to the foreground in the aftermath of traumatic change are also part of functional societies that grow and develop over time. Next, we examine the various actions that are part of rebuilding. By focusing on the activities and roles that people can play in the overall process of developing functioning social structures in the aftermath of trauma, we realise that virtually anyone can perform parts of the roles that make up the rebuilding process. Every individual can contribute in some way to rebuilding his or her society. Third, we consider first the varied actors, then the partnerships, and finally the roles of individuals involved in rebuilding. Those who rebuild are a variety of individuals working alone and within their home communities or in organisations or government structures whose activities in some way help meet one or more of the basic human needs we typically turn to society to support. We look at people partnering with each other in these activities, acknowledging that creating social bonds is indeed a social process.

Finally, even while acknowledging partnerships, we also consider individual agency, and the ways that a recognised or emergent leader can exercise what John Paul Lederach (2005) refers to as the 'moral imagination' to be part of creating history within their community. The individual's role is important in the reimagining of society. At a time when seemingly nothing works, when all that functioned has been decimated by war, people find ways to imagine what can work. We reinvent new ways to meet the basic functions of society. That imagination and invention are roles that local people play within their own societies. Living in a traumatised society, people consider what is working, and build on that to replace the shattered ruins of previous systems of interactions.

The following case study brings these concepts to life, providing concrete examples relevant to the actions, actors, partnerships and individual agency discussed later in the chapter.

Case Study: rebuilding Georgian–South Ossetian relationships

I have worked with South Ossetians and Georgians on peace-building programmes since 1998. The following short analysis of efforts to rebuild Georgian–South Ossetian relationships draws substantially on my experience, including my role as convener and facilitator of a Georgian–South Ossetian dialogue process that met from 2008–15.

In 2008, South Ossetia was thrust into international headlines. Most Western media reported that Russia had invaded South Ossetia, and that Georgia was engaging to counter the Russian attack. Russian commentators described a Georgian attack that required a Russian response to protect Russian citizens living in South Ossetia. Later, an investigation requested by the European Union (Tagliavini 2009) concluded that Georgia had indeed attacked prior to the large-scale Russian invasion, and that the conflict had been brewing for weeks prior to the 8 August 2008 confrontation. Understanding these competing narratives of events requires some insights into the history of the area. South Ossetians feared Georgian domination, while Georgians feared Russian domination. Since the late 1980s, Georgians and South Ossetians have clashed over differences pertaining to rights, independence, territorial integrity and the overall Georgian–South Ossetian relationship. The brief war in August of 2008 came on the heels of an escalation of tensions from 2004–8, and previous fighting in the 1990s. Thousands of people died, tens of thousands of people were displaced, and a new fence was constructed to prevent contact across what South Ossetians call their international border and what Georgians call the Administrative Boundary Line. Despite these barriers, there are Georgians and South Ossetians who are intent to rebuild some sort of Georgian–South Ossetian relationship.

By considering the Georgian–South Ossetian case, we can see a sampling of the themes developed in this chapter, such as the wide variety of actors who engage in post-war peace-building. Let us first consider several actors from a spectrum of most locally focused to most globally focused.

With a personal and family local focus, tens of thousands of individuals directly affected by the August 2008 war are taking action to rebuild their lives and their society. Some are displaced people who fled perhaps to Vladikavkaz in North Ossetia or to the Gori region of Georgia. While possibilities for returning home remain unclear and far in the future, some of the displaced have put down roots in new homes, and others have set their sights on preparing for an eventual return home. Whatever their circumstances, these individuals have made major adjustments in response to the changes to their society brought by the war. For example, a South Ossetian historian, Robert, lost his full library of historical documents and books in a fire during the August 2008 war. He is gradually rebuilding his collection by gathering new material bit by bit. His growing collection is not the same as his pre-war collection, but new access to historical material is stimulating his return to scholarly activity, and his ability to contribute his unique expertise to his university and thus his society.

A Georgian farmer, Gela, lives just a few miles from Robert's home in the major population centre of South Ossetia, the city Georgians know as Tskhinvali and South Ossetians know as Tskhinval. Gela grows tomatoes. For him to transport them to major markets on the Georgian side of the ceasefire line is costly, and the price he gets at those Georgian markets is low. But the price of tomatoes a few miles away, on the South Ossetian side of the ceasefire line, is much higher. Gela met with South Ossetians in a civil society confidence-building forum, and raised the question of how he could get his tomatoes to the South Ossetians there. The South Ossetians clearly were interested in the tomatoes, which Gela described colourfully with a farmer's deep respect for the qualities of the produce. Gela's offer of tomatoes sparked a broader discussion on possibilities for eventually opening trade across the ceasefire line.

While political decisions have not yet been made that would open up more trade across the ceasefire line, local leaders in villages and cities on both sides of the ceasefire line are mobilising community resources to recover and move on from the war's devastation. In the context of more limited access to Georgian products, and a need for bread, one village in South Ossetia came together to build a mill that they share and operate as a community resource. A small mini-grant was provided with Swiss funding through the international NGO Saferworld for the construction materials required for building the mill.

A major impediment to rapid rebuilding is that leaders of both sides of the Georgian– South Ossetian divide are trying to rebuild different visions of society. For the South Ossetian leadership, they strive to rebuild a South Ossetia independent of Georgia. The South Ossetian focus is on rebuilding within South Ossetia; any consideration of neighbourly relations with Georgia is secondary. For the

Georgian leadership, they strive to rebuild a South Ossetian society within Georgia's territorial integrity. The Georgian focus has been more on rebuilding relations with South Ossetians, with less emphasis on healing and recovery amongst the Georgian communities. Even while some focus on territorial claims, others see human relations as a necessary step towards agreeing political status. For example, the Georgian State Minister for Reconciliation, Paata Zakareishvili, has been clear he has no interest in an empty South Ossetian territory. Rather, it is the people of South Ossetia that he sees as part of the broader community of the state of Georgia (Resonance (Резонанси) 2012). Even within the leadership of the groups on each side of the conflict, there are different actors, seeking to build their own unique visions of society. These differences give rise to different ways of delineating the parameters of society. Is the society that is to be rebuilt inclusive of South Ossetia? Is it the South Ossetian people that are the focus, or the territory? These different emphases imply different approaches to rebuilding.

Beyond the immediate parties to the conflict, there are a myriad of other actors focusing on local, regional or global issues of rebuilding. Locally, civil society on both sides is part of the reconstitution of society in the aftermath of war, contributing to addressing humanitarian needs, offering psychosocial healing, rebuilding businesses ruined by war and so on. International non-governmental organisations (NGOs) engage first with humanitarian aid delivery, and then many transition to development assistance as immediate humanitarian concerns are addressed.

Much of the post-war engagement by internationals focuses on rebuilding in the aftermath of war, first immediately and then long term. First, humanitarian aid of US$4.5 billion was provided by Western donors to address direct war damage, build new housing for displaced people and other immediate concerns on the Georgian side of the divisions. Meanwhile Russia provided aid to the Abkhaz and South Ossetians. Now that, over seven years later, the immediate humanitarian needs are less urgent, interested Western countries focus their diplomats on supporting a peaceful settlement, with the Swiss Foreign Ministry representing Russian interests in Georgia while Georgia and Russia do not have direct diplomatic relations, and with several Western embassies in Tbilisi forming a Group of Friends that share analysis and strategise for peaceful settlement. Many donor countries support confidence-building measures across the conflict divide. The United Nations Development Programme

(UNDP) administers a set of many small grants for confidence-building measures funded by the European Union. The United Kingdom, the United States of America and other countries also provide support for non-governmentally based confidence-building measures that strengthen civil society and the contact between Georgian and South Ossetian civil societies.

This case also provides an illustration of the potential of drawing on partners' strengths to work with mutual respect. The Georgian–South Ossetian Point of View process was an informal dialogue process that brought Georgians and South Ossetians, both civil society and authorities, together to consider ways to be more effective in confidence-building, meeting the needs of people affected by the conflict, and increasing mutual understanding, with the ultimate goal of contributing to a peaceful settlement sometime in the future. The Point of View process convened dialogues three or four times a year from 2008 until summer 2015. While South Ossetians and Georgians found it was not culturally acceptable for them to reach out directly to each other, and that the security situation did not allow regular visits across the conflict line to each other, both South Ossetians and Georgians were appreciative of third-party efforts to convene discussions in a space outside of the immediate conflict area. In this case, it appeared from the outside of the process that George Mason University served as the most visible convener, with the author of this chapter leading a team that invited participants, printed an agenda and arranged meeting logistics such as purchasing flight tickets and identifying funding for meeting costs. However, such a view of the process would neglect the roles of the Georgian and South Ossetian co-conveners, Dina Alborov, Giorgi Kanashvili, Nino Kalandarishvili and Lira Kozaeva. Particularly in South Ossetia, direct unmediated discussions would not have been well understood throughout the 2008–15 time period of the Point of View dialogues. So, George Mason University filled a needed function as an impartial convener for the discussions. The Georgian and South Ossetian co-conveners provided substantial input into the invitation lists, the agenda of the discussions, the development of the dialogue format, and other convener functions. It would be impossible for a university far from the region to know the local actors and local conversations as well as these two co-conveners did. Likewise, the South Ossetian co-conveners knew the South Ossetian perspectives in a way that the Georgians could not, and the Georgian co-conveners knew the Georgian perspectives in a way that the South Ossetians could not.

All of the partners brought essential strengths that make possible the Point of View dialogues.

The broader community of international actors seeking to support rebuilding of Georgian–South Ossetian relationships also has formed ways of sharing information and analysis. The Joint Coordination Forum, convened by UNDP, is a regular monthly informal and confidential conversation amongst internationals working on related issues. The participants share their understanding of recent developments, seek to make sense of changing dynamics together and, on occasion, step back to look at the big-picture trends and consider potential strategies that many of them may wish to adopt.

There is, of course, not full consensus amongst the various international actors, as they support rebuilding differently, based on their different understandings and different relationships. Individuals do make a big difference in international organisations too. For example, Ryan Grist was working for the OSCE in South Ossetia, and was the senior OSCE official in Georgia at the time that the bombing started during the August 2008 war. Grist traveled through the area of fighting to evacuate some unarmed monitors and also to observe the situation directly. His statements that Georgian attacks on 7 August were entirely disproportionate to any South Ossetian provocations were heavily criticised by the OSCE Head of Mission Ambassador Kakala, and Grist resigned his OSCE position immediately after the war. Still, Grist's role as an individual, operating while the OSCE Head of Mission was out of the country on vacation, made a difference in how the war was interpreted internationally. While at first Western news sources blamed only Russia for the war, after Grist's comments were noticed, the Western media coverage began to acknowledge Georgia having some responsibility for the war, too (BBC News 2008; Champion 2008).

Heidi Tagliavini is another international who has made a difference in shaping international approaches to the rebuilding efforts. Tagliavini is a Swiss diplomat who had previously served as deputy head of the United Nations Observer Mission in Georgia (UNOMIG). She was appointed in 2008 to lead an EU fact-finding mission into the August 2008 war. Her report (Tagliavini 2009) noted both South Ossetian provocations in the weeks leading up to the war, and also significant Georgian military actions against the main city of South Ossetia prior to massive Russian troop movements into South Ossetia. While certainly her engagement as a representative of the EU was significant, Tagliavini was able to conduct her investigation in part because of the individual authority she held as a respected diplomat who was already familiar with the situation from her years of working there in the past. Her individual reputation and relationships made a difference in producing a report that was accepted by most as fairly balanced. In turn, this shaped international engagement in the ongoing rebuilding process.

Rebuilding roles: the actions of rebuilding

Stepping back from the specifics of the Georgian–South Ossetian case study, and before looking at who rebuilds, let us look at the actions involved in rebuilding social structures after they have been destroyed. People who seek to create a more functional life after traumatic disruption do so by taking action. It is these actions that rebuild shattered societies. It takes people talking with each other, people performing the actions of a society – reopening schools, baking and selling bread, farming, paving and policing roads, operating media sources, agreeing and implementing governance structures and so on. While it may be logical that teachers would open the schools, bakers bake the bread, farmers do the farming, road crews and police perform their roles, and journalists and politicians and so forth each perform their professional roles, let us pause for a moment to acknowledge that sometimes, in the aftermath of a tsunami or war or other catastrophe, the teachers or bakers or farmers or road crews have been displaced or worse. And, of course, some portion of the population may be so traumatised that healing their own psychological wounds must precede healthy social engagement. In such circumstances, those who have recovered sufficiently must summon a wide variety of skills and learn to play new roles, welcome help from surrounding communities, or otherwise adjust to the changed circumstances. Such actions require flexibility and adaptability.

While mediating agreements between opposing groups is only one aspect of recovery from war, we can learn from the study of mediation to understand aspects of the broader process of rebuilding. Christopher Mitchell (1993) suggests a focus on the processes involved in mediation, although much scholarly work has focused on the mediators themselves more than what roles they play. Each of the roles he outlines as part of mediating processes are relevant to rebuilding shattered societies: explorer, convener, decoupler, unifier, enskiller, envisioner, guarantor, facilitator, legitimiser, enhancer, monitor, enforcer and reconciler. Building on Mitchell's list, below I look at each of these roles one by one, analysing the ways in which each role is relevant to rebuilding, drawing on the Georgian–South Ossetian context for specific examples.

There are roles for an explorer, exploring how people want to rebuild after trauma. What new visions resonate with the communities? What resources can be drawn on as strengths during the time that other social structures are broken? Who has the energy to devote to rebuilding? What aspects of the pre-war social structures remain intact as strengths on which to build? Religious leaders, business people, journalists and political leaders are only some examples of platforms that allow performing explorer roles. In the Georgian–South Ossetian case, the first meeting of the Point of View dialogue served an explorer role: the agenda was to explore what topics, if any, were of shared interest to the participants.

There are roles for a convener, bringing together individuals who want to rebuild, who seek each other's inspiration to take the next steps in recovery, who have resources or skills to offer in collaboration with others. Individuals who have broad respect from a variety of stakeholders can play convening roles. In the Georgian–South Ossetian case, George Mason University played one convening role. Another official convening role was played by the EU, UN and OSCE as the co-chairs of the Geneva International Discussions.

There are roles for a decoupler, separating out particular aspects of recovery, and addressing these in partial isolation from all the other problems that plague a society facing the aftermath of destruction. For example, if individuals working with the International Committee of the Red Cross operating in a fragile ceasefire environment were to successfully identify healthcare restoration as a priority area of work, regardless of ongoing political or other disputes, the decoupling of healthcare provision from political questions can allow progress in at least that one area of rebuilding. In South Ossetia, the ICRC focuses purely on humanitarian issues, such as healthcare.

There are roles for a unifier, unifying communities around a vision or plan of action, developing consensus when people lack certainty as so many variables remain in flux after trauma and turmoil. For example, media outlets can spread a vision, an individual leader can bring together factions to develop a common approach, or an outsider can convene discussions amongst various locals who share some overall interests but find themselves pulling in different directions. The Georgian–South Ossetian context seems to lack a unifier.

Rebuilding also can engage the role of an enskiller. Recovery requires specialised skills, such as trauma recovery counselling, that were not in such high demand before social disruption. Training the trainers' activities, or mentored clinic programmes, can help develop skills within the affected communities to address the needs that emerge in the aftermath of destruction. Again, this role is lacking in the case-study context; South Ossetia has very few resources for trauma recovery counselling.

Rebuilding can also draw on an envisioner role. When all seems lost, family members have died, and all social structures seem to have ceased to function, a vision of how things could again become bearable must emerge. People will work towards creating healthy functioning social structures again when they see a realistic vision of how that might be possible. Someone must engage the moral imagination as John Paul Lederach (2005: ix) defines it, '[t]he capacity to imagine something rooted in the challenges of the real world yet capable of giving birth to that which does not yet exist'. Multiple brave Georgians and South Ossetians have taken on the envisioner role, but have thus far failed to bring their full home communities with them in the visioning process.

Rebuilding can further benefit from a guarantor. In the instability that reigns when social structures are shattered, when police forces may be disbanded, or other governmental structures not functioning, some sort of guarantee, even partial, can support recovery efforts. Will international observers document any human rights violations they observe? Will media report unbiased coverage of events? Will neighbours uphold culturally appropriate codes of conduct? In the Georgian–South Ossetian context, there has not been one guarantor that is accepted by all sides as impartial and reliable.

Another role is that of the facilitator. How can these many conversations be structured, the many stakeholders invited, the various agendas kept straight, and the results built on in conversation after conversation? As in any major change effort, facilitators, formal or informal, are required to focus rebuilding conversations, encourage appropriate participation, and keep the process moving constructively. The Georgian–South Ossetian context has engaged multiple facilitators.

Later in the rebuilding process, the role of legitimiser can be helpful. When tentative agreements are reached or new structures begin to emerge, who can offer them legitimacy? The local population may begin to respect a new police force, international voices may comment on the conduct of an election, a religious leader may speak about the importance of accepting the newly emergent changes. Georgians and South Ossetians have not reached that stage in rebuilding their relationship.

Further progress in rebuilding can be supported by an enhancer. As individuals make extreme efforts to rebuild their societies, who can enhance these efforts? If a community finds an old millstone that has been unused since a recent war, identifies a community need to produce flour and yet cannot find construction materials to rebuild the stand for the millstone, the wheat will not be ground into flour. (Recall that Saferworld, with Swiss support, financed a mill rebuilding effort in South Ossetia.) Financial support for rebuilding efforts is one example of enhancing. Other examples would include amplifying voices by covering efforts in national media, high-profile visits by dignitaries to enhance legitimacy of local efforts and so on.

Rebuilding may also involve the role of monitor. In times of extreme change and uncertainty, the roles of monitoring and recording events become important. For example, communities that create early warning systems of security difficulties are more able to address emerging security concerns because of their systematic monitoring of isolated events.

Another role is that of enforcer. When previous social enforcement mechanisms such as police forces or legal systems are not functional, others, such as a transitional authority, can step in to cover these functions temporarily. But, not all sides may agree on a would-be enforcer. For example, the South Ossetians see the Russian military as an enforcer, preventing Georgian military incursions. But, the Georgians see the Russian military as occupiers.

Finally, a further role is that of reconciler. When people have been on opposite sides of a gun, or seen others kill their loved ones, the rebuilding of the human relationships in a society or between neighbouring societies can be the most difficult rebuilding role of all. While no one can force others to reconcile, individuals can take on the roles of encouraging reconciliation, supporting conciliatory gestures, providing spaces for constructive discussions amongst former enemies and so on. Those who take on reconciler roles may be local leaders, individuals of mixed heritage with strong ties on two sides of a divide, outsiders who have the trust of both sides of a divide and even media figures who offer rehumanisation of the other as part of their reporting. Many different reconcilers have acted in the Georgian–South Ossetian context.

By focusing on the actions here, I intend to highlight that it is not so much *being* a certain person that allows a contribution to rebuilding society, but *acting*, or taking action, that makes a difference. For each of the actions above, there are multiple people who could take them. Those who act to rebuild are varied. The common characteristic shared by rebuilders is the actions that they take.

Those who act to rebuild

Of course, even as I emphasise the kinds of actions that rebuild shattered societies, and the kinds of partnerships that form ties, strengthening social fabric through working towards shared rebuilding goals, I must acknowledge the various actors who perform these actions. The locals are the most numerous, including officials, civil society, religious, media, business, educators and so on. Diamond and McDonald's (1996) framework of multitrack diplomacy provides an overview of some of these categories, or 'tracks', of diplomacy: government, professional conflict resolution, business, private citizens, research, training and education, activism, religious, funding and public opinion/communication.

I should note, too, that nefarious actors, such as organised crime networks, may be quick to rebuild after wars or other instability. Indeed, organised crime can thrive in the instability and uncertainty that pervades after mass destruction (Mirimanova 2006). Still, criminal networks can perform some social functions, for better or for worse. If a criminal group pledges credibly to protect an area in return for that area's loyalty, some types of rebuilding can go on in that protected area (Mirimanova 2006).

From afar, outsiders looking at shattered societies tend to focus on the national and international actors who attempt to support communities recovering from disaster. For example, the Joint Coordination Forum in Tbilisi, Georgia, draws together international actors working in Georgian–Abkhaz and Georgian–South Ossetian programmes. National actors such as official state government bodies are accessed through the channels of official diplomacy, following protocol, and through the media communications. And, internationals focused on an area consider the roles of other internationals extensively, meeting at international forums with other internationals perhaps as often as they meet with the locals most affected by a crisis and its aftermath. It is true that people working through international institutions can play highly important roles in rebuilding. Consider, for example, the roles individuals played in the

Organization for Security and Co-operation in Europe at the time of the August 2008 war between Russia and Georgia, over South Ossetia and Abkhazia, or the role of Swiss diplomat Heidi Tagliavini in chairing the Independent International Fact-Finding Mission on the Conflict in Georgia. These and other roles are noted in the case study of rebuilding Georgian–South Ossetian relations. But, such internationally focused approaches tend to leave out the billions of individuals who make choices daily about how to engage in their home communities, and the many local leaders who shape those local societies. These are also important contributors to rebuilding shattered societies. As demonstrated by the brief review of actions taken during rebuilding, there are many that require local trust, local knowledge, and location on the ground in the area concerned.

Individual agency

No single individual can rebuild society alone. However, I must also highlight that a single individual can make a difference when working in partnership with others. Individuals form the fabric that knits their societies together. Consider these recent news stories of individuals who have made an observable difference in addressing divides in their different divided societies:

In the context of black–white racial tension in the US in August 2013, African American school bookkeeper Antoinette Tuff talked a 20-year-old white mentally ill man out of his plan to shoot children at the elementary school where she worked in Decatur, Georgia. While the young man was armed with an assault rifle, Tuff was armed with love. She told him she loved him, and shared her own struggles with attempting suicide, the end of her marriage and the possibilities she found to rebuild after facing tragedy. In conversation with Tuff, the would-be shooter agreed to put down his weapons and surrender to police. A tragedy that could have ripped apart the community was averted (Walsh 2013).

In the context of Taliban threats against girls who attend school in the Swat district of Pakistan, local schoolgirl Malala Yousafzai wrote a blog about her life and her views on education for girls. She was shot in the head and neck by a member of the Taliban as she rode the school bus home in October 2012, but she survived and inspired a UN petition, 'I am Malala', calling for all children to be in school by 2015. Subsequently, Pakistan ratified a 'Right to Education' bill. Yousafzai's efforts served to at least partially bridge the social divides between educated and non-educated, between boys and girls, in Pakistan (Yousefzai and Lamb 2013). In 2014, Yousefzai was awarded the Nobel Peace Prize, which she shared with an Indian children's education advocate.

Where fighting in the Democratic Republic of Congo (DRC) has included systematic rape as a weapon of war, gynecologist Denis Mukwege directs a rape recovery programme at Panzi Hospital in Bukava in the DRC. By treating both the physical effects of rape, including repairing fistulas, and treating the psychological effects of rape, the hospital helps hundreds of thousands of women return to health. Where individual lives were shattered in large numbers by systematic rape, whole communities suffered the loss when women were traumatised and physically disabled. By helping over 200,000 women find healing and recovery, the hospital supports community recovery (Perraudin and Busari 2013).

In the context of a society not functioning to meet his basic human needs as a street vendor, Mohamed Bouazizi ignited protests in Tunisia with his self-immolation in protest of the confiscation of his wares (Abouzeid 2011). Bouazizi did not mean to become a leader. He did not plan for the major social movement his death would catalyse. However, his actions provided a focal point of shared grievances around which many desperate people coalesced and protested. While the protests that soon toppled the president of Tunisia may not be seen as typical ways of rebuilding, for the people seeking redress for years of injustice, these were part of the path to rebuilding, by highlighting these injustices through the vivid image of Bouazizi's body burning, and his lingering death in the hospital over the remaining days of his life.

Finally, drawing from the example of the South Caucasus, consider the inspirational life of Dr George Khutsishvili, who was a Georgian political scientist and conflict resolution expert. He worked on dozens of different Georgian–Abkhaz, Georgian–South Ossetian, Georgian–Russian and broader Caucasus regional confidence-building formats for two decades until his sudden passing in October 2013. At the time of his death, people from all sides of the interlocking conflicts in the Caucasus mourned his passing and noted the significant influence he had had on reaching across the conflict divides, mentoring younger colleagues who developed their own engagement across the conflict divides, and highlighting in mass media the importance of confidence-building across the fractures between communities in the Caucasus region.

Each of the above examples refers to people who have (either intentionally or unintentionally) been visible leaders in their communities. Some of their activities have been reported by news sources. Their efforts have been noticed. Of course, there are also many unreported roles in rebuilding shattered societies, and such stories remain largely undocumented. However, based on personal experience of the author, the Georgian–South Ossetian case study above includes note of one such (otherwise) 'unreported' role: the Georgian farmer's offer of tomatoes to South Ossetians. This is clearly just one of many, many individual efforts to reconstruct after social destruction. Most likely, the number of unreported contributions to rebuilding shattered societies far exceeds the number of reported contributions.

All of these examples of individual contributions to rebuilding involve creativity. Individual creativity contributes to the reimagining of society (Arai 2009). At a time when all that functioned has been wiped out by war, people find ways to imagine what could work. We reinvent new ways to meet the basic functions of society. When we notice what is working, we can build on that to replace the shattered ruins of previous systems of interactions. In a relational space that both honors what *is*, and imagines what *could be*, we can decide to build that future that could be. Creativity is required to move from old ways of social interactions, through a period of destruction, and into a new way of providing for the common good. In the absence of any roadmaps through these times of uncertainty, a strong moral imagination (Lederach 2005) and community leadership (Shmueli et al. 2009) can support the brave initial steps towards rebuilding.

Partnerships

Partnerships between local and international actors can draw on the strengths that each brings (Cohen 2013). While local actors may know their local culture, history, and local sentiments, and have trusting relationships with influential people in their community, outsiders may bring a fresh perspective, the ability to ask fundamental questions that insiders may take for granted and perhaps also some stories of how other people have addressed similar situations in other contexts (Camplisson 1999). We might see the local as knowing each individual tree, and the outsider as seeing an overall forest. Or, the local may see the trends over centuries, while the international may see the window of opportunity offered by a one-year tour of duty in the area. In both cases, contrasting perspectives can help shape constructive conversations. Genuine learning can take place in constructive partnerships based on respectful engagement.

In contrast, some partnerships are exploitive relationships in which a powerful party (often an international actor) dominates another party (often a local actor) (Cohen 2013). Power differences, or perceptions of power differences, can make partnerships difficult. But, when partners recognise that they each bring necessary insights and skills to a team effort, both become more powerful as they work together.

Particularly powerful partnerships can be formed by individuals who come from two different sides of a divide. Referred to as 'unusual pairs' (Gopin 2013) when they combine their expertise, these individuals bring the strengths of inside knowledge of both sides of a divide. By developing strong partnerships with each other as individuals, they can forge a bridge across the divide. For example, Zheng Wang and Tatsushi Arai partnered to co-facilitate several Chinese–Japanese dialogues regarding the dispute over islands in the South China Sea. Wang and Arai found their partnering process helped them develop more understanding of the approach of both sides towards the islands, and thus of possibilities for transforming the conflict. As Wang and Arai developed trust in each other, they began to feel comfortable asking each other very difficult questions, such as '[w]hy do the Japanese think the islands belong to Japan?' and '[w]hy are the Chinese so angry?' Through the bi-communal partnership facilitating Chinese–Japanese dialogues on these issues, Wang and Arai developed highly nuanced understandings of Chinese and Japanese perspectives. On the basis of these understandings, they made joint recommendations for addressing the conflict (Arai et al. 2013; Arai et al. 2015; Wang and Arai 2013).

Even without forming in-depth long-term partnerships, individuals come together to create relational spaces in which they can imagine together and envision ways their collective efforts can add up to more than the sum of the parts. Considering society as a complex adaptive system (Coleman 2011; Vallacher et al. 2013), it is clear that awareness of the system dynamics can help us engage more constructively. Coordination amongst the various actors performing diverse actions allows a more multifaceted view of the system dynamics, and thus can strengthen an overall rebuilding process.

There are many types of coordination, both sequential and simultaneous. The different initiatives involved in rebuilding can complement each other through sequentially building on each other's progress, with one picking up where the other leaves off. Also, they can build on each other with simultaneous complementary efforts, such as when several separate initiatives achieve a critical mass by separately building momentum that adds up to a shift in national sentiment. Beyond the sequential and simultaneous distinction, there are five basic approaches to coordination (Nan 1999; Nan 2003):

1. sharing information, or communication;
2. sharing analysis, or consideration;
3. planning together, or coordination;
4. resource sharing, or cooperation;
5. working in collaboration, or collaboration.

Think of these as the '5Cs' of working together, as a way of distinguishing that not all work together must be of the close partnership that is collaboration. Coordination lies within a spectrum of various other ways of working together. Even basic information sharing can strengthen a rebuilding process, and lies at the communication end of the spectrum. As the people involved begin to shift their thinking based on input from others, they move along the spectrum to shared analysis, or consideration. Consider the example of the shared analysis that is part of the work of the Joint Coordination Forum noted in the extended case study of Georgian–South Ossetian rebuilding. As plans are developed together, even simply the schedule of meetings is adjusted so as not to conflict with others, people begin acting based on their shared analysis and coordination occurs. When people begin supporting each other's work with shared resources, they are cooperating. And, finally, in partnerships in which the work becomes shared, people collaborate. The spectrum develops along a continuum of how much the other can influence one's own work, from information sharing where the influence is up to the one receiving information all the way to collaboration in which it is not always clear how to distinguish one's own work from another's.

Conclusion

This chapter has focused on local roles in rebuilding after war or other disaster. Beyond rare natural disasters, this chapter has clarified that it is people who shatter societies, and also people who rebuild, drawing on our human resilience in the aftermath of trauma. But, note that even the healthiest of societies are undergoing constant rebuilding in some way. As societies face new challenges, people adapt new approaches as needed. There is an ongoing process of rebuilding as we adjust to changing needs that naturally arise as we change and our world changes. Healthy societies can make these adjustments without catastrophic traumas such as war. Where political openness and freedom of speech are sufficient, new needs can be identified and addressed before they become rifts that tear societies apart.

Human beings are remarkably resilient and resourceful, as we have demonstrated in our abilities to create healthy societies from the shards left after destruction. We are interconnected in society, and in the repair of our social ties too. Just as it 'takes two to tango', broken ties cannot be repaired in a one-sided way. People must reach towards each other to connect. No one reaching out can form a bond if the others are not receptive. But, in the aftermath of massive social trauma, people want to be receptive, as we are social and we need functioning societies. When our social ties are broken through war or another disaster, we work together to rebuild those ties. The common task of recovering from the disaster can bring people together again as they work together to meet their shared human needs.

In war, the potential or actual destruction of large populations presents the possibility of annihilation of a people or a culture. But, in rebuilding after war, we must accept coexistence: not only do we need to accept each other's presence, but we need to make ourselves available to each other. When people from opposite sides of a war partner together to provide basic food or healthcare or meet some other basic human need, there is a shift. When we recognise our coexistence, it becomes clear that no one in a post-war environment will have a stable future unless most people do. It is this basic inter-connectedness that draws local people to rebuild beyond the confines of their own home, rebuilding their own societies from the inside-out.

Note

1. I want to thank Andrea Bartoli, Zachariah Mampilly and Wilfredo Torres for helpful discussions of these topics and constructive comments on earlier versions of this chapter.

References

Abouzeid, R. (2011), 'Bouazizi: The Man Who Set Himself and Tunisia on Fire', *Time*, 4 October, available at: http://content.time.com/time/maga zine/article/0,9171,2044723,00.html, last accessed 2 January 2017.

Arai, T. (2009), *Creativity and Conflict Resolution: Alternative Pathways to Peace*, London: Routledge.

Arai, T., S. Goto and Z. Wang (2013), 'The Daioyu/Senkaku Dispute as an Identity-Based Conflict: Toward Sino-Japan Reconciliation', in T. Arai, S. Goto and Z. Wang (eds), *Clash of National Identities: China, Japan, and the East China Sea Territorial Dispute*, Washington, DC: Wilson Center, pp. 97–107, available at: https://www.wilsoncenter.org/sites/default/files/asia_china_seas_web.pdf, last accessed 2 January 2017.

Arai, T., S. Goto and Z. Wang (eds.) (2015), *Contested Memories and Reconciliation Challenges: Japan and the Asia-Pacific on the 70th Anniversary of the End of World War II*. Washington, DC: Wilson Center, available at: https://www.wilsoncenter.org/sites/default/files/ContestedMemories.pdf, last accessed 2 January 2017.

Bandura, A. (1977), *Social Learning Theory*, New York: General Learning Press.

BBC News (2008), 'OSCE "Failed" in Georgia Warnings', BBC News, 8 November, available at: http://news.bbc.co.uk/2/hi/7717169.stm, last accessed 2 January 2017.

Camplisson, J. (1999), personal interview, Belfast, 6 June.

Champion, M. (2008), 'British Monitor Complicates Georgian Blame Game', *The Wall Street Journal*, 19 December, available at: http://www.wsj.com/news/articles/SB122963718776319647, last accessed 2 January 2017.

Cohen, S. (2013), 'International North–South Peacebuilding Partnerships: Practitioner Stories from the Field'. Fairfax: VA: George Mason University.

Coleman, P. (2011), *Five Percent: Finding Solutions to Seemingly Impossible Conflicts*, New York: Public Affairs.

Diamond, L. and J. W. McDonald (1996) *Multi-Track Diplomacy: A Systems Approach to Peace*, 3rd edn, West Hartford, CT: Kumarian Press.

Gopin, M. (2013), 'Unusual Pairs – Clips', *Zej Media*, available at http://www.zejmedia.com/video-playlists/unusual-pairs-clips/, last accessed 2 January 2017.

Harre, R. (1983), *Personal Being*, Oxford: Blackwell.

Lederach, J. P. (2005), *Moral Imagination: The Art and Soul of Building Peace*, Oxford: Oxford University Press.

Mirimanova, N. (2006), 'Corruption and Conflict in the South Caucasus', London: International Alert, available at: http://www.international-alert.org/sites/default/files/Caucasus_CorruptionConflict_EN_2006.pdf, last accessed 2 January 2017.

Mitchell, C. (1993), 'The Processes and Stages of Mediation', in D. Smock (ed.), *Making War and Waging Peace*, Washington, DC: United States Institute of Peace Press, pp. 139–59.

Nan, S. (1999), 'Complementarity and Coordination of Conflict Resolution

Efforts in the Conflicts over Abkhazia, South Ossetia, and Transdniestria'. PhD thesis, George Mason University, Fairfax, VA.

Nan, S. (2003), 'Intervention Coordination', *Beyond Intractability Knowledge Base*, available at: http://www.beyondintractability.org/essay/intervention-coordination, last accessed 2 January 2017.

Paris, R. (2004), *At War's End: Building Peace after Civil Conflict*, Cambridge: Cambridge University Press.

Perraudin, F. and S. Busari (2013) 'Nobel Peace Prize: Congo Rape Trauma Surgeon among Favorites', CNN, 10 October, available at: http://www.cnn.com/2013/10/10/world/africa/nobel-prize-congo-surgeon-mukegwe/index.html, last accessed 2 January 2017.

Resonance (Резонанси) (2012), 'Закареишвили: Вернуть людей, чтобы вернуть территории', *Закареишвили: Вернуть людей, чтобы вернуть территории*, available at: http://abkhazeti.info/news/1349591738.php, last accessed 2 January 2017.

Shmueli, D., W. Warfield and S. Kaufman (2009), 'Enhancing Community Leadership Negotiation Skills to Build Civic Capacity', *Negotiation Journal*, 25(2), pp. 249–66.

Tagliavini, H. (2009), 'Report of the Independent International Fact-Finding Mission on the Conflict in Georgia', Brussels: Council of the European Union.

Vallacher, R. R., P. T. Coleman, A. Nowak, L. Bui-Wrzosinska, L. Leibovitch, K. Kugler and A. Bartoli (2013), *Attracted to Conflict: Dynamic Foundations of Destructive Social Relations*, New York: Springer.

Walsh, J. (2013), 'The Story Bigots Hate: Antoinette Tuff's Courage', Salon, 22 August, available at: http://www.salon.com/2013/08/22/the_story_the_right_hates_antoinette_tuffs_courage/, last accessed 2 January 2017.

Wang, Z. and T. Arai (2013), 'China, Japan, and the East China Sea Territorial Dispute: An Experience of Bi-National Initiatives for Conflict Resolution', presentation at the School for Conflict Analysis and Resolution, George Mason University, 8 October.

Yousafzai, M. and C. Lamb (2013), *I Am Malala: The Girl Who Stood Up for Education and Was Shot by the Taliban*, New York: Little, Brown and Company.

12

Transforming the Discourse of Civil-Military Interaction in Humanitarian Environments

Vandra Harris

Introduction

With the securitisation of aid, the changing nature of conflict and the connecting and informing effects of globalisation, the increasing intersection between military and humanitarian is becoming recognised as an important global security issue. While NGOs and militaries are inherently different actors, the role of each is evolving in response to changes in both the environments they work in and approaches to meeting development and security challenges. These changes bring with them the ever-increasing likelihood of working in the same space and thus needing at the very least to be aware of each other's actions, though the spectrum of engagement ranges from collaborating to deliver assistance, to an absolute rejection of contact.

Discourse on civil-military interaction tends to view militaries as dominant partners in the relationship in light of their authority to carry out government policy and their focus on specific tasks and the strategies required to complete them. The civilian side of the interaction is most often understood as government and government agencies, and sometimes police. Only rarely are civil society, private enterprise and non-government organisations seriously addressed under the 'civilian' banner, despite the fact that each of these groups plays an important role in achieving and sustaining the stability and return to normality that are key to the broad military end-goal of creating an environment that is secure enough for them to withdraw completely.

This chapter explores the key non-governmental and military approaches to interaction, and how these point to civilian leadership in humanitarian environments. A range of guidelines, doctrine and policies provide clear frameworks for interaction, but NGOs and militaries are comprised of human individuals, whose experience, attitudes and beliefs shape their engagement, and these must also be understood when considering interaction. This discussion therefore explores NGO-military interaction and how it can be reframed to improve outcomes for communities, drawing on qualitative research with NGO and military personnel as well as civilian and military guidelines. Pointing to military doctrine and humanitarian guidelines, the chapter illuminates the primacy given to NGOs in most non-military guides, but points to ways in which military goals appear to have precedence. Reflecting on the claim that NGOs are the military's 'force multipliers' – additional tools that increase the impact of the military force – it argues that even turning this concept around is unhelpful. What is needed instead is greater clarity around humanitarian and humanitarian-like action and actors.

With governments funding both defence and development – the latter increasingly under a foreign affairs banner and with an explicit 'national interest' agenda – it can be understood that they view both as valuable in shaping international environments. While national militaries in functioning democracies are fully funded by government and come under government control,[1] development actors generally receive their funds from both government and individual donations. As such, while this gives NGOs greater autonomy than militaries have, they remain subject to extensive funding conditions that deeply shape the assistance they deliver and how they deliver it (for example participatory, inclusive and secular). At the same time, governments are expanding how they define development funding: just one example is that Australia funds international policing (training, capacity-building and frontline policing) from the development budget (Harris and Goldsmith 2012: 1024). With changes in military and humanitarian environments and broadening acceptance of the notion that security and development are fundamentally connected (see World Bank 2011; Duffield 2013; Pugh et al. 2013), the future of NGOs and militaries will be increasingly entwined. It is therefore important to have a clear understanding of how they relate to each other, and how that relationship can function best.

Humanitarian space and actors

The complex nature of humanitarian environments renders it extremely difficult to establish a neat division of labour between humanitarian and military pursuits. NGOs and militaries may find themselves in shared space in diverse environments, yet they may not fully comprehend each other's role and goals. Given the vastly different nature of the entities involved, this is not surprising, even in the context of whole-of-government approaches. Apart from their ubiquitous deployment in interstate conflict, foreign militaries are characteristically to be found in contexts where police and government are unable to meet security needs – often most evident in cases of civil conflict or war. This may also be the case when the peak of the conflict has passed (or been averted) and the transition to stability has begun, but police and government need assistance due to either the scale of the stability challenges or their capacity to respond, as for example in the protracted stabilisation mission in Timor-Leste.

A third environment is the case of disasters and complex emergencies, in which militaries have a rapid response capacity surpassing that of many other agencies, and they can be rapidly deployed to meet government objectives of saving lives and re-establishing infrastructure and services to enable the population to begin recovery. Disasters may be natural, human induced (e.g. large-scale terror attacks) or a combination of both, and onset may be sudden or gradual. In complex emergencies, the crisis results from 'a combination of political instability, conflict and violence, social inequities and underlying poverty' (FAO 2015), and militaries may be among the range of actors required to respond effectively.

The diverse environments in which militaries and NGOs both operate can be broadly termed as humanitarian, and an oft-heard refrain is that they are becoming increasingly crowded with a range of actors, which in turn leads to calls to respect the 'humanitarian space' (Hubert and Brassard-Boudreau 2014: 21). Just as humanitarian can be defined differently (from simply 'helping others' to providing assistance according to specific principles), so too the notion of humanitarian space, which fundamentally concerns 'the context of humanitarian action and the context of needs to which humanitarian actors are seeking to respond' (Collinson and Elhawary 2012: 2).

To respect the humanitarian space is to give precedence to the humanitarian aspect of the intervention. Humanitarian organisations have set out a charter and principles for humanitarian action, published in the *Sphere Handbook* (Sphere Project 2011). It is grounded on the fundamental principle that 'all human beings are born free and equal in dignity and rights', including the rights to life with dignity, to receive humanitarian assistance, and to protection and security. This gives rise to the absolute imperative to 'prevent and alleviate human suffering arising out of disaster or conflict' (Sphere Project 2011: 20–1).

The humanitarian space thus encompasses not only a physical space in which humanitarian assistance is delivered, but also a protected notion of the way such assistance is targeted and delivered. As affirmed in United Nations General Assembly Resolutions 46/182 (1991) and 58/114 (2004), humanitarian actions must observe the principles of humanity, impartiality, neutrality and independence. Under these principles, assistance must be delivered without distinction regarding personal or collective attributes and beliefs, including sides taken or participation in a conflict. Participating organisations cannot take sides and must remain independent from the various objectives at play in the environment, including political, military and economic ones. To many humanitarian organisations these principles demonstrate that humanitarian action is much more than simply helping people in need, and is therefore distinct from actions by militaries and private enterprise that might claim the humanitarian label. By this understanding, the military mandate renders it impossible for military personnel to fulfil the humanitarian principles of neutrality and impartiality, precluding militaries from performing humanitarian functions.

Notwithstanding the clarity of this definition in the eyes of the humanitarian sector, 'humanitarian' is a term that has broader applications. It is an adjective applied to a seemingly limitless array of nouns, from actors to environment, emergencies to interventions, and so on. At its broadest, the dictionary definition is 'relating to or characteristic of people who work to improve the lives and living conditions of other people' (Merriam-Webster: n.d.). Militaries describe their humanitarian assistance as 'support provided to host governments, humanitarian and development agencies by a deployed force whose primary mission is not the provision of humanitarian aid' (ACMC-ACFID 2012: 54). This goes beyond the basic definition of humanitarian as helping, and frames humanitarian action clearly within a revised military orientation. To the consternation of many NGOs, military strategies have broadened well beyond war-fighting to encompass strategies that place them clearly in humanitarian and development spaces. Speaking as Australia's then-Chief of Defence Force, Admiral Chris Barrie clearly outlined an expanded understanding of the role of the Australian Defence Force (ADF), stating that 'while there is no doubt that our core business is to provide traditional military options to Government, the Defence Force has also become an important resource which provides Government with a range of options not associated with force-on-force considerations. In short, we have a dual role: we must actively work for peace, as well as prepare for war' (Admiral Chris Barrie 1999, cited in ADF 2009: 1).

This shift in approach is not necessarily welcomed by humanitarian actors, which may accuse militaries of 'mission creep', and of using humanitarian strategies to meet non-humanitarian goals (see Duffey 2000: 155; Fast 2014: 95). Perhaps it is the mythology of the heroic soldier and narratives of violent warfare throughout history that lead us to assume that militaries have never wished to be humanitarians, and that they should not attempt to do so, yet militaries have long recognised the benefits to their mission of gaining the trust and support of local populations. The reality is that this reflects the changing nature of conflict and the prevalence of asymmetric, intrastate conflict, which necessitates new strategies. In this regard, so-called 'unconventional warfare' has long been the context for national military action, and if militaries are to protect citizens, they need to engage a wider spectrum of approaches. Writing in 1962, Lindsay reflected that 'militarily inferior guerrilla forces' – unconventional forces – must 'win control of the state by first winning control of the civilian population'. It follows that if national militaries are to defeat these enemies, they too must focus on the civilian population.

It is clear, therefore, that military focus on the population is not a passing (or even recent) fad but rather is fundamental to contemporary military action, under various labels. The term 'hearts and minds' is credited to British General Sir Gerald Templer in 1952, it was a catchphrase of Lyndon B Johnson's US presidency, and it has been widely adopted to refer to military actions that seek to gain local confidence by identifying and meeting the needs of communities beyond basic security. More recently, counterinsurgency (COIN) approaches have emerged to respond to subversive conflicts with non-state actors characterising the military terrain. The COIN approach explicitly adopts both military and civilian action to target not only the conflict itself but also the root causes, based on the principle that while security is an essential prerequisite, 'non-military means are often the most effective elements, with military forces playing an enabling role' (BPMA 2009: 2). These convictions lead to military actions that are consistent with development strategies and the Responsibility to Protect approach promoted by the United Nations.

Indeed, this consistency is acknowledged in the *U.S. Government Counterinsurgency Guide,* which also clearly explains the limits of that apparent connection, stating that:

> the capabilities required for COIN may be very similar to those required for peacekeeping operations, humanitarian assistance, stabilization operations, and development assistance missions. However, the intent of a COIN campaign is to build popular support for a government while marginalizing the insurgents: it is therefore fundamentally an *armed political competition* with the insurgents. Consequently, control (over the environment, the population, the level of security, the pace of events, and the enemy) is the fundamental goal of COIN, a goal that distinguishes it from peace operations or humanitarian intervention. (BPMA 2009: 12, original emphasis)

Military strategies will continue to evolve, and COIN will be sidelined by the next round of 'military fads and fashions' (Kilcullen, cited in Ricks 2014) – if indeed this has not already happened. Given the nature of warfare, military models will long remain 'human-centric', whether a 'human domain model' or other configurations (Cleveland et al. 2015: 31). It is also true that NGOs and militaries will continue to reflect on each other's actions and need to negotiate territory in humanitarian environments.

Pivotal in humanitarians' concerns about the impact of military engagement in humanitarian action is the fact that the same (or very similar) strategies are used for very different goals. Thus a military may undertake actions that mirror humanitarian assistance, with the aim of securing control over the population in order to ultimately overcome insurgents, rather than meeting their right to dignity, assistance and protection. This is also why NGOs, with their ability to build popular support, may be viewed as potential assets in human-centric military strategy.

Given the clarity of the above statement on the goals of COIN, one of the key concerns must be the conflation of military and humanitarian actors, and the impact of this. While militaries adopting human-centric approaches evidently recognise and seek to replicate the legitimacy NGOs garner through their activities and engagement with communities, NGOs fear that rather than increasing military legitimacy, these acts decrease NGO legitimacy. They are also concerned that 'armed humanitarian operations do not meet civilian needs efficiently and ignore potentially deserving recipients who do not fit the strategic goals of the aid distribution' (Lischer 2007: 107).

Additionally, they fear that military engagement in humanitarian roles will blur the distinction between military and humanitarian action, therefore reducing the security humanitarian actors assume through not taking sides in the conflict (Anderson 1999). Together this forms a significant body of concern that demands response, and this research contributes to that by clarifying the distinctions and parallels in military and NGO practice and proposing a pathway to improved mutual understanding.

Fundamental to this discussion is the very real distinction between the actions and goals of militaries and NGOs. As a rule, NGOs have a long-term presence in a community or region, building ongoing relationships of trust and seeking significant engagement from local communities and organisations. Their work is focused on building local capacity, and they often pay particular attention to the needs of marginalised groups with a view to greater inclusion, or improving equality (see Atack 1999). Many of these attributes are also central requirements for receiving government funding (see, for example, DFAT 2015: 12). Hilhorst (2003: 6) notes that the term NGO is 'a claim-bearing label', meaning that it is not merely descriptive but speaks to features of this kind of development organisation, making a moral claim that they are 'doing good for the development of others'. This chapter specifically addresses humanitarian and development NGOs, which seek a 'comparative advantage in delivering develop-ment services' (Hudock 1999: 8) through unique characteristics such as flexibility and responsiveness, understanding of local needs and aspirations, and proximity to local communities. These NGOs' com-mitment to local communities and those in greatest need means they engage in conflict- and disaster-affected environments despite the inherent dangers, and they work there long before and after a peak in international concern brings foreign military engagement (Anderson 1999: 19; Goodhand 2006).

Humanitarian NGOs are a particular subsection of this group, distinguished by a focus on immediate needs, though the prevalence of complex emergencies requiring long-term humanitarian responses means that many humanitarian NGOs work with communities in crisis for decades to ensure that those needs are met. Even those making short-term interventions, particularly following disasters, are often well networked with existing local groups, and coordination of humanitarian NGOs is significantly improved under the UN OCHA cluster system (Stephenson 2005; Stumpenhorst et al. 2011). These ongoing relationships mean that NGOs draw on extensive knowledge developed through long-term presence, remain in the communities to see the impact of their choices, and must be more accountable to communities as a result. Further to this, the development and humanitarian sectors have built a significant body of knowledge and theory regarding the interaction between conflict and assistance.

While population-centric military strategies focus on impact on military goals, development and humanitarian approaches focus on impact on local communities, particularly the least powerful. As such, each perspective will identify very different benefits and drawbacks from particular strategies. For example, militaries may see community benefits in quick-impact infrastructure projects such as building roads and schools, which are expected to convert communities to becoming allies and sharing important information that helps build security in the area. In contrast, NGOs identify the negative impacts of these actions, such as increasing the access of warring parties to otherwise isolated communities, providing buildings without skilled people to staff them, or turning a community into a target by appearing to align them with a particular side of the conflict.

This difference immediately sets up a challenge to interaction between the two, which is augmented by NGO beliefs that their protection comes from their neutrality and broader recognition of their goals. In a pivotal text, Mary B Anderson (1999) explores the interaction between aid provision and conflict, and points to the protection afforded NGOs by their neutrality and independence. More recently, in an extraordinary challenge to this orthodoxy, and in light of increasing attacks on aid workers, Larissa Fast challenges that NGOs' emblems of neutrality (even indeed the Red Cross emblem) no longer bear protective qualities (2014: 188). Fast and Anderson both argue that contemporary non-state combatants view NGOs and the assistance they provide as tools that can be utilised in the conflict. This can be as simple as the appropriation of humanitarian goods (e.g. blankets, food) for use by combatants, or for sale to purchase weapons; it can be as complex as apparent conferral of legitimacy through negotiating with warlords for safe access to vulnerable communities.

Civil-military interaction

In what has become a ubiquitous quotation in discourse surrounding NGO-military interaction, then-US Secretary of State Colin Powell declared at a national conference of NGO leaders that NGOs are 'such a force multiplier for us, such an important part of our combat team' (2001). This statement is often repeated as the quintessential illustration of the way militaries and departments of defence mis-understand how others perceive them, and how this can impact on those associated with them. This notion of NGOs as force multipliers continues to be used in literature on civil-military interaction (see, for example, Voget 2008: 145) and is echoed in military doctrine on civil-military interaction, as detailed below.

While Powell's claim to NGO action as critical to military goals has been widely decried as representative of a voracious military expan-sionism devouring the humanitarian sector, it reflects neither humani-tarian guidelines nor military doctrine on civil-military interaction. Just as their roles and approaches differ, so too do the approaches of militaries and NGOs to interaction. Broadly speaking, militaries understand interaction with non-military actors as key to achieving their goals, while NGOs may engage only reluctantly because fulfill-ing their goal of meeting the needs of the most vulnerable 'necessarily draws them into unstable environments where militaries are more likely to be present' (Thompson 2008: 6). In a neat response to Powell, the President of the International Council of *Médecins Sans Frontières* (MSF), an organisation renowned for its fierce independence, reflected that 'it should be obvious to you in the military that if we are part of your team, if we are on your side, if we are providing you with infor-mation, if we are advancing towards the same goals as you, then we fall directly into the crosshairs of the other side. It's nothing personal, but we can't afford this sort of unity' (Fournier 2009).

Militaries have long recognised the importance of non-military (civilian) individuals, groups and agencies to their mission, codified in military doctrine as civil-military interaction (CIMIC). The civil-military doctrine of most Northern countries and alliances is remark-ably similar, often sharing common wording making clear that this interaction is undertaken 'in support of the [military] mission' (see NATO 2000; EU 2002; ADF 2009). Australia's ADF describes civil-military operations as the diverse range of measures that further a mission by facilitating operations and building 'support, legitimacy and consent' amongst the population (2009: s. 1.4). Within this context, CIMIC is 'the *coordination and cooperation*, in support of the mission, between the Joint Commander and civil actors, includ-ing the national population and local authorities, as well as interna-tional, national and non-governmental organisations and agencies' (ADF 2009: s. 1.6, emphasis added). These statements illustrate both the primacy of mission goals, and the absolute centrality of the military commander in determining whether specific actions enable the achievement of those end-goals within the defined strategy. Militaries are thus guided by a fundamental orientation towards engagement with civilian actors where this will facilitate meeting mission goals.

In contrast, the approach of NGOs is diverse and not always well articulated. A key starting point is the role of the United Nations Office for the Coordination of Humanitarian Affairs (OCHA) in coordinating humanitarian action and facilitating engagement and understanding between humanitarian organisations and militaries. OCHA and the Inter-Agency Standing Committee (IASC, the key coordinating body of UN and non-UN humanitarian agencies) have several essential publications regarding civil-military interaction in disasters and complex emergencies, in specific countries and regions and for the use of military escorts (see OCHA 2015). OCHA's approach is known as UN Humanitarian Civil-Military Coordination (CMCoord), defined as 'the essential *dialogue and interaction* between civilian and military actors in humanitarian emergencies that is necessary to protect and promote humanitarian principles, avoid competition, minimize inconsistency, and when appropriate pursue common goals' (OCHA 2012a: 1, emphasis added).

A key corollary to the notion of CMCoord is the 'principle of last resort'. This is the principle that military and civil defence assets (MCDA) may be used *in support of* non-military humanitarian efforts, and only as a last resort: that they may be temporarily utilised in support of a civilian-led humanitarian response where there is a 'humanitarian gap' (when civilian assets cannot meet the need), where foreign MCDAs complement the civilian capabilities, *and* where military capabilities are unique in 'capability, availability and timeliness' (OCHA 2012b: 1).

The larger international NGOs have developed their own policies for civil-military interaction, notable amongst them World Vision, which developed a decision-making model for use by its staff and available to other organisations (Thompson 2008). Nonetheless, there remains a lack of coherence within the humanitarian sector. While CMCoord spans a spectrum from simple coexistence to active cooperation (OCHA 2012: 1), the majority of NGOs have no clearly articulated position on interaction with militaries, with a minority either 'refuseniks' (rejecting all contact), or 'principled pragmatists' (pragmatically engaging within a firm framework of the humanitarian principles) (Rana and Reber 2007: 7). Complicating this, the context of military involvement also plays an important role in NGOs' willingness to engage with militaries. Where the military is a party to conflict (generally environments where the conflict is ongoing), NGOs are most likely to seek a clear separation of roles. Where the military role is stabilisation, NGOs tend to be more willing to engage, and they are most comfortable with interaction following disasters, where military goals are much closer to their own.

This complexity of NGO positioning is one of the largest challenges in civil-military interaction, particularly for militaries attempting to understand the humanitarian sector and how to engage with it. If anything, the diversity and independence of NGOs and humanitarian bodies will increase over time with the sustained increase in the number of individuals and organisations working on humanitarian issues. Thus, while militaries such as the ADF recognise that NGOs 'understand and avoid the use of' the term CIMIC (ADF 2009: 1.9), they require a sophisticated understanding of the sector to manage engagement effectively.

In spite of this challenge, CIMIC and CMCoord are clear: military goals and strategies must be determined by militaries and humanitarian goals and strategies by humanitarians. There is a role for military support to humanitarian action, but not for humanitarians in executing military strategy. Where it becomes increasingly blurred is in the actions of militaries that mirror humanitarian action but are in fact population-centric military strategy, such as building schools and other infrastructure items. This creates potential confusion in host communities as well as verifiable confusion amongst NGO and military personnel, as revealed in the research results reported in the following section. Importantly, militaries are adaptive organisations that place great importance on learning from experience, and this provides an opportunity for humanitarian organisations to influence civilian-focused strategies through interaction. This must be complemented by increased humanitarian understanding of military approaches, as the foundation for critical dialogue on how humanitarian action and population-centric military approaches can coexist (and evolve) without compromising the vital goals of each or the security of all actors in the space.

Understanding the mission

Building on the above discussion, this section of the chapter draws on interviews conducted in a research project exploring NGO and

military perspectives from within an Australian context on the interaction in disaster and conflict-affected environments.[2] Using what
Stake (2005: 445) describes as an instrumental case study approach
to draw broader insight from a specific example, this research uses
a grounded theory approach to the collection and analysis of data
'with each informing and focusing the other throughout the research
process' (Charmaz 2005: 508). The seventy-two interview participants were drawn from NGO staff, regular and reserve members
of the Australian Defence Force (ADF), and senior staff of international organisations and Australian government agencies. All had a
minimum of three years' experience, many with over twenty, and in
a range of roles within their respective organisations. Each person
participated in a semi-structured interview of approximately one
hour concerning his or her personal experience and views on NGO-
military interaction in these environments, with particular attention
to international interventions in Afghanistan, Timor-Leste, Pakistan
and the Philippines (representing a range of military engagement
including party to conflict, stabilisation operations and disaster
response).[3]

Australia constitutes a valuable case study that can provide lessons
applicable to the broader international community. Australia is a
middle-level power that has deployed its military to peacekeeping
operations since 1947 and continues to be involved in (and at times
lead) international operations from peacekeeping to active combat
and humanitarian crises. Australia's NGO community is strong, and
whilst the nation's aid budget focuses primarily on the Asia-Pacific
region, many NGOs have a more global focus, particularly those that
are part of international confederations or networks such as Oxfam
and Save the Children.

This section of the chapter draws out responses that illustrate
understanding of the mission of NGOs and militaries, on the basis
that it reveals participants' comprehension of not only the broader
mission context but also the nuances within it such as humanitarianism and COIN and other human-centric strategies. Understanding
this helps develop a fuller picture of how the actors interpret, apply
and affect the policies and practices of their organisations. Examining
an in-depth snapshot in this way allows us to understand how these
interpretations and interventions may be occurring on a global scale,
and to devise strategies to continue to improve civil-military interaction in humanitarian environments, in turn improving outcomes for
affected communities.

The doctrine and guidelines on civil-military interaction discussed above speak very clearly to the role of each organisation in the humanitarian environment. Military doctrine sees civil-military interaction as a supportive tool for reaching the military goal, and locates military humanitarian action in the context of supporting non-military missions. Humanitarian guidelines also view military action as supporting a broader civilian-led and implemented humanitarian mission. Despite the clear guidelines from both militaries and civilian actors that military should operate in a support capacity in humanitarian action, this was not replicated in the interviews.

As would be expected, security was the main area named by ADF personnel as the ADF's mission in Timor-Leste and Afghanistan, though it was rarely stated as simply as that. For example, speaking of Afghanistan, one ADF respondent stated that 'there were two very distinct operations going on. One was deliberately targeting the insurgents; the other one was deliberately targeting the security and stability of the people, and also developing and mentoring the establishment of the security forces from the Afghan government' (A10, AFG, TL). Both of these facets are aspects of security provision: one acts to remove sources of insecurity, while the other focuses on developing local capacities for security. As a stabilisation operation, the mission in Timor-Leste tended to be characterised as building security capacity, as in the statement that 'these guys, we're trying to provide them with enough forces to create their own security so that they can then continue to develop their life, not have everything handed to them on a silver platter, which is what we are doing' (A01, AFG).

As in Timor-Leste, capacity-building and mentoring were equally characterised as central to the missions in Afghanistan, Pakistan and the Philippines. This skill-building work was targeted primarily at local military and police, but also other areas including government, with several statements such as 'well, I'd describe [our role] as mentoring them, trying to actually teach them how to do things better, sort of more efficiently' (A04, AFG). Humanitarian and infrastructure goals were rarely mentioned, though those who did so often identified the links with other goals, for example:

> I think it's the same mission . . . it's just long term. We turned around and said we need to provide mentoring, we need to provide leadership to these people and give them teaching and guidance. We can't do that without any infrastructure, can we? We can't do that without a governor's residence. We can't do that without schools. We can't do that without police

stations. How about we go in there and build them for crying out loud. (A14, TL, AFG)

Perhaps surprisingly, war-fighting was mentioned by only a single ADF respondent, with a small number noting that 'predominantly Australia goes in to aid countries rather than to fight wars, and that's what we're renowned for' (A13, AFG). Only three ADF respondents addressed the clear military goal of withdrawal, as in the statement that the purpose of the mission was 'just trying to settle them, in order for us to be able to leave and then hopefully they won't revert back to what they were doing' (A03, TL).

Population-centric strategies were mentioned as part of the ADF role by one in four ADF respondents, of whom four (all senior officers) talked about elements of such an approach. Fast (2014: 118) describes the argument by military commanders that humanitarian-like activity performs three functions: building troop morale, winning community support and increasing troop security. Interviewee A10 (AFG) painted a clear picture of how this strategic approach can be understood by military members as fulfilling a helping or humanitarian motivation:

> [in Afghanistan] they desperately want their people to prosper, and the way they see that is getting their children educated, and getting their children the ability to either get a trade or have a future in terms of work. So if we can supply that initially, to at least give them a rudimentary capability to do that, then as your stability and security footprint improves and you normalise that area from enemy influence or criminal influence, then you then empower them, through the use of civilian contractors or civilian experts, to help them help themselves . . . What they want is someone to tell them how to do it, give them the expertise, and then get the hell out of there. (A10, AFG)

In sum, ADF personnel saw their role as much bigger than a narrow interpretation of stability and security measures that might typically have been seen as central to the ADF's principal tasks. The development language of capacity-building was used comfortably by ADF interviewees with respondent A15 (AFG) explaining in clearer terms than most of the mission (in this case Afghanistan over several deployments) was 'basically trying to make the world a better place for those people that lived in Uruzgan province'. This implies a broad understanding of security, but also that the ADF is tasked with enhancing lives in a manner one might expect from humanitarian and development actors, or perhaps under civilian direction in support of humanitarian action.

NGO respondents understood military missions in a similar manner in that they were equally likely to name security and stabilisation as core to the military mission in these countries (under an umbrella of political motivations), with capacity-building, warfighting, providing infrastructure and meeting humanitarian goals mentioned by a small number of respondents.

It was clear to NGO respondents that military missions differ, dependent on the environment in which they take place, as in the response that:

> in Afghanistan I understood their purpose to be much more related to I guess stabilisation, but also a kind of defence purpose . . . much more as that they would actually be involved in active combat potentially and that they were still involved in trying to identify and isolate Taliban cells . . . Whereas in Timor . . . the objective I felt was much more around supporting the Timorese Military and around capacity building and contributing to government stabilisation purposes and peace keeping. (N05, TL, AFG)

Interviewee N24 (TL) noted that mission focus also changed in response to the level of difficulty in the area, stating that 'I think at first [the military mission in Timor-Leste] was to bring stability, and then I think it shifted to building the capacity of the local defence force'. There was a strong sense that these military actions to stabilise and provide security could enable NGOs to do their work by ensuring NGOs could safely access communities, and helping to create an environment in which individuals and communities felt safe accessing NGO programmes as well as re-establishing 'normal' lives.

NGO respondents also tended to identify the political nature of military engagement, which for some related to a direct financial benefit ('everyone wanted it to go well because they put in so many billions of dollars and also the gas industry. It was in Australia's best interest to make sure that things went ahead and were succeeded at', N25, PAK, TL). Others addressed the political machinations behind government decisions to deploy militarily, as in the following statement: 'look the reasons to me are not entirely clear, it's such an enormous financial investment, it's such an enormous investment of life and limb that it's unclear to me why you would choose Afghanistan over any of the other countries that had despotic regimes or authoritarian governments, that did grave injustices to their own people' (N19, TL, AFG).

As such, NGO respondents understood the military role in a narrower sense of security and stability. They acknowledged that capacity-building approaches had been adopted as a strategy for improving local capacity to secure and maintain that stable environment, but only as it related to capacity to achieve and maintain security at various levels. In that sense, NGO respondents maintained a strict delineation of military tasks, with exceptions tolerated primarily in disaster response. Like ADF respondents, they did not generally refer to military strategies, but neither did they legitimise humanitarian-like approaches within a military mission.

In comparison, there was greater consistency when turning the spotlight on NGO missions, with half of the ADF responses and all of the NGO responses centring on improved living standards. Many ADF responses were spoken with a level of uncertainty, as in the statement that 'I would hope [their mission] would be to improve the standard of living across the board, be it through religious, pastoral care, or be it through bare essentials, shelter, food, water, that sort of stuff, be it through education. It's to better the standard of living from when they arrive to when they leave' (A2, TL).

While there was recognition of the diversity of NGOs and the tasks they fulfil, about a quarter of ADF responses identified infrastructure projects as central to the NGO mission. For example, A08 (AFG) reflected that the NGO mission in Afghanistan is 'to basically try and help their way of life, culturally, [and through] education. Just to repair farms, bridges, roads and just basically help out with the aid to the area'. Interestingly, he interpreted these actions within a hearts-and-minds framework, stating that: 'obviously if you're going to do that to them and they see that then they're going to lean towards governance instead of the Taliban'. This implies that the end-goal of the action is to secure community support and thus decrease support for destabilising groups. It contrasts with a development approach that might undertake similar actions but focus on community goals, within 'a range of holistic activities in an integrated process designed not only to reactivate economic and social development but also to create a peaceful environment that will prevent a relapse into violence' (Barakat 2010: 11). Responses consistent with this confirm the earlier proposition that military and NGO actors appear not to have focused on the distinction between humanitarianism and human-centric military approaches. Their similarity makes them easy to conflate while at the same time reinforcing the imperative to develop a clear delineation between the two.

Many ADF responses were critical of some or all NGOs and their ability to achieve valuable outcomes, as in the comment that some

NGOs are 'just trying to make themselves look good' (A03, TL). Perhaps the most interesting critique of NGO mission and approach, however, was one that perfectly reflects NGO concerns about military projects and understanding, stating that:

> dependency creation is the biggest problem that any NGO's got and I'd be interested to know whether or not they have any view towards a mentoring approach. Like when they go in, do they view their end state as ... them leaving, and leaving whatever organisation or service they were providing, being now run by a local organisation, providing those same services without providing a dependency? I don't know if they have that long-term aim. I suspect many of them don't even think about that. They just want to meet a need, they get in there and they provide a need, especially in an emergency or humanitarian disaster ... I'd be interested know whether or not they have. . . a withdrawal plan or something like that ... an understanding that once certain conditions are met, we're leaving. I suspect most of them go in without that idea. (A09, AFG, TL)

Coming from a senior ADF member with extensive experience, this reflects awareness in ADF leadership of some of the key concerns in development and humanitarian interventions, namely dependency, mentoring and capacity-building. It reflects the comment by a respondent from an international organisation, that 'it's a measure of [recognition of] a successful approach to working in unstable and disaster-affected environments, that [militaries] begin to adopt these sorts of ways of talking and thinking, and acting as well' (I06, PAK, AFG).

The question regarding a withdrawal plan is an interesting one, and is answered by some of the NGO respondents. Discussing the cycle of implementation, evaluation and redesign, respondents talked implicitly of the way ongoing evaluations inform changes to projects: 'the mandate revises as conditions change as well' (I03, AFG). Given a mandate of improving living standards, this evolution is self-evident as it is relative – if basic needs of nutrition and shelter are met for a community, the focus can shift to other important areas such as education and human rights rather than declaring the mission complete.

Reinforcing distinction

Drawing together these strands, it is clear that even when militaries and NGOs operate in the same spaces, the way they understand their respective roles within international interventions is superficially similar but rests on fundamentally different goals. Humanitarian action strives to meet the right to dignity, assistance and redress of all people affected by disaster and conflict, using strategies focused on locally identified needs, sustainable development and the interconnected components of human security. Human-centric military strategies seek to identify and fulfil local needs in order to wrest support away from insurgents and thereby minimise their capacity to inflict damage through non-traditional warfare. The eventual military goal is to achieve broad-based security and support for governance in order that the military can withdraw.

This distinction is key to understanding NGO and military versions of humanitarianism, which in turn influences their willingness to work together and their approaches to such interaction. Improving humanitarian practice in complex humanitarian environments requires a response that builds on this understanding to develop strategies that will enhance communication and practice of both groups. Practitioners would benefit from greater clarity in three areas: language around humanitarian action; articulation of approaches to civil-military interaction, especially from NGOs; and of roles and leadership in humanitarian environments.

Work has been done to explicate the different use of terms by civilians and militaries, as, for example, in *Same Space – Different Mandates* (ACMC-ACFID 2012), a reference guide that includes a section on terms that are commonly used but understood differently by civilians and militaries. On this foundation, it would be more helpful to define the approach to humanitarian and humanitarian-like activity taken by militaries and humanitarian organisations as 'strategic humanitarianism' or 'principled humanitarianism' respectively. At its most basic, principled humanitarianism describes those actions performed in accordance with humanitarian principles, while strategic humanitarianism describes those actions that benefit communities whilst meeting strategic military goals.

Military action cannot be classified as principled humanitarianism as it cannot be performed neutrally (not taking sides in the conflict) and independently (free of political, military, economic and other objectives at play in the environment) and therefore does not satisfy the humanitarian principles. These actors may nonetheless have a strong humanitarian motivation in the dictionary sense of desiring to help others, and they may provide real assistance to populations through activities performed as legitimate human-centric military strategy to respond to asymmetric warfare and the difficulties of combating local insurgencies. Articulating this, the term strategic

humanitarianism encompasses these aspects and clearly communi-
cates the dual motivation.

Applying the terminology of strategic and principled humanitarianism opens opportunities for NGOs and militaries. For humanitarian agencies, it prompts further consideration of the degree to which
they would seek engagement and influence regarding the community
interaction side of strategic humanitarianism, in line with the concerns of development and principled humanitarianism. For militaries
it constitutes an opportunity to clearly articulate and explore their
strategies within a humanitarian context and develop an explanation that speaks more effectively to the humanitarian sector about
the need for a more flexible understanding of conflict and warfare in
current environments.

There is still some way to go in developing mutual understanding,
not only of function but also of factors such as the long-term presence of NGOs in these environments and the dangers they perceive
in engaging or associating with militaries. While a coherent approach
to civil-military interaction has been articulated by national militaries and coalitions, it is very difficult for militaries to discover the
approach of the many NGOs they may encounter. It is unrealistic
to demand greater coherence in NGO approaches to interaction,
however humanitarian practice could be greatly improved if more
NGOs and humanitarian workers were to clearly identify and communicate their own positions on civil-military interaction. Such a
process could allow them to identify areas where they benefit from
military actions (for example logistics and resources in large-scale
disasters) and strategies for communication and interaction – even if
this is just to communicate clearly that they do not wish to interact,
and why. This would help militaries understand NGOs better and
respond accordingly.

The fact that strategic humanitarianism is founded on military
goals does not mean that military actors disregard the needs and
aspirations of local communities – indeed, precisely these concerns
were raised by many military respondents. Their roles and mandates
expose military actors to a range of information and observations
of local conditions, however this becomes just one of many areas
of importance. NGOs and humanitarian organisations often build
on long-term relationships in these areas, together with training and
professional orientation towards local concerns and issues of marginalisation and visibility of vulnerable people, together with engagement with research and organisational lessons regarding what does

and does not work in similar environments. These factors position 'principled humanitarians' in a logical leadership role for the humanitarian component of an intervention – just as military training and experience position military personnel for leadership on combat and physical security.

Militaries will never subordinate their mission goals to those of a humanitarian lead, however they can accept the leadership of humanitarian organisations as it relates directly to humanitarian action, and adapt their own humanitarian-focused work to a broader plan (particularly where it is determined by local and host-nation goals). There is increasing military knowledge and use of the OCHA cluster system and how it can function as a conduit for military support to humanitarian action. It provides a vehicle for greater communication whilst maintaining neutrality when it is most needed. Direct military participation in cluster meetings is often not allowed, but militaries can still use the cluster and the cluster lead as a point of contact and communication. As the cluster system is invoked in cases of declared humanitarian crisis or disaster, there remain numerous contexts in which this will not be available – as, for example, in the protracted conflict in Afghanistan. NGO umbrella organisations are one vehicle for coordinated civil-military interaction in such cases, but this will not always be welcomed, further reinforcing the need for NGOs to examine and clearly articulate their approach to interaction.

More distinct terminology and clearer articulation of approaches and leadership will facilitate clearer thinking and more useful dialogue. The outcome of this will be determined by the civilian and military professionals already expertly involved in these interactions, but developing improved mutual understanding will be an important stepping stone to a response that embraces the complexity that characterises contemporary interventions.

The notion that NGOs are force multipliers for militaries is unhelpful because it makes blunt claims that obscure the complexity of the context and of NGO and military approaches. Civil-military interaction in humanitarian environments is complex and requires diverse approaches, and this is why it is important to recognise that while the work may be complementary, neither is a tool of the other. Using the notions of strategic and principled humanitarianism, clearly identifying NGOs' approaches to interactions with militaries and clarifying humanitarian leadership opens opportunities for learning and growth. These actions will enable practitioners to reorient the engagement once more to focus on stability and development for individuals and communities affected by conflict and disaster.

Notes

1. This set of characteristics is assumed when referring to militaries through-out this chapter.
2. 'The NGO-Military Interface In Post-Conflict and Post-Disaster Contexts', with funding from the Australian Civil Military Centre (Smith/2011/032986). The project received ethics approval from RMIT University (2000583-10/11) and the Australian Defence Human Research Ethics Committee (652-12).
3. In the interests of confidentiality, participants are referred to using a letter classifying them as ADF ('A'), NGO ('N') or government/international organisation ('IG'), followed by an interview number, for example, A10 is ADF interview 10. Letters after the number indicate the relevant countries worked in: AFG is Afghanistan; TL is Timor-Leste; PAK is Pakistan; PH is Philippines. Many had served in other countries as well, and these are not indicated.

References

Anderson, M. B. (1999), *Do No Harm: How Aid Can Support Peace – Or War*, Boulder, CO: Lynne Rienner.

Atack, I. (1999), 'Four Criteria of Development NGO Legitimacy', *World Development*, 275, pp. 855–64.

Australian Civil-Military Centre and Australian Council for International Development (ACMC-ACFID) (2012), *Same Space – Different Mandates: A Civil-Military Guide to Australian Stakeholders in International Disaster and Conflict Response*, Canberra: Australian Civil-Military Centre and Australian Council for International Development.

Australian Defence Force (ADF) (2009), *Australian Defence Doctrine Publication 3.11: Civil-Military Operations*, Canberra: Australian Defence Force.

Barakat, S. (2010), 'Post-war Reconstruction and Development – Coming of Age', in S. Barakat (ed.), *After the Conflict: Reconstruction and Development in the Aftermath of War*, London: I. B. Taurus, pp. 7–31.

Charmaz, K. (2005), 'Grounded Theory in the 21st Century: Applications for Advancing Social Justice Studies', in N. K. Denzin and Y. S. Lincoln (eds), *The Sage Handbook of Qualitative Research*, London: Sage Publications, pp. 507–22.

Cleveland, C. T., S. S. Pick and S. L. Farris (2015), 'Shedding Light on the Gray Zone: A New Approach to Human-centric Warfare', *Army*, 65(9), pp. 30–2.

Collinson, S. and S. Elhawary (2012), *HPG Report 32: Humanitarian Space: A Review of Trends and Issues*, London: Humanitarian Policy Group, Overseas Development Institute.

Department of Foreign Affairs and Trade (DFAT) (2015), *ANCP Manual: Australian NGO Cooperation Program*, Canberra: Department of Foreign Affairs and Trade.

Duffey, T. (2000), 'Cultural Issues in Contemporary Peacekeeping', *International Peacekeeping*, 7(1), pp. 142–68.

Duffield, M. (2013), *Development, Security and Unending War: Governing the World of Peoples*, Cambridge: Polity Press.

European Union (EU) (2002), *Civil-Military Co-operation (CIMIC) Concept for EU-Led Crisis Management Operations. ESDP/PESD COSDP 67*, Brussels: European Union.

Fast, L. (2014), *Aid in Danger: The perils and Promise of Humanitarianism*, Philadelphia: University of Pennsylvania Press.

Food and Argiculture Organization of the United Nations (FAO) (2015), 'FAO in Emergencies: From Prevention to Building Back Better', available at: http://www.fao.org/emergencies/emergency-types/complex-emergencies/en/, last accessed 2 January 2017.

Fournier, C. (2009), 'NATO Speech – Rheindalen, Germany. 8 December 2009', available at: http://www.msf.org/article/nato-speech-christophe-fournier, last accessed 2 January 2017.

Goodhand, J. (2006), *Aiding Peace: The role of NGOs in Armed Conflict*. London: ITDG Publishing.

Harris, V. and Goldsmith, A. (2012), 'Police in the Development Space: Australia's International Police Capacity Builders', *Third World Quarterly*, 33(6), pp. 1019–36.

Hilhorst, D. (2003), *The Real World of NGOs: Discourses, Diversity and Development*, London: Zed Books.

Hubert, D. and C. Brassard-Boudreau (2014), 'Is Humanitarian Space Shrinking?', in M. Acuto (ed.), *Negotiating Relief: The Politics of Humanitarian Space*, London: C. Hurst & Company, pp. 13–21.

Hudock, A. C. (1999), *NGOs and Civil Society*, Cambridge: Polity Press.

Lindsay, F. A. (1962), 'Unconventional Warfare', *Foreign Affairs*, 40(2), pp. 264–74.

Lischer, S. K. (2007), 'Military Intervention and the Humanitarian "Force Multiplier"', *Global Governance*, 13(1), pp. 99–118.

Merriam-Webster (n.d.), 'Humanitarian', *Merriam-Webster Dictionary*, available at: http://www.merriam-webster.com/dictionary/humanitarian, last accessed 2 January 2017.

North Atlantic Treaty Organization (NATO) (2000), *NATO Military Policy on Civil-Military Co-operation (CIMIC). CIMICWG 001-00, WP(MC411)*, Brussels: North Atlantic Treaty Organization.

Office for the Coordination of Humanitarian Affairs (OCHA) (2012a),

'OCHA on Message: Civil-Military Coordination', available at: http://www.unocha.org/what-we-do/coordination-tools/UN-CMCoord/overview, last accessed 2 January 2017.

Office for the Coordination of Humanitarian Affairs (OCHA) (2012b), 'Foreign Military and Civil Defence Assets in Support of Humanitarian Emergency Operations: What Is Last Resort?' OCHA/ESB/CMCS in consultation with the Consultative Group on the Use of MCDA, available at: https://docs.unocha.org/sites/dms/Documents/Last%20Resort%20Pamphlet%20-%20FINAL%20April%202012.pdf, last accessed 2 January 2017.

Office for the Coordination of Humanitarian Affairs (OCHA) (2015), 'Humanitarian Civil-Military Coordination: Publications', available at: http://www.unocha.org/what-we-do/coordination-tools/UN-CMCoord/publications, last accessed 2 January 2017.

Powell, C. L. (2001), 'Remarks to the National Foreign Policy Conference for Leaders of Nongovernmental Organizations', United States Department of State Archive, 26 October, available at: http://2001-2009.state.gov/secretary/former/powell/remarks/2001/5762.htm, last accessed 2 January 2017.

Pugh, J., C. Gabay and A. J. Williams (2013), 'Beyond the Securitisation of Development: The Limits of Intervention, Develomentisation of Security and Repositioning of Purpose in the UK Coalition Government's Policy Agenda', *Geoforum*, 44, pp. 193–201.

Rana, R. and F. Reber (2007), 'CIVMIL Relations', NGO VOICE Seminar on Civil-Military Relations, 3–4 December, Brussels.

Ricks, T. E. (2014), 'Kilcullen speaks: On COIN Going Out of Style, his Recent Book, Syria, and More', *Foreign Policy*, available at: http://foreignpolicy.com/2014/02/12/kilcullen-speaks-on-coin-going-out-of-style-his-recent-book-syria-and-more/, last accessed 2 January 2017.

Sphere Project (2011), *The Sphere Handbook : Humanitarian Charter and Minimum Standards in Humanitarian Response*, Rugby: Practical Action Publishing.

Stake, R. (2005), 'Qualitative Case Studies', in N. Denzin and Y. Lincoln (eds), *The Sage Handbook of Qualitative Research*, London: Sage Publications, pp. 443–66.

Stephenson, M. (2005), 'Making Humanitarian Relief Networks More Effective: Operational Coordination, Trust and Sense Making', *Disasters*, 29(4), pp. 337–50.

Stumpenhorst, M., R. Stumpenhorst and O. Razum (2011), 'The UN OCHA Cluster Approach: Gaps Between Theory and Practice', *Journal of Public Health*, 19(6), pp. 587–92.

Thompson, E. (2008), *Principled Pragmatism: NGO Engagement with Armed Actors*, Monrovia: World Vision International, Humanitarian Emergency Affairs.

United States Bureau of Political-Military Affairs (BPMA)(2009), *U.S. Government Counterinsurgency Guide*, United States Government Interagency Counterinsurgency Initiative, available at: http:// www.state.gov/documents/organization/119629.pdf, last accessed 2 January 2017.

Voget, B. G. (2008), 'Civil-Military Cooperation of the German Armed Forces: Theoretical Approach and Contemporary Practice in Kosovo', in C. Ankerson (ed.), *Civil-Military Cooperation in Post-Conflict Operations: Emerging theory and practice*, London: Routledge, pp. 143–72.

World Bank (2011), *World Development Report 2011: Conflict, Security, and Development*, Washington, DC: World Bank.

Index

Page numbers in **bold** indicate tables.

Abu-Lughod, Lila, 261
Afghanistan
    and al-Qaeda, 123–4, 160, 171
    Australian role, 299–302
    justification for war, 19
    narco-terror complex, 105–6
    post intervention, 27, 99
    Soviet–Afghan War, 146–8
    transnational feminism, 260–2
    use of technology, 34, 218, 222,
      231
Africa
    boycotts, 83–4
    forms of intervention, 74–5, 80–2
    political and criminal violence,
      102–5, 108
    regional organisations, 9, 194,
      204–8, 210
    slave trade, 76–7, 79–80, 85
    see also Burundi; Congo; Liberia;
      Libya; Rwanda; Sierra Leone;
      Somalia; South Sudan
African Union (AU), 32, 77, 134, 202,
    204–6, 209, 210
AFRICOM, 104
agency
    individual, 268, 275, 279–81
    local, 10, 21, 139, 248, 259–63
    and power, 48, 50, 59, 281–2
    subaltern, 46–7, 52
*Agreement on Provision Arrangements
    in Afghanistan Pending the Re-
    establishment of Permanent
    Government Institutions* (UN),
    261
aid intervention, 18, 22–3, 80–2,
    84, 86–8, 152–3, 157; see also
    NGOs

al-Qaeda, 103, 105, 123, 171, 218
al-Qaeda in the Islamic Maghreb
    (AQIM), 103–4
Al-Shabaab, 104, 105
Alborov, Dina, 272
Alexandrov, Stanimir A., 171
Algeria, 103
Alston, Philip G., 220
Anderson, Mary B., 294
Annan, Kofi, 7, 117–19, 130–1, 250
Arab Spring, 102, 138, 216, 280
Arai, Tatsushi, 282
arms trade, 79–80, 98–9, 101–3, 107,
    127–8, 207
al-Assad, Bashar, 99, 100, 181–2
atrocity crimes
    context, 122, 201–2
    current, 127, 139
    Kosovo, 99
    'manifest failure' to protect, 164,
      166, 169–70
    prevention, 20, 168, 192–3, 200
    role of regional organisations,
      135
    Syria, 180, 226–7, 230
    transnational solidarity, 209–10
    see also crimes against humanity;
      ethnic cleansing; genocide; R2P;
      war crimes
Australia, 151, 179–80, 288, 290, 295,
    298–303
Autesserre, Séverine, 139
authoritarianism, 45, 48, 51, 63, 128,
    138, 247
autonomous weapons systems, 222–5,
    233–4; see also technology
Azawad National Liberation Movement
    (ANLM), 103–4

311

al-Baghdadi, Abu Bakr, 97
Ban Ki-moon, 7, 117–18, 119, 125,
    133–4, 137, 169, 230
Barrie, Chris, 290–1
Beijing Consensus, 51
Belgium, 81, 198
Bellinger, John B., 175
Berlin Conference (1884), 79
'Beyond Failed States and Ungoverned
    Spaces' (Mallett), 25
Bhabha, Homi K., 197
Biafran War (1967–70), 81
Boko Haram, 34, 104–5, 108
Bosnia, 145, 216
Bouazizi, Mohamed, 280
Boutros-Ghali, Boutros, 249, 251
boycotts, 78, 83–4, 86, 88, 130
Brennan, John O., 229
Brussels Conference (1890), 79
Buchanan, Allen, 231–2
building
    capacity-building, 288, 293, 299–303
    and human security, 10–11, 247–51,
        255–7, 262–3
    identity of the 'builders', 257,
        267–70, 278–9
    individual agency, 279–81
    infrastructure, 294, 297
    international actors, 271–4
    mediation, 274–8
    national ownership, 259–62
    partnerships and coordination, 281–4
    priorities, 258–9, 270–1
    state-building, 28, 43, 55–6, 77, 82
    see also peace-building
Bull, Hedley, 51, 55, 56, 133
Burma (Myanmar), 77–8
Burundi, 253–4, 259
Buzan, Barry, 96, 98, 123

Cadbury Ltd, 83, 84
Cain, Peter J., 76
Cambodia, 98
Cameron, David, 15
Can Intervention Work? (Stewart and
    Knaus), 133
Canada, 179
capitalism
    and economic interventions, 83, 85–6
    and emancipation, 53
    and imperialism, 75–6, 155
    and liberal peace, 45–6
    and power structures, 22, 48, 51–2,
        58, 59, 123
Carr, Edward H., 45
Chandler, David, 21–2, 35, 149–50,
    252, 256

Charlie Wilson's War (film), 146–7
China, 46, 100, 102, 231, 234, 282
civil-military interaction (CIMIC)
    Australian case study, 298–303
    description, 287, 295–7
    mutual understanding, 304–6
    NGOs as force multipliers, 294–5,
        306–7
civil society
    and legitimacy, 67–8
    and nation-states, 32–3
    perspectives, 136–7, 271–2
    responses, 139, 174, 278
    see also NGOs
Cold War see post-Cold War era
colonialism
    economic and military control, 77,
        79–80, 81, 87, 88, 210
    and power structures, 58–9, 75–6,
        155, 198
    and solidarity, 204, 207
    structural violence, 48–9, 146
    see also imperialism
Columbia, 108
commonwealth, 45, 54–5
Condemned to Repeat? (Terry), 153,
    157
Congo, 81, 145–6, 198, 228, 280
The Consequences of Modernity
    (Giddens), 30
consumer ethics, 83–7, 88
corporate social responsibility (CSR),
    84
Cortright, David, 78
Côte d'Ivoire, 168, 210
Cottey, Andrew, 131
counterinsurgency (COIN), 46, 108,
    291–2, 298
crime, 100–3, 105–8, 127–8, 206, 207,
    278; see also atrocity crimes
crimes against humanity, 167, 202,
    203, 205–6; see also atrocity
    crimes
critical theory, 2, 59
Curtis, Devon, 254

Dead Aid (Moyo), 82
Deeks, Ashley, 172–3, 179, 181
defence industries, 224–5; see also
    technology
democracy
    African, 204–5, 207
    and capitalism, 53
    elections, 27–8, 253
    and legitimacy, 50–2, 68–9, 230,
        259–60
    and post-liberal peace, 57–8, 63

and regime change, 74, 98, 99
and the right to intervene,
    202–3
and the social, 48–50
Democratic Republic of Congo *see*
    Congo
Deng, Francis M., 196
development
    funding, 81–2, 88, 288
    and individual action, 85–7
    and intervention, 299–303
    and security, 120–1, 126, 207–8
    and underdevelopment, 75–7
    *see also Human Development Report
    1994* (UNDP); NGOs; Sustainable
    Development goals
difference, 59, 158, 159
disasters and emergencies, 232–3, 236,
    289, 296
displaced persons, 18, 94, 127, 128,
    138, 269–70
'Do Muslim Women Really Need
    Saving?' (Abu-Lughod), 261
D'Onofrio, Alyoscia, 228
drones *see* technology
'Drones 'R' Us?' (D'Onofrio), 228
Duffield, Mark, 21–2
Dymski, Gary A., 124–5

East Timor *see* Timor-Leste
Easterly, William, 82
Ebola, 84
ECOMOG (Economic Community
    of West African States Military
    Observer Group), 32, 78
economic intervention
    commercial, 83–7
    development aid, 81–2
    and power, 5–6, 34–5, 74–5, 87
    sanctions, 77–80, 86–8, 150, 169
    supersanctions, 76–7, 80
    wartime aid, 80–1
'The Efficacy and Ethics of US
    Counterterrorism Strategy'
    (Brennan), 229
emancipation
    and liberalism, 51, 53
    and the nation-state, 207, 211–12
    and power, 5, 43–4, 48
    and R2P, 200–1, 203, 209–10
    subjectivity, 69
equality
    and legitimacy, 50–1, 67
    and power, 44, 59, 68–9, 198–9
    and progressive politics, 56–7, 60,
    62–4
    and R2P, 200, 201

and security, 104
    see also social justice
ethics
    and consumption, 83–5, 86–7
    culpable ignorance, 224–5
    and global governance, 54, 57–8,
    60–1
    of intervention, 7–8, 11, 148–50,
    155–60, 200–1, 230–1
    just war, 3, 156, 219–20, 229–30
    and military technology, 218–19,
    221–5, 232–3, 236–7
    see also social justice
*The Ethics of Armed Humanitarian
    Intervention* (Scheid), 20
Ethiopia, 102
ethnic cleansing, 19, 132, 147; *see also*
    atrocity crimes
Europe, 32, 54, 79–82, 198
European Union (EU), 58, 60, 65, 135,
    273, 275
Evans, Gareth, 147, 149, 201

failure of intervention
    and complexity, 146–8, 152–3
    Libya, 15–16, 98, 99, 102, 138
    Syria, 138, 226–7, 230
Falk, Richard, 136–7
Fast, Larissa, 294, 300
Feinstein, Andrew, 102
feminism, 260–2
Firestone Rubber Company, 83–4
Foucault, Michel, 43
France, 77, 81, 88, 176, 179–80, 181,
    210
Freedberg, Sydney J., Jr., 235

G77, 59–60, 61
Gallagher, Adrian, 170
Galtung, Johan, 126, 251
Gela (Georgian farmer), 270, 281
genocide
    justification for intervention, 19, 20,
    153
    Rwanda, 145, 230
    Sudan, 83
    threshold for intervention, 138, 226
    see also atrocity crimes
George Mason University, 272, 275
Georgia
    2002 air strikes, 175
    conflict resolution, 280
    and South Ossetia, 269–74, 275–9,
    281
Germany, 176–7, 181
Ghana, 84
Giddens, Anthony, 30–1, 95, 96

Gilligan, Carol, 159
Glenville, Luke, 196
Global South, 57–60, 76, 154–5, 193, 202–11
globalisation
  aberrant, 6, 94–7
  global imaginary, 31, 33–4
  and the nation-state, 4, 16–17, 30–1, 31–3, 34–5
  and political power, 48, 52, 55, 123–5
  and violence, 29–30, 35–6, 64, 106–9, 127–9, 137, 153–5
'The Globalization of Responses to Conflict and the Peacebuilding Consensus' (Richmond), 22
governance
  crime and security, 100–9, 125–6
  elections, 27–8
  hybrid political orders, 25–6
  and international intervention, 46–52, 58, 60, 64
  and power, 5, 44–5
  regional, 54–5, 133–5, 139, 197, 210–11
Grameen Bank, 82
Grant, Kevin, 83
Grist, Ryan, 273
Grovogui, Siba N., 197–8, 206
Guatemala, 58, 59
guided missiles see technology

Haass, Richard N., 125
Habermas, Jürgen, 59
Hammond, Philip, 202
Hauerwas, Stanley, 131
hegemony
  and emancipation, 44
  and liberalism, 47, 51–4, 57–9
  regional, 135
  and stability, 124–5, 129
  and structural war, 55–6
  and use of force, 122, 131
Hettne, Björn, 134
The History of Development (Rist), 51
Hobson, John M., 198
Hofmann, Stephanie C., 211
Hopkins, Anthony G., 76
Hufbauer, Gary C., 78
Human Development Report 1994 (UNDP), 120–1, 152, 249, 256
human rights
  and capitalism, 51–3, 58
  and economic intervention, 74, 77–9, 82, 88
  and international relations, 49–51, 60–1, 136–7, 166, 226–7

and the military, 105, 108
principles, 289–90
and regional organisations, 135, 139
and sovereignty, 45–6, 48–9, 59–60, 118, 192–3
and state rights, 119–21, 126, 129–33
and technology, 229–30, 232–3
see also R2P; social justice
'Human Security as a Military Security Leftover' (James), 255–6
'Human Security Now' (UNCHS), 250
Humanitarian Intervention (Weiss), 19
humanitarian-military intervention
  definition, 16–17, 19–23, 80, 129–30, 149–52, 304–5
  principles, 155–6, 290
  trends, 17–19, 131–2, 146
  see also economic intervention; military intervention; R2P
humanitarian space, 289–90
hybrid peace, 46, 52, 56–64, 65–7, 69; see also liberal peace
hybrid political orders, 25–6

identity and new wars, 30, 128, 137
imperialism
  and capitalism, 75–6
  and liberal hegemony, 52, 55, 57, 59, 131, 133
  and R2P, 192, 195–6, 201–2, 210
  Soviet, 146–7
  see also colonialism
India, 46, 107, 154, 231
infrastructure
  building, 258–9, 294, 299–300, 302
  destruction, 147
  growth and funding, 18–19, 30
  North–South economic relations, 76, 82, 86
Intergovernmental Authority on Development (IGAD), 205
International Commission on Intervention and State Sovereignty (ICISS), 8, 164, 167, 195, 196, 202
International Committee of the Red Cross (ICRC), 139, 157, 275
international community
  consensus on R2P, 6–7, 117–18, 119–20, 168–70
  and democracy, 63
  and liberal peace, 54, 57–61
  motivation for intervention, 80–1, 98–9, 202–3
  role in rebuilding, 271–4, 278–9

sovereignty as responsibility, 192–3, 195–7, 210
  see also United Nations (UN)
International Conference on the Great Lakes Region (ICGLR), 207–8
International Criminal Court (ICC), 169, 184n
International Monetary Fund (IMF), 82, 123
international relations (IR), 5, 44–9, 57, 60–1, 95, 121–3, 150–1, 198–9
internationalism, 44, 54–5, 57, 192
Iran, 99, 100, 107, 138, 236
Iraq
  and ISIS, 97, 100–1, 176, 177–9
  justification for war, 7, 19, 137
  and Syria, 102, 138, 181
  use of drones, 218–19, 222, 236
Islamic State of Iraq and Syria (ISIS, a.k.a. ISIL)
  in Syria, 100, 177–82
  'unwilling or unable' formula, 164–5, 176–7, 182
  use of technology, 218, 234, 236
  as a viral threat, 96–7
  weapon supplies, 101
Israel, 146, 175

James, Paul, 255–6
Japan, 250, 282
Jütersonke, Oliver, 211

Kaag, John, 220
Kalandarishvili, Nino, 272
Kaldor, Mary, 30, 105, 128, 137
Kanashvili, Giorgi, 272
Kandiyoti, Deniz, 261
Kant, Immanuel, 46, 54, 67
Kenya, 102, 175
Keohane, Robert O., 95, 231–2
Kerry, John F., 178
Khutsishvili, George, 280
Knaus, Gerald, 132–3
Koh, Harold, 175
Kosovo, 1, 99, 118, 136, 145, 147, 216
Kozaeva, Lira, 272
Krasner, Stephen D., 195
Kreps, Sarah, 220

law
  CIA 'kill lists', 228–9
  and consent, 63, 67–8
  culpable ignorance, 225
  definition of intervention, 80
  and human rights, 119–20, 139
  and military intervention, 3, 99–100, 176–7, 178–9

and military technology, 218–19, 231–4, 236–7
rule of law principles, 26–7
'unwilling or unable' formula, 164–5, 170–4, 183
  see also sovereignty
Lawson, George, 123
'Learning From Termites' (Freedberg), 235
Lederach, John Paul, 268, 276
legitimacy
  and consent, 53–4, 67–9, 120, 130, 230
  global leadership, 61, 132, 133–4
  and peace, 48–9, 63, 66–7
  and pluralism, 47, 52, 56
  and rebuilding, 276–7
  state, 50, 154, 165–6, 196
Lessing, Doris, 147–8
lethal autonomous weapons systems (LAWS), 222–3, 225, 233–6, 237
liberal peace
  description, 65
  elections, 27–8
  evolution, 55–9
  and power relations, 16–17, 21–4, 45–9, 51–2, 59–60
  see also hybrid peace; neoliberal peace
liberalism
  and the aftermath of intervention, 147–8, 247, 259
  civilian protection, 194–5
  and emancipation, 43–4, 51, 53
  ideology, 23–4, 29, 35–6, 87–8
  and internationalism, 54–5
  and modernity, 25–6
  and structural war, 55–6
  see also hybrid peace; sovereignty
Liberia, 33, 79, 83–4
Libya
  and the African Union, 202, 204, 208–9
  arms trading, 101, 102
  economic intervention, 80–1, 88
  failure of intervention, 15–16, 20, 99, 138, 146
  'manifest failure', 168–70
  regime change, 2, 98, 210–11
  social transformation, 27, 29, 61, 202–3
  threshold for intervention, 238n
  use of technology, 34, 227
Libya: Examination of intervention and collapse and the UK's future policy options (House of Commons Foreign Affairs Committee), 15

Lord's Resistance Army (LRA), 104
Luck, Edward C., 195
Luhmann, Niklas, 96
Lynch, Colum, 228

Mabus, Ray, 234–5
MacIntyre, Alasdair, 157
Mali, 103–4
Mallett, Richard, 25
Mamdani, Mahmood, 199
'manifest failure', 164, 166–70, 183
Marshall Plan, 51
Marshall, Thomas H., 49
Marxism, 44, 45, 48, 54, 55, 75–6
Médecins Sans Frontières (MSF), 32–3, 84, 295
media
  assigning blame, 269, 273
  depiction of intervention, 146
  depiction of violence, 126–7, 155
  influence, 33–4, 84, 138, 275, 277
mediation, 61, 135, 204–5, 274–8
Midlarsky, Manus I., 96
military intervention
  aftermath, 145–7
  Australian case study, 298–303
  counterinsurgency, 291–2
  and economic intervention, 74, 77, 78, 80–1
  future direction, 61, 135, 236
  and globalisation, 6, 94–7, 153–4
  humanitarian grounds, 7, 98–9, 119, 136–7
  legality, 171–2, 173, 176–7, 180
  motives, 99–102, 122, 131–2, 138, 216
  and NGOs, 11, 22–3, 287–91, 292–7, 302–7
  paramilitaries, 107–9
  see also humanitarian-military intervention; R2P
Mitchell, Christopher, 274–5
modernity
  and emancipation, 43–4, 47
  and globalisation, 4, 31
  and ideology, 23–4, 29
  and the nation-state, 16, 21, 28, 33
  spatiality and temporality, 25–8, 30–1
Moravcsik, Andrew, 122
'A More Secure World' (UN), 251
Movement for the Emancipation of the Niger Delta (MEND), 105
Moyo, Dambisa, 82
Mugabe, Robert, 88
Mukwege, Denis, 280

nation-building *see* building
nation-states
  as basis for intervention, 32–3, 151
  and globalisation, 4, 30–2, 34–5, 123, 125
  legitimacy, 50, 154–5
  and modernity, 25–6, 28–9
  and peace, 16–17, 64
  and transnational sovereignty, 207–8, 211–12
  see also sovereignty
national interest, 3, 11, 20–1, 131–2, 288
'The National Security Strategy of the United States of America 2010' (Obama), 168
NATO (North Atlantic Treaty Organization)
  in Kosovo, 99, 136, 145, 147
  in Libya, 20, 34, 98, 169, 204, 227
  membership, 32
  and Syria, 100
neoliberal peace, 46, 57, **65**; *see also* hybrid peace
neoliberalism, 47–8, 53–8, 84, 86, 124–5, 128, 153; *see also* capitalism; hybrid peace
Netherlands, 176, 179
new wars, 29–30, 55, 105, 127–8, 137
NGOs (non-government organisations)
  and humanitarian infrastructure, 18
  and the military, 11, 22–3, 236, 287–90, 292–9, 301–7
  and politics, 122–3, 125
  role in rebuilding, 270, 271–2
  see also civil society
Nigeria, 76, 81, 104–5, 108; *see also* Boko Haram
9/11, 2, 170–1
non-intervention, 119–20, 131–3, 135, 165–6, 195
Northern Territory National Emergency Response, 151
Nsanze, Augustin, 253
Nussbaum, Martha C., 159
Nye, Joseph S., Jr., 95

Obama, Barack, 124, 168, 175, 178, 229
OSCE (Organization for Security and Co-operation in Europe), 273, 275, 278–9

Pakistan
  capacity-building, 299
  education for women, 279–80

narco-terror complex, 105–6
use of drones, 173–4, 218, 231, 233
Palestine, 218
Pape, Robert A., 155–6
paramilitaries, 105, 107–9, 128, 146–8
Paris attacks (November 2015), 176
Paris, Roland, 17–18
partnerships, local and international, 134, 137, 267–8, 281–4
Pattison, James, 157
PBC (UN Peacebuilding Commission), 18, 251–5, 257, 260, 262
peace-building
  agencies, 22–3
  in Burundi, 253–4
  in Central America, 58
  local turn, 2–3, 10–11, 60, 139, 248, 267–8
  outcomes, 247
  positive and negative peace, 65–7, 69, 202–3
  UN policy, 249–53, 254–5, 260, 262–3
  see also building; hybrid peace; liberalism
Philippines, 107–8, 299
Pictet, Jean, 157
Pillay, Navi, 233–4
Ping, Jean, 204
politics
  hybrid political orders, 25–6
  and R2P, 195–6, 199–200, 202–4
  system reform, 49, 55–60, 62–4, 67, 68–9
  transnational solidarity, 205–10
  violence and authority, 102–3, 105, 128, 154–5
  see also democracy; globalisation; liberalism; neoliberalism
'The Politics of Gender and Reconstruction in Afghanistan' (Kandiyoti), 261
The Politics of Humanitarian Technology (Jacobsen), 35
positionality, 43–4, 46, 49, 53, 69
positive relationality, 8, 157, 158–60
Poss, James O., 221
post-Cold War era
  economic intervention, 78, 80–1, 87–8
  and globalisation, 122–3
  ideology, 35, 36, 51–2
  increase in intervention, 17–18, 45–6, 131–2
  new wars, 29–30
  social justice, 60–1, 121
  see also hegemony

post-liberal peace see hybrid peace
poverty, 86, 88, 104, 126; see also equality
Powell, Colin L., 294–5
power relations
  asymmetry, 44, 220–1, 255
  and globalisation, 30, 34–5, 153
  and intervention, 4–6, 16–17, 20–4, 47–8, 259–63
  and partnership, 281–2
  and political representation, 63–4, 67–9
  post-Cold War era, 122–5
  and progressive peace, 52, 57–60
  and violence, 97, 99–100, 126, 154–5
  see also agency; economic intervention; emancipation; hegemony; sovereignty
progress
  and intervention, 46–8, 52
  and liberal peace, 53–6, 60–1
  and post-liberal peace, 56–9, 62–3, 68–9
  and systemic reform, 49–50

al-Qaddafi, Muammar, 2, 88, 98, 169, 170
Qaddafi, Saif al-Islam, 15

'The R2P Is Dead, Long Live the R2P' (Chandler), 150
R2P (Responsibility to Protect)
  and counterterrorism, 8, 201–2
  criteria for intervention, 20, 97–8, 131–2, 155–6, 167–8, 182–3
  definition of intervention, 80, 148–52
  and human rights, 48–9, 119–20, 226–7
  and regional organisations, 9, 138–9, 203–5, 208–11
  resourcing, 18
  and the right to intervene, 202–3
  significance, 1–2, 164
  and sovereignty, 46, 117–18, 192–7, 199–200, 211–12
  see also 'manifest failure'
'A Rare Disagreement with Ignatius, on the Deployment of Armed Predators to Libya' (Ricks), 227
regime change, 2, 7, 20, 74, 94, 146, 210
'Regimes of Sovereignty' (Grovogui), 197–8
regional organisations (ROs)
  and global governance, 139, 210

regional organisations (ROs) (cont.)
  local and international roles, 18–19,
    133–5, 196–7
  solidarity, 203–5, 209–10, 211
  and sovereignty, 9, 193–4, 205–8
The Responsibility to Protect (Evans),
    149
Review of the United Nations
    Peacebuilding Architecture (UN),
    260
Richmond, Oliver P., 21–2
Ricks, Thomas E., 227
The Rise of the Global Imaginary
    (Steger), 31, 32
Rist, Gilbert, 51
Robert (South Ossetian historian),
    270
Roff, Heather M., 235
Rosenau, James N., 95
Rousseau, Jean-Jacques, 54
Russett, Bruce, 135
Russia
  arms trade, 102, 103
  and Georgia, 175, 269, 271, 273,
    277
  paramilitaries, 107
  sanctions, 88
  and Syria, 20, 100–1, 138, 176, 178,
    182
  see also USSR
Rwanda, 79, 81, 145, 153, 216, 230

Same Space – Different Mandates
    (ACMC-ACFID), 304
sanctions see economic intervention
Saudi Arabia, 99, 100, 176
Saunders, Christopher, 80
Savà, Peppe, 43
Scheid, Don E., 20
Schörnig, Niklas, 34
Scott, David, 204
security
  and crime, 100–3
  and globalisation, 95–6
  and human rights, 119–21, 125–6,
    152
  NGOs and the military, 287–9,
    303–4
  and power, 63–4, 122, 128–9,
    259–60
  privatisation, 7, 108–9
  as rationale for intervention, 18,
    299–302
  and (re)building, 10, 247–9, 255–7,
    259, 262–3
  state-centred, 98, 129, 207–8
  UN policy, 249–55

see also United Nations Security
    Council
Sennett, Richard, 161n
Serbia, 99, 118
Sharkey, Noel, 225
Sierra Leone, 32, 78
Singer, Peter W., 220–1, 224, 230
slave trade, 76–7, 79–80, 82, 83–5
social justice, 53, 55, 56–60, 68–9; see
    also equality; human rights
social relations
  and elections, 27
  and globalisation, 30–1, 95–6, 153–4
  and intervention, 16, 87, 157, 160
  and modernity, 23–4
  reciprocity, 158–9
solidarity, 54, 157, 196, 199–201,
    203–5, 207, 209–11
Somalia, 32, 33, 79, 81, 102, 145, 174,
    218
Sommerville, Quentin, 262
Sorkin, Aaron, 147
South Africa, 82, 83, 108
South Ossetia, 269–74, 275–9, 281
South Sudan, 27, 28, 29, 104, 205, 211
sovereignty
  and globalisation, 30–1, 34–5, 123,
    150–1
  and human rights, 45–6, 59–60,
    119–20, 133
  and intervention, 6–7, 19–20, 74,
    138
  and the liberal international order,
    51, 57, 60–1
  redefining, 117, 118
  as responsibility, 165–7, 192–200,
    203–6, 208–10
  transnational, 9, 135, 206–8, 211–12
  see also nation-states; R2P; regime
    change
Sphere Handbook (Sphere Project),
    289–90
state-building see building
Steger, Manfred B., 31, 32
Stewart, Rory, 132–3
STTEP (Specialised Tasks, Training,
    Equipment and Protection
    International), 108
Sudan, 77–8, 83, 102; see also South
    Sudan
Sustainable Development goals, 49, 56,
    60
Syria
  complexity of situation, 1, 99–102,
    146
  deaths and displacement, 230
  economic sanctions, 77–8

military robotics, 234
role of Russia, 20, 100
Security Council debates, 177–82
'unwilling or unable' formula, 164–5,
    175, 176, 179–82
will to intervene, 16, 17, 138, 216,
    226–7

Tagliavini, Heidi, 273–4, 279
Taliaferro, Jeffrey W., 131–2
Taliban, 160, 171, 231, 279; see also
    Afghanistan
technology
    accountability, 231–3, 236–7
    and the dehumanisation of death, 9,
        148, 153, 156, 220–1
    drones, 216–20, 226–9
    and ethics, 8, 149, 224–5, 230–1
    globalisation, 32, 34–5
    machine autonomy, 222–3, 233–6
    sanctions, 79
Templer, Gerald, 291
temporality and spatiality, 25–6, 27–8,
    30–1
terrorism
    in Africa, 103–5
    CIA 'kill lists', 228–9
    and counterterrorism, 164–5, 167,
        170–3, 176, 182–3, 201–2
    and crime, 105–6, 127–8
    and economic sanctions, 78
    Global War on, 2, 123–4, 132, 216
    ideology, 96–7
    in Pakistan, 279
    and paramilitaries, 108–9
    and political fragmentation, 155
    in Syria, 178–80, 182
    and technology, 218–19, 233
    see also Islamic State of Iraq and
        Syria; Taliban
Terry, Fiona, 153, 157
Thailand, 107, 108
Thakur, Ramesh, 160n, 168
Timor-Leste, 27, 33, 118, 216, 289,
    299, 301
truth and reconciliation commissions,
    26
Tuff, Antoinette, 279
Tullow Oil plc, 84
Tunisia, 138, 280
Turkey, 174–5, 176, 179–80

Uganda, 104
Ukraine, 234, 238n
United Kingdom (UK)
    and Libya, 15, 202
    military robotics, 234, 235–6

and Nigeria, 81
and R2P, 168
role in international relations, 46, 61,
    88, 272
and Sierra Leone, 32
slave trade, 77, 82, 83
and Syria, 176–7, 178, 179–80, 181
welfare state, 53
United Nations Security Council
    (UNSC)
    authorising intervention, 119, 136,
        171, 176–7
    and Burundi, 253
    debates about ISIS, 177–81
    inability to act, 17, 100, 123
    and Libya, 2, 169–70, 208–9
    'manifest failure', 166–70
    and the Peacebuilding Commission,
        251
    'unable or unwilling' formula, 173,
        181–3
    use of drones, 228
    use of sanctions, 79
United Nations (UN)
    2005 World Summit, 117, 164, 167,
        194
    arms embargoes, 79
    Capstone Doctrine, 48
    Commission on Human Security, 250
    Conference on Trade and
        Development (UNCTAD), 58
    Development Programme (UNDP),
        120–1, 152, 249–50, 271–2
    failed responses, 145–6
    G77, 59–61
    and human rights, 50, 53, 121,
        130–1, 166
    humanitarian principles, 290
    International Covenant on Economic,
        Social and Cultural Rights, 44
    leadership, 61–2, 132, 133–4
    Office for the Coordination of
        Humanitarian Affairs (OCHA),
        293, 296, 306
    Peacebuilding Commission, 18,
        251–5, 257, 260, 262
    reform, 135, 139
    and regional actors, 196–7, 211
    see also Annan, Kofi; Ban Ki-moon
United States
    AFRICOM, 104
    CIA 'kill lists', 228–9
    economic intervention, 77–8, 82, 83,
        84, 87, 88
    hegemony, 51–2, 55–6, 122, 124–5,
        129, 131
    international relations, 46, 47, 48, 61

United States (*cont.*)
and Mali, 103
military intervention, 7, 33, 97,
101–2, 132, 226–7
military robotics, 234–6
progressive thinking, 53
and Russia, 100–1, 138
Soviet–Afghan War, 146–8
'unwilling or unable' formula, 164–5,
168, 174, 175–81
use of drones, 218–21, 233
see also War on Terror
unmanned aerial vehicles (UAVs), 217,
222–4, 227–8, 231–3, 236; *see also*
technology
'Unmanned Warfare' (Schörnig), 34
'unwilling or unable' formula, 8,
164–5, 167–8, 170–6, 178–83
*U.S. Government Counterinsurgency
Guide* (BPMA), 292
USSR, 87, 105, 122, 146–7; *see also*
post-Cold War era; Russia

Vietnam, 97, 98
violence
and extremism, 96–7, 100–1
and globalisation, 30, 33, 35–6
individual response, 279–81
level and kind, 19, 20, 126–8
and power relations, 126, 201
and religion, 160
and revolution, 54, 138
and social integration, 25, 29
structural, 49, 50, 55–7, 63–4, **67**,
137
targeted killing, 218–19, 228–9
see also arms trade; atrocity crimes;
genocide; terrorism; war

Walzer, Michael, 229
Wang, Zheng, 282
war
counterinsurgency, 291–2, 304
displaced persons, 18, 127
effect on civilians, 121, 130, 147,
269–70, 274, 280
and globalisation, 106–7, 154–5

just war, 3, *156*, 230
in the Middle East, 1–2, 19–20,
98–100, 138
military technology, 6, 34, 216–23,
226–9, 233–6
new wars, 29–30, 105, 127–8,
131–2, 137
role of contractors, 224–5
structural, 49, 55–6
wartime aid, 80–1, 101
see also genocide; military
intervention; violence
war crimes, 100, 164, 166, 167, 225;
see also atrocity crimes
War on Terror, 2, 123–4, 132, 171,
201, 216, 233
Washington Consensus, 51, 86
'Weapons Autonomy is Rocketing'
(Roff), 235
Weiss, Thomas G., 19, 184n
Welsh, Jennifer, 80
the West
decline in influence, 51, 61
dominance, 16, 22, 34, 54, 198,
210
economic intervention, 82, 86–7,
202, 271–2
increase in intervention, 17, 132
progressive politics, 60
see also globalisation; hegemony;
imperialism
Westphalian sovereignty, 58, 129, 195,
198
'When Duty Calls' (Pape), 155–6
Wilder, Gary, 207
Williams, Gareth D., 172
Wilson, Charlie, 146
The Wind Blows Away Our Words
(Lessing), 147–8
women, 87, 254, 260–2, 279–80
World Bank, 61, 82

Yemen, 107, 173–4, 218
Yousafzai, Malala, 279–80
Yunus, Muhammad, 82

Zakareishvili, Paata, 271

EU representative:
Easy Access System Europe
Mustamäe tee 50, 10621 Tallinn, Estonia
Gpsr.requests@easproject.com

www.ingramcontent.com/pod-product-compliance
Lightning Source LLC
Chambersburg PA
CBHW050628280326
41932CB00015B/2560

9 781474 444422